RAILWAYS, URBAN DEVELOPMENT AND TOWN PLANNING IN BRITAIN: 1948–2008

Transport and Mobility Series

Series Editors: Professor Brian Graham, Professor of Human Geography, University of Ulster, UK and Richard Knowles, Professor of Transport Geography, University of Salford, UK, on behalf of the Royal Geographical Society (with the Institute of British Geographers) Transport Geography Research Group (TGRG).

The inception of this series marks a major resurgence of geographical research into transport and mobility. Reflecting the dynamic relationships between socio-spatial behaviour and change, it acts as a forum for cutting-edge research into transport and mobility, and for innovative and decisive debates on the formulation and repercussions of transport policy making.

Also in the series

Transit Oriented Development
Making it Happen
Edited by Carey Curtis, John L. Renne and Luca Bertolini
ISBN 978 0 7546 7315 6

The City as a Terminal
The Urban Context of Logistics and Freight Transport
Markus Hesse
ISBN 978 0 7546 0913 1

Ports, Cities and Global Supply Chains
Edited by James Wang, Daniel Olivier, Theo Notteboom and Brian Slack
ISBN 978 0 7546 7054 4

Achieving Sustainable Mobility
Everyday and Leisure-time Travel in the EU
Erling Holden
ISBN 978 0 7546 4941 0

Policy Analysis of Transport Networks
Edited by Marina Van Geenhuizen, Aura Reggiani, and Piet Rietveld
ISBN 978 0 7546 4547 4

For further information about this series, please visit www.ashgate.com

Railways, Urban Development and Town Planning in Britain: 1948–2008

RUSSELL HAYWOOD
Sheffield Hallam University, UK

ASHGATE

Published by
Ashgate Publishing Limited
Wey Court East
Union Road
Farnham
Surrey, GU9 7PT
England

Ashgate Publishing Company
Suite 420
101 Cherry Street
Burlington
VT 05401-4405
USA

www.ashgate.com

British Library Cataloguing in Publication Data
Haywood, Russ.
  Railways, urban development and town planning in Britain,
  1948–2008. -- (Transport and mobility series)
  1. Railroads and state--Great Britain--History--20th
  century. 2. City planning--Great Britain--History--20th
  century. 3. Urban policy--Great Britain--History--20th
  century.
  I. Title II. Series
  385'.0941'09045-dc22

Library of Congress Cataloging-in-Publication Data
Haywood, Russ.
  Railways, urban development and town planning in Britain : 1948–2008 / by Russell Haywood.
      p. cm. -- (Transport and mobility)
  Includes bibliographical references and index.
  ISBN 978-0-7546-7392-7 (alk. paper) -- ISBN 978-0-7546-9042-9 (ebook) 1. Railroads--Great
Britain. 2. City planning--Great Britain. 3. Urbanization--Great Britain. I. Title.

  HE3015.H39 2009
  385.0941'09045--dc22

                                                                                          2009008160

ISBN 978-0-7546-7392-7
eISBN 978-0-7546-9042-9

Mixed Sources
Product group from well-managed
forests and other controlled sources
www.fsc.org Cert no. SA-COC-1565
© 1996 Forest Stewardship Council

Printed and bound in Great Britain by
MPG Books Group, UK

Contents

To Jen

List of Figures

List of Tables

List of Appendices

Acknowledgements

Between 1970–72 I undertook a two year master's course in urban and regional planning at the University of Nottingham and an interest in planning and transport was planted by Roy Cresswell, one of the few contemporary planners concerned to build a bridge between the two. After working in local government as a town planner between 1972–85, I moved into the education sector. In the late 1980s there was renewed interest in planning around rail networks, but opportunities for substantial involvement in research and academic writing did not come along until I moved to Sheffield Polytechnic in 1991, which became Sheffield Hallam University the following year.

The research thread which eventually led to publication of this book began at that time, facilitated by a developing research culture around planning, transport and urban regeneration led by Professors Peter Townroe and Paul Lawless. Paul set up what became one of Hallam's leading research institutes, the Centre for Regional Economic and Social Research (CRESR). All the contract research I have carried out which has provided material for the book has been with the support of CRESR and I would like to thank Paul and three of CRESR's research assistants with whom I worked over the years and who have always been absolutely thorough and reliable in their work: these are Karl Dalgleish, Clare Greensmith and Elaine Batty. Sue Mason of Sheffield Hallam produced many of the excellent maps and diagrams which have been reproduced in the book and, as ever in academic research, library staff at Hallam and elsewhere have provided their usual excellent service in securing the various arcane references which I have requested.

As part of its staff development programme, Sheffield Hallam funded my work on a part-time PhD between 1995–2000, which produced material on which the book has drawn. I was lucky to have Professor Ted Kitchen as my director of studies. I had worked with Ted during my time with Manchester City Council and Ted subsequently became city planning officer at Manchester, before moving into academia at Hallam. Ted is not only very knowledgeable about planning and transport, but is also a master of the craft of PhD writing.

Help and encouragement is essential to sustain one when engaged in research over many years and I would like to offer thanks to all those in local authorities, the railway industry and academia who have provided that. Several people have been particularly supportive at various times and I would like to extend specific thanks to them. This includes: Steve Atkins (formerly of the SRA), Lord Tony Berkeley (Chairman of the Rail Freight Group), the late Professor Gordon Cherry (University of Birmingham), Julia Clarke (formerly Director of Freight at the SRA), the late Sir Martin Doughty (formerly Leader of Derbyshire County Council), Robin Gisby (of Railtrack and now Network Rail), Professor Michael Hebbert

(University of Manchester), Professor Richard Knowles (University of Salford), Mark Livock (formerly of Railtrack), Allen Marsden (formerly of English Welsh and Scottish Railway Ltd), Paul Salveson (formerly of the Transport Research and Information Network and now Northern Rail), Robert Upton (Secretary General of the Royal Town Planning Institute) and Kevin Williams (Derbyshire County Council).

Finally I would like to thank my wife, Jen, for her continuous support over the many years during which I have been engaged in the research for the book. Her managerial role demanded fine judgement as to the balance between how much time I should be allowed to pursue my lonely quest and when I should pack it in and participate in society. She has exercised this flawlessly, with love and patience.

List of Abbreviations

APT	Advanced Passenger Train
BR	British Railways (1948–61)
BR	British Rail (after 1962)
BRB	British Railways Board
BTC	British Transport Commission
CBD	Central Business District
CDA	Comprehensive Development Area
CfIT	Commission for Integrated Transport
CMDC	Central Manchester Development Corporation
CPO	Compulsory Purchase Order
CRESR	Centre for Regional Economic and Social Research
DEMU	Diesel Electric Multiple Unit
DETR	Department of the Environment Transport and the Regions
DfT	Department for Transport
DLR	Docklands Light Railway
DoE	Department of the Environment
DoT	Department of Transport
DMU	Diesel Multiple Unit
ECML	East Coast Main Line
EMU	Electric Multiple Unit
ERDF	European Regional Development Fund
EWS	English Welsh and Scottish Railway
EZ	Enterprise Zone
FOC	Freight Operating Company
GGTS	Greater Glasgow Transport Study
GLA	Greater London Authority
GLC	Greater London Council
GMPTA	Greater Manchester Passenger Transport Authority
GMPTE	Greater Manchester Passenger Transport Executive
GO	Government Office
GWR	Great Western Railway
HLOS	High Level Output Statement
HST	High Speed Train
ITA	Integrated Transport Area
LDDC	London Docklands Development Corporation
LDF	Local Development Framework
LIFE	London International Freight Exchange
LCC	London County Council

LMS	London Midland Scottish Railway
LNER	London North Easter Railway
LPAC	London Planning Advisory Committee
LPTB	London Passenger Transport Board
LTP	Local Transport Plan
MALTS	Merseyside Area Land Use Transportation Study
MHLG	Ministry of Housing and Local Government
MoT	Ministry of Transport
MPG	Minerals Policy Guidance
MTCP	Ministry of Town and Country Planning
NAO	National Audit Office
NCB	National Coal Board
NSE	Network South East
ODPM	Office of the Deputy Prime Minister
OPRAF	Office of Passenger Rail Franchising
ORR	Office of Rail Regulation
PAG	Planning Advisory Group
PPG	Planning Policy Guidance
PPP	Public Private Partnership
PPS	Planning Policy Statement
RDA	Regional Development Agency
RDS	Railway Development Society
RPG	Regional Planning Guidance
RSS	Regional Spatial Strategy
RTS	Regional Transport Strategy
RUS	Route Utilisation Strategy
SAG	Sites Appraisal Group
Serplan	The London and South East Regional Planning Conference
SFO	Station Facility Operator
SNCF	Société Nationale des Chemins de fer Français
SoFA	Statement of Funds Available
SPV	Special Purpose Vehicle
SPZ	Simplified Planning Zone
SR	Southern Railway
SRA	Strategic Rail Authority
TfL	Transport for London
TOC	Train Operating Company
TOD	Transit Oriented Development
TGV	Train à Grande Vitesse
TUCC	Transport Users Consultative Committee
UDA	Urban Development Area
UDC	Urban Development Corporation
UDP	Unitary Development Plan
WCML	West Coast Main Line

WMPTE   West Midlands Passenger Transport Executive

Chapter 1
Introduction

Birth of an idea

There has to be a moment in time when the idea at the core of a book first crackles into life. In this case the catalyst was a phrase in 'This Common Inheritance', the seminal White Paper published in 1990, during Chris Patten's time as Secretary of State for the Environment. This marked a turning point at the end of a decade during which the government had ignored the basis of much land-use and transport planning policy developed since the mid-1960s. The phrase followed a discussion of the proposed use of planning to guide development into locations which would reduce the need for transport and/or permit use of public transport, as an alternative to the motor car:

> However, not enough is known about the relationship between choice of housing and employment location and transport mode to allow the Government to offer authoritative advice at this stage (Secretary of State for the Environment et al. 1990, 87).

This marked a welcome resurgence of commitment to policies which would seek to bring about a planned relationship between land-use and transport networks, rather than just bending to market forces to produce development patterns dominated by the demands of the motor car and lorry. However, the statement seemed to deny decades of work by academics and practitioners to understand relationships between land-use patterns and transport networks and, on the face of it, this seemed odd. So a review of this work was timely.

But why write a book with a focus on the relationship between land-use planning and the *railway* network? The reasons for this are twofold. Firstly the railway network is a product of the nineteenth century and, from the 1920s onwards, had tended to be seen as old fashioned and not very relevant to the lives of most people. Although, post 1955, modernisation had clearly taken place, there was a continuing air of decay and dereliction around much of the network and the 'railway problem' was, seemingly, a constant feature of post-war Britain. But, and this is the second reason, the economic boom of the second half of the 1980s had been accompanied by increased demand for travel and the result was growing congestion on the road network. In turn and especially in the south east, this had led to growth in ridership on the British Rail (BR) and London Underground networks: 'This Common Inheritance' noted the nine per cent increase in rail's market share for commuting into London. Even outside the south east, steady work by local transport authorities and BR had produced some remarkably positive results: new stations and the reopening of passenger services on lines which had lost them, years previously. It was noted in 'This Common Inheritance' that:

> The major public transport operators do extensive research into areas where they can expand their markets … British Rail's reopening of local stations for commuters is one result of this work. The Government will continue to support efforts like these (Secretary of State for the Environment et al. 1990, 76).

Initial research in the early 1990s showed that town planners were centrally involved in these developments too, with regard to strategic policy development and local matters, such as station location (Haywood 1992). Suddenly the railway network had come to be seen in a different light; there was talk of a renaissance and a more central role as part of a more holistic approach to transport planning, despite a falling off in rail traffic in the recession of the early 1990s. From a planning point of view there would be challenges though, if there was to be a move from a paradigm of relative decline to one of growth and expansion. A critical review of the relationships between land-use planning and railway planning over previous decades would therefore be a valuable contribution to the new dialogue. An additional factor was that, just as this research started, the privatisation of BR began to look increasingly likely, so a review of the relationships between land-use and railway planning, during the period of public ownership, would be timely.

The shift in planning and transport policy in the early 1990s

The road congestion issue had been brought to a head by publication of revised National Road Traffic Forecasts (Department of Transport (DoT) 1989a), which projected increases in traffic over 1988 levels of between 83 and 142 per cent by 2025. The DoT responded to this, and the accompanying political pressure from the road lobby,[1] by announcing an expanded and very ambitious programme of motorway building (DoT 1989b). This typified the single-minded support for 'the great car economy' and lack of enthusiasm for state backed public transport characterised by previous 'Thatcherite' governments. During his term as Secretary of State for Transport (1983–86), Nicholas Ridley, one of the leading free market theologians, had symbolised this approach with his 1985 Transport Act which deregulated stage bus services outside London, thereby flying in the face of historic aspirations to secure integration between different forms of public transport through public sector control.

But the political mood towards transport was changing. The 1980s had also seen growing public concern over the environmental impacts of rising road traffic

---

1   The British Road Federation pointed out that; 'the 1980–86 growth in car traffic was 8% higher than the most optimistic forecast' (1987, 7).

and loss of countryside from road building and sprawling new development. This led to development of the 'new realism' (Goodwin et al. 1991) in transport policy, whereby the view that ever rising volumes of traffic could be accommodated through road building, characterised as 'predict and provide', was to be fundamentally challenged. The negative environmental impacts of transport were thoroughly explored in another seminal publication, the Eighteenth Report by the Royal Commission on Environmental Pollution (1994). Amongst a whole range of recommendations, this called for significant modal shift from road to rail for passenger and freight traffic. It was the resultant political pressures from these transport related environmental issues, and concern over others such as acid rain, marine pollution and global warming, which led to the wider changes in government attitudes towards the environment, transport and the planning system. In the early 1980s planning had been seen by Thatcher's Tory government, first elected in 1979, as a brake on enterprise and economic growth which;

> imposes costs on the economy and constraints on enterprise that are not always justified by any real public benefit in the individual case (Department of the Environment (DoE) 1985, 10).

By 1986, when Ridley moved to become Secretary of State for the Environment, an Enterprise and Deregulation Unit was operating which was looking at reducing the 'unnecessary burdens' of planning control through reducing its scope and developing a positive approach to development:

> recognising that there is always a presumption in its favour, unless that development would cause demonstrable harm to interests of acknowledged importance (DoE 1986, 21).

Although it was the threat of widespread housing development on greenfield sites across the south east which led to a political furore around Ridley and placed limits on this deregulatory stance, the wider environmental debate had its impact too. Publication of Patten's 'This Common Inheritance' was a crucial part of the move away from it, towards seeing the planning system as playing a positive role as part of what eventually became the 'Strategy for Sustainable Development' (DoE 1994a), marking a major policy U-turn as compared with the early 1980s. So, in the early 1990s, there was an expectation of change with regard to the planning system and the railway network.

An important component of this change was a desire to lessen the growth and environmental impact of road traffic through what came to be known as 'demand management'. In light of the claimed lack of a firm knowledge base for offering authoritative advice about relationships between transport demand and land-use, the DoE sponsored research (DoE 1993a) which informed the development of planning policies aimed at reducing demand for travel and facilitating travel by a variety of modes other than the car. These became a central part of the government's sustainable development strategy and reflected a major shift away from the deregulatory policies of the 1980s towards a more prescriptive regime. With regard to the relationship between land-use and transport and the desire to reduce car dependency, this culminated in publication of the revised version of Planning Policy Guidance Note 13 (PPG13), which stated that:

> ... local authorities should adopt planning and land use policies to:
> * promote development within urban areas, at locations highly accessible by means other than the private car;
> * locate major generators of travel demand in existing centres which are highly accessible by means other than the private car (DoE DoT 1994, 3).

One important goal of these new policies was the promotion of patterns of urban development to increase the utility of the railway network: after years of being marginal to the concerns of land-use planning, there was to be an attempt to integrate the two. The optimism around rail, coupled to the policy shift towards better integration between land-use planning and transport planning, formed the rationale for the research which would eventually lead to publication of this book.

A gap in the literature

A literature review carried out at the start of the research in the early 1990s revealed a great deal of material that dealt with the post-war history of the railway system, with Allen (1966) and Gourvish (1986 (and later 2002)) as outstanding examples, and land-use planning, with Cherry (1974) and Hall (1989a) as outstanding examples. However, there were few publications which focused on relationships between planning *and* transport, with Tetlow and Goss (1965) as significant, and very few which looked specifically at contemporary relationships between the railways and urban development, as Kellett (1979) did with regard to the Victorian period. Only Hall has researched the latter consistently over the post-war period, and that was often as part of more broadly based research into strategic planning and decentralisation, largely focused on the South East (Hall 1971; Hall et al. 1973a and b; Hall 1988; Hall 1989b), with only one significant publication which looked at railways and land development in provincial cities (Hall and Hass-Klau 1985).

There has been a fairly continuous stream of literature concerned with the economic impacts of new urban transit systems. This is dominated by North American publications (as reviewed in Cervero and Landis 1995, and Giuliano 1995) and is not directly relevant to the UK situation. However, one strand of it was concerned with using land-use change as evidence of property impacts and for considering its impacts on transport behaviour. For example, Heenan (1968) highlighted the concentration of high-rise apartments and office developments within a five-minute walk of stations on Toronto's Yonge Street subway. The importance of policy and institutional contexts was emphasised by Knight and Trygg, who pointed out that:

> ... the achievement of major land use 'impacts' around transit stations must require the concerted action of other powerful forces in addition to transit-induced accessibility increases (1977, 233).

However, even British publications in this area, as reviewed in Grieco (1994), were not specifically focused on the role of town planning. The absence of a strong thread in the literature with regard to the relationships between British town planning and management of the nationalised railway meant that the rationale for the book came into view: an historical overview of the relationship between urban development and the railway network, with a focus on evaluation of the impact on this of the planning system created by the 1947 Town and County Planning Act.

Initially the likely product of the research seemed self-evident: the railway system was, at best, a marginal influence on the land development process during this period, and land-use patterns were permitted, or promoted, to develop in ways which largely ignored the potential utility of the railway network. This view arose from a consideration of official transport statistics. These showed that relative patronage of the railway system for the carriage of passengers, and absolute patronage with regard to freight, declined from a position of dominance to a relatively marginal position when compared with the huge growth in road traffic (see Table 1.1 for passenger data). In addition, whereas the road network had grown in length as well as in the volume of traffic it carried, the railway network was considerably smaller in 1994 than it was in 1948; it had been 'undeveloped'. Popular consciousness about planning and transport was dominated by images of burgeoning suburbanisation characterised by road-oriented patterns of development, typified by the 'edge city' of the 1980s (Sudjic 1992).

But more careful consideration of the interrelationship showed that it merited closer study because:

- although rail transport had been overshadowed by road transport, it was still significant, and this significance was very variable spatially;
- although certain parts of the railway network had been undeveloped, other parts had received significant investment, new railways had been built, closed railways and stations had been opened, some lines had experienced real growth in traffic;
- although land development had been dominated by road based transport considerations, there were some notable exceptions wherein the transport properties of nodes on the operational railway system had been an important consideration and there had been a clear intention to integrate land development with rail access;

- land and buildings had been released for development as a result of the contraction of the railway industry and had presented significant opportunities for the planning process; evaluation of the way these were treated was a significant element of any overall evaluation of post-war planning, as well as being of special significance in considering the relationships between land-use planning and the railway network.

Table 1.1 The growth of passenger travel in Great Britain: 1952–1994

billion passenger kilometres (percentage)							
Year	Buses and coaches	Cars, vans and taxis	Motor cycles	Pedal cycles	Air (UK)	Rail[1]	Total
1952	92 (42)	58 (27)	7 (3)	23 (11)	0.2 (0.1)	38 (18)	218 (100)
1960	79 (28)	139 (49)	11 (4)	12 (4)	0.8 (0.3)	40 (14)	282 (100)
1970	60 (15)	297 (74)	4 (1)	4 (1)	2 (0.5)	36 (9)	403 (100)
1980	52 (11)	388 (79)	8 (2)	5 (1)	3 (0.6)	35 (7)	491 (100)
1990	46 (7)	588 (85)	6 (1)	5 (1)	5.2 (0.8)	40 (6)	690 (100)
1994	44 (6)	614 (87)	4 (1)	4 (1)	5.5 (0.8)	35 (5)	706 (100)

Note: [1] British Rail plus urban metros and light rail.

Source: DfT Transport Statistics Great Britain 2007.

The relationship between the railway and land-use planning sectors in the post-war period was therefore, perhaps, not as clear-cut as it first seemed and further study was justified. Also the commitment from the early 1990s to bringing about a closer relationship between urban development patterns and the railway network through integrated planning, meant this research held the promise of informing contemporary policy making.

Methodology and structure: thirteen steps

The research was concerned with the railway and planning sectors and it was clear from the outset that, before any analysis could take place, it was necessary to establish the basic facts and chain of events in each sector post-1947. As these were fundamentally bound up with public policy making, as opposed to the sorts of subject matter which other kinds of transport research might be focused upon, it was clear that the research was policy oriented. The literature on research methodology showed that it would be likely to focus on 'actionable factors', to be 'multi-dimensional' in order to obtain a well rounded and balanced picture, and to be 'nationally representative' (Hakim 1997). It was also clear that the research would be primarily qualitative, concerned with describing, analysing and evaluating the institutional structures in which policy was developed, policy itself, and the outcomes from the interaction between institutional structures and policy i.e. the juxtaposition of urban development and the railway network. As the research was essentially historical, source material would be archival, primarily contemporary official documents. As the book aims to explain the findings, it was also necessary to review publications which offered analysis of and commentary on the subject matter, particularly contemporary publications, as it was important to differentiate between comment and criticism which was made at the time, and that which was made with the benefit of hindsight. The overall development of the methodology can be presented as a serious of steps.

Step one. This was to fix the scope of the research with regard to space and time. Given that the vast majority of railway lines in the country, referred to as the 'main line railways', had been operated by the state owned industry since nationalisation under the 1947 Transport Act, then it was this network which was central to the research. However, where it has been fruitful with regard to understanding the subject matter and developing arguments to consider other railway systems, such as the London Underground, then these have been considered too. Given the fact that the nationalised railway operated in England, Wales and Scotland, then Great Britain was the geographical context for the study. Under the respective legislation, the main line railways came into public ownership and the planning system came into operation in 1948: this fixed an initial point in time for the start of the study. The initial end point was easy to identify; the moves in the early 1990s to privatise British Rail had massive implications for the way in which it would be managed and would fundamentally change the organisational relationship with state land-use planning. Under the 1993 Railway Act, April 1st 1994 was the date on which the shadow structure for the privatised railway came into effect, so this marked the end point of the core research.

Step two. After fixing these overall parameters the second step was to sketch out 'key events' with regard to development of the railway network and operation of the planning system between 1948–94 and to consider the possible interrelationships between them.

Step three. In doing this it quickly became clear that, in order to begin to understand these interrelationships, it was necessary to consider the period before 1948. This was because the railway network, patterns of urban development, the relationships between the two and, to a limited degree, the practice of town planning, had all existed for many years beforehand. Understanding these was an important precondition for studying the post-1948 era. Therefore the third step was the realisation that analysis of interrelationships before 1948 became necessary to produce a position statement of where things stood in 1947 and to identify analytical factors around which to develop the research into the 1948–1994 period.

The historical review showed that, in the time of its development between 1830–1914, the geographical relationships between the railway network and its operating contexts were generally positive, given that the network grew, the amount of traffic it carried increased, and most of this was commercially profitable. By 1914 the period of railway construction was largely over and the basic geography of the network showed little change thereafter. But the economy continued to change and in response to this, and to the rising importance of road transport, the country's urban geography and the institutional arrangements with regard to transport began to change too. The relatively unchanging main line railway network found itself increasingly out-of-step with the economic, geographical and institutional contexts within which it was operating. This book is an exploration of the factors affecting the *spatial* dimension to the readjustment which was necessary to reintegrate the railway network with its operating context, which itself would continue to change, in the aftermath of nationalisation in 1947.

Step four. The pre-1947 review explores: the relationships between railway management and the management of urban growth, particularly with regard to the development of town planning ideology; the developing role of the state; the institutional manifestations of the latter, and the co-ordination it produced or failed to produce. This review led to the fourth step in the methodology, the use of the concept of the *interface* between the railway system and the land-use planning system and a realisation that this needed to be defined in ways which enabled the formulation of a set of specific and interrelated research questions as shown in Table 1.2.

Because, post-1947, the management of the railway network and the land-use planning system were both carried out by agencies of the state, it was concluded that two important dimensions to the interface between them were concerned with institutional arrangements and public policy. In addition, the product of the two activities was the operation of the railway network and land development patterns, which are both discrete, physical entities with distinct geographical characteristics which are likely to exhibit varying degrees of spatial association. The analysis and evaluation of this physical outcome was therefore adopted as a third dimension to the interface.

Table 1.2 The research questions with regard to the three dimensions to the interface between the railway and land-use planning sectors

1. What were the institutional structures for railway management and land-use planning and to what extent did these facilitate the development of positive relationships between the two sectors?
2. What were the main features of policy for the two sectors and to what extent was policy in each concerned with the relationship between them, as opposed to other matters, and was this concern likely to be positive or negative in its impacts on utilisation of the railway network?
3. What was the outcome of the interrelationships between institutional structures and policy for the two sectors as measured by: the geographical characteristics of the railway network and the intensity of the service on it; patterns of land use; and the degree of spatial association between patterns of land-use and the railway network?

Step five. This was the utilisation of the product of the review of the pre-1947 period to provide a position statement which acted as a point of departure for analysis of the post-1948 period. This contains:

- an analysis of the geographical characteristics of the railway network which was nationalised in 1947; it was particularly important to identify those aspects of the network geography which required attention in the post-1948 period in order to increase its utility and spatial association with patterns of urban development;
- an understanding of the interrelationships between the railway network and urban development during the period when the railway network was the most important transport influence on urban growth. It was particularly important to identify the positive and negative elements of this interrelationship as they stood in 1947 because, in the post-1948 era, synergy between land-use and transport planning would be expected to focus on the former and reduce the impact of the latter, if the two activities were to be working in harmony;
- an overview of the institutional framework under which the private railways were managed, including an analysis of the development of the role of the state with regard to the railway system and the control of land development, and the relationship between the two sectors;
- an analysis of the development of town planning ideology and railway management ideology with regard to the interface between the two sectors.

Step six. This was to study in depth the 1948–94 period, using the benchmarking exercise as a point of departure, and seeking to answer the questions set out in Table 1.2. With regard to institutional arrangements, this showed that, although the railway system was state owned and the planning system was state operated, these activities took place in quite separate organisational domains; the central state and the local state. Conventional wisdom about the management of BR characterised the industry as centralised, hierarchical, introverted, traditional in outlook and production oriented.[2] Although subject to political influence, this was at the national, as opposed to local, level and was direct from government as opposed to arising from any wider political process. The conclusion was that the industry was not sensitive to the changing characteristics of its wider operational context and that, as a nationalised industry subject to central political control, there was not an effective independent railway lobby seeking to promote the industry's interests and maximise its integration into the land development process. However, given what has been said already about the continuing significance of the rail mode, the research sought to test this conventional view. In particular, the aim was to identify those situations where the institutional relationships were more favourable, or where similar relationships were used in different ways as a result of the interplay of different personalities and/or local contexts.

Although a function of the central state with nationally derived policy priorities, with periodic outbursts of activity at the regional scale, British town planning has been predominantly associated with local government and, as such, has been more open to political influence through pressure groups and political parties. It would be expected, therefore, that the two sectors were managed largely in isolation from each other. But a brief review of the institutional arrangements for the railways and local government showed that they were dynamic, raising the question as to how and why they changed, how the changes impacted on each other, and what the outcomes were for the relationship between the sectors. As both sectors were governed by statute, it was important also to identify what the statutory requirements were with regard to interrelationships between them and how these changed over time.

Step seven. This developed from the initial analysis of institutional arrangements and was based on the realisation that, owing to the creation of passenger transport authorities/executives and other factors, 1968 was an important benchmark in the 1948–94 period. As a result, it would be analytically beneficial, and more practical, to handle the analysis of the period in two parts: 1948–68 and 1969–94.

Step eight. With regard to policy, the review of the 1830–1947 period threw up a list of items which would be expected to be on the policy agenda if railway and land-use planning were intended to operate harmoniously, and which could be used to evaluate policy in the 1948–94 period. The initial policy research for the latter, showed that the agenda for the railways has been characterised by a tension between the internal priority for the industry – how best to run the railway, and

---

2   The term 'operator-driven' has been used to characterise British public transport generally.

that imposed by government – how to run the railway at minimum cost to the Treasury. The policy agenda for planning was dominated by the pressures exerted by various lobby groups: those for social housing, private housing, commercial property development, farming, countryside protection and, with regard to transport, the road lobby. The fact that the railway lobby was largely neutralised through nationalisation meant that its cause was only taken up by proxy, largely by those on the periphery or outside the industry, typically when a route was threatened with closure or, later, by the environmental movement. Railway trade unions lobbied on behalf of the industry, but this always ran the risk of being seen as self-serving by others and could work to the industry's detriment. However, despite the generally negative implications of these factors, there were obvious examples of policies which had historical antecedents and which were aimed at producing synergy between the two sectors: the location of new towns along rail routes; the improvement of local rail services serving city centres; the resistance, until the 1980s, to out-of-town shopping centres; and the location of some major commercial redevelopment schemes at large railway stations. The research aim was to put these into context and evaluate their weight, as compared with policies which were not focused on integration between the two sectors.

The final element of the initial approach to the research was concerned with the physical out-turn of the institutional and policy interfaces. The research focused on the location of development, the impact this had on the utility of the railway network and, in turn, the changing geography of the railway network and the impact this had on the nature and location of development. At the strategic level, the research investigated the location vis-à-vis the railway network of major blocks of new development such as new towns, town expansion schemes, over-spill schemes, city centre redevelopment projects, major areas of suburban development, airport developments and port developments, as well as the impacts of green belt policy. At the local level, the research investigated the location and design of new development with regard to its precise interrelationships with the railway network, its stations and freight handling facilities. As, during much of the period under study the railway network was in decline, research with regard to the disposal of redundant railway land and its after-use produced particularly important material from which to draw conclusions.

The foregoing analysis led to the development of key themes which could be employed to analyse and explain the findings. Three themes were selected: politics and political ideology; the influence of the professions and professional ideology; governance and management theory. This facilitated the eighth step in the development of the methodology, the creation of the overall analytical structure for the core of the book which is illustrated in Table 1.3.

Table 1.3 The structure for the analysis of the railway sector-planning sector interface: 1948–68 and 1969–94

Explanatory themes	Institutional arrangements	Policy	Spatial outcomes
Politics and political ideology	Analysis of relationships at three spatial levels: national, regional/sub-regional, and local		
Professions and professional ideology			
Governance and management			

Step nine. This was the decision to utilise a refinement of Table 1.3 to summarise progress with the analysis at the end of each chapter. This is illustrated in Table 1.4 with regard to its use in Chapter 3 showing how this tool enabled progress to be summarised and, by reference back to Table 1.3, benchmarked with regard to the position in the overall methodology.

Table 1.4 The analytical structure to be utilised to summarise the analysis in each chapter: example for Chapter 3 – 'Institutional Arrangements 1948–68'

Explanatory themes	Railway sector	Interrelationships between the two sectors	Planning sector
Politics and political ideology			
Professions and professional ideology			
Governance and management			

Step ten. The subject matter of the book is very broad owing to it dealing with a long time span, two sectors of state activity and ranging over the national theatre. It was recognised at this stage of the development of the methodology that it would reinforce the product of the research if the analytical tools developed could be employed in a single case study area to show, in some detail, what actually happened in a typical city region. This would serve to 'ground' the whole exercise and add depth to the analysis by exploring the relationship between the general themes identified in the main analysis, and the particular and unique forces at work in a given locality, on the understanding that these forces can work in both top-down and bottom-up ways.

Step eleven. Whereas the chronological approach seemed best for the general analysis of the post-1948 period, it was not necessarily the best way to handle the case study. A significant characteristic of the research subject matter was the hierarchy of spatial domains within which the three dimensions to the inter-sectoral interface were interacting: these were the national level, the regional/ sub-regional (conurbation) level, and the local level. For example, at the national level the research was concerned with the locus within government of railway planning and land-use planning, the organisational structure for the railways and its relationship to the national structure for the operation of the land-use planning system. It was also concerned with the major thrust of policy for each sector and the out-turn with regard to the general geography of the railway network and interregional patterns of land development. At the regional and conurbation level, the research was concerned with the degree to which there was scope for institutional co-operation between the two sectors, whether there was evidence that the geography of the railway network was managed in ways to maximise its utility in the plans for urban decentralisation and urban regeneration, and the physical out-turn in terms of the relationship between the changing nature of the railway network and broad patterns of urban development. At the local level, the research was concerned with institutional arrangements for each sector, the local policy framework and the outcome in terms of the detail development of specific sections of the railway network and areas of land. The issue of surplus railway land and how it had been used was particularly noteworthy in this respect. The spatial dimension to the research was therefore a unifying theme which reflected the geographical thread running through it. The eleventh step in the development of the methodology was, therefore, the decision to employ a spatially hierarchical, or 'embedded', approach to the case study (Yin 1989, 50).

Step twelve. This step was selection of the Greater Manchester conurbation for the case study as it represented the 'critical case' (Yin 1989, 47). Whereas London is the British city most influenced by railway development, it is a unique case. It will be shown in Chapter 2 that the extent of railway development and its impact on urban growth and decentralisation, varied significantly amongst the major provincial cities. Glasgow, for example, developed the most complex railway network which had a significant relationship with urban growth, whereas the network in Birmingham played a much lesser role than in many other major cities, although its network exhibited features which, in the long term, became very advantageous. Liverpool was geographically a special case because of its estuarine location which meant that it could be perceived as being only 'half a city' with its urban geography dominated by the riverfront. Manchester can be seen as a model conurbation in that it developed a complex railway network and the city radiated out along it in all directions on the level plain of the Manchester Embayment. It will be shown that the network exhibited prototypical strengths and weaknesses and played a significant role in urban decentralisation. In the 1948–94 period there was a great deal of change to this network, of both a positive and negative kind; this took place in the context of extensive land-use planning activity which had identifiable impacts upon urban form. Manchester, therefore, presented all the right conditions for the case study.

Step 13. Finally, since this research commenced in the early 1990s, railway privatisation has taken place and there has been over ten years of economic growth before the recent down turn. In addition, with over ten years of New Labour government, much has changed on the wider institutional, ideological and policy front too. To give the analysis additional weight and currency, it was desirable therefore to extend the analysis to the post-privatisation era.

Table 1.5 The thirteen steps in the evolution of the research methodology

1	Fixing the scope of the core of the research with regard to space and time: the main line railway network, and other systems as appropriate, and land-use planning in Britain between 1948–94.
2	Sketching out of key events with regard to the railway system and the land-use planning system between 1948–94 to scope the research.
3	Recognition of the need for research of the period 1830–1947 to create a base line for the core research and develop analytical tools.
4	Development and definition of the concept of the interface between the railway system and the land-use planning system utilising three dimensions: institutional arrangements; policy; and spatial outcomes.
5	Utilisation of the 1830–1947 research to benchmark the position in 1948 as a point of departure for the core research.
6	Utilisation of the three dimensions to the interface between the railway and planning systems to carry out an in-depth study of the 1948–94 period.
7	Acting on the product of initial core research to make the decision to split the 1948-94 period into two roughly equal parts, either side of the 1968 Transport Act.
8	Utilising the product of initial core research to generate three explanatory themes: politics and political ideology; the professions and professional ideology; governance and management.

9	Further refinement of the utilisation of the three explanatory themes to summarise and benchmark the analysis in each chapter.
10	The decision to carry out a case study to ground the research.
11	The application of a spatially hierarchical approach to the case study.
12	Selection of Manchester conurbation for the case study.
13	The development of the analysis into the post-privatisation period.

Conclusions

The methodology produced a book with 13 chapters, including this introduction. Chapter 2 reviews the 1830–1947 period, documenting the development of the railway system and its interrelationships with patterns of urban geography. The analysis draws particular attention to the development of planning ideology and railway management practice, with regard to their stance towards these interrelationships and to the role of the state in each sector. The chapter concludes with a review of the strengths and weaknesses of the geography of the railway system vis-à-vis its relationship with urban development and the derivation of a set of analytical criteria for the following analysis. Chapter 3 reviews the development of the institutional arrangements for the railway network and the planning system for the period 1948–68. Chapter 4 reviews sector policy for the same period, and Chapter 5 analyses the spatial outcomes with regard to the interrelationships between the railway network and patterns of urban development. Chapters 6, 7 and 8 repeat this process for the 1969–94 period, and the summary diagrams are used to benchmark progress with the analysis. Chapter 9 is the case study of the Manchester conurbation and analyses the specific impacts of the interplay of the factors reviewed in the previous chapters as they crystallised in this conurbation. The spatially hierarchical approach leads, firstly, to an analysis of the broad geography of the Manchester railway system and its macro relationships with the growth patterns of the conurbation. Secondly, the analysis moves on to consider how regional, and particularly sub-regional, considerations impacted on the development of the railway network serving Manchester's central business district (CBD) and its relationship to the development of that CBD, especially with regard to patterns of development close to stations. The third element of the case study considers two local matters: detail patterns of development in a high growth area on the outer fringe of the conurbation and the re-use of surplus railway land.

Chapters 10, 11 and 12 comprise the post-privatisation analysis reviewing, in turn, institutional arrangements, policy and outcomes. Since privatisation, the railway network has enjoyed unprecedented growth in traffic and there has been further development of land-use and transport policy to seek, or so it would seem, even closer integration between the two sectors. The pros and cons of privatisation have been hotly debated but it is not the purpose of this book to explore them per se. Rather the product of the analysis of the nationalised era is used to develop commentary on the specific impacts of privatisation for integration between land-use planning and railway management, and the outcomes from this in terms of spatial relationships on the ground. Finally Chapter 13 is a brief postscript offering some reflections on planning around rail over the period studied and their implications for the future.

Chapter 2

The Railway Network, Urban Development and Town Planning: 1830–1947

Introduction

The aim of this chapter is to develop a critical understanding of the geography of the railway network and its relationships with patterns of urban development, and to evaluate the degree of integration and/or dislocation between the two by 1947. It will also consider how town planning ideology developed during this period with regard to its stance towards the relationships between railways and urban development. The chapter will develop an explanation of these findings by reviewing the development of political ideology concerning state intervention in management of the railways and the land development process, and how professional ideologies with regard to railway management and town planning came to view the relationships between the two sectors. The chapter concludes with: consideration of how attitudes to governance and industrial management influenced the way in which the two sectors were structured at the start of the post-1948 period; a policy overview which will be used as a point of departure for the core of the book; and the production of a set of criteria to be utilised in the subsequent analysis of the 1948–94 period.

The development of the railway network: 1830–1914

Britain's population increased from 10.5m to 37m between 1801–1901 (Royal Commission 1940), and this was mostly an urban phenomenon. The geography of industrialisation, so strongly associated with the coalfields, cities and ports, was interwoven with that of the railway network. With the emergence of service industries after 1860 and the onset of urban decentralisation, the railway network became associated with central business districts (CBDs) and suburbs too. Country districts jostled for the attention of railway builders so that their products could get access to the burgeoning urban markets and, when mass travel for the working class became the norm, coastal resorts were tied into the network too (Simmons 1986). The network radiated out from London and was dense in the major urban and industrial areas with similar radial networks around provincial cities, but its tentacles reached out to all but the remotest rural areas. Network mileage and the volumes of goods and passengers carried grew steadily throughout the period, as shown in Table 2.1.

The railways were built when *laissez-faire* was the dominant ideology: the initiative was with private commercial interests and competition between companies was the norm. The administrative mechanism was the Parliamentary Bill (Biddle 1990, 27-57), which on becoming an Act gave the promoting company the right to compulsorily purchase the line of route from existing landowners. The conflict of interest between the railway promoters and aristocratic landowners was a point of serious political conflict in the early years and the focus of much parliamentary activity:

> The power of horse and aristocrat was challenged by the railway but both learned
> to recognise an ally as well as a rival in its influence (Thompson 1963, 1).

Table 2.1 Growth in railway network and traffic (Great Britain): 1870–1912

Date	Length of line open for traffic	Millions of passengers carried	Tons of freight carried	Gross receipts (£m)	Working expenses (£m)	Net receipts (£m)	% of working expenditure to gross receipts
1870	13,565[a]	322.2	166.5[b]	42.9	20.6	22.3	48.1
1880	15,563	596.6	231.7	62.8	32.1	30.7	51.1
1890	17,281	796.3	298.8	76.8	41.4	35.4	53.9
1900	18,680	1114.6	419.8	101.0	62.5	38.5	61.9
1912	20,038	1265.2	513.6	124.0	78.4	45.6	63.2

Notes: [a] Mileage constructed; [b] 1871.

Source: Railway Returns, reproduced in Aldcroft (1968).

It is worth recalling that the birth of the railways came towards the end of the period of Parliamentary Enclosure of the open fields (Hoskins 1955; Shoard 1987), a process of ownership consolidation which was indicative of the power of the land owning classes. With regard to railway building, this power was exercised to develop a complex statutory code which empowered the companies to acquire land, whilst protecting private property rights. In particular, railway companies could not retain land not required for operational purposes, known as 'surplus lands', and were thereby excluded from enjoyment of any increase in value, or betterment, associated with its development. These matters were drawn together by the Land Clauses Consolidation Act of 1845 (Frend and Hibbert Ware 1866) and came to be of great significance in the relationship between the railway companies and the housing reform and town planning movements which, themselves, became much concerned with the land development process. A side-effect of the power of the landowners was that development of railways had to be driven through by strong minded individuals who imposed their will on colleagues, opponents and employees. This was a significant factor in the development in the industry of a tradition of centralism, hierarchialism and introversion (Vaughan 1997).

In 1844, in reaction to the growing influence of the railway companies, Gladstone, then President of the Board of Trade, promoted a Railway Bill[1] which proposed an extension of state intervention[2] in the industry, but was fiercely resisted by the 'Railway Interest' (Alderman 1973). The most lasting feature of the subsequent Act was the provision for third class passengers to travel at a fixed rate of one penny a mile. This laid the foundation for the mass transit of the working classes which would eventually impact on the nature of urban development. By 1845 the exploratory phase was over and trunk routes linking London with Birmingham, Liverpool, Manchester, Leeds, Newcastle, Bristol and Southampton were in place: railways were established as profitable enterprises. The defeat of Gladstone's attempt to manage network development meant that subsequently:

> The Road was clear for the chaos of the Mania, for future construction of blocking lines by rival companies, and of hundreds of uneconomic branches …
> (Ellis 1960a, 155).

When the speculative bubble which drove the Mania burst it took a while for investment to recover, but between 1850 and 1875 some 13,700 kms (8,500 miles) were added to the network, giving a total of nearly 24,140 route kms (15,000 miles). Growth continued right through to 1914 to give an eventual total of 32,200 kms (20,000 miles) (Freeman and Aldcroft 1985) (Figure 2.1). Most of the later additions were rural branch lines, often known as 'farmers lines' as they were built with locally raised finance:[3] few were profitable. Other branch lines were those which intensified the suburban networks around major cities. Beginning in 1863, the development of the London underground as a system largely segregated from the main line network was a very special case of this: for the most part new suburban lines were conventional, surface running routes of the main line companies. It was not unusual by this time, however, for landowners to offer inducements of various kinds to the companies to build lines to access their estates

---

1   During Gladstone's time at the Board of Trade, the Select Committee on Railways and a Railway Board, under the Chairmanship of Lord Dalhousie, developed public interest principles for the consideration of railway bills: these represent the first articulation of ideas about state involvement in railway planning. (See Select Committee 1844; Railway Department of the Board of Trade 1845.)

2   This included provisions for nationalisation, although the preconditions were sufficiently complex for these never to be implemented.

3   By contrast local routes in France, known as 'Chemins de fer d'Interet Local' were built using local and national sources of public funds, only strategic routes, known as 'Chemins de fer d'Interet National' were privately funded, although even these were centrally planned.

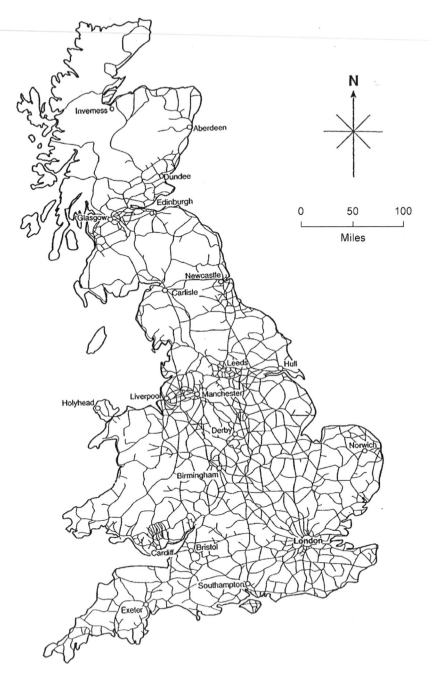

Figure 2.1 The railway network 1914

Source: Biddle, G. (1990), *The Railway Surveyors* (London, Ian Allan Ltd).

so that they could be developed for housing; the provision of land for a station was typical (Jackson 1999 a and b).

In the closing decades of the nineteenth century the 'water gaps' in the main line network were closed by some remarkable feats of engineering. Brunel had set the standard in 1859 with his innovative Royal Albert Bridge at Saltash, and the Severn Tunnel and Forth Bridge were worthy successors. The extremities of the network were completed by the opening of lines to Kyle of Lochalsh in 1897, Padstow in 1899 and Mallaig in 1901.[4] A surprising, late development was the building of a new, well engineered,[5] main line between Annesley in north Nottinghamshire (with existing links back to Sheffield and Manchester) and London Marylebone, opening in 1899 as the Great Central Railway. This was the product of a long campaign by one of the most influential and visionary 'railway kings', Sir Edward Watkin (Hodgkins 2002), and was intended to be part of a Liverpool–Paris route which would include construction of a Channel Tunnel (this was in fact started but never seriously got underway). The railway then entered its Edwardian heyday and the emphasis changed to fine tuning with construction of 'cut-offs' (short cuts) typified by the last piece of main line railway built until the 1980s, the Great Western and Great Central Joint Line opened in 1906 between west London and Aynho Junction near Banbury, via High Wycombe (Edwards and Pigram 1988), which shortened the Paddington-Birmingham route by 30.6 kms (19 miles).

The geographical and operational characteristics of the mature network in 1914

Laissez-faire meant that the mature railway network came to exhibit certain key characteristics. Route duplication was one: for example there were two between London and Exeter/Plymouth, two between London and Birmingham, and four between London and Manchester. Duplication extended to the lines between provincial cities too: there were two between Manchester and Leeds, two between Manchester and Sheffield, and five between Manchester and Liverpool. There was route duplication at the local level as exemplified by Clydeside, which developed the densest network outside London (Smith and Anderson 1993): Barrhead and Renfrew had two routes to Glasgow and Paisley had three.

A second feature was that the focus of the main lines on London meant that cross-country routes were usually engineered to a lesser standard, leading to journeys at slower speeds than on the main lines, with few through trains.[6]

---

4   As an illustration of the growing involvement of the state in railway development in Britain, the lines from Strome Ferry to Kyle of Lochalsh and Fort William to Mallaig were financed by the government for social/political reasons (Thomas 1991, 109-123).

5   Gentle gradients and curves and an absence of level crossings allowed sustained high speed running.

6   Bonavia (1995, 105) refers to the Oxford-Cambridge route which had the potential to facilitate 'cultural exchanges' between the two universities, whereas the reality was that

There were exceptions, though, and the most notable included the York-Sheffield-Birmingham-Bristol route, Edinburgh-Glasgow, and the routes across the Pennines linking Liverpool and Manchester with Leeds, Sheffield and Hull.

Although the companies resisted state-led planning, they did engage in their own planning to meet corporate goals. As the network developed, lines connected and companies developed common interests leading to the creation of the Railway Clearing House in 1842 (Bagwell 1968), which facilitated further co-operation. This led to amalgamations to secure territorial supremacy, the maximisation of traffic and economies of scale, demonstrating what has been seen as the natural tendency towards monopoly in the transport sector. This process was initiated by formation of the Midland Railway in 1844, with an empire stretching from York through Sheffield to Birmingham and Bristol. Amalgamations proliferated and, by 1870, 83 per cent of total railway revenue accrued to only fifteen companies (Freeman and Aldcroft 1988, 33), although there were over a hundred companies in business. The largest company, the London and North Western, had an empire stretching from London Euston through Birmingham, Manchester and Liverpool to Carlisle and claimed to be the world's largest joint stock company at the time. The creation of large companies with ample resources led to a third characteristic of the network, duplication of facilities: if different companies had lines serving a particular city, typically each had separate passenger and goods facilities as increasing state regulation of prices restricted competition to quality of service. Duplication reduced network benefits and increased overheads.

Territoriality was associated with a fourth characteristic, gaps in the network which were usually at the interface between company territories: these typically occurred around city centres, where companies approached from different directions. Because of the expense of making a connection across the city centre, probably by tunnelling, this was often never achieved: Manchester, Liverpool, Bradford and Glasgow (in the north-south direction) were prime examples, with London as a special case.

Railway network development and operation 1914–39

This period was a watershed for the railways as their status as the dominant transport mode ended. Competition from tram and motorbus networks led to the reduction, or even complete withdrawal, of passenger services from some inner urban stations in most conurbations and some closures in rural areas too. Road haulage of freight grew rapidly too and, as a deregulated industry, it had the freedom to cherry pick the most profitable cargoes. In 1928 the railway companies were empowered to develop their own fleets of buses and lorries, which potentially facilitated co-ordination between road and rail services, but the extent of this was

---

these were usually effected via the waiting room at Bletchley as one had to change trains en route.

limited. As road infrastructure developed and began to influence patterns of urban development, the issue for the railway system was whether or not its operational role could be successfully adjusted to the new conditions, and whether its spatial integration with its markets would be successfully maintained.

During the Great War a Railway Executive Committee managed the railways as a unified system and significant economies were achieved (Aldcroft 1968, 31). In 1919 the Ministry of Transport was established and the drift politically was towards nationalisation. The first Minister of Transport was Sir Eric Geddes who during the 1914–18 war had been sent in by the Prime Minister, Lloyd George, to sort out logistical problems on the Western Front (which were very much associated with the rail network, of course) and he was a supporter of central control. However, the companies fought against this and, instead, to secure a more rational business structure whilst perpetuating private ownership, a compromise was struck by the 1921 Railways Act which grouped them into the 'Big Four' companies in 1923. These comprised regional monopolies radiating out from London: the London Midland and Scottish Railway (LMS), the London North Eastern Railway (LNER), the Great Western Railway (GWR), and the Southern Railway (SR).

Table 2.2 British railways passenger and freight traffic: 1919–38

Year	Passenger Journeys[1] Million	Freight Tonnes Million	of Which Coal and Coke Million	Freight Tonne – kilometres Billion
1919	2,064	310	183	–
1923	1,772	349	226	31.0
1928	1,250	331	190	29.0
1933	1,159	255	168	24.6
1938	1,237	270	176	26.6

Note: [1] Figures include free-hauled (i.e. departmental) traffic on revenue earning trains.
Source: DoT, *Transport Statistics*, London, HMSO, 1984.

Competition from road modes and loss of traffic associated with the Great Depression, meant that the railway companies had their backs to the wall. These difficulties and structural problems arising from the Grouping, meant that managements were pre-occupied with internal matters. Between 1920–38, the number of rail passenger journeys fell by 40 per cent (Table 2.2), although passenger mileage increased by a small amount: but this was totally eclipsed by the increase in bus and coach travel (Table 2.3). Freight tonnage lifted fell by

16.8 per cent and freight tonne kilometres decreased by 13 per cent. Also the financial performance of the railway companies failed to live up to expectations as, although they remained in profit, net receipts were below those for 1913 for every year between 1923 and 1939. The decline of the railways, the growth of road traffic and the pursuit of integrated transport became the subject of both popular (The Times 1932) and official (Hurcomb 1935) debate.

Table 2.3 Estimated number of passenger miles travelled by final consumers on public land transport in the U.K 1920–38 (m)

Mode	1920	1929	1938
Railways	19,214	18,912	20,009
Tramways and trolleys	8,058	9,494	8,148
Buses and coaches	3,457	11,307	19,037
Taxis and hire cars	1,624	929	587
Horse drawn vehicles	216	63	13
Total	**32,569**	**40,705**	**47,794**

Source: Stone R., and Rowe D.A., 1966, The Measurement of Consumers' Expenditure and Behaviour in the UK, 1920-38, Vol. 2; reproduced in Aldcroft, 1968, 56.

Technologically the period saw refinement of steam locomotive design. Some suburban services were electrified, particularly on the Southern, and there was experimentation with the use of diesel power. But there was nothing like the development of main line diesel and electric traction as occurred in the USA where, by 1940, they were used to operate the majority of express passenger services (Allen 1941). During the economic recovery of the late thirties there was competition for public attention through the operation of high profile express services, typified by the 'Silver Jubilee', the 'Cheltenham Flyer' and, most famously, the 'Flying Scotsman'. These earned the railways a romantic place in the heart of the nation, but most services saw little improvement and most suburban services were typified by slow speeds and grimy carriages.

The handling of freight saw little change; even in 1939, it was still based on wagonload traffic[7] wherein wagons had to be shunted and re-shunted into different trains as they slowly made their way from origin to destination, with

---

7   Wagonload traffic occurs where a train is made up of wagons having consignments with different origins and final destinations, so that marshalling is usually required at both ends of the trunk trip. Trainload traffic, on the other hand, occurs where all wagons have

goods often getting delayed and/or damaged in the process. There was investment in automated marshalling yards at Toton, March and Feltham, and containerisation was introduced but, generally, innovation in freight handling was limited. The traditional methods were vulnerable to competition from road haulage with its ability to move goods door-to-door and failed to build on the competitive advantage of railways: the capacity to move large volumes quickly over medium and long distances. The railways remained hamstrung by their common carrier obligation[8] too; this was such a burden that the companies belatedly launched the 'Square Deal' campaign in 1938 to have it removed. The MoT was sympathetic but the outbreak of war prevented progress.

The Grouping improved efficiency; between 1928–38 the number of locomotives was reduced by 17 per cent, more standardised approaches to locomotive building were introduced, and the railway workforce was reduced from 735,870 in 1921 to 588,517 in 1939. Some companies, particularly the GWR, developed an extensive network of feeder bus and lorry services. But, generally, the heavy investment by the railway companies in bus companies[9] did not lead to bus-rail integration, but to bus services complementing, or even competing with, rail. The railway companies were mainly looking to increase their revenue. One positive outcome was that the companies[10] became members of Joint Operating Committees with the local authorities which ran the municipal bus services, so that new bus services running *into* the towns could be properly co-ordinated with those running wholly *within* the towns. This was one of the few ways in which institutional relationships were developed to embrace the railway companies and local authorities (Hellewell 1996) although, ironically, buses were the focus. But generally across the network, there was no fundamental innovation to create a base on which the railways could compete with road modes which were developing technologically at a quicker pace (Joy 1973; Hamilton and Potter 1985).

The relationships between the railways and urban development 1830–1914: the industrial districts

Bulk freight haulage, particularly coal, was the underlying rationale for the network. In the coalfields, the complexity and duplication of routes was remarkable: in the Welsh Valleys, for example, five companies served 72 collieries and there was at

---

the same origin and destination and no marshalling en route is required. The latter is clearly the most cost effective.

8   This was a duty laid on railway companies by parliament in return for the monopoly on freight transport which passage of a railway act bestowed on them: they had to accept for carriage any item submitted by a customer.

9   They had an interest in 47 per cent of the 41,500 buses on British roads in 1931 (Aldcroft 1968, 86).

10   This was a particular feature in the territory of the LMS.

least two or three company networks in each valley serving the same collieries. The railways were also closely involved with development of the iron and steel industries, heavy engineering, town gas plants, breweries and the like. Industrial activity created demand for labour, leading to the development of industrial townships and demand for passenger services.[11] As for the railway companies themselves, engineering complexes and associated townships developed at Crewe, Doncaster, Derby, Swindon and their many counterparts. In the larger cities huge agglomerations of rail-served industries and railway engineering industries developed (Kellett 1979; Simmons 1986) as did large port complexes with their own internal railway systems: the largest was, of course, London, and all the major railway companies sought to gain access. In other areas specific ports were associated with particular companies, notable examples being the London and South Western with Southampton and the Great Central with Immingham.

So there was a close correlation between the location of industry and the geography of the railway network, although this is not to say that every factory was rail connected. Most were not and the short distance carting of raw materials and part-finished or finished goods through the streets was important in every industrial area. Where goods needed to be moved by rail to or from premises which were not rail connected, the railway companies provided a network of public goods depots (also known as 'stations' in the Victorian period) and these were found in all settlements, large and small, along the railway network.

The lack of control over urban development meant that industry was often associated with appalling environmental conditions. It was not uncommon for railway routes approaching city centres to be elevated on brick viaducts so as to avoid interference with street level traffic. Frequently these fixed the limits of city districts and, usually, they were associated with railway goods facilities, areas of sidings and railway maintenance facilities, areas of noxious industry and sub-standard housing, as for example in Ancoats, Manchester (Kellett 1979, 338). Concern over the poor environment and low standards of public health in these areas triggered calls for state intervention and, through association, led to railways being seen in a negative light by those concerned with public health, housing and town planning, a point of view which was to persist:

> It was unfortunate that just at this period of lowest ebb in England's control of urban growth and when the onrush of town building was commencing, the Railways should enter upon the transport scene. Hailed as the prime symbol of industrial success and so armed with despotic powers, they became a new tyrant dominating our cities with much less regard to the general convenience than the old aristocratic planner (Abercrombie 1944a, 81-82).

---

11   That around Denaby and Cadeby Collieries in South Yorkshire was typical (Booth 1990).

However because of the necessity for rail access to large industrial premises, the model industrial settlements such as Saltaire, Bournville and Port Sunlight built by the industrial philanthropists and which came to inspire the town planning movement, were rail connected, with a passenger station too.

The relationships between railways and urban development 1830–1914: the CBDs

As city centres grew in size and the range of services they supported expanded, the employment they provided grew in parallel, as did the number of business visitors and other travellers. This demand for movement fuelled the growth in railway traffic and led to a close relationship between CBD growth and railway development. Railway stations were directly associated with hotels, warehousing facilities, retail and office developments and, by 1890, railway companies were owners of up to nine per cent of city centre land in the five biggest cities, and directly influenced the function of up to 20 per cent (Kellett 1979, 318). The locations of major city centre stations became a factor of enduring significance for town planning, because of their particular juxtaposition with the regard to the final destinations for railway passengers and the difficulties involved in altering this, if it became problematic: it was often not optimised from the outset.

Competition for access to central London was particularly fierce: high land values and parliament's policy (see later) of restricting surface railway construction, produced the now familiar pattern of termini around the 'quadrilateral', the roughly oblong shaped, continuously built-up area comprising the City and West End. Eventually the *laissez-faire* approach and the failure to adopt the practice of building joint stations on the German *Hauptbahnhof* or American *Union* station models, led to the building of 15 surface termini: more than in any other European city. This led to the need to change to another mode of transport for movement between the termini to make journeys beyond London and for access into the City and West End. Part of the solution was a local, underground railway system and the first line, opened in 1863[12] and running east to west between Farringdon and Paddington, was built by the Metropolitan Railway along the line of Farringdon Street, King's Cross Road and Euston Road, thereby connecting up Paddington, Euston and King's Cross stations as well as providing a convenient means of transport for residents in the west seeking employment in the City. This was built by 'cut and cover' techniques and was really a 'sub-surface' railway as, for ease of construction, it was buried at no great depth under existing roads and ventilation shafts were provided, along with sections of open air running to help with removing the noxious smoke from the engines. Following construction of a similar east to west route by the District Railway between Mansion House and

---

12 For a detailed history of the development of the London Underground see Barker and Robbins 1963, 1976 and Wolmar 2004.

the prosperous south western suburbs (Kensington, Brompton and Hammersmith), encouragement by parliament (Select Committee 1863, 1-2) led to these routes being extended and connected to become the Inner Circle, completed in 1884. In 1890, following the invention of the Greathead shield which facilitated deep tunnelling and the application of electric power to the running of trains, came a new generation of deep 'tube' railways which criss-crossed the quadrilateral rather than run around its periphery, as their alignment did not depend upon suitable surface roads; they were free, subject to geology, to follow the most profitable alignments. By 1907 these underground railways were linking new suburbs with the heart of the City and West End (Croome and Jackson 1993) (see Appendix 1 for a chronology of their construction).

In the first decade of the twentieth century the street tramway networks, built under the 1870 Tramways Act, were being electrified so successfully that they took a slice out of the inner suburban railway traffic of the main line companies in many cities, owing to their greater convenience for shorter journeys. The response of the railway companies was to develop their outer suburban services, but also they began to electrify their inner suburban services with the first examples being in Liverpool and Newcastle and, a little later, in London itself (see Appendices 2 and 3): so, despite the competition, rail traffic continued to grow. Electrification meant faster, cleaner and more reliable services.

London's dominance of the urban hierarchy and the severity of its urban problems mean that it had paradigm status as a planning problem (Haywood 1997a). The railway network was a principal component of this: the debate about overcrowding, the need to provide land for commercial expansion and to widen access to the suburbs, all hinged around the capacity of the network, with congestion throughout much of it indicating the stress it was experiencing. In the absence of any state directed co-ordination, trains, trams and buses competed with each other. However, the more astute managers of the various private undertakings began to realise that there were commercial benefits to be gained from amalgamation, as exemplified by the creation of the Underground Electric Railway Company (UERL) in 1902 by American railway financier, Charles Tyson Yerkes. The work for the UERL by the young Frank Pick[13] (Barman 1979), typified the approach: he developed a livery, poster and branding campaign to promote the Underground as a unified network and, after 1912, when the Underground took over the London General Omnibus Company he:

> … began to develop feeder buses from the tube termini, on the model of Yerkes' original tramways plan. Within six months, with a new slogan 'where the Railway Ends the Motor Bus begins' he more than doubled the number of routes, and extended the service area five times (Hall 1988, 64).

---

13   Albert Stanley, later Lord Ashfield, was Managing Director of the Underground Group at this time and he and Pick began a lifelong association which reached its climax in their work on the underground in the 1920s and 1930s.

There was not prolonged competition by railway companies to penetrate deeper into the heart of most provincial CBDs; the traffic potential was not there to make such huge investments viable. For the most part railway stations remained where they had been located from the outset, or re-established soon afterwards, with a general absence of tunnelling, either for main line railways or 'tube' lines. As in London, the *laissez-faire* approach usually meant that companies each had their own station and their juxtaposition could make onward rail travel very inconvenient. But in some cases, owing perhaps to intervention by a local authority or an agreement between companies, city centres came to be served by a single station, with Newcastle and Bristol as the most notable examples. Cambridge, Derby, York and Chester were examples in smaller cities, although sometimes secondary stations appeared later, as in Derby and Chester, as a result of an incursion by a new company (Biddle 1986).

Stations, generally, were located on the periphery of the centres they served because of the high costs involved in buying up city centre property to secure a more central location, although this was often resisted by local authorities in any case. So journeys had to be completed by a walk, tram, omnibus or cab ride. Sometimes stations were very peripheral as at Derby where the main station was located about 1.6 kilometres (one mile) from the town centre. In a situation like Sheffield, its two stations were about 500 metres (550 yards) from the centre, but the latter was on higher ground making the walk a challenge for many. A notable exception was Glasgow, where bridges were built to bring lines from the south over the Clyde into the city centre termini at Central and St Enoch's to complement Queen Street and Buchanan Street, located on the centre's northern edge about a half mile (800 metres) away. Also in Birmingham, lines from north and south were linked by tunnels with a large excavation to create the centrally located New Street station. Glasgow had standard gauge tunnels running east-west under the city centre which facilitated the operation of steam hauled services linking the eastern working class housing areas with industrial complexes down the Clyde to the west[14] and was the only provincial city to see construction of a circular, electric underground railway around the city centre. Liverpool had an electrified, elevated 'overhead' railway connecting suburbs on the Mersey riverside to the docks, warehouses and factories and an electrified line under the Mersey linking the city centre with Birkenhead.

Although the earliest stations tended to be designed as a long, single platform accessed by trains moving in each direction (Cambridge is the only surviving example), eventually, as stations expanded and were rebuilt, a format was arrived at where each of the two main running lines would have a platform face and larger stations would have multiple lines and platforms. Although there may well have been buildings on each platform, there tended to be a dominant side for through stations and this was important for onward movement to final destinations beyond

---

14   Travel along the north-south axis continued to demand travel by road across the CBD between Central/St Enoch and Queen Street/Buchanan Street.

the station, as most passengers would move through this side. A common format was arrived at for termini too where, although again there would be platforms alongside the several running lines, there would be a connecting platform and circulation area at the 'head' of the station at right angles to the other platforms, through which passengers would pass as they moved in and out of the station. Station architects used these operational factors to inform their designs and the grandest architecture was reserved for the areas where footfall was highest and where the station presented its most public face (Biddle 1986). These characteristics also had implications for town planning, as these parts of stations were usually the most important in terms of the integration of the station with the rest of the city centre and those involved would want to optimise this relationship, as far as they were able.

The railway companies were keen to make grand statements about their corporate power through the size and quality of design of their stations and were also aware that this would reassure passengers who might have concerns about the safety of such high speed travel. The perfection of the use of iron and glass by Sir Joseph Paxton for his hall at the 1851 Great Exhibition, provided the technology for the creation of the great 'train sheds' at major stations which would both provide shelter for passengers and, along with an adjoining station building, provide the kind of grand, modern structure which the companies desired. This combination of the engineers' skills in designing the train sheds with those of the architects who designed the station buildings was a grand alliance: it produced structures all over the country in a range of styles, from the classicism of Newcastle Central to the Gothic of Liverpool Street and St Pancras. Erection of these structures continued right up to the 1914–18 war and slightly beyond, with the rebuilding of Birmingham Snow Hill completed in 1912 and London Waterloo, not finally completed until 1922. The grand stations with their train sheds, which were found on a lesser scale in towns throughout the country, were a very significant transportation and architectural legacy which would raise some serious issues for future generations (Biddle 1986).

The relationships between the railways and urban development 1830–1914: suburban housing and planned suburban settlements

Even in London, where areas such as Richmond and Hounslow had lines by 1850, the initial pace of suburban expansion was slow (Dyos 1973). However, suburban traffic was actively promoted by the companies from the 1860s, and was associated subsequently with rapid inter-censal population growth in Outer London. Railway companies to the south and east of London (Jackson 1999a and b; Kay 1996) were much more interested in suburban traffic than those bringing long distance traffic into north and west London, as the latter had little spare capacity. This affected the scale and timing of suburban development and the nature of the railway networks. As the influence of the early town planning movement grew, the railways came to be associated with planned suburbs too. Bedford Park was the first such railway suburb, with the most notable being the association between the arrival of the tube at Golders Green in 1907 and subsequent development of Hampstead Garden Suburb, a showcase development for the new town planning movement (Ikin 1990).

Construction of lines to city centre termini often involved demolition of much working class housing which was the cheapest to compulsorily purchase (Kellett 1979). Few of the occupants were re-housed by the companies, the majority being displaced into adjacent areas leading to more overcrowding: these negative impacts were well understood by parliament (Royal Commission 1884, 20). Political concern over the housing question grew under Gladstone's Liberals and Disraeli's new Tories, as the ideological pendulum swung towards collectivist and interventionist strategies (Black 1969). This produced various statutes which are seen as part of the ancestry of modern town planning (Ministry of Town and Country Planning and Department of Health for Scotland 1950; Ashworth 1954; Cherry 1974, 1988; Lawless and Brown 1986).

Despite the legislation, the housing problem remained, but reformers saw a solution in facilitating access through cheap rail fares to better and affordable housing built on cheap suburban land. The first statutory provision was in 1861 (Royal Commission 1884, 49) but mass access to London's railways did not arrive until the Cheap Trains Act of 1883: 'the twopenny fare brought an entirely new travelling public on to the railways' (Dyos and Aldcroft 1971, 219). As a result the growth of working class suburbs accelerated, typified by those in the East End such as Walthamstow. At the turn of the century the debate around the housing problem intensified; Charles Booth led the movement which saw 'improved means of locomotion', particularly that provided by railways (Booth 1901, 15-17) as the best way of increasing access to the suburbs. Some observers saw that if the railway companies were allowed to combine land and railway development, a solution could be found to the housing problem and the associated need to finance expanded railway services, by using development profits to subsidise rail travel (Perks 1906). The growing impact of the town planning movement was reflected in the promotion, by Asquith's Liberal government, of the 1909 Housing and Town Planning Act. Although only enabling legislation, a number of schemes were submitted to the Local Government Board for approval before 1914. These included several examples of railway suburbs, typified by those for the Ruislip-Northwood estate in north west London, alongside the Metropolitan Railway's lines from Baker Street (Thompson 1913, 133 and 139).

Although, undoubtedly, railways did influence the patterns of suburban development in provincial cities, their smaller size meant that, generally, the impact was much weaker than in London and was very variable. For the majority of working and lower middle class people, the main methods of getting around were walking and using street trams. Nevertheless, Glasgow saw development of a dedicated suburban railway, the Cathcart Circle, and the tunnels under the CBD built in the 1890s improved access from the residential East End to the industrial complexes down the Clyde, typified by the Singer works which had its own railway station. Services extended out well beyond the built-up area as far as Helensburgh, Balloch, Milngavie and Wemyss Bay. Manchester developed such classic middle and upper class commuter settlements as Hale, Altrincham, Wilmslow and Alderley Edge, with their revivalist station architecture reflected in the design of the adjacent shopping parades and villas. In Birmingham the suburban developments in Sutton Coldfield were linked with the CBD by the 'Cross City Line' (Boynton 1993),[15] but rail commuting was less important in Birmingham than in any other city of comparable size (Cherry 1994, 70). Nevertheless, its network can be regarded as a model of good practice and will be revisited later in the book: two well located main stations with cross-city lines running in tunnel under the CBD, efficiently linking the outer suburbs and industrial towns with the regional centre.[16]

Overall, the most striking characteristic of railway development in provincial cities was its variability. This was well illustrated by Nottingham and Leicester; within five miles of central Nottingham there developed 35 stations, whereas within the same distance of central Leicester there was only 21. Nottingham was a good example of a local authority where the city fathers took a positive interest in railway matters and supported the development of the Nottingham Suburban Line (Marshall 1986), opened in 1889 with three new stations within the city boundary. They also developed ideas for a new central station, more accessible than that provided by the Midland Railway on low lying land to the south of the city centre. This was eventually provided by Watkin's Great Central Railway in the very grand form of Nottingham Victoria (Vanns 2004).

The relationships between the railways and urban development 1919–39

The inter-war years were marked by the development of the National Grid which freed industry from dependency on rail connections to supply coal as the key source of power. The growth of road haulage increased this locational shift away from the railways. However, new industries were developed which required rail haulage, such as iron and steel manufacture at Corby. As a response to the structural decline of traditional industries, some large 'trading estates' were developed, typically

---

15   The importance of the link between a railway suburb and its CBD was nicely demonstrated by the case of the Birkenhead to Hoylake railway opened in 1866. Initially this brought little growth to Hoylake but, in 1888, a connection was made with central Liverpool via the new tunnel under the Mersey. Hoylake grew from a population of 3,722 in 1881 to 14,009 in 1911.

16   The Cadbury's model settlement of Bournville, with its own station and freight facilities (Hitches 1992), was on the West Suburban Line and planning schemes were prepared under the 1909 Housing and Town Planning Act for Quinton, Harborne and Egbaston in association with the Harborne branch line (Sutcliffe 1981, 84).

towards the periphery of urban areas which is were much new industry did locate in this period, but unlike much of that, these were all rail connected. Examples included Park Royal (West London), Slough, Trafford Park (Manchester) Treforest (South Wales), the Team Valley (Gateshead) and Hillingdon (Glasgow). So, despite the general erosion of rail's association with industry, the outcome of change was not wholly negative.

Political unrest during the Great War led to Lloyd George initiating the 'Homes Fit for Heroes' campaign (Swenarton 1981), implemented by the 1919 Housing and Town Planning Act. Perhaps the best known of the council housing schemes developed under this was that by the London County Council (LCC) at Becontree, in east London. Construction started in 1920 and;

> By the end of the thirties, its population had reached about 116,000, accommodated in 25,769 dwellings (Jackson 1991, 235).

Despite the obvious potential for integrated land-use and transportation planning by building on such a scale, this took a long time to be realised and a station didn't open until 1932. The lack of railway connections to new council housing estates was not unusual outside London; Manchester's Wythenshawe and Liverpool's Speke were largely left off the railway network. It was significant that from around 1900, the municipalities developed their own tram and omnibus services and that the importance of linking council housing schemes to these had been emphasised by the Tudor Walters report (Local Government Board 1918).

Despite the intensity of local authority house construction, three quarters of the four million houses built between 1919 and 1939 were erected by private builders. Because of imbalances in regional economies, most were in the Midlands and South East, particularly around London. It was here that concerns increased over loss of farmland and the failure to produce balanced settlements with community facilities and employment. New motor bus services and the increasing use of cars by the middle classes led to 'ribbon development' along arterial roads: this became the subject of particular criticism and statutory control under the 1935 Restriction of Ribbon Development Act. There was widespread condemnation by architects and other arbiters of public taste of the poor architectural quality of this suburban sprawl (see chapter 3 in Hall, 1988).

There were some important exceptions to the relatively declining role of the railways, particularly around London, where railway companies were centrally involved in suburban growth. The Metropolitan Railway Company had underground lines in central London and a surface extension out to Aylesbury, opened in 1892, and was unique in circumventing the general ruling that railway companies should not develop their surplus lands for non-operational uses (Jackson 1986 and 2006). Electrification to Uxbridge was complete by 1905 and, by 1914, housing development on surplus lands had commenced at Pinner. In 1919, in order to provide a more legally watertight basis for its development activities, the Metropolitan set up the Metropolitan Railway Country Estates Company (MRCE) and marketed its developments under the banner of 'Metroland' (Jackson 1991, 2006). This was a significant contribution to the massive population growth in Middlesex which experienced 'five times the (percentage) increase for England and Wales, and the highest recorded for any county' (Cherry 1988, 95). The MRCE encountered no serious opposition to its activities but other railway companies did not follow suit, despite the Metropolitan's call for general legislation to enable them to do so (Selbie[17] 1921). Nevertheless, south of the Thames, the Southern demonstrated that it shared a common interest with house builders and this acted as a spur to the improvement of services. Booth and his associates had recognised some years before that:

> Inner South and Outer South London are like two cisterns, the one brimming over and the other empty; a junction pipe is all that is needed to redress the level in one, and make the other serve a useful purpose (Browning Hall 1902).

Electrification of existing lines to secure faster, more frequent and more reliable trains and construction of new routes was the answer, with the added bonus that removal of dirty steam trains made the system more attractive to passengers, something which the railway industry came to call 'the sparks effect'. Appendix 2 shows that, under the inspired management of Herbert Walker (Klapper 1973), the most outstanding of the Big Four managers, the Southern electrified the routes out as far as Orpington, Sutton, Dorking, Guildford and Windsor by 1930.[18] Subsequently electrification reached the South Coast allowing the introduction of that most famous commuter train, the Brighton Belle. The attendant suburban growth around south London (Jackson 1999a) led to massive increases in the numbers of passengers carried (Haywood 1997). Over a third of the new stations opened in the London area after 1919 were on the Southern and almost all of them enjoyed subsidy from developers (Bonavia 1987; Jackson 1991): pressure from landowners was partly responsible for the opening of new branch lines too (Jackson 1999b). The Southern actively promoted its trains to access the new suburbs and produced a free 'Residential Guide' from 1926 onwards (Jackson 1999a and b). The Southern Railway also became widely recognised for excellence in the design of some of its new stations which employed the modernist 'Southern Odeon' style, with Surbiton as the best known example.

After 1918, Pick began to pursue the sort of strategy for the Underground endorsed in contemporary professional journals:

---

17   Selbie became general manager of the Metropolitan Railway in 1908 and promoted electrification and extension out to Harrow. He initiated the Metroland marketing campaign and formation of Metropolitan Railway Country Estates Ltd.

18   Bonavia (1987, 83) refers to the marketing slogans used by the Southern: 'Live in Surrey, Free from Worry' and 'Live in Kent and Be Content'.

The electric railways in the north of London are becoming congested and new direct railways from the north-west to the south-east and the north-east to south-west through central London, pivoting on Piccadilly Circus, are a necessity. These lines should be constructed on a high speed basis of average speeds of at least 25 m.p.h., with stops not more than one per mile, with interchange facilities where they bisect the slower lines and with omnibus and tram services to feed the comparatively widely separated stations (Thomas 1922, 114).

New tunnels under central London were not financially viable, so the Underground built surface extensions of the existing lines out into green fields (Appendix 1) thereby spawning new suburbs, and rail catchment was maximised by integration with feeder bus services on the Pick model. When London's public transport was taken into public ownership under the London Passenger Transport Board (LPTB) in 1933, the New Works Programme was launched, with a budget of £40 million: this was facilitated by the government underwriting the necessary loans as part of its anti-unemployment strategy.[19] Most of the work was completed before being curtailed by the War (Appendix 1) and facilitated further suburban growth, public and private:

> The Edgware, Cockfosters and Stanmore extensions, and the tube routes to Uxbridge and Hounslow ... traversed areas that were quickly covered with private enterprise housing ... and of course the Edgware line also served the big LCC estate at Watling (Jackson 1991, 190-192).

The LPTB was also notable for its success in co-ordination of the design of stations, associated buildings, rolling stock, bus interchanges and promotional literature. Pick, who became the LPTB's Vice Chairman, was very influential in this field and had long recognised the commercial importance of the attractiveness of stations and a good public image of the system:

> ... if the cinemas were temples of entertainment, the Underground stations were the temples of travel. Frank Pick, Vice-Chairman of the Underground Group, had called his stations 'inviting doorways in an architectural setting that cannot be missed by the casual passer-by'. To live near an Underground station was considered by many people to be the 'acme of convenience' (Edwards and Pigram 1986, 17).

Stations, such as Charles Holden's Arnos Grove on the Piccadilly Line extension to Cockfosters, with their integrated bus facilities, were widely acclaimed as models of transport provision and practical but tasteful modern architecture.

---

19   The relevant legislation was the 1929 Development (Loans, Guarantees and Grants) Act which the Big Four companies also took advantage of. This was an imaginative initiative for the period.

As on the Southern, the stations were frequently part of a suburban node which comprised shopping parades and other local services and the surrounding green fields quickly filled up with houses. However, even in London, modernisation had its limits and one of the densest commuter flows, that between the eastern suburbs and Liverpool Street, remained steam hauled with all the unpleasantness for passengers and people living alongside the railway which that entailed. The only improvements in provincial cities which approached the achievements in London were electrification of the Manchester to Altrincham line and the extension of the electrified Mersey Railway from Birkenhead to West Kirkby on the Wirral. The latter involved the rebuilding of Hoylake station, where a striking art deco style was utilised. A number of main line stations were rebuilt in the art deco style too, but usually in isolation from their surroundings. However the experiences of the period did facilitate the drawing up of principles for the design of new stations in the immediate post-war period as set out in Table 2.4, but these did not address matters outside the station (Barman 1947).

Table 2.4 New standards for station design 1947

a	Free and comfortable circulation planned as a result of scientific study of passenger movement; circulation unencumbered by luggage trolleys for which separate means of access will be planned.
b	The various station and platform buildings grouped into compact and continuous blocks.
c	Clearly distinguishable signs, illuminated where necessary, to guide and inform passengers at all points between their entering and leaving.
d	Escalators to and from different levels, wherever the traffic is sufficient to justify their operation.
e	Island platforms to allow direct interchange from one train to another, without climbing stairs.
f	Full-length platforms to avoid double stopping, protected from the weather for most of their length, and fitted with windscreens to protect passengers from cold winds and draughts.
g	Plentiful lighting in hours of darkness in all parts where passengers may tread.
h	At very large stations, interesting and well-stocked shops in which last-minute shopping will become a pleasant experience.
i	Shops, kiosks, automatic machines and advertisements arranged in compliance with a general station design and rigorously controlled so that order and dignity may never be lacking.
j	Light, airy waiting rooms, well heated, well ventilated, welcoming in appearance, decorated in light, cheerful colours.
k	Tea and coffee served in the waiting room, or in refreshment rooms next door.

l	Bright, welcoming refreshment rooms and restaurants, with soft, intimate lighting, scrupulously clean underfoot, without advertisements, lined where necessary with absorbent materials that will reduce noise and clatter.
m	The windows of waiting rooms, refreshment rooms, buffets and restaurants arranged so as to give a full view of platforms and trains.
n	Lavatories lined with delicately coloured tiles and kept spotlessly clean at all hours of the day and night.

Source: Barman, 1947, 64.

State intervention in the railways and urban development: 1830–1918

Despite the failure of parliament to take strategic control over the development of the railway network, it was inexorably drawn into the industry's affairs. The fact that, initially, railways were built to different gauges was an obvious shortcoming which would undermine network benefits. The major variations were Stephenson's gauge and Brunel's 'broad gauge': in 1846 the Gauge Act was enacted, despite Brunel's vigorous opposition (Vaughan 1991), whereby Stephenson's 'standard gauge' was adopted for all future construction.[20]

The railway companies had powerful opponents amongst the traders who wanted goods carried at the lowest price and equitable treatment as compared with their competitors. Despite the common carrier obligation, 'railway rates' became the dominant transport issue. The traders wanted a transparent set of rates which all the companies would have to adhere to, with no display of 'undue preference' between customers. This was eventually put in place by the Railway and Canal Traffic Act of 1894 (Dyos and Aldcroft 1971) and effectively ended competition on price between railway companies.

Parliament was also concerned with safety. The records of the Railway Inspection Department of the Board of Trade go back to 1840 (Rolt 1998) when it was given the power to delay openings if the required standards were not met. As traffic became denser, serious accidents occurred: debate around the causes focused on signalling, lack of brakes on rolling stock, and railwaymen's excessive hours of work. The growth of safety culture was another source of the introversion and hierarchical discipline which came to characterise the industry. The drift of public affairs meant that, by 1900, legislation was enacted covering all these areas[21] and the state was involved in its enforcement (Parris 1965; Bagwell, 1968; Dyos and Aldcroft 1971).

---

20   The gauge debate was focussed around the width between the rails and not the 'loading gauge', the vertical clearance under bridges and tunnels, which in Great Britain was very low by comparison with Continental railways: this came to be a problem after 1948.

21   Brakes capable of being operated by the engine driver at the front of the train were only made compulsory on passenger carriages, not freight wagons, a shortcoming which

There was one issue which the state was drawn into from a very early date which was directly related to the development of town planning: the impact of railway construction on public amenity. In the provinces extensive destruction of historic buildings occurred, such as the part demolition of Newcastle's mediaeval castle (Biddle 1986). Intrusion did not always evade critical comment: in 1840 Ruskin bemoaned construction of the Midland Railway through the beautiful Wye Valley in Derbyshire:

> every fool in Buxton can be at Bakewell in half-an-hour, and every fool in Bakewell at Buxton, which you think a lucrative process of exchange – you fools everywhere (Cook and Wedderburn 1996, 86-87).

The eighteenth and early nineteenth centuries had seen a flowering of Renaissance inspired, privately sponsored town planning schemes for the wealthy classes throughout Britain, from Bath to Edinburgh. These were characterised by residential squares and crescents comprised of grand terraces with uniform frontages, often with several of these linked together to form a whole new city district, typified by Edinburgh's New Town. This had some impact on railway development as the whole line built by Brunel through Bath:

> ... was prominent and great care was taken to ensure that as far as possible it fitted into the city. Cuttings and viaducts were given classical or Gothic forms ... (Biddle 1986, 62)

Similarly in Edinburgh, the railways coming in from east and west had a struggle with the civic leadership before they were allowed to connect up by construction, in deep cutting, through Princes Street Gardens. In London, owing to this longstanding 'Spirit of Improvement' among the city's rich and influential property owners (Summerson 1962), the companies had a much more difficult time and a Royal Commission (1846) came down firmly against penetration of surface railways into the central 'quadrilateral'. Although some of the first termini, such as Euston and King's Cross (and later St Pancras and Marylebone), were located along its northern edge, the New Road (Euston Road) having been built in the mid-eighteenth century as a by-pass, London did not experience planned rebuilding on the Parisian scale with stations becoming foci for a new network of interconnecting boulevards (Carmona 2002).This concern to protect central London from intrusive railway building was picked up again in the 1860s by a Select Committee (1863, 2) which encouraged the development of a diversionary orbital rail route, particularly in East London to serve the docks. However, this was only built on a piecemeal basis, the biggest omission being a link under the Thames

---

limited the speed of freight trains and was eventually to become a serious weakness vis-à-vis road haulage.

to the east of Wapping.[22] The exception to the restriction on railway construction across central London was the link between Blackfriars and Moorgate via Snow Hill tunnel, opened in 1866. This was the final thrust in a long battle between the companies serving south London to outflank each other in gaining access to the City and West End. It produced the series of termini along the Thames: Victoria, Charing Cross, Blackfriars (originally St Paul's), Cannon Street, Waterloo and London Bridge. These were accessed by miles of brick arch viaducts which, along with bridges over the Thames, attracted contemporary criticism from the arbiters of public taste owing to their visual intrusiveness (Haywood 1997b).

Elsewhere, in 1883 the successful campaign to prevent construction of the Ennerdale Railway, led by Canon Rawnsley, was instrumental in the formation of the National Trust and was the culmination of a long struggle to protect the Lake District by the group which included Wordsworth, Ruskin and Morris (Wheeler 1995). Opposition to railway construction became increasingly sophisticated and, by 1914, the town planning movement was able to develop a detailed and successful environmental case against the proposed Northern Junction Railway, an orbital route in north west London. However, the North Circular Avenue which was proposed at the same time by the Traffic Department of the Board of Trade and would run roughly parallel to this railway, did not come in for similar criticism (Reade 1913). This imbalance by planners in their attitude towards the environmental impact of roads and railways was something which came to characterise British planning.

By the 1890s Parliament had become so entwined with railway management that it became difficult to see where government ended and private enterprise began. There was a growing lobby of those who wanted this to develop to its logical conclusion – nationalisation, which would allow operation as a single, unified network, wholly in the public interest. The Society for Railway Nationalisation was formed in 1895 and the case was soon fully articulated and written up (Edwards 1898). By 1912 the leading contemporary railway economist was of the view that:

> The conclusion, therefore, that I most reluctantly arrive at is that we cannot go on as we are, that there is little hope for the establishment of an adequate and clearly thought out system of State control, and that, therefore, the only alternative – State ownership – is inevitable (Acworth 1912, 9).

Popular concern about transport problems in London led, in 1903, to the appointment of the Royal Commission on London Traffic with a study area of up to fifteen miles from Charing Cross. Its reports (Royal Commission, 1905, 1906)

---

22   This outcome contrasted with the situation in France and Germany where, owing to military considerations, the state was centrally involved in the development of railway networks; construction of the orbital Ceinture around Paris was completed by 1867 with a similar line around Berlin completed by 1877.

were a milestone with regard to their articulation of the relationship between the railway network and urban development and the policy recommendations for its further development. Tables 2.5 and 2.6 reproduce evidence submitted by the Statistical Officer of the London County Council (LCC) which contained very useful summary measures of network characteristics. This is the sort of data which, in subsequent years, one would expect to find in land-use and transportation plans if the aim of state planning was to integrate land-use planning with the railway network. The Royal Commission recognised a number of features of the network and its relationship with urban development as worthy of attention:

- the general geographical characteristics of urban railway networks including features such as route duplication and strategic gaps;
- the precise alignment of railways with regard to urban geography;
- the timing, frequency and cost of passenger services along the component parts of the network;
- the spacing and catchment of stations and the density of development around them;
- the precise location of stations with regard to passengers' destinations;
- the design of stations and their aesthetic relationship to other elements of the urban environment;
- the relationship between railway lines and the location of new development and the cost of railway services to such development;
- the relationship between railway services and other urban transport modes.

The report showed that *laissez-faire* had been replaced by recognition of the need for planning and effective institutional arrangements, recommending the creation of a 'Traffic Board' (1905, 97), the precursor to the London Passenger Transport Board (see later). The report also endorsed more interventionist mechanisms for the provision of cheap fares, to ensure that the railways made a bigger contribution towards solving the housing problem; these included local authority subsidies and railway companies being allowed to engage in land development. Despite these recommendations, action by Parliament was minimal and, with regard to town planning, only produced the permissive 1909 Housing and Town Planning Act. This was the first piece of legislation with the words 'town planning' in its title but, despite the aspirations of the contemporary town planning movement, this only provided for the drawing up of town planning schemes for *new suburban developments* and, even then, only if local authorities so wished. This was a very damp squib.

Table 2.5 Number of stations in Greater London – according to sections

Section	Number of Stations			Number of Stations per Square Mile			Number of Inhabitants per Station		
	In Administrative County of London	In 'Extra London'	In 'Greater London'	In Administrative County of London	In 'Extra London'	In 'Greater London'	In Administrative County of London	In 'Extra London'	In 'Greater London'
Western	53	60	113	3.14	.38	.64	15,603	7,001	11,036
Northern	70	55	125	3.52	.43	.84	16,332	7,582	12,482
Eastern	46	51	97	3.62	.34	.90	17,747	13,241	15,378
Total, north of the river	169	166	335	3.42	.43	.77	16,489	9,111	12,833
South-eastern	60	47	107	1.46	.45	.74	13,964	6,294	10,595
South-western	46	43	89	1.78	.48	.77	19,761	5,576	12,908
Total, south of the river	106	90	196	1.59	.47	.76	16,480	5,951	11,645
Grand Total	275	256	531	2.36	.44	.77	16,485	8,000	12,394

Table 2.6 Length of railways in Greater London – according to sections

Section	Length of Railway in Route Miles			Length per Square Mile			Population per Route Mile		
	In Administrative County of London	In 'Extra London'	In 'Greater London'	In Administrative County of London	In 'Extra London'	In 'Greater London'	In Administrative County of London	In 'Extra London'	In 'Greater London'
Western	35.3	100.1	135.4	2.09	.63	.77	23,427	4,196	9210
Northern	43.7	67.3	111.0	2.20	.52	.74	26,161	6,196	14,056
Eastern	26.6	65.3	91.9	.99	.69	.85	30,691	11,524	16,231
Total, north of the river	105.6	232.7	338.3	2.11	.61	.78	26,388	6,692	12,707
South-eastern	66.7	86.4	153.1	1.62	.84	1.06	12,582	3,424	7,404
South-western	49.3	58.9	108.2	1.91	.66	.94	18,438	4,071	16,617
Total, south of the river	116.0	145.3	261.3	1.74	.75	1.01	15,059	3,686	8,735
Grand Total	221.6	378.0	599.6	1.90	.66	.86	20,458	5,516	10,976

Source: Mr Harper, Statistical Officer of the LCC, Royal Commission on London Traffic, Vol 111, Appendix No 6, , p160, Table 31.

State intervention in the railways and urban development: 1918–48

It took the upheaval of the First World War to trigger more radical measures as outlined above. With regard to the railways this produced the Grouping which '... brought to a logical conclusion the trend towards concentration in the late nineteenth and early twentieth centuries' (Aldcroft 1968, 41). The most complex part of the 1921 Act was that which dealt with rates and charges which, not withstanding the new competitive environment, continued the nineteenth century regulatory tradition, including the common carrier obligation. Rates were fixed at a level to yield an annual net revenue, known as the 'standard revenue', equivalent to that of 1913. However prices were still fixed at a level relative to the value of the commodity being carried, rather than the costs of carriage, which discouraged the railway companies from finding out more about the real costs of different kinds of traffic (Aldcroft 1968, 45). However, the road haulage industry had a much clearer idea and used it to cherry pick the most profitable traffic. The Grouping deflected the attention of the MoT away from the railways, perhaps permanently (Council for the Protection of Rural England 1992) and it focused on the growing bus and road haulage industries and development of the road network. The Ministry did, though, respond to growing public concerns about road safety, pricing regimes and unfair competition for the railways, by regulating the bus and road haulage industries under the 1930 Road Traffic Act and the 1933 Road and Rail Traffic Act.[23] The latter gave the railway companies some rights to object to the granting of licenses to road haulage companies. A particularly significant development was the 1936 Trunk Roads Act which, for the first time, gave a central government ministry, the MoT, the duty to develop a strategic transport network, reinforcing the emphasis on road planning.

With rising road traffic, London's traffic problems worsened and the large, privately owned public transport companies were the focus of intense political debate over the conflicts between private profit and public interest. As the Labour Party gained political influence, one of its leading ideologists developed the case for public ownership (Morrison 1933). This came to pass in 1933, interestingly under the National Government which replaced Ramsay McDonald's second Labour government (1929–31), and the LPTB took over all London's trams, buses, the Underground, the Metropolitan Railway and MRCE. During the Second World War the railways were again placed under the control of the Railway Executive Committee (Aldcroft 1968). There was a moratorium on investment and a huge increase in traffic carried. The railways suffered extensive bomb damage and were stretched to breaking point and the network emerged with a huge investment backlog (Pearson 1967). The end of the war was marked by a rapid fall off in traffic

---

23   A Royal Commission on Transport was appointed in 1928 to consider issues surrounding the growth of unregulated bus and road haulage services and the 1930 Road Transport Act was passed as a result of its endeavours, even before their final report was published in 1931.

and the availability, again, of ex-army lorries and drivers, meant that, despite a large increase in costs, the railways could not raise prices too much, without fear of losing traffic.

Once the wartime emergency passed, the two main political parties re-opened hostilities and a debate around nationalisation was firmly on the agenda. However, the rhetorical cross-fire tended to mask the deeper issues with regard to the future of the railways: matters such as the appropriate balance between road and rail transport and how they could be best integrated; what form railway modernisation should take; and the relationship between the network and patterns of urban development. Once Attlee's[24] Labour government was returned in 1945 with a landslide majority, nationalisation was inevitable and this was enacted by the 1947 Transport Act, taking effect on January 1st, 1948.

Accelerated suburbanisation in the inter-war period, facilitated by the new transport technologies, stimulated the debate about town planning. Although 928 planning schemes had been drawn up by 1930 under previous legislation, these were unable to effectively manage suburbanisation (Pepler 1949). The 1932 Town and Country Planning Act consolidated all previous legislation and extended the powers of the local authorities to produce planning schemes for any land, although the powers were enabling rather than compulsory. Nevertheless, many local authorities drew up planning schemes which sought to limit suburban growth and they did have an impact, but their effectiveness was limited as the right to develop land remained with the landowner and, if a local authority sought to restrict this against the landowner's wishes, it would be liable for compensation payments for loss of betterment. When faced with this, councils backed down and development took place (Hall 1989a).

The Blitz had a major impact on the planning debate, as the destruction meant that the task of rebuilding was so great that only the state would be able to manage it. This provided the political stimulus for further intervention. In addition, the potential of planning to produce homes for all, typified by garden cities, created a wave of popular support, largely amongst the educated middle class: Thomas Sharp's *Town Planning* was published in 1940 and sold 1/4 million copies (Cherry 1974, 130). The changed political context meant that consideration was given to the thorny problems of property rights, land values and betterment (Ministry of Works and Planning 1942). The election of the Attlee government in 1945 added a new dimension, as its commitment to the Welfare State meant that there would also be a need for sites for the schools, colleges, hospitals and so on which would be its physical manifestation. The new government passed the New Towns Act in 1946, followed by the 1947 Town and Country Planning Act which became effective from July 1st 1948.

---

24   Clement Attlee was leader of the Labour Party between 1935–55 and was Churchill's Deputy Prime Minster between 1942–45.

Planning ideology and the railway network

Although the eighteenth and early nineteenth centuries had been a high point for privately sponsored town planning, generally these ideas did not inform the location and design of railway stations and their relationship with surrounding development. Although the railway companies built many architecturally striking stations, typically these were not integrated into grander pieces of civic design, even in London. Euston had started out quite well but, not untypically, the operational demands of rapid growth in railway traffic came to outweigh concern for town planning:

> When it was finished in 1838, it fronted the large open space of Euston Square which ideally set off the view of Philip Hardwick's great Doric Arch and four flanking lodges from Euston Road, but then the London and Birmingham railway spoilt it all by building a pair of hotels in front. The arch and two lodges were still visible between them but the overall effect was ruined and, in 1881, completely obliterated when the hotels were joined by a connecting block (Biddle 1986, 37).

There were a few exceptions, such as the North Staffordshire Railway's Stoke-on-Trent station which was part of Winton Square, the other sides of which were made up by the railway company's hotel and housing for railway workers, all built in neo-Jacobean style. Also the original Liverpool Lime Street station had a classically colonnaded frontage to Lime Street which was matched by the adjacent St George's Hall built soon afterwards, although this frontage was subsequently demolished and replaced by a station hotel in the French renaissance style and somewhat undermining the overall composition. Huddersfield was another situation where a classically inspired station frontage came to fit in well with the adjacent property, although Biddle (1986) considered that this was by good fortune rather than integrated planning.

Writing towards the end of the railway building era, one of the leading planners of the day, Raymond Unwin, recognised the opportunities which had been missed and was critical of the location and design of city centre railway stations and described how station approaches should be integrated with the centres they served (1909, 173). This was the contemporary norm on the European mainland where central and local governments had tended to exercise greater control over railway development:

> In Europe the central station could form the focal point of town planning ... Indeed, in most large continental cities the station was deliberately fronted by a square to set it off (Biddle 1986, 37).

Unwin's design for the town centre in Letchworth, the first garden city, utilised the railway station as a focal point, albeit within a scheme of modest proportions (Figure 2.2).

Given the association between the social housing movement and 'improved locomotion', it is hardly surprising that those who first articulated town planning ideology around what became its main focus in Britain, the planned dispersal of population from major cities to smaller garden cities, should have had a perspective on the railway network. However it was the overall design of the built environment, especially residential areas, which formed the mainstream of contemporary planning ideology, not its specific relationship with transportation systems: the infant profession was dominated by architects. Ebenezer Howard, the radical reformist who developed the ideas of the public health and housing movements into his garden city vision (Howard 1898), saw the solution to the problems of the big cities as out-migration of population to free-standing small towns, where houses would have gardens, land would be owned by the community and the increase in value resulting from its development would be used to benefit the community. As people would move by public transport between the various settlements which, together, would comprise the 'social city' offering the range of facilities people would need, there was a need for a planned relationship between walking, electric trams and railways:

> Those who have had experience of the difficulty of getting from one suburb of London to another will see in a moment what an enormous advantage those who dwell in such a group of cities as here shown would enjoy, because they would have a railway system and not a railway chaos to serve their ends (Howard 1898, 107-108).

It was no coincidence, therefore, that the first creations of the garden city movement, Letchworth and Welwyn, were located on a main line. However, despite this generally positive stance, Howard's schema marked the beginning of the divergence between planning ideology and the interests of the railway system, as there was an implicit assumption that demand for regular travel out of town would reduce substantially, as compared with life in the expanding suburbs.

Much of the debate about the advantages of garden city housing was carried out at a fairly generalised level, but Unwin used his architectural skill to examine the comparative costs of by-law terraces and garden city housing. He was aware that an argument against building at lower density was that it would lead to an unacceptable increase in travel costs, but countered this by a simple argument:

> ... the fact that the area of a circle increases not in proportion to the distance from the centre to the circumference but in proportion to the squares of that distance, it follows that the increased radius required to give an area sufficient each year for a given increase to the population of a town is a rapidly diminishing one ...

> It will be seen, therefore, that the total additional distance to be travelled as
> a result of preventing overcrowding is a comparatively unimportant matter ...
> (Unwin in Creese 1967, 121 and 123).

Unwin's arguments about the viability of lower densities were reinforced by those of others, such as the Royal Commission on London Traffic and the Metropolitan Railway Company, about allowing railway companies to become involved in suburban development in return for cheap fares. There was the potential for a close ideological relationship between the two sectors therefore, but this did not materialise. By 1913 Howard had developed a more explicit critique of the social costs of rail commuting (Howard 1913) and the gap between the two sectors began to widen thereafter.

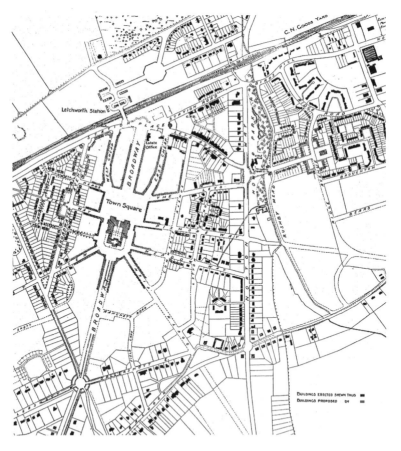

Figure 2.2 Unwin and the station plâce at Letchworth

Source: Creese, W.L. (1967), *The Legacy of Raymond Unwin: A Human Pattern for Planning* (Mass., MIT Press).

Although the first planning statutes were focused on housing, a new form of planning emerged, regional planning. This was initiated by Patrick Geddes and broad, geographical analysis enabled him to appreciate the real extent of urban decentralisation and coalescence, and he coined the term 'conurbation' to describe it (Geddes 1915). His analysis led him to the view that environmental problems had to be tackled strategically and his ideas fell on fertile ground, as the Depression produced widespread dereliction. Regional planning was potentially beneficial for the railway network, which needed rationalising, and its future utility depended upon its continuing integration with urban development. However, rail access was not a priority in contemporary regional planning ideology: the main issues were economic restructuring and job creation; land for housing; and the protection of agricultural land. The main transport issue was road planning since, even before 1914, there had been a realisation that the road system needed to be improved and that this could only be achieved by co-ordination and strategic planning by local authorities. Regional planning schemes were produced through joint committees of local authorities and, generally, the railway companies were not involved (Abercrombie 1923; Abercrombie and Johnson 1923).

Planners were excited by the challenge of creating new environments to accommodate growing road traffic and the ideology of the small planning profession meshed with that of the much bigger architecture and civil engineering professions, which were similarly pre-occupied. The work, in the 1920s, of Clarence Stein in Radburn, New Jersey showed how the low density residential areas favoured by planners in the garden cities, could be adapted to the era of the motor car. This vision of lush, green suburbs and garden cities with carefully planned roads was very attractive, as even high capacity roads could be built as heavily landscaped 'parkways'. But the ambitious ideas of the Modernist movement brought radical ideas with regard to existing cities too, and there was a tension between these and those of most planners which were focused around decentralisation to lower density garden cities. Le Corbusier considered that the old cities would have to be completely rebuilt (Le Corbusier 1929). He envisaged high rise blocks of flats separated by a grid-iron network of local roads linked to high capacity roads. But, interestingly, railways were a part of the Corbusian vision, with a complex, three tier underground network, with all routes converging at a multi-level city centre station:

> The only place for the station is in the centre of the city. It is the natural place for
> it, and there is no reason for putting it anywhere else. The railway station is the
> hub of the wheel (Le Corbusier 1929, 166).

However, this aspect of the vision was overlooked in Britain owing to the growing inter-professional focus around road building. Plans for building new roads around London were developed by a civil engineer, Sir Charles Bressey, who used a leading architect, Sir Edward Lutyens, as consultant (Bressey and Lutyens 1937). The traffic police became involved too, with Sir Alker Tripp of the Metropolitan

Police developing his plans for road network hierarchies and segregating traffic and pedestrians through the use of precincts (Tripp 1942). This was reinforced by further architectural ideas for the reconstruction of city centres using large, Modernist multi-level structures (Tatton Brown and Tatton Brown 1941, 1942).

Although there isn't space in this book to dwell at length on theoretical developments with regard to the association between railways and urban development, it is worth making the point that because of the widening scope of planning concerns in 1919–39 period, the field of human geography was, arguably, becoming as important to the development of planning ideology as its historical roots in architecture and the working class housing issue. It is significant, therefore, that geographers were taking cognisance of the general impacts of transport infrastructure on patterns of urban geography, as well as considering the specific geographies of railway networks. This work can, in fact, be seen as linking back to the ideas of one of Howard's contemporary visionaries, Spain's Arturo Soria, who was aware of the relationships between public transport networks and patterns of urban development and developed his theory of transit-oriented linear cities (Velez 1982). The Chicago school of human ecology developed models of city growth which evolved to show a growing understanding of the effect of transport corridors with evolution from the 'Concentric Ring' model (Burgess 1925) to the 'Sector Theory' model (Hoyt 1939) being particularly significant. This tension between ideas based on concentricity (CBD, inner suburbs, outer suburbs, etc) and those taking account of the corridor impacts of transport which cut across and break up concentric rings, will be picked up in later chapters. Further work was produced by Beaver (1937), who compared and contrasted the railway networks of a number of major European cities including London, Paris and Berlin and their relationships with patterns of urban geography. He noted the piecemeal nature of the orbital route around London, as compared with the two complete orbital routes around Paris; the petite ceinture and the grand ceinture. However there is no evidence of these developments in geography having any impacts on British planning ideology, wherein architectural concerns remained dominant and concerns about transport were firmly focused on the developing road network.

The wartime reports

The regional problem and the furore over unrestrained suburban growth led to louder calls for state intervention and this presented opportunities for planners to show that they had some answers. In 1937 the concerns culminated in the appointment of the Royal Commission on the Geographical Distribution of the Industrial Population, known after its chairman, Sir Anderson Montague-Barlow, as the Barlow Commission, which served as a focus for debate about the relationship between railway development and the growth of London. Pick gave extensive evidence which revealed that, despite being a supporter of town planning (Pick 1927), his opinions were fundamentally different to those of mainstream planners. He dissented from the Commission's view that the growth of London was a 'national menace' and questioned its terms of reference which spoke only of its 'strategic disadvantages' (Royal Commission 1940, 1). Pick thought that London should continue growing to accommodate up to twelve million people inside its green belt, and that the efficiency of the transport network should govern its size, the key factors being the cost and time of travel:

> The conclusion from these two approaches to the problem is broadly, so far at any rate as the centrifugal movement of the population is concerned, that London cannot become fully developed beyond a zone stretching roughly 12 to 15 miles from the centre (Pick 1938, 358).

Frederic Osborn gave evidence on behalf of the Garden Cities and Town Planning Association and did not see Pick's data on per capita growth in journeys as indicative of an improving quality of life:

> Industrial techniques shorten hours, and this ought to mean more leisure. But in the great towns much of the released time gets used up in longer travelling – a fantastic way to waste the benefits of progress (Osborn 1938, 742).

He had no truck with the idea that land-use zoning should be manipulated to balance flows along public transport corridors and considered that city growth of the type envisaged by Pick led to increased waste of money, time and human energy. He favoured decentralisation to self-contained satellite towns where, with a population of 50,000 at 25 persons per acre, the average distance between home and work or countryside would be half a mile.

The Barlow Report's watchwords were 'redevelopment, decentralisation and dispersal' (Royal Commission 1940, 196). It was imbued with the view that 'Railway transport ... is one of the largest contracting industries' (1940, 41) and had much more to say about road traffic and its impact on urban form. It expressed concern at the increasing amount of travel and congestion in London which it saw as a product of railway-oriented suburbanisation. The final recommendations, which formed the background for the development of the ideology to underpin the planning of post-war reconstruction, called for population dispersal to self-contained garden cities and satellite towns, where home and work would be in close proximity, obviating the need for lengthy journeys. Such strategies were to be developed by a new 'Central Authority, national in scope and character' (1940, 201). Interestingly in an additional minority report by Abercrombie and two others, there was a recommendation that this new Ministry should also take over, 'Some part of the planning functions of the Ministry of Transport' (1940, 222).

Concerns over the threats to the countryside led, in 1941, to the Minister of Works and Planning, Lord Reith, appointing the Committee on Land Utilisation in Rural Areas, known after its chairman as the Scott Committee. The Scott Report (Ministry of Works and Planning 1943) showed a keen awareness of the effects of roads in facilitating development in the countryside which was seen as an undesirable aspect of 'suburban drift'. The report bemoaned this but noted that new trading estates were rail connected. But it did not draw the conclusion that, by restricting industry to rail accessible sites, the rail option could be kept alive and there would be a rationale for resisting rural road building.[25]

The Honourable Mr Justice Uthwatt chaired the Expert Committee on Compensation and Betterment appointed, in 1941, to resolve the problems over development rights and land values. The Committee produced a fascinating report (Ministry of Works and Planning 1942) which was crucial in developing the case for effective planning and the legal and financial means by which it could be achieved. It would be unreasonable to expect such a broad study to dwell at length on the particular matter of railways and land. But it is notable that, despite a complete historic review of the role of the state in constraining the rights of landowners, the issues concerning surplus lands and access to social housing were not mentioned, and neither was Howard's model of local community ownership of betterment: there were no planners on the Committee, only lawyers and valuers. In line with their terms of reference, the Committee's report was wholly focused on how to secure effective state control of the use of land and had nothing to say about what betterment might be used for, other than to compensate landowners for loss of development rights. This failure to directly link development value with investment in physical or social infrastructure can, with hindsight, be seen to be a fundamental flaw within the post-war planning system created subsequently.

The wartime plans for London

The wartime government and local authorities showed remarkable foresight in promoting plans for reconstruction, during a period when they had to prioritise matters relating to national survival, and these provided further opportunities for planners to promote their ideas. The County of London Plan focused on five major defects in London: traffic congestion; poor housing; poor open space provision; unsatisfactory mixing of land-uses; and outward sprawl. It was produced by Forshaw and Abercrombie: Forshaw was the County Architect, reflecting the continuing dominance of architectural concerns within planning ideology. As a result the stance towards the railway system was familiar:

> To the planner the most obvious defects are the overhead lines carried on viaducts which impede redevelopment; the out-of-date character of some of the terminal stations, especially their faulty connection with main road planning and the large area of central land locked up in sidings (Forshaw and Abercrombie 1943, 6).

---

25   It is worth recording that in the index to the Scott Report there were four references to jam making, but only one to railways, indicative perhaps of the dominance of the romantics in the development of rural policy.

Although the Plan recognised the need for modernisation and rationalisation of the network, the dispersal of population presaged a reduced role: the main physical works envisaged were aimed at removing the bridges across the Thames and their associated viaducts. The Plan recognised the difficulty of this and suggested that a specialist body be set up to consider its proposals. Despite the expected reduction in demand for rail services, the Plan embraced road building ideology and contained proposals for two orbital and nine arterial roads with flyovers, pedestrian footbridges and subways. This vision was developed from the Bressey plan, but tried to relate this to the perception of London as a network of villages. Building on Tripp's work, the plan proposed construction of American-style parkways allowing through traffic to be diverted away from the retained village cores and newly redeveloped precincts, through green backwaters. None of this was perceived as unacceptably intrusive.

The LCC Plan raised strategic issues of central concern to the Greater London Plan, also produced by Abercombie, (1944b) which, recognising the need to plan for the whole sub-region, covered an area up to 50 miles from central London.[26] This also was critical of continued suburban growth and was ambivalent in its attitude towards the LPTB which:

> ... now pioneer, now camp follower, plays a vigorous, if sometimes uncertain, role. It creates new suburbs and then finds itself unable to cope with the traffic: extensions in other directions aim at further spread of the population. On routes overcrowded beyond cure, it asks the straphanger to exercise patience beyond limit (Abercrombie 1944b, 3).

The planned dispersal of over 1,000,000 people and the associated jobs to self-contained new towns was at the heart of the Plan, with a green belt around London to prevent further sprawl. This meant that:

> Extensions of suburban lines and tubes, which may have been begun or for which parliamentary powers have been obtained, may no longer be required, and congested lines, it is hoped may be relieved (Abercrombie 1944b, 10).

There were more proposals for new roads, but the Plan was not totally negative towards the railways and envisaged electrification of outer suburban lines as far as places like Aylesbury, as well as better orbital routes, particularly around the north eastern quadrant to the docks, and a rail link to the proposed airport at Heathrow. Abercrombie saw the need to reduce freight costs by mechanisation, larger wagons and containers; he was alert to the industry's problems. But, again, he called for the creation of a special railway industry body to consider the ideas. The fact that, despite all his extensive research and consultations Abercrombie fell back on referral to a specialist body, is symptomatic of the failure to integrate the private

---

26   The two plans comprised 'two sides of a seamless web of cloth' (Hall 1995, 230).

railway industry into the planning process. A railway manager, Bonavia, cruelly recalled later that:

> Progress from the cloud-cuckoo land of planners trained as architects, lacking any transport experience, towards more realistic forms of planning, came in stages (1981, 188).

The Railway (London Plan) Committee was set up in 1944 and responded vigorously to the planners' downbeat view of the railway's prospects. It objected to the basic tenet that dispersal would lead to a reduction in demand for travel into central London:

> ... we do not believe that the expectation of a reduction from this cause is likely to be realised ... we feel confident that a greater dispersion of population will mean a greater volume of traffic (Ministry of War Transport 1946, 10).

Their investment proposals reflected operational requirements rather than the planners' priorities of removing elevated railways on aesthetic grounds.

Wartime plans in provincial cities

There were planning concerns similar to those in London in all the conurbations and the solutions of green belts and planned decentralisation were common currency. As has been shown, in provincial cities trams and motor buses were the dominant transport influences on patterns of urban development: this and concerns over growing traffic congestion, meant that road building was the dominant transport theme. Given the ideological gap between town planning and the railways which has been shown to exist in London, it would be reasonable to expect that few of the plans for the provincial cities would have much to say about it.

The general case, which will be illustrated later in the Manchester case study, is that railway content was based on minimal expectations about development of the local network, but did embrace consideration of the location and character of main line stations and, in some cases, their rationalisation. The Abercrombie Plan for central Plymouth (Watson and Abercrombie 1943) was unusual because the extent of bomb damage demanded almost complete rebuilding and had particular implications for the station. The central axis of the classically inspired plan linked the Hoe in the south with the main station on the city centre's northern periphery, thereby tying it into the grand scheme of things in a way that would have pleased Unwin.

A major exception to the generally minimal attention given to railways was Glasgow: the City Engineer's First Planning Report (Bruce 1945) did contain extensive road building plans but, inspired by American practice, also envisaged construction of electric commuter railways along the central reservations of six radials, with two other roads already having parallel railways which would be electrified. Peripheral housing developments at locations such as Pollok, Castlemilk and Drumchapel were to be rail linked with the city centre too. In an echo of London, the plan also proposed the cutting back of the railways approaching the city from the south, to a new 'South Station' on the south side of the Clyde. The Bruce plan was only concerned with Glasgow and was based on decentralisation within the city boundaries. Abercrombie, in his Clyde Valley Regional Plan (Abercrombie and Mathew 1946), took a much more strategic approach and proposed decentralisation to new towns which would be self-contained growth centres. The plan envisaged a new strategic road system but, also, electrification of the local railway network which included Glasgow suburban lines, lines from Glasgow to towns such as Paisley, Motherwell and Hamilton, and lines out to proposed new towns at East Kilbride and Cumbernauld. Abercrombie also identified certain lines as being redundant, including the Subway. As in London, he called for the setting up of a special commission to consider his proposals. Although there was a conflict between the Bruce and Abercrombie decentralisation strategies, the fact that they both saw a significant role for the railways had a special influence on subsequent railway policy for the Glasgow region.

Conclusions

This chapter has shown that during the long, formative period, between 1830–1947, the railways moved from dominance in the transport market to a position where they were successfully challenged by road modes. In the early years, despite *laissez–faire*, Gladstone and others tried to develop the case for the state to have a greater role in planning railway network development, but the 'Railway Interest' successfully opposed this. Interestingly though, the 'Railway Interest' met its match in the 'Landed Interest' and that clash seems to have characterised the development of a permanent fault line between the railway industry and land development which was to persist over the following decades. But the exclusion of (most) railway companies from land development did not preclude railways from becoming deeply embedded in patterns of urban development: their primacy in the transport market ensured that they would. Initially there was a convergence of interests between the young town planning movement and the railway industry too, around the working class housing issue but, subsequently, the two sectors diverged as planning become more focused on urban decentralisation, self-containment and road building. Table 2.7 summarises the findings of this chapter with regard to the thematic analysis of the railway-town planning interface.

Although *laissez-faire* was the dominant ideology, there was from the 1840s an awareness that such an approach may well not produce a network best suited to the public interest. However, such doubts were initially held only by a minority and as a result, state influence on the development of the network was limited. The outcome was that its broad geography came to exhibit certain negative features.

Most of these were recognised, to some degree, as problems at the time and, eventually (post-nationalisation), they were to impact on the performance of the railway system and its ability to compete with other modes. These features were:

- too much duplication of routes at local and strategic levels;
- too much duplication of facilities, particularly stations and goods depots;
- poor location of many stations with regard to town and city centres;
- failure to maximise network benefits, such as leaving strategic gaps and the poor development of cross-country routes;
- the restricted vertical loading gauge (this wasn't perceived as a problem at the time, but grew to become one in the post-1948 era).

It has been shown that there was an inexorable increase in state intervention in the railway industry, largely as a result of factors internal to the industry, and this was a part of a broader swing in political ideology towards intervention and collectivism. This began in the late nineteenth century and received two subsequent fillips as a result of the socio-political impacts of the First and Second World Wars. It is also important to note that, with the exception of the London Underground, intervention in the railway industry was through organs of the central state; the Board of Trade and, later, the Ministry of Transport.

In parallel to the political discourse around railways, there was a discourse around state influence over urban development. By 1900 the two were linked with regard to the working class housing question, as manifested by cheap trains, the debate around betterment and surplus lands, and the location and design of new suburbs, with the model settlements as a special case. The railways came to be seen as not only requiring control in the public interest in light of their role as the dominant transport mode, but that special control was required with regard to the housing question and other matters of interest to the town planning movement. It is significant, though, that town planning arose out of the public health and housing movements which were essentially a function of local government, and that legislation placed town planning within the municipal domain. Intervention in the railways and land development was a function of quite different realms within the state's institutional structure.

Despite the development of a number of ideas, models and techniques to secure closer relationships between railways and the areas they served, they were not an essential component of British town planning ideology which crystallised around the notion of the garden city. This was essentially an anti-urban or, at best, small town, vision which sought to disperse the city and, thereby, undermine the railways which had been central to its development. This divergence of interest increased during the inter-war period, when the primacy of the railways came to be challenged by road transport and the demands of the road network began to exert a powerful influence on planning ideology. This was also a time when the calls for countryside protection and planned decentralisation became more influential in government circles. Despite the planners' focus on urban decentralisation to small towns, powerful visions were promoted, largely by architects and the Modern Movement, as to how cities should be redeveloped at high densities. But planners' and architects' views about urban railways were dominated by concerns over their visual intrusiveness, rather than the operational implications of their functional association with towns and cities and concentrations of residential, commercial and industrial development. However, they were excited about how to create new urban environments to accommodate growing road traffic and this inter-professional, road oriented ideology came to dominate the transport content of contemporary city plans.[27] With profitable private railways which were seemingly central to the country's survival, there was no awareness that prioritising road-oriented planning contained the seeds of the geographical marginalisation of the railway network.

In 1945 deeper state involvement with the railways and land development was facilitated by a broader interventionist thrust by the new Labour government. Nationalisation of the railways was a part of the socialist agenda of bringing the 'commanding heights' of the economy under public control. But the locus of professional and political debate about the railways was largely restricted to matters internal to the transport sector, i.e. what form nationalisation should take and how to best manage the various publicly owned transport modes in the public interest. The reason why Pick's ideas about integrating land-use and railway planning were so notable, is that there were few other leading figures who shared them, and he died prematurely in 1941. Herbert Walker of the Southern was someone who did, and another was Barman[28] (1947) of the GWR who was well aware of the importance of relating stations to the development around them. Somewhat over optimistically, however, he considered that:

> To the town-planner, few buildings in a modern city are more important than the railway station. Its physical extent bulks large in the city plan (Barman 1947, 69).[29]

---

27   The exception was an unofficial plan for London produced by the Modern Architectural Research Group (Korn and Samuely 1942: Gold 1995).

28   Barman had rare qualities with regard to knowledge of the interface between planning, design and the railway network and awareness of the need for communication across the disciplines: he was an architect, who later worked as publicity officer at the LPTB under Pick, and then moved to the GWR. Payne (1947) is further evidence of the unique role of the LPTB in producing such cross-cutting professionals.

29   This was a book about and sponsored by the GWR, presumably as part of Chairman Sir James Milne's rear-guard campaign against nationalisation: it seems that Barman's optimism about planners stemmed from Abercrombie's plan for Plymouth and its rather unique focus on the company's station there.

Perhaps a more accurate reflection of the state of planning ideology came from another contemporary railwayman who, many years later, reflected that even with regard to the Southern Railway:

> Overall, however, the close social inter-relation between transport and land use had scarcely been appreciated ... (Bonavia 1987, 84).[30]

However, this chapter has shown that by 1947, such was the intrinsic state of knowledge and understanding of the strengths and weaknesses of the railway network and its relationships with patterns of urban development that, if there had been the motivation to do so, it would have been perfectly possible to draw up a policy agenda for development of the network and the reinforcement of its relationship with planned patterns of urban redevelopment and growth. Such an agenda is set out below and will form a template against which to evaluate policy and practice in the 1948–94 and post-privatisation periods. A pre-condition was the creation of institutional arrangements which would have facilitated collaborative working between the land-use planning and railway sectors at national, regional and local levels. With regard to the railway network, the policy agenda would have included the following:

1. *rationalisation of the network*: to selectively remove duplicate routes and facilities, but with an eye on both contemporary diseconomies and the potential for future use to accommodate growth in traffic, or the need to retain capacity to provide diversionary routes;
2. *development of railway services*: to ensure that their pattern and quality would be managed to be competitive and/or integrated with that offered by road modes;
3. *closing strategic gaps in the network*: particularly with regard to CBD penetration and access across cities;
4. *development of a programme of station enhancement*: to maximise their convenience and attractiveness to travellers, and station building so as to ensure that new urban areas would be located close to points of access to the network.

The town planning policy agenda would have included:

5. *patterns of urban development*: the general articulation of expectations about changing patterns of urban development in ways which would identify the implications for the potential utility of existing main line,

---

30   Bonavia began working for the LNER in 1945 and became a senior officer in the BTC and BR: he was one of the few employees to write extensively about the railways with official blessing.

suburban, cross country and rural railway routes, and the utility of new routes, so as to ensure integration between them;

6. *management of the redevelopment process in existing urban areas*: to maximise access to railway stations and rail freight facilities, with appropriate guidance for the location, layout, and density of development;

7. *management of the location and character of greenfield site development*: so as to ensure accessibility to the railway network, with appropriate guidance for the location, layout, and density of development.

Table 2.7 Summary of thematic analysis of 1830–1947 period

	Institutional structures	Policy	Outcomes
Political ideology: railway sector	Market based development of oligopoly, accelerated by the State in 1921, followed by creation of nationalised industry. LPTB the exception with regard to urban rail systems.	No overall network plan: recognition of the need for planning came too late for most of it. Even post-1945 the vision of integration restricted to transport sector.	Market forces led to railway being well integrated with C19 urban form, but increasing dislocation post-1919: by 1948 network characterised by strategic weaknesses.
Political ideology: land-use planning sector	Association with public health and housing led to planning becoming a function of the municipal domain under central government direction.	Planning seen as largely concerned with housing and countryside protection. Effective legislation only came about as a result of bombing and the drive for the Welfare State.	Despite a growing body of statutes, no commitment to effective planning control. No possibility therefore for use of planning powers to reduce the dislocation of the railway post-1919.
Professional ideology: railway sector	Emphasis on infrastructure reflecting the dominant civil and mechanical engineers, and general business matters internal to the industry.	Main concerns with matters internal to the industry: locomotives, signalling, mergers. Few personalities with the vision of Pick or Walker.	Little re-adjustment of the network post the Grouping, with notable exceptions in London. Railways perceived by other professionals as old fashioned and not essential to the 'brave new world' of post-war planning.

	Institutional structures	Policy	Outcomes
Professional ideology: land-use planning sector	Focus on public health, housing and land development led to focus on municipal sector. Strong association with architects and highway engineers.	Initial convergence of interest with railway network, but development of garden city ideology led to hostility towards /ignorance of railways, whilst embracing road ideology.	Initially garden suburbs/cities integrated with network, but post-1919 progressive disengagement of planned developments from the rail network.
Governance and management: railway sector	Emphasis on business efficiency in structures led to mergers between rail companies and diversification into other transport sectors. Lack of linkages between railway industry and local government – LPTB the exception.	Companies focused on internal matters and resistance to state intervention. Public interest focused on a balance between efficient units whilst restraining their power. Integration between modes came to be seen as demanding nationalisation.	Post-1923 emphasis on internal managerial problems and little rationalisation or improvement of the network. Activities of MRCE and LPTB unique, more limited association with land development by SR.
Governance and management: land-use planning sector	Planning initially in voluntary sector, then became a function of local government, set within broad national guidelines	Planning in a policy locus associated with public health and housing, roads, buses and trams, not railways.	Local government agencies for planning, even at the strategic level, and even in London, excluded railway companies. Ideas referred to specialist rail industry bodies.

Chapter 3

Institutional Arrangements: 1948–68

Introduction

The railway companies remained under the control of the Railway Executive Committee until nationalisation, which was announced as a policy goal by Herbert Morrison in 1945 and, despite opposition from the companies and the Conservative party, was enacted by the 1947 Transport Act. The railways passed into state hands and became British Railways (BR) on 1st January 1948.

During the War, serious consideration was given to how the legal obstacles to effective state control over land development could be overcome and what the goals of an effective planning system should be. Town planning was seen by Attlee's administration as playing a central role in reconstruction, developing the Welfare State, and protecting the countryside. The new towns, which embraced a vision of the good life previously unattainable to the working class, were particularly attractive in setting the tone of what the Brave New World might look like: the 1946 New Towns Act was Labour's first piece of planning legislation. The Town and Country Planning Act followed in 1947 and provided the state with effective teeth to control patterns of development. In future, if land owners wanted to 'develop' land or buildings, they would have to apply to the state for 'planning permission'. The state could refuse this, if to do so was in the public interest, and the land owner would have no grounds for compensation for loss of betterment.

The aim of this chapter is to analyse the institutional structures which were created between 1947–68 for the management of the railways and for the operation of the land-use planning system, and to evaluate and account for the degree to which they were co-ordinated to secure the maximum utility of the railway network.

The British Transport Commission

The 1947 Transport Act nationalised the railways, the inland waterways, some of the larger private bus companies and the long distance (over 40 miles) road haulage industry (Aldcroft 1975). Each mode was put under the management of an 'Executive' responsible to the British Transport Commission (BTC) which, in turn, was responsible to the Minister of Transport. The LPTB was wound up and placed under the control of the London Transport Executive. This creation of a separate body for London ensured the continued separation of management of the Underground and London's main line commuter railways. The BTC was charged with the duty to provide:

... an efficient, adequate, economical and properly integrated system of public inland transport and port facilities within Great Britain for passengers and goods with due regard to safety of operation.

Sir Cyril Hurcomb, former Permanent-Secretary of the Ministry of Transport and a supporter of greater transport integration (Hurcomb 1945), was installed as Chairman of the BTC, and Sir Eustace Missenden, former General Manager of the Southern, became Chairman of the Railway Executive. In the provinces the municipal bus, trolleybus and tram fleets remained under local authority control outside the BTC empire. Although the Labour Party was thoroughly imbued with the notion of building an integrated transport system, there was a tendency to think that nationalisation would deliver this automatically. There was awareness amongst the professionals though that it would take time to work out what integration would mean in practice: 'this is a period of transition towards "a properly integrated system of public inland transport"' (Lamb[1] 1948, 5). The task of managing BR as a single organisation was daunting enough:

> The Railway Executive alone had inherited between 632,000 and 649,000 staff (no-one seemed quite sure of the exact figure), together with 20,000 steam locomotives, 1,223,000 wagons (half of which had been inherited from private owners), 56,000 coaches, 19,414 miles of track ... and 7,000 horses (Henshaw 1991, 41).

With each mode under the control of a separate Executive, it is difficult to see how Government expected the institutional structure to deliver integration. In addition, there was a clash of interest between the BTC and the Railway Executive over who should control strategy (Bonavia 1971,1981; Gourvish 1986).[2] In theory, with state control over all sectors, integration was a matter of deciding which mode could best be used to transport a particular traffic and setting the rates accordingly. But, in practice, rates were controlled by a Transport Tribunal, not the BTC. So the BTC could only use quality to influence the choice between modes, a tool which historically had served the railways poorly. So in practice competition continued, despite nationalisation.

As the railways were nationalised so that they might be operated in the public interest, a mechanism was created whereby the public could influence the managers. In what for its time was a surprisingly enlightened initiative, the Transport Act created regional Transport Users' Consultative Committees (TUCCs), the membership of which, though appointed by the Minister, was intended to be representative of users (Cameron 1953). Although

---

1   This was David Lamb's Presidential address to the Chartered Institute of Transport.

2   By contrast, despite their failings, the Big Four had become regionally based multimodal transport enterprises, owning railways, docks, hotels, shipping fleets, lorry fleets and bus companies under a single, unified management (Bonavia 1971).

useful talking shops, the TUCCs had no powers and had to report through a Central Transport Consultative Committee (CTCC), partially staffed by the BTC. Access to the Railway Executive was therefore circuitous and open to BTC influence. Subsequently the TUCCs and the CTCC became important bodies in the struggles against rail closures. They were one of the few channels available for lobbying in defence of rail transport, in an industry whose managers, as public servants, were gagged:

> One of the difficulties that nationalisation has brought to the railways is the abolition of the directors who were also Members of Parliament and could speak in both Houses for the industry when required. Under nationalisation the railways have no one who can speak for them at all times (Pearson 1953, 121).

Although their numbers were to dwindle over the years, at the time of nationalisation the railway trade unions had thirty MPs (Morris 1948), all within the Labour Party of course. However, this influence on Labour governments was not necessarily in the long term interests of the competitiveness of the railway industry against an aggressive road transport industry and, of course, identification with Labour could become an added incentive to a Conservative government to intervene in railway management.

The land-use planning system

Prior to the 1946 New Towns Act, three types of institutional mechanism had been employed in the creation of new settlements. The first was the actions of industrial philanthropists, as in Bournville and Port Sunlight. The second was voluntary organisations with members ideologically committed to the garden city movement, as in Hampstead, Letchworth and Welwyn. The third was action by local authorities, as in the garden city satellites of Wythenshawe and Speke. However, the mechanism created under the New Towns Act was the 'development corporation', based on the Reithian model of the British Broadcasting Corporation. Membership of development corporations was to be by ministerial appointment and they were vested with powers to compulsorily purchase land and produce and implement master plans, largely outside the influence of local authorities.

As part of the planning for post-war reconstruction a Ministry of Town and Country Planning (MTCP) had been set up in 1943 and this continued into the post-war era. Under the subsequent 1947 Town and Country Planning Act the process of 'development control', whereby prospective developers have to apply for planning permission from the relevant local planning authority, became the most familiar face of the planning system to the general public. To help them make decisions which would be technically sound and which would have public confidence, planning authorities also had duties laid upon them to carry out surveys and consultations and to present their proposals as statutory development plans. These public documents, which would comprise maps and written statements, were also to be used to co-ordinate investment in publicly owned infrastructure with public and private sector development projects. Development plans, and other statutory instruments, circulars and policy documents from central government, were to be used as the basis upon which individual planning applications would be considered. These two arms of the planning system – forward planning and development control, were inextricably linked. The important point for this book is that the Act gave local planning authorities powers to make decisions as to where land should be developed and what it should be developed for so that, if authorities so wished, a close spatial relationship could be achieved between land-use patterns and particular transport networks.

In light of what has been said in Chapter 2 about the potential relationship between betterment and the development of infrastructure, it is worth saying more about these aspects of the Planning Act. The report of the Uthwatt Committee (Ministry of Works and Planning 1942) provided the intellectual point of departure: the argument was that just as the state should not be liable for a payment of compensation to a landowner refused planning permission, one who did receive permission should surrender the betterment through taxation. This became known as the 'development charge' and was levied in the Act at 100% of the betterment. But this money disappeared into the Treasury pot. As an application of the ideas mooted at the turn of the century by Perks, hypothecation could have included modernisation of rail services to serve new developments, but this was never proposed and the Treasury has always resisted hypothecation as a matter of principle.[3]

Although the planning system was to be overseen by the MTCP, detailed operation was to be in the hands of 'local planning authorities' which comprised the then existing upper tier of local government; the county councils in the shires and the county boroughs in the major urban areas. It is clear therefore that, from the outset, there would be difficulties in achieving co-operation between the bodies involved in railway management and land-use planning. They were the product of quite different models of public governance. The railways were perceived as an industry, similar to the nationalised utilities, with a focus on production, dominated by complex technologies and operational matters internal to the industry. On the other hand land-use planning, although steered by national government, was to be carried out by local councils and was seen as a service for local communities, closely related to other services.

Also there were relatively few town planners in the early years as membership of the Town Planning Institute was reported as 2,500 in 1950, some 700 of whom were students. Many practitioners were in fact architects or surveyors, with little knowledge of transport and the focus on design still prevailed; 'Emphasis is placed on design, because that must be the focus of knowledge' (MTCP and Department

---

3   Changing this principle has been a significant factor in the development of transport policy since 1997 although, tellingly, the change has not been implemented.

of Health for Scotland, 1950, 34). Municipal engineers held a special place as; 'the majority of chief officers to local authorities responsible for planning are engineers' (MTCP and Department of Health for Scotland, 1950, 25). Transport was therefore barely within the professional gaze and, where it was, the focus was on roads. In addition statutory undertakers, such as BR, were given special status under the Planning Act whereby they could engage in 'development' associated with railway operation without the need to formally obtain planning permission. Where BR wished to engage in new railway building, or other major civil engineering works, then they continued to seek powers through the historic parliamentary bill process. These facts reduced the need and opportunities for the growth of mutual understanding and co-operation between the two sectors.

The initial relationship between the railway and planning sectors

Despite the barriers there was some evidence that the early post-war commitment to integration led to limited contact between the two sectors which was aimed at achieving co-ordination. For example, the annual reports of the BTC for 1948–52 contained sections reporting on the activities of the London Transport Executive (LTE) entitled 'Population, Planning and Future Developments': these reviewed activity with regard to new towns, reported on the London Plan Committee, and referred to contemporary population projections. In the annual report for 1950 the LTE section stated: 'The Executive regularly review progress in the development of local authority housing estates, so that transport facilities may be provided as new traffic needs arise' (BTC 1950, 164). However there were very few references to such matters in the annual reports with regard to the main line network outside London, although the 1949 report refers to an approach by the City of Glasgow with regard to the electrification of local services. This liaison continued over the years and did eventually bear fruit. The most heartfelt references to the impact of planning legislation in the annual reports were about the workload created for the estates section in submitting claims under the compensation provisions. Generally, despite the recommendations of Abercrombie within the Barlow Report, transport planning and land-use planning were in separate government departments and, specifically, no integrative mechanism was set up at national, regional or local levels with the explicit role of securing integration between urban development and the railway network.

Conservative reaction to Labour's initiatives

The long, grey years of austerity made it very difficult for Attlee's Government to deliver on its bold promises and, by 1950, the socialist dream was wearing thin. As an indication of the difficulties, the financial pressures led in 1951 to Hugh Gaitskell, who had replaced Stafford Cripps as Chancellor, introducing prescription charges. As a result Aneurin Bevan, former Minister of Health who had masterminded the creation of the National Health Service (NHS), the jewel in the government's crown, resigned his post and the Labour Party was split between left and right wings. With regard to transport:

> After six years of Labour Government, the Holy Grail of road/rail integration remained as elusive as ever. The high hopes of the 1947 Act were never realised ... (Henshaw 1991, 56).

In 1951 the Conservatives were returned to power and 'the post-war consensus' (Smith 1990) was tested: although it included support for the NHS and council housing, it did not extend to transport and the road haulage industry was promptly denationalised by the 1953 Transport Act. The railways remained in public ownership as there was no practical alternative and became the dominant concern of the BTC. Although road haulage was freed to pursue the most profitable traffic, the railways retained the common carrier burden, with some relaxation, and were prevented from operating road haulage services to railway depots. There had been widespread criticism of the two tier structure of Executives and the BTC (Pearson 1953), so the former were abandoned and the railways came under the sole management of the BTC. Management of London Transport remained as a separate body under the BTC umbrella. With the retirement of Hurcomb, General Sir Brian Robertson was appointed as Chairman of the BTC, continuing the long association of the military with railway management.

As well as being supporters of a free enterprise road haulage industry which would expose the railways to competition, the Conservatives:

> returned to power obsessed with euphoric recollections of life in the late 1930s. They sighed for the LMS, LNER, GWR and SR, and the supposed stimuli of old identities, liveries and rivalries (Allen 1966, 15).

Under the 1953 Act the BTC was therefore required to develop a devolved, regional structure for the railways comprising 'Area authorities', 'which were clearly intended ... to be as much like the old railway companies as was feasible under nationalisation' (Bonavia 1981, 88). This structure was introduced by the government in 1954 (Ministry of Transport and Civil Aviation, 1954) and bore some striking similarities to the geography of the Big Four, thereby facilitating the continuation of pre-nationalisation corporate cultures. The regions were the Southern, Western, London Midland, Eastern, North Eastern and Scottish. These had been in existence for operating purposes since nationalisation, but now the six Area Boards became statutory bodies with full powers to manage the railway, with day-by-day operation through a General Manager. Although local authority associations were consulted as part of the preparation of the relevant White Paper, its content was wholly focused on railway matters and did not refer to any need for liaison between the Area Boards and local planning authorities. Robertson was concerned about the lack of control over the boards at the centre and created a 'General Staff' and, below it, a 'Central Staff' at the BTC to counteract the power of the regional managers and co-ordinate their actions, producing a labyrinthine decision making structure (Bonavia 1971, 1981) Other former army officers were drafted in reinforcing the militaristic and introverted culture of the organisation and its focus on production and 'man management'.[4]

Operation of main line commuter services into London remained under the control of BR and were in fact distributed amongst four regions: the Southern, Western, London Midland and Eastern. Despite increasing patronage on the commuter routes, some years later Hall highlighted the failure to bring about improvements and bemoaned the lack of integration between London Transport and British Rail services:

> In 1955, after seven years of nationalisation during which integration should have taken place, the Committee of Inquiry into London Transport recommended strongly that facilities for interchange should be improved. Yet still nothing is done (Hall 1971, 141).

The totality of the 1947 Planning Act was also beyond the Conservative's interpretation of consensus, particularly that element of it concerning taxation of betterment which was dismantled by Planning Acts in 1953, 1954 and 1959 (Parker 1985). However, other actions by the Conservatives broadened the scope of planning, particularly the 1952 Town Development Act. Pressure for this came from local councils, especially in the South East, which looked jealously at the benefits enjoyed by localities arising from new town designation: the act empowered local councils to enter into agreements to accept large overspill populations from exporting authorities such as the LCC. As a result the Conservatives only designated one further new town during the 1950s. As further evidence of their desire to distance themselves from the socialist connotations of planning, the Conservatives also wound up the MTCP and its functions were absorbed into the Ministry of Housing and Local Government (MHLG), which would inevitably lead to some dilution of purpose.

In the previous chapter there was discussion of the emergence of the regional focus for town planning activity in the inter-war years. The deliberations of the Barlow Commission had reinforced this and, in the late 1940s, such was the scale of activity by local councils with regard to both housing and town planning activity, that the MTCP created a network of regional offices. However, there was no creation of a more formal tier of elected government at this level and, in fact, very early in their term of office the Conservatives closed these regional

---

4 The BTC headquarters were located in the former Great Central Hotel adjoining Marylebone Station and became known in the industry as 'the Kremlin': dining facilities were known as 'messes' and salaried staff continued to be known as 'railway officers', a situation which continued to the end of BR.

offices. So, despite the development of a regional structure for BR, the institutional arrangements for regional co-ordination between the planning and railway sectors worsened.

Growth of the road lobby

As the new structure for the railways bedded down, major changes developed in the balance of competition between transport modes. Mass car ownership sat comfortably with Conservative ideology and characterised 'Super-Mac' (Prime Minister Harold Macmillan) and the 'you've never had it so good' years, in contrast to the austerity under Labour (Sked and Cook 1993). Road transport interest groups had existed since the turn of the century, typified by the Society of Motor Manufacturers and Traders (SMMT) and the Royal Automobile Club (RAC). Many became members of the overtly lobbyist British Road Federation (BRF), founded in 1932, whose influence was reaching new heights in the 1950s (Council for the Protection of Rural England (CPRE) 1992; Hamer 1987).

There was a direct link between local government and the road lobby as the County Surveyors' Society had been developing plans for a national motorway network for years, and local authorities worked closely with the BRF. Sir James Drake, the County Surveyor of Lancashire, had been instrumental in securing passage of the Special Roads Act in 1949: it was no coincidence that Britain's first stretch of motorway was the Preston by-pass, opened in 1958. The 1950s also marked a shift in power within the trade union movement as heavy industries declined and manufacturing expanded. The balance of power between the transport unions shifted away from those of railway workers, typified by ALSEF and the NUR (McKenna 1980), towards the Transport and General Workers Union (T & GWU), to which lorry drivers and car workers belonged. This growing political influence of the road lobby was a significant factor which, along with problems within the railway industry itself, led the Government to pursue further major changes in the institutional arrangements for management of the railways.

In 1959 Ernest Marples, owner of Marples Ridgeway a road building company, became Minister of Transport. Government concern over BR's finances was increasing at this time and, despite the fact that a Parliamentary Select Committee was investigating its activities, Marples set up his own committee of inquiry headed by Sir Ivan Stedeford, Managing Director of Tube Investments Ltd. The committee comprised private businessmen and two civil servants: its deliberations were shrouded in secrecy lending credence to the conspiracy theory of history (Henshaw 1991, 122-129). But it significantly influenced the direction of subsequent events, such as the appointment of Dr Richard Beeching, a Committee member and former Technical Director of Imperial Chemical Industries (ICI), to the chairmanship of the BTC. The importation of personalities from private industry was a feature of the Marples-Beeching era. Beeching's appointment caused a furore as his salary, at £24,000 twice that of Robertson's, was seen as a portent of difficult times ahead.

One significant innovation introduced by Beeching, though previously suggested by the BTC, was the creation of a subsidiary to develop railway property interests. Interestingly the name chosen was 'Railway Sites Ltd.', taken from a company created by the LNER in 1937 (Biddle 1990). Though chaired by railwaymen, this company did include personalities from the world of property on its board, notably Harold Samuel of Land Securities Investment Trust. There were no planners, but at least it symbolised a more pro-active stance towards the extensive land holdings.

In the early 1960s, when transport policy became dominated by road building, the MoT began to broach the idea of joint working on transportation studies to major local authorities in the conurbations. In the West Midlands for example, a 'West Midlands Conurbation Highways Committee' already existed and, in 1963, the Ministry wrote to Birmingham City Council suggesting working together in 'formulating a programme of road improvements for the next 15-20 years' (Birmingham City Council 1963, 333): this sort of initiative was in stark contrast to the institutional relationships which existed between the Ministry, BR and local government.

Creation of the British Railways Board

The 1962 Transport Act disbanded the BTC and separated control of the nationalised elements of road and rail transport. Control of the railways was recentralised and vested in the British Railways Board (BRB) with the following remit:

> It shall be the duty of the Railways Board ... to provide railway services in Great Britain ... and to provide such other services and facilities as appear to the Board to be expedient, and to have due regard ... to efficiency, economy and safety of operation.

The overall aim was to create a simpler and more accountable organisation, charged with the task of having all the businesses at the 'break even' point within five years. Theoretically the industry was finally freed from statutory restrictions on its ability to fix rates and fares but, in practice, political control increased. Although the other nationalised transport operations remained in public ownership, and a National Transport Advisory Council was set up whereby the successor Boards could meet and develop policy, the 1962 Act was widely seen as destroying any potential co-ordination between the nationalised undertakings (Bonavia 1971, 100). The Act gave the Minister many powers to intervene in the work of the BRB and, no doubt with a view to coming battles over closures, severely curtailed the powers of the TUCCs. In future, where closures were mooted, they would only be able to oppose them on the specific grounds of 'hardship' to individuals affected by the closure proposal. Section 87 of the Act required the BRB to submit development proposals on surplus land to the MHLG and Railway Sites provided a convenient vehicle for this. To create an even more development-oriented stance towards the estate, the offices of the Chief Estates Surveyor and Railway Sites Ltd were merged in 1965.

A renaissance for integrated land-use and transport planning

The 1960s were years of major upheaval for the railway network. Public transport in general was in relative decline as a result of rising car ownership, and the whole notion of operating railways and bus services as commercially profitable enterprises was undermined: publicly owned transport as a whole needed to be thrown a lifeline. This came in the late 1960s as the product of a wider debate about urban problems and the need for new institutional structures. The Labour Government elected in 1964 under the leadership of Harold Wilson, was much more interventionist than its Conservative predecessor: it was committed to accelerated slum clearance, rejuvenation of the new towns programme, and economic planning at the regional and national levels. However, with regard to transport, the new Government was still subject to the intense pressure of the road lobby, the general popular aspiration towards car ownership and, within the party, the growing influence of the Transport and General Workers Union, ably led by Jack Jones. There could be no turning around of the underlying growth of private road transport therefore, but there was an attempt to look at the railway problem more strategically. The commitment to regional policy led to the creation of Regional Economic Planning Councils and, after April 1965, railway closure proposals were submitted to them for consideration: 'The climate was clearly more restrictive' (Gourvish 1986, 441).

With the commitment to planning which so characterised this Government, and Labour's long-standing commitment to social justice, perhaps a skilful politician could put publicly owned transport on to a firmer foundation. This turned out to be the first woman to play a significant governmental role in transport,[5] Barbara Castle, who 'was part of the intellectual left-wing of the Labour party, eager to fuse the reforming zeal of the 1940s with the central planning obsession of the 1960s' (Gourvish 1986, 351). Castle produced a series of White Papers (MoT 1966, 1967a, 1967b, 1967c) which drew some fundamental lessons from the experiences of the previous twenty years and introduced significant innovations in institutional arrangements. The learning went deep: it was understood that; 'The nature of urban transport systems must be based on our ideas of the kind of cities we want' (MoT

---

5   Although women had been employed by railway companies from the 1830s, their history has been disregarded by most historians and 'is a history of exploitation as cheap labour, and of segregation in women's work' (Simmons and Biddle 1997, 564-566). Their employment on 'men's work' was a temporary occurrence during both world wars.

1967b, 1), and crucially; 'We have neither the physical space nor the economic resources to rebuild our cities in such a form that all journeys can be made by private car ...' (MoT 1967b, 2). The conclusion was that land-use and transport planning needed to be much more closely integrated, with the aim of reinforcing the potential to use public transport in cities, and that new interventionist bodies were required in the major conurbations to plan, co-ordinate and operate public transport. These were to be called 'passenger transport authorities' (PTAs) which would make policy, to be implemented by 'passenger transport executives' (PTEs). New legislation was proposed which would address this wide range of matters and this became the 1968 Transport Act: in particular this revised the remit given to the BRB and took the hard edge off the 1962 version, as it became:

> ... to secure that the combined revenues of the authority and of its subsidiaries taken together are not less than sufficient to meet their combined charges properly chargeable to revenue account, taking one year with another.

In response to the general thrust towards more sophisticated planning, the BRB created a 'Central Planning Department' with the object of working on the internal corporate plan and co-ordinating other work such as the 'conurbation studies' and 'planning such as that for the Channel Tunnel' (BRB Annual Report 1967, 2).

At this time there was increasing concern too about the effectiveness of the structure of local government inherited from the nineteenth century. Regional geographers had a clear understanding of the implications for city governance of the decentralising trends which were so apparent in the city regions (Dickinson 1972). The fit of the territories of existing institutional structures with the changing geography of the conurbations was increasingly unsatisfactory. In addition, a managerial revolution was taking place throughout the western world in pursuit of the economies of scale achieved by large organisations, lubricated by the application of new computer technology, typified by such giant agencies as NASA and the American multi-nationals. Harold Wilson enthused over the 'white heat of the technological revolution', and there was a desire to bring these benefits into local government. Change had already taken place in London as, in 1963, the LCC had been replaced by a new strategic authority, the Greater London Council (GLC), with local services delivered by a lower tier of 32 boroughs and the City of London Corporation. So in 1966 the Government set up Royal Commissions on Local Government for England (under Sir John Redcliffe Maud) and Scotland (under Mr Justice Wheatley), and these reported in 1969. A common theme was recognition of the need for much bigger units of government, but there was debate over the advantages of a simple unitary structure, as opposed to the need for an upper tier of GLC type strategic bodies in the major conurbations. The majority of the English commissioners, seeing a need for simplicity, only accepted a need for an upper tier in the major conurbations, whereas the Scottish commissioners saw a need for one everywhere. These matters would not be finally resolved until the 1970s and will be reviewed in Chapter 6.

Castle was a pugnacious politician but, despite her commitment to the nationalised railway and her demonstration that she was the 'man' for the job (MoT 1970), nevertheless she was also subject to the political pressure of the road lobby. In response, in order to accelerate construction of the motorway network, one of her final initiatives was the creation in 1968 of the Regional Road Construction Units, which combined staff from the Ministry of Transport with those seconded from local government. This was another fusion which, if applied to the railways, would arguably have enabled the BR regions to develop closer liaison with strategic land-use planning and regional economic policy making.

Conclusions

This chapter has shown that, between 1947–68, although management of the railway network and operation of the planning system were both state activities, their institutional structures were quite different. They were associated with different parts of the governmental regime and there were few points of contact between the two, as shown in Figure 3.1. Table 3.1 summarises the explanation for this utilising the three core themes.

In the immediate post-war period transport integration was the priority for the Labour government and this produced the complex structure of the BTC and the various Executives. On denationalisation of the road haulage industry, the Railway Executive was removed from the structure by the Conservatives but a backward look towards the Big Four produced a statutory regional structure. Eventually the drive for a more commercially efficient organisation led to the abolition of the BTC and its replacement by the BRB, which was left intact by the subsequent Labour government. The professional cultures within the nationalised railway continued to be introverted, disciplined and hierarchical. Although, in the early 1960s, the Conservatives progressively sought to replace the public service ethos with a commercial one, this did not alter the view about the need for a centralised structure, rather it served to reinforce it.

Because of its involvement with reconstruction and the Welfare State, planning was seen as essentially a local service to be delivered through locally elected councils with a need to be sensitive to local demands. Although initially a flagship activity by the Attlee Government with its own Ministry to guide the local authorities, the Conservative's lesser enthusiasm saw the absorption of this by the MHLG. Towards the end of the period the renewed enthusiasm for planning and the intention to reform the structure of local government, held the promise of a more distinct place for planning within local government. Planning ideology was comfortable with the institutional structure and the links with local authority road builders and council house designers. In terms of the internal structure of local government, planning was usually subsumed within the local authority technical services sector, typically the engineer's department, and this reinforced these professional synergies.

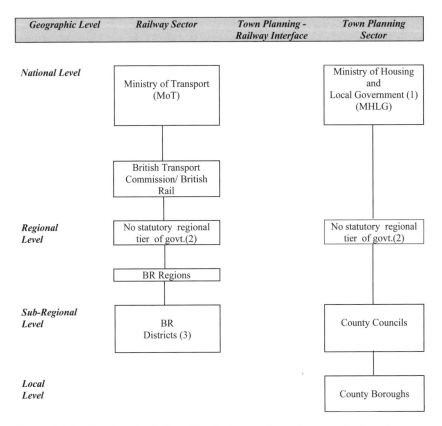

Geographic Level	Railway Sector	Town Planning - Railway Interface	Town Planning Sector
National Level	Ministry of Transport (MoT)		Ministry of Housing and Local Government (1) (MHLG)
	British Transport Commission/ British Rail		
Regional Level	No statutory regional tier of govt.(2)		No statutory regional tier of govt.(2)
	BR Regions		
Sub-Regional Level	BR Districts (3)		County Councils
Local Level			County Boroughs

Figure 3.1 Institutional relationships between the railway and planning sectors in England 1948–68

Notes [1] The Ministry of Town and Country Planning was absorbed into the Ministry of Housing and Local Government in 1953. [2] The Conservative Government elected in 1951closed the regional offices of the MTCP. Serplan (Serplan, 1992) was created in the South East region in 1962 and the advisory Regional Economic Planning Councils were created in the mid-1960s. Scotland had its own locus of government throughout the period, whilst the Welsh Office was created in 1965. [3] Used for operating purposes only. Generally managerial decisions were made at regional headquarters, which in most cases were in London, or by the BTC/BRB.

Table 3.1 Summary of thematic analysis of institutional structures 1948–68

Explanatory themes	Railway sector	Interrelationships between the two sectors	Planning sector
Politics and political ideology	Initially seen as a public service: focus on integration with other transport modes. Separated out by Conservatives, eventually with a more commercially oriented business structure.	Generally weak and minimal, but realisation that a need for more integrative structure at the end of the period.	A local service closely related to others, especially housing. Initially a flagship service, withdrawal from this by Conservatives. Search for a more efficient structure by Labour by 1968.
Professions and professional ideology	Focus on internal functions; traditional, introverted and hierarchical structures maintained. New influences were from private business, this reinforced the introverted, national identity.	Few points of contact between professions in the two sectors which knew little of each other.	Planning was embedded in structures which were dominated by professionals concerned with road building, and planners looked towards these on transport.
Governance and management	Centralised, production oriented body under Labour. Rivalry between regional bodies created by Conservatives, followed by creation of BRB on private sector model.	The two activities were seen as quite different; tied to different parts of the State structure with little need for contact; change of view with regard to passenger services in main conurbations by 1968.	Initially a separate government department, then subsumed in a Ministry dealing with other centrally steered local services. But essentially a local service: awareness of need to update geography of local government by 1968.

These poor institutional relationships between the railways and planning meant that, even if policy makers in each sector were looking to co-ordinate their activities, delivery of this would not be easy. It was only towards the end of the period, and only in the major conurbations, and only with regard to passenger traffic, that the combination of a political opportunity with changing political and professional ideologies, produced a consensus around the creation of intermediary bodies, the PTAs/PTEs. The segregation throughout most of the period between land-use planning and the railways can be contrasted with the much more widespread and closer relationship that existed between local government, particularly the highway authorities, and the private sector road lobby.

Chapter 4
Policy: 1948–68

Introduction

Commentators have seen the railways as experiencing net disinvestment since the late 1930s (Gourvish 1986, 68): during the 1939–45 war the network suffered extensive damage and received minimal maintenance. In 1947 the operating ratio (the ratio of costs to income) stood at 103 per cent, so there was no internal source of capital accumulation. Britain was experiencing severe austerity and the economy was weak leading to the Chancellor of the Exchequer, Stafford Cripps, devaluing the pound in the crisis of 1949. Railway management, like much else in contemporary Britain, was on the basis of make-do and mend.

The major tasks for the planning system were:[1] reconstruction of the war damaged cities; new housing; providing sites for development associated with the Welfare State; new towns; and protecting agricultural land from development. The overriding concerns of contemporary planning ideology with regard to transportation, were remodelling cities to mitigate the effects of road traffic and a reduction in daily commuting through dispersal of population to self-contained satellites. The prolonged period of austerity, including severe restrictions on the availability of building materials, meant that little progress was made in realising this ambitious agenda: the early achievements were largely limited to designation of the first generation new towns with little actual development taking place and, in the cities, the erection of thousands of prefabricated houses to meet the immediate housing crisis.

When the economy improved in the 1950s, the political context meant that transport and planning policy developed in ways which were markedly different: under the Conservatives, integrated transport and state managed decentralisation were largely abandoned. However, the re-election of a Labour government in the mid-1960s led to a resurgence of commitment to both areas of policy and, significantly, the relationship between them. But this was in a context where the nature of transport infrastructure and society's transport behaviour were markedly different from those of 1948. The aim of this chapter is to review how policy for the railways took account of planned changes in urban development patterns, and the degree to which planning policy was influenced by considerations about access to the railway network.

---

1   These were extensively reviewed in the introduction to a planning white paper in 1944: see Appendix 4.

The railways: a difficult start

One of the most urgent tasks facing the Railway Executive was modernisation of the motive power fleet: although Continental and American railways had been replacing steam with electric and diesel locomotives since the 1930s, Robert Riddles, the Railway Executive's Chief Mechanical Engineer, ordered a new generation of steam locomotives and the last of them was not delivered until 1960. This decision was a source of tension between the BTC and the Railway Executive, illustrating the inability of the Commission to influence strategy (Bonavia 1981, 45-55). It locked the railways into a form of traction which, although comparatively cheap to build, was labour intensive in operation, filthy, and thoroughly Victorian in image. The overall intention of the Railway Executive seemed to be to recreate the railway as it existed in 1939, and the average speeds of the express trains of that period were used as a benchmark against which to measure progress in reconstruction: the mind set was backward looking.

The Railway Executive was concerned about loss making rural branch lines, there having been few closures since the 1923 Grouping (Appendix 5): a Branchline Committee was set up in 1949 to expedite closures and the annual reports of the BTC contained a section on 'Closing Lines and Stations'. Securing closures was no easy matter, not at this time because of public opposition, but because of legal complexities over land ownership dating from the time of railway construction (Henshaw 1991, 49): but the important point is the emphasis on closures, not openings.[2]

Planned decentralisation and urban renewal

The location of the new towns was fixed by central government and, in continuation of the locational characteristics of their antecedents, the sites designated around London were on the main line network. This was in fact a recommendation of the New Towns Committee:

> It is better for a town to be on a through railway line than at the end of a branch; and in view of the importance of the rail traffic generated by a new town, or a group of such towns, the possibility of adding to and extending existing railways should not be ruled out (Ministry of Town and Country Planning et al. 1946, 12).

However, location on a railway was, typically, the limit of the consideration given to planning around rail. For example, in the master plan for Harlow (Gibberd 1952), one of the most self-consciously design-oriented plans, although the large area designated for the town centre abutted the station site, the area closest to it

---

2   A small number of new routes were planned, but these were freight links to new collieries, such as to Calverton in Nottinghamshire.

was zoned for a park and playing fields, with the commercial area being the most distant (Figures 4.1 and 4.2[3]). This was not a plan based on maximising access to the station, despite Gibberd's awareness that the railway was a contender for electrification, and was contrary to the advice given by the New Towns Committee wherein it had seemed that the tradition of Unwin lived on:

> It (the station) should be an outstanding feature of the town ... The siting and approaches will be part of the general scheme for the town, but the passenger station should be located as near as possible to the main shopping centre, and the railway and main bus station should be designed for easy interchange of traffic (New Towns Committee 1946).

In other conurbations location on a railway line was also seen as desirable, but commitment to rail was minimal as, for example, at East Kilbride. This was a village of 3,000 population at the time of designation for Glasgow overspill, but had an initial target of 45,000,[4] more than enough to sustain a train service, especially as the density was to be 40 persons per acre. There was an operational station adjoining the historic village core, but the area designated for the new town centre was about half a mile away: the master plan noted that, notwithstanding the huge amount of road building proposed:

> The form of the ground does not lend itself, without major cutting, to a realignment of the track to bring the passenger station nearer the centre of the town (East Kilbride Development Corporation 1950, 16).

Despite Labour's commitment to planning, it was not until after the election of the Conservatives in 1951 that, because of economic growth, the pace of reconstruction accelerated. In 1954 building licenses were abolished and money became available for major projects. Local authorities embarked on massive slum clearance and redevelopment programmes and employed batteries of young, Modernist architects to design their new housing. Building high allowed for surface uses other than housing, whilst keeping population densities relatively high and minimising the loss of agricultural land was in line with the pursuit of urban containment. But when the inner cities were redeveloped, despite high density construction, it was rarely possible to get more than half the number of people back onto a given area of land because of the need to provide land for non-housing uses.

---

3   Figure 4.1 shows the semi-circular town plan which failed to maximise accessibility to the station, and the failure to include access to the station as a key component of the internal road circulation systems. Figure 4.2 shows the poor access from the station to the commercial core of the town centre.

4   This was later raised to 70,000.

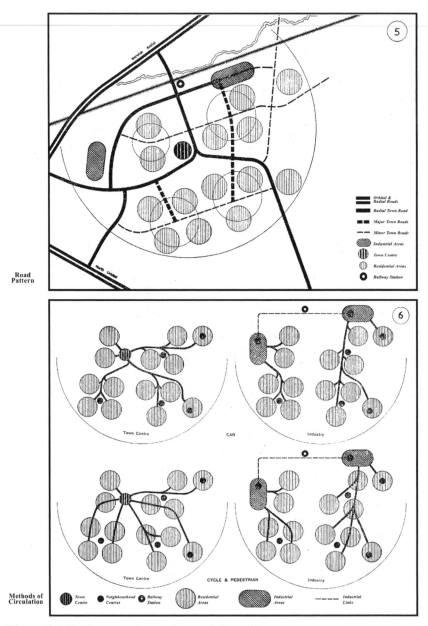

Figure 4.1 Harlow new town plan and the railway

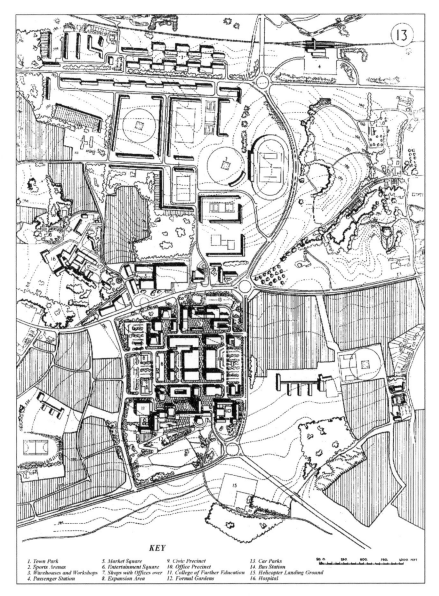

KEY

1. Town Park	5. Market Square	9. Civic Precinct	13. Car Parks
2. Sports Arenas	6. Entertainment Square	10. Office Precinct	14. Bus Station
3. Warehouses and Workshops	7. Shops with Offices over	11. College of Further Education	15. Helicopter Landing Ground
4. Passenger Station	8. Expansion Area	12. Formal Gardens	16. Hospital

Figure 4.2 Harlow new town: the station and the town centre

Source: Gibberd, 1947.

Dispersal to new towns was, increasingly, not possible as they were expensive owing to the need for infrastructure, and generating the growth of jobs at the same pace as the public sector could build houses was difficult too. So, extensive as it was, the programme could not meet all the demands. The Conservatives had no intention that it should, in any case, as they preferred the other element of Abercombie's strategy, the expansion of existing towns, to be facilitated by the Town Development Act of 1952.[5] Therefore, many authorities had to use their own peripheral land or negotiate with other local authorities to acquire land and build overspill estates and town expansion schemes.

All cities had good public transport systems at the beginning of the period, often including extensive tram and trolleybus as well as bus and railway networks. But the upgrading of the tramways was not pursued, even though many of the 1930s peripheral estates had been served by extensions to the Edwardian systems: closure programmes were drawn up and it was not unusual for local planning authorities to initiate these (Sheffield Transport Department 1960, 27). This was because it was felt that trams were dangerous, owing to passengers boarding in the middle of the road, and a restriction on traffic circulation. But at least the inner districts had good bus services: most of their residents had never been regular users of the railways in provincial cities in any case.

The primary role of the first generation of development plans was to manage the land-use aspects of the housing renewal process. This involved rezoning the inner urban redevelopment areas so as to provide sites for housing and its various ancillary uses, separating housing from incompatible uses such as industry, providing sites for new schools and other social facilities, and identifying green field sites for new peripheral estates. By and large, there was little consideration of the public transport needs arising from the location and density of development, despite the obvious potential which such compact housing forms had for association with railway systems. The mind set of BR meant that there was little attempt to engage with this process in any case. The political priority of the city councils was to build housing units, although because of the importance attached to road building and the fact that many development plans were produced within highways engineer's departments, alignments for new roads were accommodated as they had been in the wartime plans which informed the post-war planning process. The County of London Development Plan (LCC, 1951, 8) was typical in that its only reference to railways was to locate and zone operational railway land.

The Clyde Valley was a significant exception as the BTC produced a report (BTC 1951) on the network and, as in London, the committee which produced this was chaired by Inglis and its terms of reference required it to be mindful of Abercrombie's plan. This was embraced enthusiastically and the report

---

5   This was facilitated by the fact that a bill was already under preparation by the previous administration (Hall and Ward, 1998, 56). The Scottish equivalent, the Housing and Town Development (Scotland) Act 1957, was utilised for the decentralisation of Glasgow overspill population.

researched into experience on the network in the inter-war years and noted the increases in rail ridership at townships which experienced population growth, in a context where ridership generally had fallen; three new stations had in fact been opened to serve Glasgow City Council housing estates in 1949. The report, therefore, accepted the need to integrate railway and land-use planning by building new stations quickly to serve new developments, and by electrifying the local network to the north and south of the Clyde. In addition, it was recommended that municipal bus services and those operated by the BTC (Scottish Bus Group), should feed into rail hubs.

The reality of statutory planning in Glasgow was in stark contrast to the boldness of Abercrombie and Inglis: the draft City of Glasgow Development Plan was produced in 1951 and, like the Bruce plan, sought to solve the city's housing problems within its boundaries through a combination of 29 comprehensive development areas (CDAs) and peripheral housing developments; the only transportation element of any significance was an extensive new road network. At the public inquiry Abercrombie expressed his bewilderment as to what the written statement was all about and considered that the city's approach was 'contrary to the spirit of the Act' (MHLG 1953, 728-729). This situation graphically illustrated the limitations placed upon the planning system by embedding it within local government: this prevented the development of more strategic approaches which might have more easily linked a land-use strategy with a rail network plan.

In the mid-1950s, despite plans for government investment in the railways (see below), planning ideology with regard to rail transport remained unchanged. For example in the master plan for the one new town designated in the period, Cumbernauld, the designated area had a railway line along its southern periphery, rather than the area sitting astride the rail route. The town centre, despite being an innovative multi-level, high density structure, was remote from the station, as was most of the proposed settlement (Cumbernauld Development Corporation 1958). Even in the South East, a plan by the LCC for a high density new town at Hook for 100, 000 people, also placed the station on the periphery of the town, remote from the proposed town centre (LCC 1961). However, the projected expansion at Basingstoke from 26,000 to 76,000 which was substituted for the abortive Hook plan, was focused around the existing town centre with its centrally located station. But this was more a product of the Victorian inheritance than conscious rail-oriented planning (Butler 1980). By the early 1960s, the planning process managed the remarkable feat of designating a site for Skelmersdale new town in south Lancashire, with its complex network of railways, with no rail access at all (Skelmersdale Development Corporation 1964).

Roads, cars and suburbs

Not all public sector housing in the period was Modernist and the new towns, in particular, were a test bed for the development of Garden City ideology. As well as using traditional, two storey house designs, the concept of the neighbourhood unit had always been important to the Garden City movement and it was shown in Chapter 2 that, historically, the garden city idea had been associated with the development of suburbs, or neighbourhoods, focused on railway stations. However, in the post-war era it was the needs of motor traffic which attracted planners' attention and the neighbourhood concept was appropriately updated (Tetlow and Goss 1965). The neighbourhood unit:

> … was an American idea developed in the 1920s by Clarence Stein and others who were strongly influenced by the work of Unwin and Geddes. The elements of the neighbourhood unit, which were applied (though the scheme was not finished) at Radburn, NJ, as well as a few other places, were derived from Unwin's cul-de-sac layout of houses at Hampstead Garden Suburb and other early Garden-City type settlements. They were linked with modern road planning ideas to form the main components of the unit: 'superblocks' of houses encircled by distributor roads, on which the houses were turned inwards; the segregation of pedestrians and vehicles; and a network of pedestrian routes, including 'green spines' which linked the superblocks (Ravetz 1980, 51-52).

Attlee's government envisaged the public sector taking the lead in house construction, and this was the case until the late 1950s when rising incomes made home ownership more accessible and rising property values made it financially attractive too. Private housing became increasingly important and construction companies acquired land speculatively and then pressurised the planning system to grant permission to build. The Garden City movement had wetted the public's appetite for low density houses with gardens and this had fuelled the suburbanisation process in the 1930s, but private builders had jettisoned the carefully crafted designs and created the sprawl which had fuelled the calls for effective planning. Now the process began again, and despite planning control, the quality of the new suburbia was heavily criticised by contemporary commentators:

> … by the end of the century Great Britain will consist of isolated oases of preserved monuments in a desert of wire, concrete roads, cosy plots and bungalows. There will be no real distinction between town and country … Upon this new Britain the Review bestows a name in the hope that it will stick: SUBTOPIA (Nairn 1955, 365).

The builders favoured greenfield sites which were relatively cheap to buy and were uncomplicated by ground problems, unlike redevelopment sites in the cities. As the houses were built for sale, they were aimed at more affluent households who, increasingly, were car owners and this was becoming of increased locational significance:

The other vital environmental factor (in addition to newness of housing and location RH) was how housing was connected physically to the rest of the city. In a period of declining public transport this meant, in effect, whether a household had only a house, or a house-plus-car (Ravetz 1980, 152).

This need to make private housing attractive to car owners affected layout design. The speculative builders rarely used architects, relying on a small selection of standard house plans. As qualified planners were thin on the ground, it was often highway engineers who designed estate layouts and their primary consideration was vehicle circulation: the principles underlying this were developed into official guidelines by the mid-1960s (MoT 1966b).

From the mid-1950s there was relentless pressure, from within local authorities and by private builders, for the release of greenfield sites. Although this demand had to be met, in part if not in full, what planning authorities could do was protect good quality farmland and prevent the ribbon and sporadic development which had characterised the inter-war years. One of the tools which they began to utilise was green belt, officially introduced by Minister of Housing Duncan Sandys (MHLG 1955), wherein there would be a blanket presumption against development which would either have to locate between existing urban peripheries and inner green belt boundaries, or leapfrog over the green belts to sites outside them. In Greater London the latter typically included the new towns but, increasingly, housing came to be provided by the private sector in estates built on the edge of existing towns and villages located outside the green belt. Although, owing to the glacial speed at which planning documents were processed by central government, it often took many years for green belts to be formally adopted within approved statutory development plans (Elson 1986). But, nevertheless, they were effectively employed around all the major conurbations, as well as around historic towns such as Oxford, Cambridge, York and Chester. They came to have significant impacts on transport, as will be shown.

Railway modernisation

There was increasing awareness in the BTC of the competition from road transport and a realisation that diesel and electric power were an urgent necessity. With investment plans already in place for other nationalised industries by the mid-1950s, the government looked to the BTC to produce one. This was done within six months by a Planning Committee comprising headquarters staff and regional managers: there was no one from outside the BTC empire, not even major customers. The Modernisation Plan, as it was popularly known, was approved in January, 1955 (BTC 1955), with a price tag of £1,240 million. It included proposals to replace steam locomotives, including electrification of the East and West Coast

Main Lines (ECML, WCML),[6] and certain suburban services in London and Clydeside: for the latter the Inglis Report was specifically referred to, the only reference to an extant planning document in the whole Plan.

With regard to land requirements, the major impact was the programme for closure of 150 freight yards and construction and/or reconstruction of a network of 55 large marshalling yards to expedite the handling of wagon load traffic. The new yards were planned to incorporate 'humps' and 'speed retarders' to allow automatic marshalling of trains with minimum use of locomotives and manpower (Allen 1966; Fiennes 1967). There is no disputing the fact that there was a major problem of outworn infrastructure and archaic working practices (Rhodes 1988, 10), but a freight strategy needed a much more incisive appraisal of future demand for rail freight, and this should have been clear at the time. For example, back in 1944 Abercrombie, hardly a railway expert, had alluded to the importance of containerisation. Wagon load traffic was already being lost to road haulage with its door-to-door service and diminishing journey times, but there was no fundamental debate within the BTC as to whether there should be a more selective approach. Debate focused on whether the new yards should be within conurbations and close to traffic generators such as in London, or at major junctions on the trunk routes, such as at Carlisle (Fiennes 1967). Only weeks after the Plan was published, the MoT announced a four-year scheme of road improvements, including £212 million for motorways.

A similar situation developed with regard to investment in locomotives where the intention was to phase out steam in 15 years. The Regions were given their head[7] and, just like the old days of the Big Four, each had its pet designs: so after the drought came the deluge with too many locomotive types, no standardisation, and many failed designs.[8] In one respect though there was evidence of awareness of the importance of the views of external customers as Sir Brian Robertson set up a 'Design Panel' in 1956, 'to advise on the best means of obtaining a high standard of appearance and amenity in the design of its equipment': but historically railway engineers had typically always had 'a good eye'.

As the introverted culture of the BTC and overall institutional arrangements did not provide good links with other agencies, such as local planning authorities who were implementing their vision of the future (not well informed about the

---

6   The ECML runs from London King's Cross to Edinburgh via Newcastle and was formerly the LNER's main line. The WCML runs from London Euston to Glasgow via Crewe with branches off to Birmingham, Manchester and Liverpool. It was the former LMS main line.

7   Encouraged by the government's liking for historic continuity, the Western Region, for example, had already embarked on a programme of painting its carriages in GWR 'chocolate and cream'.

8   The new traction fleet was to include electric and diesel-electric locomotives, and diesel and electric multiple units (DMUs and EMUs), with a small number of diesel-electric multiple units (DEMUs).

railway network), the BTC was poorly placed to develop a strategic vision for the railway system in the context of rapid socio-economic and land-use change. The overall strategy was driven by the aspirations of the engineers who maintained and operated the railway and did not address the shortcomings of the geography of the network identified at the end of Chapter 2. As a result the strategy was deeply flawed:

> ... apart from the modest proposals for passenger withdrawals ... and the closure of a number of goods depots, the modernisation plan set out to rebuild the existing railway, whether there was a demand for its services or not (Joy 1973, 44).

Or to put it in the rather plainer language of one of the few contemporary railway managers to commit themselves to print: 'We had made the basic error of buying our tools before doing our homework on defining the job' (Fiennes 1967, 77).[9] In addition the financial impacts of key matters such as rising labour costs were overlooked (Joy 1973, 48).

As the saga of the Modernisation Plan unfolded it did nothing to reassure an increasingly sceptical government, and senior civil servants became distrustful of BR's managerial capabilities. BR went into deficit in 1956, a position from which it never recovered. It was the concern over its finances that led the BTC to bring forward more lines for closure and these began to attract organised public opposition. The protracted closure of the East Grinstead to Lewes line between 1955 and 1958 was a notable example: eventually this was taken over by preservationists, becoming 'the Bluebell Railway'. However, 1958 also saw the closure, with minimal opposition, of the longest route considered by the TUCCs up to this time, the former Midland and Great Northern Joint Line running across rural north Norfolk between Spalding and Great Yarmouth. Although the rate of closures increased, the public mood was still relatively passive compared with what was to come.

London Underground

At this point it is necessary to make a brief diversion to consider the London Underground, as certain issues arose which were of wider relevance. This network emerged from the War in the same rundown state as the main line railways, although ridership in 1948 was above inter-war levels (Barker and Robbins 1976, 339). From the start the BTC made it clear that its priority was the main line network and London's needs would have to be funded from other sources. London Transport, therefore, had to develop investment cases sufficiently convincing to

---

9   Fiennes was in fact sacked in 1967 after publication of his book which contained reflection on and informed criticism of railway policy.

prise money out of central government. The Victoria Line saga serves to illustrate the sort of arguments used and the difficulties involved in raising funds on this basis. This had its roots in Route 8 of the Inglis Committee report and first appeared as Route C in the London Working Party's report of 1948. The proposal marked a significant change in Underground planning as, unlike the suburban extensions of the inter-war years, this was a new route to be tunnelled under the central area. Previous funding mechanisms had included straight commercial profit and, between the wars, Keynesian inspired demand management (the New Works Programme). In the post-war period underground railways could not be built as straight commercial enterprises, and there was a labour shortage, so the old rationales were no longer relevant. Therefore, the wider benefits of railway investment which could not be captured through the fare box would have to be taken into account if new investment was to be justified.[10] Cost benefit analysis techniques were developed to inform the appraisal process for the Victoria Line involving complex, socio-economic analyses which were so innovatory and wide ranging (Beesley and Foster, 1965) that they slowed the decision-making process down considerably. The handling of the Victoria Line proposal therefore:

> shows characteristic features of public handling of investment projects in mid-twentieth century Britain: general acceptance of the intention as desirable; delay for argument on constantly changing bases; final approval under temporary pressures which were largely irrelevant to the arguments (Barker and Robbins 1976, 344).

What is significant with regard to the ideological context for planning, is that this project marks the first utilisation of welfare economics to underpin railway investment. This became very significant as events unfolded and would be used to justify, not just *construction* of new railways, but the *operation* of a significant part of the extant network. In addition, cost benefit analysis showed the significance to the viability of railways of securing property development around stations.

The railways in crisis

Owing to the onset of recession in 1958 and growing competition from road transport, railway losses increased. The costs of the BTC's most prestigious project, electrification of the WCML, escalated from an estimated £75m to £165m and its completion was brought into doubt. Government began to ask difficult questions about the return on investment and other major projects, such as ECML

---

10   The development of the motorway network ran into similar difficulties with regard to choosing which route to build from several alternatives: the problem with motorways was more fundamental though, as they were to be toll-free and would generate no direct income (Coburn, Beesley and Reynolds, 1960).

electrification, were abandoned. The report on BR by the Select Committee on the Nationalised Industries (Select Committee 1960) explored the principles[11] which should underpin the management of the railway network and, in particular, recognised that certain services could be run on commercial principles, whilst others could not. The Committee advised that it may well be in the public interest to underpin the costs of the latter: the important point was to have clarity of purpose and transparency of accounting. This constituted the first articulation of a new approach to financing the railways and eventually, along with cost benefit analysis, became part of the ideological bedrock of a new funding regime.

The review process which Marples had set in motion, reached its conclusion in 1963 with publication of Beeching's 'The Reshaping of British Railways' (BRB 1963), popularly, or perhaps unpopularly, known as the Beeching Plan. There was an objective need for some incisive thinking, but transport policy under Marples had developed on the basis of ideological commitment to road transport and a reductionist stance towards the railways. Far from any desire to develop a balanced and integrated transport policy, there was a simple goal of cutting back the loss making railway system as far as public opinion would allow. However, notwithstanding the shortcomings of this ideological context, Beeching tried to apply a structured and analytical approach to the railway problem (Table 4.1).

The basis was to test, as quantitatively as possible, how far the operation of the railway departed from these conditions. The report analysed different traffics and routes to identify the costs and income of each. The results were very revealing showing that one third of route mileage carried only one per cent of passenger miles and one per cent of freight tonnage. Roughly half the network could be seen as losing money, whereas the most heavily used part showed substantial returns. The lightly used part included most of the single track branch lines, of which there were 5,900 route miles (9495 kms). The Report also produced data showing that only express passenger services and coal traffic were profitable. London suburban services approached profitability, but local passenger services in other conurbations were major loss makers. Beeching identified the high costs and poor competitiveness of wagon load freight and highlighted the need to develop train load business (siding to siding flows with no marshalling en route) and to develop new freight handling technologies, such as containerisation.

Given that there was contemporary awareness of the failure of the Modernisation Plan to take into account the future impacts of changes in urban and economic geography, it would have been reasonable to expect that Beeching would have considered their impact on potential demand for railway services. But he only mentioned this briefly and it was soon dismissed:

> No novel assumptions have been made about the future distribution of population and industry in the country as a whole.

---

11   The relevant extract from the Committee's report is in Appendix 6.

... Therefore, in formulating proposals for line closure, all the Railway regions have taken account of any developments which are sufficiently specific to be probable, but have not been influenced by quite unsupported suggestions that something might happen some day (BRB 1963, 56).

Table 4.1 Beeching's approach to railway rationalisation

The logical approach to the problem of shaping, or reshaping a railway system is:	
a	to determine the basic characteristics which distinguish railways as a mode of transport;
b	to determine under what conditions these characteristics enable railways to be the best available form of transport;
c	to determine to which parts of the total national pattern of transport requirements these conditions apply;
d	to shape the railway route system and services so as to take advantage of favourable circumstances wherever they exist ...
Railways are distinguished by the provision and maintenance of a specialised route system for their own exclusive use. This gives rise to high fixed costs. On the other hand, the benefits which can be derived from possession of this high cost route system are very great.	
Firstly, it permits the running of high capacity trains, which themselves have very low movement costs per unit carried. Secondly, it permits dense flows of traffic and, provided the flows are dense, the fixed costs per unit moved are also low. Thirdly, it permits safe, reliable, scheduled movements at high speed.	
In a national system of transport we should, therefore, expect to find railways concentrating upon those parts of the traffic pattern which enable them to derive sufficient benefit from these three advantages to offset their unavoidable burden of high system cost (Beeching, 1963, 4).	

Beeching's brief was to consider then current levels of traffic in shaping his proposals and he, in fact, considered his closure proposals to be restrained. His recommendations were a mixture of good and bad news, but undoubtedly it is the bad which has entered national folklore. This included: the withdrawal of many passenger and freight services; the targeted closure of 2363 stations and freight depots and 5000 route miles (8046 kms); a withdrawal from the seasonal holiday business; a dramatic reduction in the amount of rolling stock; and the possible withdrawal of provincial commuter services. However, the good news, which underpinned the development of more successful traffics, included: the selective improvement of inter-city passenger services; co-ordination of suburban train and bus services and charges, in collaboration with municipal authorities; the development of siding-to-siding 'block' freight trains; the development of a network of 'liner trains' carrying intermodal containers between a limited number of mechanised terminals; and the accelerated replacement of steam engines by modern locomotives.

Contemporary criticisms of Beeching

The major objections to the 'Beeching Axe' focused on the lack of regard for the social role of the railways:

> The application of strict economic principles of pecuniary demand and cost (au Beeching) emphasises this anti-democratic influence (of the motor car RH) ... the purely monetary calculus of demand and supply has a definite bias against public transport (Dickinson 1964, 6).

Also there were technical objections to some of the techniques and costings used to underpin the plan. The Railway Development Association (RDA)[12] developed two main criticisms, around the issues of contributory revenue and operating costs.[13] The RDA argued that with modern traction and concerted efforts to reduce operating *and* track costs, the case for retention of many lines could be greatly strengthened as compared with Beeching's presentation of 'the facts'. Criticism of Beeching's methodology included the significance of only counting ticket *sales* at stations and not numbers of passengers *arriving*: this was felt to tip the scales against branch lines because these served seaside resorts and so on which were more likely to be destinations than origins. Similarly there was criticism of the timing of the collection of passenger figures, this being over a single week in April 1961, two weeks after the Easter holiday and hardly the peak of the tourist season. Critics felt that branch line operating costs tended to be overstated: Beeching was seen to take a dogmatic view of track costs as fixed and not susceptible to significant cost reductions. This was something that Fiennes (1967) pursued in rural East Anglia: the 'basic railway' with single track, automatic level crossings, minimal signalling and unstaffed stations. However in later closure hearings, Beeching's estimated costs were sometimes quoted to counter even harsher costings put forward by zealous railway managers keen to please their political masters (Henshaw 1991, 159).

If the social cost arguments can be seen as coming from the liberal, pro-public transport social welfare lobby, and opposition to specific closures as coming from

---

12   The RDA had been formed in 1951 to argue the case for the development of modern lightweight diesel railbuses and multiple units to sustain retention of the branch lines: Sir John Betjeman was one of the founders. The RDA became the Railway Development Society and continues to operate today, now known as Railfuture.

13   Contributory revenue is the contribution to income on the trunk routes made by traffic feeding from the branch lines: if the latter are closed then the trunk services lose that traffic.

rail passengers, criticism of Beeching also came from a more unexpected source, an eminent railway economist:[14]

> ... vital years were lost while the management shunted round looking for excuses when it became obvious that the Beeching prescriptions were not even relieving the symptoms, let alone curing the disease. Straight talk and analysis in 1962 could have saved much wasted effort later, by directing scarce management resources into areas of really high pay-off, instead of scratching for negligible returns in trying to close rural branch lines. By this I mean areas such as:
>
> 1.   Maximising the profits from the Inter-City passenger business ...
> 2.   Obtaining continuous true improvements in labour productivity ...
> 3.   Demanding improved performance from the non-rail subsidiaries ...
> 4.   Commencing a fundamental analysis of the future of the freight business ...
> 5.   Getting the capital structure right ... (Joy 1973, 79)

Despite the criticisms, Beeching had many supporters amongst railway managers as, coming from outside the industry, he had no particular axe to grind, and he introduced a market oriented culture[15] which promised a way out of the financial crisis:

> How did we, the railwaymen, react? ... Most of us shrugged and got on with the job for we knew, although things would never be the same again, that Beeching was right (Hardy 1989, 83-84).

Town planning and road transport

Contemporary publication of another seminal document, Buchanan's 'Traffic in Towns' (MoT 1963) reflected the government's rising expectations with regard to the role of the private car. Marples had already increased the target for motorway construction from 800 miles (1287 kms) to 1000 miles (1609 kms) by 1972. However, the environmental problems associated with road traffic were recognised in the wartime plans and had been more rigorously analysed subsequently (Smeed 1961). It was accepted that some sort of balance had to be struck between accommodating road traffic and protecting the quality of urban life. Buchanan's terms of reference were:

---

14   Stewart Joy was a consultant to the MoT during the policy making period which culminated in the 1968 Transport Act and was subsequently BR Chief Economist for three years.

15   The language used in the BRB annual reports characterised this and progressively through the mid and late 1960s embraced terms like 'market research', 'product', 'product development', 'branding' and 'market sectors'.

to study the long term development of roads and traffic in urban areas and their influence on the urban environment (MoT 1963, 7).

It was clear that this was not to be a multi-modal view of the urban transport problem: the Buchanan and Beeching Reports were mutually exclusive. Nevertheless, there were a number of points about the former which make it worthy of discussion. The commissioning of the report resulted from recognition of the predominance of road traffic and the statistics which summarised that fixed the context of the policy debate:

> ... in 1959, road travel represented 81% of all inland passenger travel. Of all inland goods transport (during 1958), about 72% by tonnage or 45% by mileage, was by road (MoT 1963, 12).

Buchanan demonstrated that car ownership would increase substantially over the following ten years and a significant increase in road space was necessary, even if only a part of the increased demand was to be catered for. He was well aware of the negative effects of motor traffic arising from congestion, accidents, noise, and atmospheric pollution (Buchanan 1958). As Buchanan saw it, society had to decide what levels of external costs it was prepared to tolerate, and implement the balance of road building and vehicle restraint necessary to achieve those levels. The Buchanan Report represented the maturing and coalescence of professional ideologies which stretched back to the 1930s, as reviewed in Chapter 2. There was nothing remotely like this sort of inter-professional ideological convergence around planning for the railway network.

However Buchanan was not blindly in favour of unbridled road building. Stemming from his sensitivity to the negative aspects of motor traffic, he developed the concepts of the 'environmental area' and 'environmental capacity' which were defined as:

- Environmental area – an area having no extraneous traffic, and within which considerations of environment (in the specialised sense, as defined) predominate over the use of vehicles.
- Environmental capacity – the capacity of a street or an area to accommodate moving and stationary vehicles having regard to the need to maintain the environmental standards.

Overall his message was subtle: increased road traffic could be accommodated, but there would be an environmental price to pay and society had to decide what the limits should be. However, the problem with his environmental concepts is that they were just that, concepts, which were not operationalised and were thus vague and subjective.

Despite his brief, Buchanan made a number of significant references to public transport, the need to integrate different transport modes, and to integrate transport and land-use planning. He also suggested that development plans needed to be supplemented by statutory transportation plans, concluding that:

> In the long run the most potent factor in maintaining a "ceiling" on private car traffic in busy areas is likely to be the provision of good, cheap public transport, coupled with the public's understanding of the position (MoT 1963, 193).

The report contained some interesting references to the use of railways and street trams as part of integrated transport and planning strategies, particularly in Germany and Sweden. Stockholm[16] was noted as a city where the railway network was being developed along with road building, in line with the plan from 1941:

> It is very significant that a city of this size should have found it possible to finance the construction of an underground system, and to reach the bold conclusion that in the general public interest it should be a subsidised undertaking (MoT 1963, 177).

But Buchanan's message was too subtle given the political realities of the time: a huge development machine was rolling and it was not susceptible to the niceties of his arguments:

> Behind Buchanan came the traffic engineers with their plans for urban motorways: hundreds of miles for London, similarly vast networks for every provincial city (Hall 1988, 316).

The report's major impact was that the leadership of civil engineers in urban transport planning was reinforced and they utilised the new computer technologies to model[17] traffic flows in a new generation of 'land-use transportation plans': the vacuum left by the failure of the integrated transport paradigm of the 1940s was filled by 'predict and provide' and accelerated road construction. The outcome was most typically characterised by events in Birmingham, where the plans developed by Manzoni dovetailed with the MoT's plans for the national motorway network, to unleash an amazing burst of activity. At the time this had the support of politicians and most of the public.

---

16   See Cervero (1995) for a later reflection on Stockholm's plan.

17   In the 1960s the use of theoretical models, such as the gravity model, and quantitative techniques to represent transport networks and settlement patterns, caused a paradigm shift in human geography, a subject which grew even closer to planning in this period (Chorley and Haggett 1965, 1967).

Table 4.2 Beeching's approach to trunk route planning

Examination of the present pattern of trunk transport of freight on rail, in relation to the national demand for freight transport between main centres, and of the present inter-city flows of passenger traffic.
Consideration of those changes in the national economy and in the disposition of population and industry which are likely to affect the future demand for public transport, and in particular, rail transport.
Assessment of the probable pattern of transport demand between main centres by 1984, and of the traffic flows favourable to trunk movement by rail.
Consideration of the potential capacity of rail trunk routes when developed technically and operated in the manner best suited to the types of traffic foreseen.
Selection from existing routes of those which can best be developed to provide the network and capacity required to handle the future trunk traffic demand (BRB 1965, 9).

Railway investment in the 1960s

Publication of the Trunk Routes report, BRB (1965), was, as Beeching saw it, the logical and positive concomitant to the Reshaping Report and had a twenty year planning horizon. The problem with the 7,500 miles (12,070 kms) of trunk route was the historic one of duplication: with declining traffic and the potential for increased capacity through modernisation, there was an obvious need to make choices, although Beeching emphasised that because a route was not selected for investment, that didn't mean that automatically it would be closed. Beeching set out his usual methodical approach as shown in Table 4.2. The report was notable for its 27 maps showing the relationship of the recommended core network of approximately 3,000 miles (4,828 kms) to major traffic sources such as power stations, oil refineries, steel works and coalfields, as well as the relative population densities of the conurbations. In keeping with the optimism of the time, there was an assumption of an annual 4 per cent growth rate in the economy, and of a 15 per cent rise in population by 1984. In this case Beeching was attentive to the work of the planning system and quoted from a contemporary study:

> "The South East Study 1961–81", which deals with the growth and distribution of population and industry in the South Eastern Region, was issued last year by the Ministry of Housing and Local Government. One significant feature of this report, and of the White Paper (Cmnd.2308) which accompanied it, is the evidence which it provides of the strong urge of the government to damp down the main migrational movement which is apparent at the present time, namely the migration to the South East (BRB 1965, 15).

From his consideration of these matters Beeching made two important assumptions which underpinned his strategy:

In relation to population it was assumed that the rate of growth would be comparatively even throughout the country and that no major redistribution would take place. In relation to industry, although some change was foreseen in the commodity pattern of production, the assumption was made that the geographical spread of general industrial activity would remain the same, and that growth would be uniform throughout the country (BRB 1965, 16).

Therefore an attempt was made to accommodate some of the factors influencing demand for railway transport in the long term. Beeching was also aware that the focus for investment shouldn't be too narrow:

A system too neatly tailored to the estimated future traffic level might well prove inadequate to carry a substantial part of the profitable traffic on offer. A measure of surplus capacity must therefore be provided for … In the case of the system indicated this surplus amounts to about one-third (BRB, 1965, 46).

But one issue conspicuous by its absence was urban road traffic congestion: there was no connection with the Buchanan Report. Overall Beeching painted a rather pessimistic picture of the potential for rail passenger traffic and saw it as squeezed between competition from the airlines, for journeys over 200 miles (322 kms), and from road transport for distances below 100 miles (161 kms):

It is estimated that the total volume of demand for inter-city travel on rail will fall slightly from its present level … (BRB 1965, 32-33).

His vision did not encompass high speed trains, despite contemporary development of the Japanese Shinkansen (Allen 1966), although he did countenance the possibility of a Channel Tunnel, but raised no specific expectations about its impact on traffic. The issue of the vertical loading gauge was not addressed although its constraining impacts on carriage of freight, particularly intermodal traffic, were recognised at the time (Calvert 1965, 41-47). The report was Beeching's swan song as by mid-1965 he was back at ICI, four years after he left. He was succeeded by a career railwayman, Stanley Raymond:[18] the quantum change in railway policy was complete.

Regional planning in London and the South East

On its return to government in 1964, Labour had no coherent transport policy but was resistant to the Beeching closures. The new government was marked by a commitment to accelerate slum clearance which, along with the need to accommodate economic and population growth, set the scene for a period of

---

18   Raymond's salary at £12,500 was just over half of Beeching's.

intensive strategic planning, typified by several plans for London and the South East as shown in Table 4.3.

Table 4.3 Strategic plans for London and the South East

1	'The South East Study' (MHLG 1964), (obviously this had been under preparation by the previous Conservative Government);
2	'The Conference Area in the Long-term', by the Standing Conference on London and the South East Regional Planning, (Standing Conference on London and the South East Regional Planning 1966); (the Standing Conference was a voluntary grouping of all the local planning authorities in the region, and became known as SERPLAN).
3	'A Strategy for the South East', by the South East Economic Planning Council (South East Economic Planning Council 1967); (this was one of a number of Regional Economic Planning Councils set up by the Labour Government reflecting the renewed commitment to economic and land-use planning: Peter Hall was a member).
4	'Strategic Plan for the South East', (South East Joint Planning Team 1970) produced by an independent study team set up by central government under the direction of the Chief Planner at the MHLG, Dr Wilfred Burns.

One of the major issues with which these wrestled was the location of major growth areas and their relationship to London. Experience showed that these would have to be larger and further from London than first generation new towns if they were to meet the needs of a growing population and achieve a higher degree of independence from London. With planning at this scale there were crucial interrelationships to consider between development and transport infrastructure, so there was obvious potential to interrelate railway and land-use planning.

The 1964 South East Study (MHLG 1964) envisaged the development of fairly small market towns such as Newbury and Ashford, but also substantial expansion of existing county towns such as Northampton, Peterborough and Ipswich. In addition a completely new city, much larger than previous new towns, was envisaged to the north of Bletchley (Milton Keynes), as well as substantial growth in the Portsmouth-Southampton corridor. This notion of the 'planned agglomeration', as opposed to the development of free standing settlements, was an idea which developed rapidly. In the 1967 Strategy for the South East (South East Economic Planning Council 1967) three such agglomerations were envisaged: one at about 70 miles (113 kms) to the south-west of London in South Hampshire; one between 50 and 70 miles (80.5-113 kms) to the north-west of London based on Northampton-Milton Keynes; and a third area based on Colchester-Ipswich and the growing ports of Felixstowe and Harwich.

With regard to the development of planning models, in addition to the 'planned agglomeration' there was also the 'transport corridor' in the 1966 report of the

Standing Conference[19] on London and the South East Regional Planning (1966), as noted later by Hall:

> Its authors argued that the concept of a self-contained town or community had broken down, to be replaced by the notion of different communities welded into an organised pattern of inter-relationships. Therefore, they argued, a study of communications and of movement patterns was fundamental to preparation of a strategic plan. This pointed to the fact that any plan must be related, first to plans for major regional, inter-regional and international routes, so that non-local movements could be catered for efficiently; and secondly, to developing clusters of settlements closely related to transport routes. They concluded:

> "This may point to the advantages of establishing corridors (on regional or sub-regional scales) in which road and rail routes and services would be closely associated with axes of urban development (existing and new)" (Hall 1971, 190).

The 1967 Strategy for the South East utilised the agglomeration and corridor ideas, although the word 'sector' was used to indicate breadth as well as length. Four major sectors were envisaged, radiating from London towards planned 'counter magnets': in the direction of Southampton-Portsmouth, Northampton-Milton Keynes, Colchester-Ipswich, and Canterbury. Each of these was to be paralleled by a minor sector also leading to counter magnets, which in this case would be free standing towns, not agglomerations. These radiated from London towards Swindon, Peterborough, Basildon-Southend, Ashford and Brighton. The underlying transport rationale was undoubtedly the development of the motorway network, but the sectors were well related to main railway lines radiating from London too.

All the sectors mentioned appeared in the map of routes selected for development in Beeching's second report (BRB 1965, map 21), apart from the London to Canterbury/Ashford, and London to Southend sectors, which were commuter routes and did not fall into Beeching's classification as trunk routes. Although the sector idea was a good one for building a broad strategic relationship between patterns of land development and strategic transport routes, it is interesting to note that they were defined solely in terms of their relationship with London. Their relationships to each other were not mentioned and there was no discussion of new orbital rail routes in these plans and no serious examination of existing rail services *between* the centres mentioned: this failure to relate railway and planning policy was criticised at the time (Allen 1966, 38).

---

19   The Standing Conference had been formed in 1962 and later became known as Serplan and was very influential with regard to strategic planning in the south east (see also Chapter 7).

The final plan in the series emerged from the MHLG in 1970 (South East Joint Planning Team 1970a).[20] Coming at the end of a period of intense strategic planning activity and being produced as a result of a joint commission by the Secretary of State for Economic Affairs, the Minister of Housing and Local Government and the Minister of Transport, as well as the Chairmen of the Standing Conference and the Economic Planning Council, it is obvious that this Plan was of much greater standing than any of its predecessors and can be seen to represent the most interventionist and prescriptive strategy that the planning system could then achieve. A number of specialist studies were produced and Volume 3 (South East Joint Planning Team 1970b) dealt with Transportation. Paragraph 1.4 of this stated: 'There has been no previous transport study of this kind, or on this scale, in the United Kingdom...'.

The institutional context facilitated BR involvement in this study, which was a step forward, but the differing treatment given by central government to the road and rail networks was soon revealed:

Major road plans are already in hand for the period up to the late 1970's ... There was not comparable long-term commitment to the allocation of resources to railway improvements ... (para 1.7).

Section 2 was wholly concerned with the railway system and the limited horizons were clear:

The rail network is considerably less dense than the road system. Changes over the last few years have been in the form, on the one hand, of technical improvements to infrastructure, traction and rolling stock and, on the other hand, of closures of lightly used sections. This pattern is likely to continue, because the network already covers the main corridors of movement, and because high utilisation – and therefore major urban development in an area previously not served by rail – would be needed to make entirely new lines an economic proposition. For the purpose of this study the Team have therefore been concerned with changes in the loading and operation of the existing network, as opposed to changes in its form ... (para 2.23).

Paragraphs 2.24 and 2.25 went on to look at the organisational structure of BR noting that, for the most part, it followed the geography of the routes radiating from London apart from a small number of cross country services such as Southampton-Reading-Oxford-Birmingham, and Southampton-Severnside. Further comment was added about their quality:

20   Although strictly outside the time period of this chapter this document is an integral part of the sequence of plans being reviewed here.

In most cases the cross-country services offer a lower frequency of service than the radial routes, and in very few cases is it possible to make a cross-country journey of any length without changing trains.

So the historic problems associated with cross-country and orbital rail services were recognised, but the conventional wisdom was that this situation was not going to improve. Section 3 of the study looked at 'New Developments in Transport Systems' and the involvement of BR staff is evidenced by comment on the likely impact of improved signalling, automated control techniques and improvements in passenger handling. But the overall conclusion was downbeat:

> The Team consider that these changes could lead to considerable improvements but doubt whether their impact on interurban travel will be significant.

The recommended strategy was that development should be steered towards a number of major and minor growth points. The major growth points were envisaged as eventually having a population of 1 million each and included South Hampshire, Reading-Aldershot-Basingstoke, Crawley, Milton Keynes-Wellingborough-Northampton, and South Essex. The minor growth points were envisaged as eventually having populations of 0.25 to 0.5 million and included Bournemouth-Poole, Eastbourne-Hastings, Ashford, Maidstone-Medway, Chelmsford, Bishops Stortford-Harlow and Aylesbury. This strategy was accepted by government as the basis for regional planning in the South East and brought a decade of frenetic strategic planning activity in the region to a close.

Regional planning in the provinces

Outside the South East the need for regional plans was perceived to be less because of lower rates of growth and the spheres of influence of provincial cities were smaller than London's. Chapter 2 showed that, historically, the role of railways in the growth of provincial cities had been less too, so even where strategic planning did take place, there was comparatively little positive comment on the role of the railways. As an example of this, and because of subsequent events in the 1980s which are reviewed in chapters eight and nine, it is desirable to consider the Nottinghamshire-Derbyshire Study (Nottinghamshire County Council et al. 1969).[21] This was concerned with the changing socio-economic characteristics of Nottingham and Derby and industrial decline in the Erewash Valley coalfield along the county border. It was the problems in the border area, and the presence of the new M1 Motorway along it, which were the catalysts for the joint exercise. There were two trunk railways in the area: the ECML running between Newark and

---

21   Although published just after the end of the period which this chapter reviews this study was carried out within it.

Doncaster, and the Midland main line running from Leicester to Loughborough, with branches to Nottingham and Derby which conjoined near Chesterfield en route for Sheffield. The northward extension of the Nottingham arm ran through the Erewash Valley en route for Chesterfield. There were a number of mineral lines in the area, mainly serving collieries, but the Beeching closures had removed much of the local passenger network focused on Nottingham, as well as the Great Central main line from Leicester, through Nottingham to Sheffield. Mansfield lost its passenger service to Nottingham in 1964 and entered national folklore as the largest town with no rail service. There were few references to railways at all in the Study, although it did demonstrate awareness of the potential for concentrating development in rail corridors, but discounted this as a viable option (Nottinghamshire County Council et al. 1969,78). The absence of an inter-city service to Mansfield was remarked upon in a way which demonstrated awareness of the strategic importance of this, and the lack of direct involvement by BR in the Study:

> Inter-regional links are essential to the prosperity of a major urban complex and should not be sacrificed because of relatively minor operational difficulties for British Rail.

> Commuter links into Nottingham are not what is sought, but a stopping place for inter-city express services ... British Rail have been asked to investigate these possibilities.

Planning ideology and the debate on urban form: the new towns

With regard to broader ideological trends in planning, the car-based decentralisation which so concerned Clark (1958) led, in America, to a radical conceptualisation of this new type of urban form, 'the non-place urban realm' (Webber 1964). This developed from sociological criticism of the planners' notion of the neighbourhood as a physical development form which had social significance because of its association with the creation of communities: Young and Wilmott (1957) pointed out that people were members of many communities which could be based on family, workplace or leisure interest, as well as, perhaps, place. Webber developed this idea and said that, with developing communications technologies and the mobility offered by the car, the traditional city centre was losing its role as the central place where people needed to congregate for social interaction and access to goods and services. Technology offered the possibility for interaction without face-to-face contact, and the dispersal of activities throughout a motorway network would mean that there would be many sub-centres for such direct contact as would be required, all equally accessible to a dispersed but mobile population – the non-place urban realm.

Running contrary to this vision and, again coming from America, was a staunch defence of the traditional city and a fierce attack on what planners and architects had done to it. This was led by Jane Jacobs (1962) who celebrated the traditional, high density inner city suburb with complex patterns of human activity, characterised by walking and the use of public transport, typically a railway or subway system. The varied activity at street level – shops, cafes, restaurants, bars, workplaces and local service outlets – created a stimulating and singularly urban environment. There was no reason why such neighbourhoods should be seething slums, as they had been portrayed.

In British planning circles debate raged as to these visions of the future and their implications for urban design and urban transport systems (Tetlow and Goss 1965). As so often happened it was in the new towns that the ideas came to be developed and applied in their purest form. The Cumbernauld master plan was dominated by roads, but the designers drew from the experience with Radburn-inspired layouts in the first generation new towns and planned for a very high degree of pedestrian-vehicular segregation: the town centre design was the sort of structure endorsed by Buchanan. The new towns, including Cumbernauld and those designated later, were dominated by car-oriented transport planning during a period when resources for road building were abundant. As one of the engineers involved stated subsequently:

> In the early years of their existence the Mark IIs and Mark IIIs[22] laid down what are arguably the best, and certainly the most comprehensive, urban highway structures to be found in Britain (Dupree 1987, 33).

It fell to the designers of Runcorn new town to produce a plan (Ling 1966) which, by utilising a 'double circuit linear' form, structured development around a dedicated public transport corridor, albeit a busway. This was because the designers[23] recognised that even with rising car ownership, there would always be a significant part of the population which would be dependent on public transport, so it made sense to embrace it as a core element of the design. The layout of residential neighbourhoods was focused around the need to provide easy pedestrian access to the centrally located bus stop. Runcorn's new town centre was to be a similar structure to that at Cumbernauld, with the addition of access by the busway.

Initial plans for Milton Keynes were for a high density monorail city but these were dropped in 1968 (Bendixson and Platt 1992) and replaced by the now familiar

---

22   New towns designated between 1955 and 1970 are Mark II and III, those designated before 1955 are known as Mark Is.

23   The design team included Roy Cresswell, one of the few town planners of the period to specialise in the relationship between land-use and public transport networks. See Ling (1967) for a fuller discussion of Runcorn and the rationale behind the target of 50/50 public/private transport modal split.

system of grid roads, with a dispersed pattern of land-uses and development at limited densities so as to maximise vehicular mobility, whilst minimising traffic generation and congestion (Milton Keynes Development Corporation 1970). It was recognised that the provision of public transport services would be difficult, but it was felt that technology would come to the rescue with a 'dial-a-ride' system. The plan came to be warmly endorsed by garden city traditionalists as a return to the original concepts of spaciousness, good landscaping and plenty of open space (Osborn and Whittick 1977): the failure to plan around public transport was traditional too.

Planning ideology and the debate on urban form: city centre redevelopment

Owing to post-war austerity there was little scope for planning authorities to act quickly on the advice of the New Towns Committee (1946) or the Ministry of Town and Country Planning (1947) with regard to station design. But, by the mid-1950s, the economy improved and town centre redevelopment became a significant focus for planning activity. There were many forces driving this: the need to make good war damage; demand for new retail floorspace and the need for better access for delivery lorries; demand for private car access and parking; the need to resolve the increasing conflicts in city streets between through traffic, local traffic, buses, cars, delivery vehicles and pedestrians; and demand for new office buildings to house the growing service sector. Architecturally, this process was dominated by Modernism and, as so many of the issues had to do with traffic, highway engineers played a central role too: the Buchanan Report reinforced this engineering-led approach. The notorious Councillor T. Dan Smith[24] was a member of the Buchanan Steering Group and his role in the dramatic redevelopment of central Newcastle which incorporated major road building plans, illustrated the close relationship between local government and the road lobby.

The case of Birmingham was particularly notable: Chapter 2 showed that, although it was a major railway hub with a model network, rail commuting had not played a very significant role in its growth. Nevertheless, the potential was there. However, the post-war planning of Birmingham was masterminded by one of the country's leading civil engineers, Sir Herbert Manzoni, who considered that:

> Unfortunately, the layout of the railway system is very meagre, and its use has probably tended to diminish rather than increase with the improving facilities for trams and omnibuses (Manzoni 1940, 112).

---

24   Smith was Leader of Newcastle Upon Tyne City Council from 1960 to 1965 and a prominent figure in the area's Labour party. He formed illegal business links with architect John Poulson which led, in 1974, to his trial for accepting bribes: he was sentenced to six years' imprisonment.

Although he was well aware of the spatial demands of rising car traffic, Manzoni's thinking was totally road-oriented. But he was tremendously far-sighted and effective: under his auspices the City Council promoted a city centre compulsory purchase order (CPO) in 1946 beginning the long process of road building through acquisition, demolition, and reconstruction. The city's statutory development plan (City of Birmingham 1960) was much concerned with problems of 'communication',[25] but the solutions embraced policies for the building of inner, intermediate and outer ring roads, link roads, by-pass roads and multi-storey car parks, with no mention of public transport. The only railway item of any significance was appendix 4 which listed 'Major Developments by Statutory Undertakers' and included rather cryptically: 'British Transport Commission – London Midland Region – New Street – Reconstruction'.

The CDA, one of the tools of the 1947 Act, was increasingly used to plan and implement large scale change which often involved the use of CPO powers to bring land into public ownership. This was deemed necessary so that local road networks could be remodelled and large retail and office buildings could be developed, in an integrated way, along with multi-storey car parks. It wasn't unusual for CDAs to be pursued in partnership with a private developer. With such thoroughgoing change occurring there was plenty of scope to alter structural relationships between land-use and transport systems and, even within the context of improving vehicular access, rail access could have been improved too. Croydon is a good example of how the central area of a traditional market town grew rapidly into a business centre as a result of massive planning-led investment but, despite the excellence of its railway services, the design of the central area was overwhelmingly dominated by road-oriented ideology.

Ravetz (1980, 48) commented that two primary concepts which underpinned urban planning ideology at this time were 'concentricity' and 'segregation'. Concentricity went back to Howard's Social City with its garden cities surrounded by open countryside and was an important element of Abercrombie's Greater London Plan, often known as 'the plan of the Four Rings', which was so closely related to orbital road proposals. The Ministry of Town and Country Planning had produced policy guidance (MTCP 1947) for town centre redevelopment which was dominated by concern to improve traffic circulation by building ring roads around town centres. It was clear that this could have negative implications for access to railway stations as their, typically, peripheral location could place them outside such roads, thereby separating them from the town centre they served (Figure 4.3). Concentricity lent itself to the idea that different planning treatment should be given to different rings of cities, and that land-uses should be segregated accordingly. For example, the design guide mentioned above found that, of thirteen possible uses, only four or five were permissible in town centres.

---

25   The written statement listed 17 'problems' with nos. 13-17 all concerned with communications.

Ravetz demonstrated how well fitted to each other were these planning concepts and the aspirations of architects and highway engineers:

> The imperatives of traffic engineering were thoroughly compatible with architectural thought, which regarded obsolete street plans as the "root evil" of modern city planning (1980, 50).

SKETCH PLAN FOR THE CENTRAL AREA

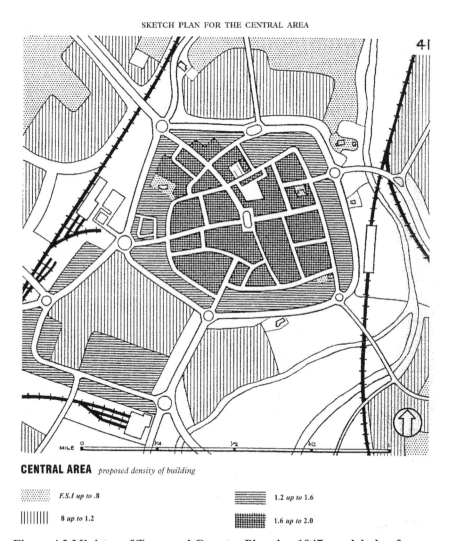

CENTRAL AREA *proposed density of building*

```
:::::::  F.S.1 up to .8              ≡≡≡≡  1.2 up to 1.6
|||||||  8 up to 1.2                 ▓▓▓▓  1.6 up to 2.0
```

**Figure 4.3 Ministry of Town and Country Planning 1947: model plan for
town centre redevelopment**

Source: Ministry of Town and Country Planning, 1947. Crown copyright.

Thus the planning approach to urban restructuring came to be founded on the concentricity of the road network. As indicated in Chapter 2, an ideological approach focused around the railway network would be quite different and be focused on railway corridors and the nodes i.e. stations and freight facilities, along them. The segregation of land-uses, particularly residential from workplaces, increased the need to travel, but the road-oriented ideology meant the process was likely to produce reliance on the private car and to reduce the convenience of rail transport. The only significant counter trend resulted from the activities of Railway Sites: the potential for securing development around main line stations, especially in London, was recognised and pursued vigorously, although the main aim was to secure cash income to offset the losses in the core business.

The social railway

Despite its stated opposition to the Beeching closures, the trunk network was not secure from closures under Wilson's Labour government. In 1967 Castle produced the 'Network for Development' plan (MoT BRB 1967) which stated that the railway network, standing at 13,200 miles (21,243 kms) would be 'stabilised' at 11,000 miles (17,702 kms), of which just 8,000 miles (12,875 kms) would be open to passenger traffic. This network comprised the profit making trunk routes and the socially necessary commuter lines, along with a handful of rural routes. But:

> The real shock came with the list of lines that fitted neither of the above categories
> … It appeared that many supposedly "safe" secondary lines were to be swept
> away, as were the majority of the marginal branch lines (Henshaw 1991, 189).

Political opposition to closures reinforced the use of rail's social benefits to justify public investment in infrastructure and the underpinning of operating costs. By the mid-1960s concern for 'the environment' was an emergent issue too (Galbraith 1958; Carson 1962), with the development of a polemical critique of the political focus on maximising economic growth and its associated, increasingly dispersed pattern of suburbanisation with its car dependency and road traffic growth:

> Chiefly, under the impetus of the automobile, the suburbs are pushing their way
> farther out into the countryside in a vain endeavour by commuters 'to get away
> from it all'. An environment is thus created in which, while it is increasingly
> exhausting to travel, it becomes increasingly indispensable for many to have a
> private car (Mishan 1967, 127).

Mishan called for a radical alternative to the Buchanan plan which, rather than accommodating increasing numbers of cars, called for a strategy based on their gradual abolition and replacement by public transport. Whilst not so radical, white papers confirmed government recognition of the continuing importance of the railway network and the need to put it on a sound financial footing. It was seen as essential to identify and secure financing of those lines which could not operate profitably, but which should be retained in the public interest. In 1967 a special Economic Unit was set up in the MoT to do this: cost benefit analysis was now employed as a core policy making tool. Castle's new broom led to casualties in the BR hierarchy and Stanley Raymond was forced out in late 1967. She wanted new blood to take the industry forward and her preferred Chairman was Peter Parker. However salary terms could not be agreed and, ironically, Castle ended up with a 62 year old career railwayman, Henry Johnson: Castle herself moved on in April 1968.

The emergence of structure plans

In parallel with the paradigm shift in public transport policy in the mid-1960s, tremors were passing through the planning system and there was increasing debate about its successes and failures. It was clear that, under the Conservatives, the system had not been used as its architects intended. One of the key points at issue was the relationship between forward planning and development control. There had been rapid economic growth from the mid-1950s with the ensuing property boom exerting tremendous pressure on the development control system. Development plans were supposed to set the context for this but often, owing to political and bureaucratic delays, they were not available as formally adopted plans. The finished product was often unsatisfactory too because their central feature was a zoning plan superimposed over an Ordnance Survey map. This detail, coupled with the impacts of planning decisions on property values,[26] meant that the focus of debate was at site level. The broad strategic issues were largely obscured.

A Planning Advisory Group (PAG) was set up in 1964 to review the situation. Membership was drawn largely from local government and was dominated by chief clerks and planners: although it included the Director of Highways and Transportation of the GLC there was no one from British Rail or the bus industry. The report (PAG 1965) recommended that two types of plans should be produced, structure plans and local plans. Structure plans for quite large areas concentrating on strategic matters, such as economic development, transportation, social welfare and demand for land. Location policy would not be site specific. These strategic plans would be supplemented by local plans which would be site specific, but could only propose patterns of development which were compatible with the structure plan. Significantly this report made no mention of railways. As a step towards implementation of the PAG report, the government produced a white paper (MHLG 1967): this drew attention to how the context for planning had changed since 1947 when expectations about population and road traffic growth

---

26 Which had risen markedly during the period giving rise to a generation of property tycoons (Marriott 1967).

had been modest. These changes to the planning system were introduced by the 1968 Town and Country Planning Act and will be reviewed in Chapter 7.

Conclusions

Although integrated transport was an important goal of Attlee's government, it was poorly conceptualised and limited to matters internal to transport. Public ownership of an integrated transport system was not part of the post-war consensus and the Conservatives acted quickly to denationalise the road haulage industry. Once car ownership began to increase they were quick to see the implications and to make political capital out of road building plans. Policy towards the railway network initially marked time, owing to austerity and the need for the organisational implications of nationalisation to be worked through. When investment plans came in the mid-1950s they were poorly conceived and backward looking, with no deep understanding of how the competitive position of the railways was changing, or how the network needed to be developed to accommodate socio-economic and spatial change. The rise of the road lobby and the escalating costs of railway modernisation combined to trigger Conservative plans for the undevelopment of the network. This was accompanied by development of a vision, albeit a limited one, for the remaining core network: there was no aspiration for a Japanese-style high speed network, and no firm plans to improve the penetration of city centres by tunnelling or building urban metro systems. Although whilst in opposition Labour had opposed the Beeching cuts, once in power they found it hard to stop the momentum of the closure process and, in any case, were equally supportive of the roads programme. The critique of Beeching developed by his opponents tended to focus on matters internal to the industry, rather than any potential to reinvigorate lines mooted for closure through manipulating patterns of land-use change.

Chapter 2 demonstrated that, historically, there was an absence of railway oriented thinking in British planning. This did not change in the 1947–68 period, although planning ideology did change dramatically. The public sector oriented ideology of planned decentralisation and self-containment of the early period, was overridden by a focus around the management of private sector suburban growth and town centre redevelopment, facilitated by road building. However, planning ideology was not completely devoid of concern for the railway network: in London and the South East, and to a much lesser extent on Clydeside; the geography of the network did influence strategic planning, particularly the location of new towns and growth poles.

The development of strategic planning in the 1960s, strengthened the case to invest in the core network of radial routes serving London. But these interrelationships between the planning and railway sectors were fairly minimal and were not tied to any proposals for major extensions to the core network and did not prevent the development of proposals to close strategic routes as well as rural branch lines. Outside the South East there was more limited strategic planning activity. With weaker historical associations between urban development and railway networks, and with so many closures taking place, the scope for developing interrelationships between the two sectors was limited.

The findings with regard to the thematic analysis are summarised in Table 4.4 and the following summarises the outcomes with regard to the points on the policy agenda developed at the end of Chapter 2. With regard to railway policy:

1. *rationalisation of the network*: plans were drawn up to rationalise the network and went beyond removing the excesses arising from duplication and loss of business and were based on the goal of minimising the cost to government of running the railway, and on the basis of a vision of the railway playing a fairly minimal role within the future transport network;

2. *development of railway services*: plans were drawn up to modernise the core, main line network radiating from London and linking it with other major cities, although only one trunk route was prioritised for electrification; no qualitative leaps were planned such as the introduction of high speed trains or the raising of the vertical loading gauge to facilitate the movement of significantly larger rolling stock; plans were made to upgrade those commuter services in London and other conurbations which were not scheduled for closure;

3. *closing strategic gaps in the network*: no plans were made with regard to new railways to close strategic gaps in the network, and only one new Underground railway line was planned for London;

4. *development of a programme of station enhancement*: there was a programme of station enhancement, but many stations were scheduled for closure and there were very few plans for new stations;

With regard to the town planning agenda:

5. *patterns of urban development*: planning policy generally was not articulated in ways which identified the implications for the railway network, with the exception of some strategic plans in the South East and even these concentrated only on radial routes to London;

6. *management of the redevelopment process in existing urban areas*: planning policy and ideology with regard to the redevelopment process in existing urban areas was dominated by the needs of motor vehicles, with generally negative implications for access to railway stations and rail freight facilities, and the guiding principles for redevelopment were built around the needs of road traffic movement;

7. *management of the location and character of greenfield site development*: the policy with regard to greenfield areas was to prevent their development as far as possible, but where development was planned the prime transport consideration was to provide for access by road vehicles: with the

exception of most of the new towns, there was no general attempt to ensure accessibility to the railway network.

Despite, or perhaps because of, the dominance of road building in transport policy, there was an identifiable shift by 1968 with development of the social case for the railway and recognition that all the expected growth in road traffic could not be accommodated. Creation of the PAG group showed recognition of the need to reinvigorate strategic planning, which was potentially beneficial with regard to managing the development process in ways to facilitate rail travel. But it was still clear that British planning ideology had little understanding of how to do that.

Table 4.4 Summary of thematic analysis of sector policy 1948–68

Explanatory themes	Railway sector	Interrelationships between the two sectors	Planning sector
Politics and political ideology	Public service role of the 1940s replaced in the 1960s by a commercial remit and dominance of the reductionist Treasury view. Development of the political case for the social railway by 1968.	Labour's vision of integrated transport did not embrace land use, and Tories were against integration per se. There was, however, political consensus around planning for the road network. By the late 1960s, support for strategic planning and recognition of the case for the social railway offered better prospects for the future.	Priorities linked to housing, town centre redevelopment and countryside protection. Transport elements dominated by road lobby. Public sector hegemony replaced by private sector.
Professions and professional ideology	Introverted culture focused on technical disciplines – engineering and operating. New blood came from private sector whose business culture was hostile to the public service mentality and emphasised importance of core businesses.	Very limited interface between the professions: their ideological gaze was away from each other. Main contact restricted to location of new towns and some other major developments. More contact in London and the South East than elsewhere.	Continued dominance of design oriented ideology: convergence with other professions around road planning/urban redevelopment. Minimal planning for access by public transport – Runcorn exceptional.

Explanatory themes	Railway sector	Interrelationships between the two sectors	Planning sector
Governance and management	Railways seen as a nationalised industry to be managed first as a public service but, post-Beeching, as a public corporation. Spatially, policy focused around a core, modernised main line network. Awareness by 1968 that a need for change for local services in the conurbations.	Little awareness, or concern, for most of the period that institutional structures and their internal cultures were inimical to linking the two sectors. There was an intention to change this by 1968, particularly in the major conurbations.	Major focus of activity related to other areas of local government: integration with road planning the dominant transport theme. Re-emergence of regional planning in the 1960s largely focused around land-supply and economic issues, but limited attempt to plan in co-operation with BR in the South East.

Chapter 5
Outcomes: 1948–68

Introduction

The aim of this chapter is to review the outcomes of the interplay between the institutional structures and policies of the railway and land-use planning sectors, to draw conclusions as to whether these were largely positive or negative with regard to the role and utilisation of the railway network, and to offer some explanations for these outcomes.

The overriding outcome was the huge increase in society's transport activity, passenger and freight, and the overshadowing of all public transport modes and rail freight by the huge growth in car and lorry traffic. Total passenger movement increased from 219 to 389 billion kilometres between 1952[1]–68, with that by car and light van increasing from 58 to 279 billion kilometres. The proportion of households without a car declined from 86 per cent in 1951, to 51 per cent in 1968. Total passenger movement by rail (BR plus all other networks) declined by 16 per cent from 40.4 to 34 billion kilometres between 1948–68, having reached a peak of 41 billion kilometres in 1958–59. Bus and coach travel declined 30 per cent, from 92 to 64 billion kilometres showing that, by comparison, rail was reasonably successful. With regard to freight, the total of goods lifted by all modes increased by 67 per cent from 1202 million tonnes to 2009 million tonnes between 1952–1968, but the total lifted by rail declined by 27 per cent from 289 to 211 million tonnes. Reflecting the changes in the geography of manufacturing and distribution which became more transport dependent, there was an increase in goods carried by all modes from 88 to 129 billion tonne kilometres, a 47 per cent increase. But goods moved by rail fell from 37 to 23 billion tonne kilometres, a 38 per cent decline, so by both measures, there was a substantial absolute decline in rail freight.

The railway network was cut-back by approximately one third and the closures included sections of main line as well as many branch lines as shown in Table 5.1. The number of freight depots, marshalling yards and private rail sidings was massively reduced, and the number of passenger stations was more than halved (Appendix 5). Extensive parts of rural Britain in Cornwall, Devon, Central Wales, East Anglia, Lincolnshire, the Pennines, the Southern Uplands and Highlands of Scotland were removed from the railway map, along with many urban branch lines.

---

1   DoT statistics for total passenger travel only run from 1952.

Table 5.1 Closures of main routes 1948–68

Date of closure	Route closed
1958	Midland and Great Northern Joint Line between Spalding-Great Yarmouth
1966	Somerset and Dorset Railway between Bournemouth- Bath/Bristol
1966–69	Great Central main line between Aylesbury-Sheffield via Rugby, Leicester and Nottingham. Aylesbury-London Marylebone stub retained for commuter services
1968	Cambridge-Bedford and Oxford-Bletchley sections of Oxford-Cambridge east-west route: Bedford-Bletchley and Oxford-Bicester stubs retained
1968	Matlock-Chinley section of former Midland Railway Manchester-Derby main line, leaving no direct link between the East Midlands and the North West
1968	London and South Western main line between Exeter -Plymouth closed between Okehampton-Bere Alson (near Plymouth) leaving only the former GWR coastal route between Exeter-Plymouth which is prone to sea damage

Superficially therefore, it would seem that there was limited scope for planning to link developing land-use patterns with the contracting railway network. However there was another side to the outcome, as indicated by the fact that the decline in bus and coach ridership was much steeper than for rail. The main line network received considerable investment: for example the Kent Coast electrification out to Margate and Dover was completed by 1962, WCML electrification between London and Birmingham, Manchester and Liverpool was complete by 1966, and high speed diesel-electric locomotives were introduced on to the ECML. Journey times were cut by up to a third and the WCML electrification produced spectacular returns:

> An upsurge of 50 per cent in passenger receipts and 65 per cent in passenger journeys, some of which were recaptured from air (BRB 1966, 3).

Retained local railway networks were improved with diesel multiple units (DMUs) and electric multiple units (EMUs) replacing steam services. All this meant that there were plenty of opportunities for planning policy to, selectively, concentrate activity around modernised railway corridors and nodes.

There were two major dimensions to planning practice in the period. In one the planning system was used proactively to manage major schemes such as new towns, expanded towns and overspill estates: the geography of the railway network was a significant strategic consideration in some of this. In the other dimension, which became dominant, the planning system was largely reactive, responding to pressure from the private sector for the development of green field sites for private housing and major town centre schemes for commercial redevelopment. Planning in this case was typified by the development of green belt policy, a fairly blunt instrument with which to manage decentralisation and, in town centres, the use of planning powers to assemble publicly owned sites and develop CDA plans, in partnership with private developers. Access to the road network was the overriding transport consideration in this, but there were examples of favourable outcomes for rail.

Planned decentralisation

London's historic paradigm status as a planning problem was inherited by the whole of the South East region. Between 1951–61, redevelopment of inner areas at lower densities led to population decline in Greater London (the built-up area within about 15 miles (24 kms) of Charing Cross). On the other hand the outer ring, between 15 and 45 miles (24-72 kms), increased its population by 964,000 (Hall 1971, 19-20). This growth was strongly, but by no means exclusively, associated with the planned dispersal of population and employment from inner London.

Of the areas designated for London's new towns all, except Basildon,[2] had a station at designation and even Basildon was on a radial route to London (see Appendix 7). In Harlow a new 'town centre' station[3] was opened in 1960 and its poor relationship with the town centre has already been noted. The low priority given to rail in new town planning, by both the MHLG and BR, was revealed in a contemporary publication:

> Train services are not a great problem because, apart from a few commuters, nobody needs them to get to work ... Most towns ... have reserved land for a new station; but getting the new stations built is a long job (Schaffer[4] 1970, 141).

Clearly, despite rising car ownership and personal mobility, even in 1970 Schaffer's views about the needs of new towns residents for transport were still quite contrary to those of the authors of the 1946 Inglis Report. Outside the South East the association between the railway network and new towns was more patchy: Washington station was closed in 1963 at the same time as its designation, and Corby closed in 1966 (Daniels and Dench 1980); there was no station on designation at Newton Aycliffe; and Peterlee, Skelmersdale and Glenrothes were not on the railway network at all.

---

2 Referred to at the time as one of the 'notorious examples' of the BRB vetoing new station projects (Allen, 1966, 210).

3 Now a listed building.

4 Schaffer was a senior civil servant and for seven years was in charge of the New Towns Division of the MHLG.

Town expansion under the 1952 Act was a more random process than new town designation as it depended upon reception areas volunteering to enter into agreement with the exporting authority. Appendix 8 shows that, although the towns which entered into agreements with London were all on the network and had a station at the time of making their agreement, three towns in East Anglia, (Braintree and Brocking, Haverhill, and Mildenhall), lost their stations in the 1960s. Bodmin, an unlikely overspill for London perhaps, retained only Bodmin Road. In the provinces two of Wolverhampton's partners and eight of Glasgow's did not have a station at the time of making their agreement. As a result of pre and post-Beeching closures, stations were closed at three of Birmingham's partners, both of Walsall's, three of Wolverhampton's, Burnley lost two local stations but kept its main one, three of Bristol's partners lost their stations, one of Newcastle's and eleven of Glasgow's. Despite the exhortations of the New Towns Committee, there were no extensions of railways to serve new settlements.

It is important to recall that the aim of planned decentralisation was to reduce demand for travel into London through self-containment. Although the Inglis Committee had cast doubts on the likelihood of this outcome, research (Hall 1971, 338-346) showed that the new towns stood out in terms of their relatively low levels of out-commuting. The problem with this apparent success was its relative insignificance: 'Overall, just under 4 per cent of the total housing effort had gone into the planned communities' (Hall 1971, 358-359). Notwithstanding the decentralisation of employers from London, employment there increased by about 150,000 (Hall 1971, 23) as a result of service sector growth. Public transport, particularly rail, was important in providing access to the jobs:

> … of 1,238,000 people entering central London on an average day in 1962, less than 10 per cent (123,000) used private transport (Hall 1971, 131).

This increase was accommodated by improvement to commuter services into London which included electrification of routes into Essex. This was initially to Shenfield,[5] then Chingford, Enfield, Hertford and Bishop's Stortford by 1960, and all the way to Southend and Clacton by 1963[6] (see Appendix 3 for details of electrification schemes). The investment in the Bishop's Stortford line included the opening of new stations at Southbury, Turkey Street and Theobalds Grove, a rare event during this period.[7] In 1947 another belated completion of a pre-war project was the extensions of London Underground's Central Line: eastwards from

---

5   A scheme begun by the LNER, but delayed by the outbreak of war in 1939 and completed in 1949.

6   This electrification of Eastern Region routes out of Liverpool Street was a product of the Modernisation Plan.

7   These were in fact re-openings of stations closed in 1919 when services were withdrawn on the Churchbury Loop between Lower Edmonton and Cheshunt owing to competition from street trams.

Liverpool Street, surfacing at Newbury Park to connect up with the former Great Eastern country branch lines to the growing suburbs of Woodford, Loughton and Hainault;[8] and westwards to West Ruislip (Bruce and Croome 1996). The route from King's Cross to the new and expanded towns of Letchworth, Welwyn, Stevenage and Hitchin was widened to allow a more frequent service but, although earmarked for electrification in the Modernisation Plan, this did not take place until the 1970s. The commuter routes to Kent were improved by extensive work at Charing Cross in 1954 to accommodate 10 car commuter trains[9] (Morgan 1994) and then, between1959–61, pre-war electrification was extended by the Kent Coast scheme to Canterbury, Ashford, Ramsgate, Dover and Folkestone (Appendix 2). These schemes brought dramatic improvements in services with reductions in journey times (28 minutes off the Liverpool Street-Clacton schedule), and more frequent services (those to the Kent Coast were almost doubled).

Despite the strength of the central London office market, decentralisation of offices accelerated and in the four years to the end of 1961, planning permission was given for a greater volume of office development outside central London i.e., the City and West End, than within it (Marriott 1967, 181). The single most notable feature of this was the development of Croydon which was 'the only centre worthy of the name' (Marriott 1967, 185). Central Croydon grew from more or less zero floorspace to nearly 300 000 square metres (three million square feet) built by 1964. There was a rational pattern behind the spread of decentralised offices and the locational relationship with transport networks was crucial:

> Access to transport and to pockets of white collar workers were the two decisive factors … Ideally, there had to be inter-suburban links to ferry office workers to and fro by public transport, and links of road and underground train with the West End or the City, or both (Marriott 1967, 180-181).

Whereas Croydon was not on the Underground, its growth as a surburb had long been associated with the excellence of its rail connections to central London. It was therefore an ideal location to draw in rail commuters from its own hinterland and to provide the rapid access to central London necessary for business purposes. However, despite its prime location on the south London network, the detail

---

8   As evidence of London Transport's continuing ability to deliver integrated transport, the route surfaced at Stratford to provide cross-platform interchange with BR Essex commuter trains, and three of the new stations – Wanstead, Redbridge and Gants Hill – were on the Eastern Avenue with good bus connections.

9   Because of the low vertical loading gauge, extra capacity on the British network could only be achieved by running longer trains which necessitated platform extensions at stations: two experimental, and rather compact, double-deck trains were built by the Southern Region in the 1950s, but were deemed to be unsuccessful. Double deckers were considered again in the 1960s, but the idea did not get off the drawing board (Allen 1966, 219-21).

development of Croydon was highway oriented. This comprised the archetypal Modernist townscape of high rise office blocks built alongside a new dual carriageway, Wellesley Road, which had elevated and underground sections, along with multi-storey car parks and a purpose-built shopping mall, the Whitgift Centre. Although the Council played a leading role in promoting this investment, implemented through the development plan, no special measures were taken to promote access to and from the railway station, which received no investment either, and the road schemes rendered pedestrian access from the station more difficult.

Another impact of the decentralisation process was that it tended to lead to the replacement of inner suburban journeys by long distance commuting, thereby exacerbating network capacity problems:

> ... in the present minimally planned environment, commercial migration from London tends to boomerang on BR ... Between 1962 and 1964, for example, season-ticket travellers from Basingstoke[10] to London, 48 miles out, rose by 83 per cent in number, whereas those from the commercially developing suburb of Kingston-on-Thames, 12 miles out, dropped by 13 per cent (Allen[11] 1966, 227).

So, although in a general sense decentralisation in the South East was good for BR's business, it tended to increase the problem of 'the peak' and made it difficult to reduce overcrowding, despite increases in network capacity. The opportunities to secure mutually beneficial development through the disposal of surplus land were missed too. In 1964 the MHLG requested that the BRB co-operate with the LCC, and subsequently the GLC, in making surplus land[12] available for housing and giving the local authorities first refusal: this became a general requirement following the issue of a government circular (MHLG 1966). The tensions between BRB and the planning system over the slow progress in securing financial yields from this were made clear when an annual report referred to these arrangements as 'a distinct drawback to the Board' (BRB 1968, 56).

The limitations of strategic planning

The limited commitment in the South East to integration between strategic development and the railway network meant that there were no plans for cross-London rail routes of the sort discussed during the War, and orbital routes were

---

10   Basingstoke experienced rapid growth in the 1960s and 1970s under the Town Development Act.

11   Geoffrey Freeman Allen was editor of Modern Railways and this book was widely regarded within the industry as a seminal publication.

12   The 1964 BRB annual report referred to 800 acres of land in Greater London being the subject of discussions (BRB 1964, 67).

closed. Whilst major growth was promoted in locations like Milton Keynes, Northampton and Peterborough, as well as the already well established centres of Oxford, Cambridge and Swindon, railways between them were closed. A service existed between Oxford and Cambridge, and steam had been replaced by DMUs. En route between the two towns this service offered connections with four major trunk routes: the Great Western at Oxford, the WCML at Bletchley (with easy access to Milton Keynes and Northampton), the Midland main line at Bedford, and the ECML at Sandy (for access to Peterborough). With these strategic links and the expected growth at key nodes along the route, there was obvious potential in this line, but Barbara Castle agreed to closure in 1965 and services were withdrawn as of January 1, 1968 (Allen 1966, 39). The absence of investment in new railways, even in London, meant that Heathrow was not linked to the network, although this had been suggested by Abercrombie in 1944. Two early BTC initiatives, which really were completions of former Southern Railway projects, exemplified the backward looking culture. In 1948 a new terminal for BOAC flying boat services was opened at Southampton followed in 1950 by a new Ocean Terminal for trans-Atlantic liners, and both of these were linked to London by rail services. The flying boat terminal was redundant by 1950 and the Ocean Terminal by 1960, both eclipsed, of course, by the development of Heathrow. However, as evidence that there was not total failure to integrate rail with air transport, in 1958 a new station on the London-Brighton main line was provided at Gatwick which was developed as London's second airport: there had been a long established station at Gatwick for the racecourse, so this was really a well chosen rebuilding exercise by the BTC.

The Ashford-Hastings line is another example of an orbital route which connected two growth areas and, even at this time, Ashford was envisaged as important with regard to Channel Tunnel plans. This route was slated for closure by Beeching, but survived as a result of local opposition (Moody 1979, 207), although it was one of the few Southern Region routes not electrified and was served by diesel electric multiple units (DEMUs). The fact that such gaps were left in the electrified network was indicative of the tight Treasury constraints on investment. Another area earmarked for growth which suffered large scale closures was Bournemouth-Poole: these included the former Somerset and Dorset Joint line which linked them with another area of rapid growth, Bath-Bristol. This route was closed in 1966 with a rail journey between the two conurbations subsequently necessitating a circuitous journey via either Dorchester or Southampton with a change of trains en route, always a disincentive to users. The route between Brockenhurst and Poole via Ringwood, and the direct line from Poole to Salisbury had already been closed in 1964, so the opportunity was lost to guide the growth of Bournemouth-Poole along rail axes, as well as to facilitate direct rail access to Bath-Bristol and the intervening Mendips area of outstanding natural beauty (Adley 1988, 79-103).

One notable exception to the general case of the run down of suburban services in the provinces was the Welsh Valleys lines. In the pre-grouping era five companies had run services to Cardiff and these all passed to the GWR in 1923, and were then handed on with minor changes to British Railways in 1947, so rationalisation was long overdue. The service was recast in 1953 to give regular interval services, and then steam was replaced by DMUs: these improvements seemed to reflect the self-contained nature of the Valleys where the absence of long distance main lines allowed management to be focused on local services. Despite colliery closures and rationalisation post-Beeching (Davies and Clark 1996, 6), the services survived remarkably well, given the fact that they served a sparsely populated hinterland and linked it with a city of only medium size. In subsequent years, with further rundown of the coalfield, these links with service sector employment in Cardiff were to become more important as will be shown in Chapters 7 and 8.

Transport impacts of housing location and layout design

With regard to the impacts of planning ideology on the design of residential areas, the outcomes were complex and were the product of three ideological models. The first was in the new towns and town expansion schemes where the garden city tradition lived on, but varying degrees of pedestrian-vehicular segregation were employed to bring the traditional neighbourhood concept into the era of mass car ownership. Although most new towns were located on railway lines and either had a station at designation or were provided with one, or in some cases an additional one, this was about as far as planning around the railway network went. Despite the prior practice of Unwin and official advice, stations were not always accessible, as exemplified by Harlow. Although Runcorn's new town centre was well located with regard to the busway, it was inaccessible from the railway station. A better solution was provided at Redditch, which was also notable for bus-oriented planning, as the new town centre was to be an expansion of the original which had an existing railway station. Redditch was designed by consultants Wilson and Womersley who were well aware of the growing importance of public transport to government policy in the mid-1960s, noting that BR's proposed closure of rail services to Redditch had been refused (Wilson and Womersley 1966, 59). They also produced a bus-oriented linear design for Irvine where, again, the new town centre was located at the historic town centre which had a station (Irvine Development Corporation 1971).

In the second model the large urban local authorities, encouraged by central government (both Labour and Conservative), had their massive redevelopment programmes which were typically inspired by Modernism. However, post-Beeching, local rail services were often withdrawn. As the street tramways were scrapped too, the residents became dependent on bus services. Where new developments were located on the urban fringes, this lack of rapid rail connections with the mother city placed the residents at a disadvantage with regard to their access to jobs, services, families and friends.[13]

Increasingly it was the third model which became dominant wherein private, speculative builders developed large estates of detached and semi-detached houses and bungalows, with little direct input from the design professions and with minimal planning control. Here the vision was a scaled down version of contemporary American, consumerist suburbia built around car ownership, domestic appliances and relaxation in private gardens. The role of the planning system was largely confined to fixing the location: typically this was either on the edge of large towns or cities, or of small towns and villages in the rural hinterland of major cities, out beyond the green belt. In a contemporary study of the Hertfordshire green belt, Pahl (1970) showed that the new residents of the expanding villages were more affluent and, being car owners, more mobile, than the original working class residents. Their presence tended to lead to reductions in local services and the planners' vision of the future tended to be through the eyes of car users, leading to a development pattern which depended on use of a car to gain access to necessary services:

> Planners and builder-developers may be forgiven for thinking primarily of job opportunities and communications to take the chief earner to work when making decisions in the outer metropolitan region … However, it is the chief earner's wife who actually lives in the outer metropolitan region day in and day out, and most of these women are certainly not mobile (Pahl 1970, 120).[14]

The developers were well aware that the likely purchasers of their houses would be car owners and provision for their needs was an important design consideration: there had to be space to park cars and adequate access to the main road network. For the most part proximity to a railway station was not a factor. Generally, the peripheral location maximised the distance between the new housing estates and the nearest station, which was typically in the town centre. As large numbers of smaller railway stations were closed, this suggests a tendency for an increasing average distance between the location of new housing and the nearest station, although there is no available data for this period.

Whatever ideology influenced the location and layout of housing, the one common factor which came to affect the residents' lives was car ownership. In a

---

13 Research by Wilmott and Young (1957) showed the strength of family and kinship networks in the East End and the relative isolation which could be experienced in overspill developments, particularly by women if they were not working.

14 This was a far cry from the middle class, country lifestyle portrayed in Noel Coward's 'Brief Encounter' produced in 1945, wherein Celia Johnson used the train for her weekly trips to Milford to change her library books at Boots, have coffee at the Kardomah, and illicit encounters with Trevor Howard.

thorough contemporary evaluation of planning policy there was a clear conclusion as to how road building and land-use policy had combined to benefit car users:

> Increasing car ownership's most significant effect has thus been substantially to increase the proportion of the population able to make cross-country journeys between places too small or too distant from each other to support a reasonably convenient public transport system … The type of person who has benefited most from the mobility explosion has been the car owner living in a small town or rural area. And containment policies have operated to place a substantial part of the population growth, during the 1950s and 1960s, in just such areas – thus encouraging the use of the car (Hall et al. 1973a, 418).

The generally poor location of housing developments with regard to the railway system, and the decline in railway services in most city regions, meant that rail was not an option even for the longer radial journeys which historically had been a characteristic feature of the railway's role.

Rail served housing: the exceptions

Amidst this generally poor integration between housing developments and the railway system, there were some positive outcomes. The line from Birmingham to Sutton Coldfield was built in 1862 to serve this growing suburb and was extended northwards to Litchfield in 1884. In 1948 BR inherited a frequent commuter service between Sutton and Birmingham, but this had changed little and was archaic by comparison with the pre-war Southern Electric model. In 1951 the population of Sutton Coldfield stood at 47,000, more than double the 1931 figure, and commuters were a significant part of the population. Local BR managers were aware of the need to improve what was the busiest commuter line into Birmingham and an hourly, regular interval, steam-hauled service was introduced in 1954 carrying about 2,390 passengers per day (Boynton 1993, 77-78). In 1956 the service went over to DMUs and the frequency was increased. Soon after an exceptional event took place. The "Railway Magazine" reported in November (1957):

> A temporary station, Butlers Lane, which has been experimentally installed by the LMR to meet the needs of a housing estate under development, was opened on September 30th …

The opening of a new station was an unusual event in the 1950s. There were new stations built in that decade, but most appeared on declining rural lines as last ditch attempts to attract extra traffic. They have all now vanished. Butlers Lane is the second oldest station built since the formation of British Railways in 1948 which remains today (Boynton 1993, 83). However, despite this early success and the continued growth of population in Birmingham's outer suburbs facilitated by the development plan process, even this railway service went into decline. This was because of increasingly tight investment constraints which led to lowered maintenance standards, reductions in service and no electrification. In the meantime the commuters bought cars.

The Sutton Coldfield branch line was unusual: outside Greater London any improvements to local railway services usually only came about as a result of main line investment which allowed simultaneous improvement of local services on the same route. The best examples were those associated with the WCML modernisation which facilitated electrification of local services between Rugby-Coventry-Birmingham-Wolverhampton-Stafford, Birmingham-Walsall, Manchester-Crewe/Stoke, and Crewe-Liverpool Lime Street (Nock, 1966). A notable exception was Clydeside, resulting from the Abercrombie and Inglis reports, and the lobbying by Glasgow city council. The Helensburgh-Queen Street Low Level-Aidrie cross city service was electrified in 1960: new stations were opened at Garscadden and Hyndland. This was followed by electrification from Glasgow Central to Cathcart, Neilston, Kirkhill and Hamilton in 1962, and to Paisley, Greenock and Gourock/Wemyss Bay in 1967.[15] Tables 5.2 and 5.3 show that the introduction of DEMUs and EMUs stimulated ridership, but that the superior service given by electric trains resulted in the biggest increases, the 'sparks effect' which the Southern had discovered forty years previously. To illustrate the limited horizons of rail investment even in Glasgow, the Rutherglen-Dumbarton cross-city line utilising the tunnel under the CBD via Central Low Level, was closed in 1964[16] and, despite Abercrombie and Inglis, neither the route to East Kilbride nor Cumbernauld was electrified, but at least they avoided closure.

It is disappointing to note that, despite the Corporation's support for electrification, the location of peripheral housing estates took little note of the geography of the network (Smith and Wannop 1985, 155). Despite electrification, there was no extension of the network to better serve the estates either, this was impossible given the government's stance and the overall mindset of the BTC/BRB. As in Birmingham, the city development plan was restricted to zoning existing railway land as 'operational railway land'. On the other hand, the 29 CDAs promoted for housing renewal, were also utilised to assemble land for motorway construction and extensive land allocations were included in the development plan for this (Corporation of the City of Glasgow 1960).

---

15   This latter route was the most heavily populated of all and arguably should have been electrified soonest: Allen (1966, 144) considered that the reason for the delay was a deal struck between BR and Glasgow Corporation to protect Corporation bus services from competition, a nice example of how public ownership was no guarantee of providing the best service for the public. This was a difficult time for the Corporation Transport Department as the street tramway network was closed between 1959–62 and replaced by bus services, which were themselves experiencing competition from rising car ownership.

16   This was still steam hauled at the time of closure and the atmosphere at platform level was an unpleasant throwback to the Victorian era.

Table 5.2 Impact of service improvements on ridership on Birmingham suburban services 1966–69

Route	Time period	Increase in ridership
Birmingham-Walsall*	1966–69	+51%
Stafford-Wolverhampton-Birmingham-Coventry-Rugby	1966–69	+112%
Birmingham-Lichfield (DMU)	1966–69	+22%
Birmingham-Kidderminster (DMU)	1966–69	+18%

Note:* electrified services unless indicated otherwise eg. (DMU).
Source: Greater Glasgow Transportation Study, 1974.

Table 5.3 Impact of service improvements on ridership on Glasgow suburban services 1960–73 (1960 base line=100)

	Glasgow North (Airdrie-Helensburgh)	Neilston Branch	Gourock/ Wemyss Bay	Lanarkshire Circle (DMU)
1960	100	100	100	100
1961	electrified	electrified		
1966			electrified	
1973	358	285	217	220

Source: Greater Glasgow Transportation Study, 1974.

City centre redevelopment

The product of road-oriented redevelopment for town centres was disastrous for the environment and for access to the railway network. Birmingham was typical, with its multi-level Bull Ring development opened in 1963, followed by the inner ring road around the whole city centre (Cherry 1994) which served to create a barrier and had a blighting effect. In Newcastle and Bristol, new dual carriageway roads were associated with large scale office developments with barren, first floor pedestrian decks (Aldous 1975). It has been demonstrated in Chapter 2 that planning for rail was not a significant component in the development of British planning ideology. The lack of appreciation of Victorian station design was reflected in the fact that the grand plans produced in the 1940s often included proposals for station demolition and redevelopment: even one of the quality of York, with its great train shed built over the sweeping curve of the tracks, was earmarked for this. Whether or not such plans came to fruition depended upon BR's investment plans and local property markets, but local planning authorities were usually enthusiastic when the opportunity arose. The most notorious episode was the rebuilding of Euston as part of the WCML electrification, which triggered demolition of Hardwick's Doric Arch and then the whole station, including the Grand Hall.[17] The Arch dated from the dawn of the railway age and its demolition served as a spark to ignite the popular, conservationist backlash against the developers and the Modernist ideology of the architects and planners, although this took time to mature and become effective in preventing the demolition of many notable station structures.

Euston was also a case where the BRB proposed an office development in the 'airspace' over the tracks as part of the rebuilding, but:

> Almost incredibly, the London County Council refused British Rail permission to develop office accommodation over the rebuilt Euston Station as it would increase street congestion ... while granting permission for office blocks along Euston Road remote from any station (White and Senior 1983, 114).

Space was left between the new station and Euston Road to take advantage of any change in planning policy but, despite the Labour government's pro-public transport stance, strategic policy worked against this as it was stymied by the restrictions on office development introduced in 1963 on an informal basis, and then formally under the Control of Office Employment Act of 1965. These difficulties with the planning system were referred to in the BRB annual reports with a growing sense of frustration:

> Although belatedly it became generally accepted that the most suitable places for major office developments in London are over the main-line stations, efforts to progress worthwhile schemes of this kind are frustrated by government restrictions (BRB 1968, 56).[18]

With regard to the location and general ambience of stations, the changes in city centres tended to not only promote the use of cars, but also to actively work against the use of the railway network. It will be recalled from Chapter 2 that one of the historical weaknesses of the railway system was the peripheral location of stations with regard to city centres. There was no strategy to invest in realignments, by tunnelling for example, and some existing tunnels were closed, as in Glasgow. What happened instead was that 'concentricity' led to construction

17 Euston grew in a rather haphazard fashion and, other than Hardwick's external Doric Arch, its most notable feature was the Great Hall opened in 1849. Designed by Hardwick's son, this was a classically inspired, spectacular structure built on a grand scale with a high, broad, ornamental ceiling and a sweeping staircase at its northern end.

18 This went on to refer explicitly to the illogicality of granting permission for the Euston Centre referred to above whilst refusing air space development over the redeveloped Euston station.

of inner ring roads which, because of the peripheral location of stations, often lay between them and the commercial core. This reduced the accessibility of stations by introducing another barrier and, typically, crossing the road necessitated use of pedestrian subways or over-bridges which came to be regarded as amongst the most unattractive features of city centres. This re-arranging of the road network and its relationship with stations was facilitated by statutory town maps and CDA plans. Examples were widespread and included Bristol, Hull, Gloucester, Sheffield and Plymouth.

In some cases, far from increasing the rail penetration of town centres, lines were cut back with new stations being built in more peripheral locations. Sometimes the driving force behind such rationalisation was the BRB, in pursuit of cost reduction. In other cases it was the local council, acting through its planning and/or highways committee, as the land was required for redevelopment, sometimes for road building, with the changes being incorporated into statutory plans. Closures of well located stations included Blackpool Central and Nottingham Victoria: the latter, with its great train shed, was built in a huge cutting and more conveniently located than the retained Midland Station, was completely demolished and a shopping mall, the Victoria Centre, was developed on the site. Despite the good location and access via tunnels under the city centre, the new development was granted planning permission in 1965 with a design that precluded the later restoration of a rail, or light rail, service. The acquiescence of the BRB and the planning authority in this failure to retain an option for rail reinstatement was typical of the era.

An important by-product of the changing position of the railways in the transport market was the closure of freight facilities on the periphery of city centres. In Chapter 2 it was noted that these had been provided on a massive scale, typically with duplication. During the 1960s the wagonload and general merchandise traffic collapsed and there were widespread closures: 'The result was a sudden and massive increase in redundant land' (Biddle 1990, 203). Although close to city centres, often this was not close enough to make it attractive for commercial development. This meant that the most financially rewarding use could be to lay the areas out as 'temporary' car parks for the growing numbers of commuters who either could not, or would not, use the railway. Thus redundant railway infrastructure was used to facilitate competition from the car. More generally the BRB recognised that disposal of redundant land could provide a significant income to offset its losses: in 1965, Railway Sites was wound up and the Estate Department given a more specific brief to dispose of land rather than seek its development.

City centre redevelopment: the exceptions

There were situations where integrated planning produced a more positive outcome. In London, for example, the main stem of the Victoria line between Walthamstow and Victoria opened in 1969, giving access to King's Cross/St Pancras and Euston, as well as the prime retail area of Oxford Circus. Arguably the only development where anything like the sort of high quality, multi-level scheme envisaged by Buchanan came to fruition (although not completed until the early 1970s) was the Barbican, which was also readily accessible by Underground on the Corbusian model. But even this had a downside:

London Wall – a motorway dividing the city. A completely anti-pedestrian environment despite the upper level walkway (Ward 1986, 43).

Despite the planning difficulties referred to previously, by 1968 significant commercial developments were secured at Holborn Viaduct and Waterloo, with a large airspace development at Wembley Central in the suburbs.

Outside London positive outcomes were most likely where complete modernisation of railway infrastructure was taking place, such as on the Coventry-Birmingham-Wolverhampton axis. Lord (1991) reported that in 1963, as a result of post-Beeching streamlining, the Western and London Midland Regions were merged and the new organisation took a more focused approach to securing development opportunities. New Street had always been unusual because of its central location facilitated by tunnelling and this provided a good opportunity to carry out the sort of development which should have been more widespread: the building of large retail, office and residential developments at major stations. Henry Johnson, the Chairman and General Manager of the London Midland Region, said that the intention at New Street was to emulate recent developments at Cologne and Munich to create 'an attractive social centre in addition to a modern environment for railway business' (Hellewell 1964, Modern Railways 1964a).[19] The tragedy for New Street was the architectural form which this took: the tracks were 'decked' over by a 7.5 acre (3.04 ha) slab and the inspiring ambience of the historic glazed train shed, which was completely demolished, was replaced by a gloomy, subterranean world at platform level. Commercial buildings designed in the 'Brutalist'[20] style, were erected above, with little recognition in the design of the external access points or interior layout that the shopping centre was the prime means of gaining access to the station below. Birmingham's statutory development plan had nothing to say about this project other than to allocate the whole site as 'operational railway land'.

19 The development was to be carried out by what today would be called a public private partnership comprising BR, Birmingham Corporation, Norwich Union, Taylor Woodrow and Capital and Counties property development Company. The scheme linked to the adjoining Bull Ring scheme which contained a bus and coach station.

20 Brutalism was a development within the Modernist movement characterised by angular buildings, typically with external facades of exposed concrete, often revealing the texture of the wooden forms used for the in-situ casting.

The 'modernisation' of all stations during the 1960s was dominated by this no frills approach of the Modernists which influenced the BRB Design Panel[21] in the same way that it influenced local planning authorities.[22] Because of the decayed state of many old stations, redevelopment in this style was welcomed at the time:

> Elegant new show pieces of modern architecture with model passenger facilities were put up at Tamworth and on a much grander scale at Coventry. Between Crewe and the Manchester-Liverpool terminals a good many local stations had their old buildings replaced by neat pre-fabricated structures of modern outline, to complete the image of a thoroughly up-to-date service when the electric multiple-units began to run (Allen 1966, 139-40).

In 1965 the Design Panel created the 'double arrow' totem to signpost the location of stations and this piece of functionalism has certainly stood the test of time. Overall however, despite the fact that the Victorians had understood the commercial benefits to be gained from grand stations with welcoming frontages to the cities they served and the urban design principles underpinning station location and design had been developed long ago by Unwin, they were ignored in the early post-war decades. The statutory planning system played its part in this, albeit a limited one because, in many cases, utilising its rights as a statutory undertaker and/or gaining powers by parliamentary Act, BR could rebuild stations without the need to obtain formal planning permission. But even where planning permission was required, owing to the involvement of commercial development with station rebuilding, planning authorities were ill-equipped ideologically to secure a better outcome. The overall result was that passenger access to stations tended to become more difficult and the stations themselves became less attractive as places to wait for trains.

Industrial development

In the early post-war decades, in just the same way that the old Victorian housing areas needed to be redeveloped, so the industrial areas needed attention too. However, this was a lengthy process. Although under the 1945 Distribution of Industry Act central government did get involved in industrial development, steering industries

---

21   In what was an example of the positive impact of the post-Beeching market-oriented approach, this design work involved the creation of a women's panel to advise on the design of passenger rolling stock; however there is no evidence that this extended to consultation about issues such as station design and access (Allen 1966, 55).

22   Upsurge in demand for school and other community buildings led to local authorities developing the CLASP system of prefabricated construction: the 1966 BRB annual report noted that this system of providing very utilitarian structures had provided new stations at Fleet and Sunbury-on-Thames.

to new towns or the depressed regions, by and large the state, at either central or local level, played a more passive role in the redevelopment of industrial areas compared with housing areas or city centres. During the early BTC period when the road haulage industry was being nationalised, the 1951 annual report showed that the BTC was mindful of the need to locate new road haulage depots in locations which would promote road/rail co-ordination, but such initiatives were stillborn. Owing to improvements in heavy goods vehicle technology and the development of the road network, more and more industrialists changed over to road transport: sidings were closed and internal railway networks fell into disuse.

From the 1930s, the sorts of buildings which modern industry required were large, single storey structures with a much larger footprint than the multi-storey structures of old. Post-war planning authorities were aware that more land needed to be allocated for industry but, despite the experience of the 1930s trading estates, there was little pressure from industrialists to include access to the railway network as a locational requirement in development plans. So, as in the housing areas and city centres, authorities focused on the need to improve road access and a rail link was not seen as a standard locational requirement with regard to access for freight or the workforce.

The major land development activity by BR, the construction of the new marshalling yards under the Modernisation Plan, did not require formal planning permission as they were built using development rights granted to statutory undertakers. They had a huge land take requiring sites up to three miles long and half a mile wide: the biggest was Carlisle Kingmoor which covered 2.75 square miles (7.12 sq km) of greenfield land. The overall construction programme lasted over ten years as shown in Table 5.4, and the last, Tinsley, was not opened until 1965. But this programme did not bring planning authorities and the railway industry together in jointly utilising the planning process. Liaison was only consultative and the industry worked to its own agenda. There was no development of the mutual understanding or information sharing which was necessary to develop a pro-rail culture within planning authorities, or an understanding of how land-use could be manipulated to serve the railway within the railway industry. The collapse of the wagon load traffic which inspired construction of the yards was so severe that, by late 1965, closure of Ripple Lane (east London) was in hand, seven years after it opened, and a number of major projects were quietly aborted at the planning stage.

By the mid-1960s, structural economic change was leading to closure of rail connected industrial complexes too: the railway industry itself was not immune as exemplified by closure of private engineering plants such as Beyer Peacock's in Manchester and North British in Glasgow. Electrification of the station at Singers in Glasgow was illustrative of the way in which the whole of the old railway was blindly and expensively electrified, rather than proactive policy with regard to use of the modernised railway for industrial workers: factory and station were closed in 1969.

Table 5.4 The Modernisation Plan marshalling yards

Yard	Year opened	Yard	Year opened
Bescot (Walsall)	1966[a]	Ripple Lane (London)	1958
Crewe	1961[b]	Severn Tunnel	1960/62[a]
Dringhouses (York)	1962	Tees (Thornaby)	1963
Healey Mills (Wakefield)	1963	Temple Mills (London)	1958[a]
Kingmoor (Carlisle)	1963	Thornton (Fife)	1956
Margam (Port Talbot)	1960	Tinsley (Sheffield)	1965
Millerhill (Edinburgh)	1963	Tyne (Gateshead)	1963
Perth	1962		

Notes: [a] reconstruction of existing yard(s); [b] Basford Hall yard at Crewe opened in 1901 but was electrified as part of the WCML project; Pre-existing major yards which received no significant investment under the Modernisation Plan are not listed: examples included Whitemoor, Feltham, Toton, Wath, Willesden, Cricklewood and Mossend.

Source: Rhodes, 1989.

The statutory planning process had little influence on the development of strategic transport policy and, as has been shown, by 1963 the die was cast in favour of road transport. Planners were pressured by their highway engineering colleagues[23] to prevent roads in industrial areas from becoming blocked with parked vehicles and causing difficulties for lorry access, by ensuring adequate on-site parking. Local planning authorities thereby required planning applications for the new industrial estates to include land for ample off-street car and lorry parking. The lower density development which this produced, wholly dependent on road access, was a further element of the incremental process of adapting the built environment to facilitate access by cars and lorries, whilst preventing any possibility of rail access.

Post-Beeching, the BRB seemed content to let much of its freight traffic fall away anyway, as it focused on trainload haulage of bulk products centred on a relatively small number of major industrial complexes such as quarries, collieries, power stations, steel works, oil refineries and ports. The character of contemporary rail freight was epitomised by the introduction of semi-automated 'merry-go-round' coal trains, linking new or modernised collieries with new coal-fired power

---

23   Typically, until the mid-1960s, this was the same department and often the planning was done by engineers or surveyors in any case, owing to the small number of qualified town planners and, as has been shown, City Engineers were in the forefront of the replanning of the cities in the early post-war period.

stations developed by the Central Electricity Generating Board, such as those along the Trent and Aire Valleys.[24] One of the major locational constraints was the need to place power stations at rail accessible points adjacent to rivers which were used as a source of cooling water (Allen 1966; Fiennes 1967; White 1979). This facilitated retention of the coal traffic which continued to be the core of the freight business and it was typical of the era that this involved three nationalised industries and did not require formal planning consent. BR did develop rail links into private sector oil refineries though, largely developed since 1945 in estuarine locations such as Fawley, Milford Haven, Thameshaven, Stanlow, Immingham and Grangemouth. Between 1963 and 1968 rail increased its haulage of heavy petroleum products from 4.8m to 15.0m tonnes, using the Beeching approach of high bulk wagons and block trains (White and Senior 1983, 96).

As the focus of industrial production moved towards light industry and consumer products, the rail freight business found it increasingly difficult to carry goods at competitive prices in the quantities generated, from origins and to destinations which, increasingly, were not rail connected. The liner train concept, branded as Freightliner, was a bold and initially successful attempt to compete and a network of 50 terminals nationwide was planned. The potential was recognised by some planners:

> In the early new towns much stress was placed on the need for rail communication but, although access was provided to rail sidings, little use is made of them at present. Circumstances may change in the future, as the rail service to industry is improved by liner trains and other means (Schaffer 1970, 25).

As a result of Labour's reinvigoration of regional economic policy in the 1960s, several large industrial projects were implemented where rail played a role. These included the development by Ford of the Halewood plant on Merseyside and the British Leyland development at Bathgate where rail was used to move components and finished vehicles. However this work to reduce the costs of the automotive industry was something of a mixed blessing with regard to the future prospects for the rail passenger business.

Conclusions

The major issues for management of the post-war railway system were rationalisation and modernisation. But the introverted culture of the industry, and the failure to link it institutionally with external bodies which were more deeply involved in planning for change, meant that the industry found it difficult to

---

24   This was a massive programme involving transport of coal to over a dozen new power stations: although most were close to the coal fields some, such as Didcot, involved lengthy hauls (Modern Railways 1964b).

develop a vision for its role in a rapidly changing society and ensure that societal change was steered in directions which did not marginalise rail. Instead, a start was made on rebuilding almost the whole of the inherited system as though it would continue to be central to society's needs. When things rapidly began to go wrong, changes in transport politics produced an abrupt, politically directed U-turn, and an attempt to reduce the industry down to a profitable, modernised core network with minimal call on the Exchequer. The public service paradigm was replaced by minimising cost to the Treasury. Although contraction was painful, the overall view within the industry about Beeching was positive:

> His outstanding achievements are to have jolted a hidebound industry out of morbid introspection into an aggressive confrontation of its competitors, to have trimmed it down to ideal fighting weight, and to have bludgeoned the public conscience into awareness of the crucial issues facing public transport in a motor age, even if the public has not yet had the courage to tackle all of them (Allen 1966, viii).

With the benefit of hindsight, it is clear that a more logical approach to the railway problem would have been to first carry out a Beeching-style review of the role of railways and use that as the basis for a modernisation plan. As things turned out, despite the retrenchment and concentration of investment in the core business post-Beeching, BR remained in deficit with little prospect of breaking even: profitability was a goal which turned out to be a chimera.

At the local level it was obvious that, owing to their inherent advantages over the rail mode, use of the car and lorry would have profound implications for urban planning. It does not follow, however, that: provision for road traffic should have been such an overriding concern; that the railway network should have been pruned back as far as it was; or that patterns of development should have been encouraged which were so obviously at odds with use and development of the railway network. The closures of some duplicate routes such as the Somerset and Dorset and Manchester-Derby, or routes which appeared to be in decline such as Oxford-Cambridge, were based on a minimalist view as to rail's future potential. With regard to the detail design of new development, the case of Runcorn new town shows that there was an understanding amongst some planners as to how it could be manipulated to prioritise access to public transport, whilst also facilitating use of the car. Similarly, the experiences in places as disparate as the Valleys, Birmingham and Glasgow showed that improvement of local rail services was feasible outside the South East. Also there were cases of railway managers who fought against branch line closures, even in rural areas, arguing, counter to Beeching, that both operating *and* track costs could be reduced. Supportive town and *country* planning frameworks could have been linked to the modernised main lines, suburban branch lines and low cost rural operations, but the institutional arrangements and railway and planning ideology were not conducive to such co-operation. The failure to secure more major development around main line stations characterises the relationship: the positive outcomes were notable because they were exceptional.

The findings with regard to the thematic analysis are summarised in Table 5.5 and the following summarises the outcomes with regard to the points on the policy agenda developed at the end of Chapter 2. With regard to railway system:

1. *rationalisation of the network*: rationalisation was based on short term perspectives and a minimalist view as to future capacity needs with the goal of cutting back to a commercially viable core network, rather than with an eye to maximising the network's future scope and utility as part of a broader social and environmental policy agenda;

2. *development of railway services*: services and fixed infrastructure on the main line network radiating from London were modernised, although only one trunk route was electrified; outside greater London those commuter and rural services which were not withdrawn were modernised by the introduction of some EMUs but mainly DMUs although, where travellers had a choice, the quality was unlikely to persuade them to prioritise the train over the car; those rail freight services which were retained, were significantly improved but the marshalling yard programme was not a success;

3. *closing strategic gaps in the network*: no significant sections of new railway were built and in fact some cross CBD tunnels or well located stations were closed and other strategic gaps were opened up by cross country route closures, and only one new Underground railway line was built in London;

4. *development of a programme of station enhancement*: many stations were rebuilt, occasionally as part of a larger commercial developments, but hundreds were closed and there were very few new stations;

With regard to the town planning agenda:

5. *patterns of urban development*: planning policy produced patterns of development which were generally poorly related to the railway network, with the exception of some strategic developments such as the new towns and some major industrial complexes, the most significant of which were the power stations which did not require formal planning permission;

6. *management of the redevelopment process in existing urban areas*: the redevelopment process in existing urban areas generally served to undermine access to railway stations, and the location, layout and density of development generally took little note of station location or the accessibility of rail freight facilities;

7. *management of the location and character of greenfield site development*: with the exception of most of the new towns, the development of greenfield areas generally produced settlements which were not focused around rail corridors and nodes, and the location, layout and density of

development generally took little note of station location, even in the new towns.

Table 5.5 Summary of thematic analysis of outcomes 1948–68

Explanatory themes	Railway sector	Interrelationships between the two sectors	Planning sector
Politics and political ideology	Public service paradigm led to start of rebuilding of most of the historic railway. Cost of this and the rise of the road lobby led to a U-turn towards the Treasury led approach and un-development of a third of the network.	No political champion for rail-planning integration and little evidence of the two systems working in harmony. Planning policy had no effect on Beeching closures. Change in the offing at the end of the period.	The political priorities never included integration between land-use and the railway network: examples of this were exceptional. Muted response from planning system to rail closures.
Professions and professional ideology	Dominance of the industry's technical managers produced backward looking modernisation, followed by fatalism about the Beeching closures. The infusion of private sector businessmen produced greater awareness of market segmentation, but their vision was constrained.	There was minimal contact between professionals in the two sectors and no development of an inter-disciplinary culture of planning for rail, as developed around road planning.	The goal of self-containment was readily abandoned in the face of growing car ownership, and planners were pulled along with the road oriented ideology of the engineers and architects.

Governance and management	The complex public service monolith of the early period was replaced by a streamlined, action oriented Board on the private sector model. This was used to secure rapid contraction of the industry and least cost modernisation.	The two systems were managed within different parts of the public sector realm, with little or no political or professional pressure to alter that. Activity in each sector took little note of the other. Firm proposals for change in the major conurbations were in place by the end of the period.	The development corporations secured positive locational outcomes for the new towns, and the non-statutory strategic plans for the South East embraced rail planning, on a limited basis. Elsewhere planning was largely focused around providing for road traffic.

Politically, by the end of the period, the road lobby was dominant, characterised by the 'Motorway Box' plan for London. However, there was rising concern over the growing impact of urban road traffic and the continuing decline of public transport and this was so great as to provoke action: the 'do nothing' alternative looked too unpalatable. But, as explained in the previous chapter, despite the development of a new policy thrust by Barbara Castle, Labour found it difficult to halt the momentum of the closure programme.

On the other hand, the future looked hopeful with a new deal for public transport in the major provincial conurbations to be brought about by the 1968 Transport Act and a greater emphasis on strategic planning which it was hoped would result from the 1968 Town and Country Planning Act, all to be set within a modernised local government structure. It was clear that the railway industry had developed a much better understanding of the need for liaison with the planning system too:

> Co-operation between state, local authorities and public transport to plan population and commercial resettlement around transport routes that need more use economically and can practically absorb it is a *sine qua non* for the resolution of coming problems (Allen 1966, 226).

What would be critical with regard to future outcomes would be the goals which would be set for the new arrangements with regard to the role of the railways and their relationship to land development, and the adequacy of the resources which would be brought to bear in their attainment. Would these continue to be minimal and largely focused on main lines to London and the London commuter traffic, or was passage of the 1968 Transport Act symptomatic of a sea change in attitudes and action towards better integration of urban public transport and land-use planning throughout the country?

Chapter 6
Institutional Relationships: 1969–94

Introduction

By 1968, concern over the social and environmental impacts of the growth of car traffic and the decline of public transport led to a refinement and reassertion of the policies of the 1940s which, in the following decade, cascaded through the railway and planning sectors and produced a new set of spatial outcomes. At the national level there were some important features to the pattern of institutional structures put in place to deliver this. With regard to the railways, at the broadest level there was continuity, in that the BRB remained in existence throughout the period and the railway was led by the Chairman of the Board. However this didn't preclude significant change within the organisation itself which impacted on external relationships. With regard to planning at the national level, there was a high degree of continuity too. The environmental debate led, in 1970, to creation of the Department of the Environment (DOE) and this continued to have planning as part of its remit throughout the period. However there was change in that the Department of Transport (DoT) was subsumed within the DOE as a result of the surge of commitment to integrating land-use and transport planning, but this was a temporary marriage lasting only from 1970–76. At the local authority level there was far reaching change, both at the start of the period and in the mid-1980s.

At the end of the 1970s, apart from some very notable achievements in a few of the major conurbations, the vision of integrated land-use and transportation planning allied to successful development of modern public transport systems, was still a long way from being realised. In 1968 it was possible to be optimistic about the prospects for railway-land use integration, but in 1979 the prospects became markedly pessimistic. Margaret Thatcher's 'New Right' government set its face against the post-war consensus and sought to re-affirm the primacy of market forces and roll back the frontiers of the state. This bitter economic medicine was intended to shake out inefficiency and encourage managements to break union power so as to raise productivity and profitability. It was sweetened politically with a brand of populism not previously seen in British politics which, for transport, meant the assertion of the right of the motorist to go where he or she chose, when he or she chose. Margaret Thatcher made a point of not travelling by train and she drew attention to the benefits of 'the great car economy'. This generally bode ill for strategic planning, for publicly owned public transport, for a nationalised monolith like BR and for strategic local government bodies. However, surprisingly, the development of institutional arrangements for management of BR and for integrated strategic land-use planning in the late 1980s, produced the most supportive structure of the whole post-war period.

Creation of the Passenger Transport Authorities and Executives

The 1968 Transport Act restructured BR's finances in the face of continuing deficits and attempted to put the industry on to a secure footing. Its creation of the passenger transport authority and passenger transport executive (PTA/PTE) structure in the major conurbations was crucial in developing the interface between town planning and local railway networks. The general model for such public transport bodies had a long pedigree, going back to the 1905 Royal Commission on London Traffic and the Pick/Ashfield era at the LPTB had demonstrated what could be achieved. The PTAs comprised elected councillors and became responsible for policy making; the PTEs were their officer level counterpart responsible for implementation. The PTEs were given powers under the Act (section 20) to finance the socially necessary services which BR could not run commercially. They were also given powers (section 56) to invest in public transport infrastructure, which could include railway rolling stock and fixed infrastructure: 75 per cent of the cost would come from central government. In addition, section 39 of the Act gave the Minister of Transport powers to pay BR grant for other loss making services outside the PTE areas, which is where the lion's share was; for example the Southern Region's commuter services which were treated as a single 'block'. Freight services were expected to be profitable without subsidy.

The 1968 Act also substantially changed the pattern of ownership of the bus industry. Various publicly owned coach and bus services outside the major conurbations were vested in a new public undertaking, the National Bus Company (NBC). These services were to be operated in competition with BR's InterCity services. In areas where PTEs were created, the historic municipal bus companies were wound up and their fleets vested in the PTEs. This meant that, for the first time outside London, there was a body in the major conurbations with a focus on local rail services which could also organise local bus services to feed into rail hubs. In 1969 the first four PTA/PTEs were established in the West Midlands, Merseyside, South East Lancashire North East Cheshire (SELNEC) i.e. Greater Manchester, and Tyneside. These were followed by Greater Glasgow in 1973, and South and West Yorkshire in 1974.

The structure of BR

In line with the developing corporate culture within BR, the 1968 Act abolished the statutory regional boards and the BRB produced its first 'Corporate Plan' in 1968. The development of a more outward looking planning culture with participation in the 'conurbation studies' was seen as very beneficial in a BRB annual report:

By these means, it became possible to see more clearly the significant contribution that the Board's services can make to the passenger transport needs of urban communities in the decades to come (BRB 1969, 19).

The 1968 Act also required the BRB to report back within a year with a replacement scheme of organisation. There had been concern in the 1960s about government interference with railway management for political purposes,[1] i.e. deferring increases in fares and charges as part of broader fiscal policy, and that the Board was too concerned with running the railway rather than with developing a vision for its future and promoting it externally (Bonavia 1971). Any change in the former was unlikely and outside BRB's control, but they lost no time in appointing McKinsey and Company to draw up a management plan to address the latter.

This was entitled 'Organising for the 1970s' and was adopted by government in amended form in 1969 (BRB 1969). The main principles were a clearly defined management structure and a systematic planning and control process based on the setting of objectives. The Board was to take on a non-executive role, with day-to-day management of the railway ('staff' as well as 'line' responsibilities) being handled by a Chief Executive, with the Chairman acting as principal spokesman and head of liaison with the Minister and outside bodies. The implications for reinforcing the role of the railway within society as a whole were positive and signalled a further move away from the former introverted culture. The report also proposed replacement of the six operating regions by eight 'territories'; Bonavia (1985) referred to this as an example of the disease to which BR became increasingly prone – continuous structural change as a response to crisis resulting from being given conflicting and unachievable goals by politicians. BR embarked on this change in the geography of its organisation, but it quickly ran into the sands of union opposition and was abandoned after three years; the regional structure remained intact, although non-statutory and without the prior degree of devolved decision making.

A new structure for rail freight

The 1968 Act had specific implications for institutional arrangements concerning freight: quantity regulation of the road haulage industry introduced in the 1930s was abandoned and replaced by quality control, which only regulated the safety standards of goods vehicles and their operators. The Act set up the National Freight Corporation (NFC) which comprised the rump of the nationalised road haulage industry (British Road Services), the former BR sundries business

---

1   There were particularly scathing remarks in the 1967 annual report (BRB 1967, 6) which welcomed the recognition by Government of the need to create statutory mechanisms for the support of socially necessary services which, it was hoped, would allow the Board greater freedom of action with regard to the commercial railway.

(National Carriers), and Freightliner with its road haulage fleet. The principle underlying this was that the NFC would be responsible for rail traffic where its origin was road collection, whereas BR would retain control of freight traffic which originated from rail-connected sources. This was a determined effort to try and create an organisation which was competitive in the market for general merchandise and parcels traffic. However, placing rail based services in the hands of a road transport organisation, rather than encouraging BR to develop intermodal expertise, was seen by BRB as disadvantageous to the long term interests of the rail freight business.

Creation of the BR Property Board

One very significant change which came out of the McKinsey report was the creation of the British Rail Property Board with the following remit:

> to control all property matters for the whole of the Railway Board's undertakings, with particular regard to the commercial development of its property, including the air space over stations (BRB 1969, 52).

The Property Board assumed responsibility for the sale or management of non-operational property and maximisation of revenue from operational property. The need to handle the large amounts of property which were becoming redundant and the need for BR to reduce its deficits, were the rationale for this renewed attempt at creating an effective property operation. These factors also meant that BR had a very specific need to engage with local planning authorities, which, if influenced by the right sort of policies, had the potential to stimulate ridership by locating major activity generators at, or near to, stations. The significance of this new era of management of the railway estate was not lost on the BRB and this was illustrated in 1974 when Robert Lawrence, former general manager of the London Midland Region and an operator and not a property manager, became chairman of the Property Board and remained so until his premature death in 1984. Lawrence's experience helped him prise the maximum amount of property from the operating departments. Also in 1974 the property regions were increased from five to seven:

> this put the regional estate surveyors into smaller administrative areas that gave closer contact with local business and municipal communities (Biddle 1990, 207).

Local government re-organisation: the English metropolitan counties, the Scottish regions and the GLC

In the local government arena, underpinning the deliberations of the Redcliffe Maud and Wheatley Commissions was an assumption:

> that something loosely called the city region – that is, the city or conurbation plus its sphere of influence – would be the right basis for local government reform (Hall 1989a, 176).

This concept sat comfortably with the PTA/PTE structure, but the commissioners found difficulties in applying the concept because of tensions between the design of administratively efficient institutional structures and the public's politico-geographical consciousness. The former drove the English commissioners towards the unitary concept, whereas their Scottish colleagues opted for a two tier structure throughout. Senior was alone amongst the English commissioners in his support for a comprehensive two tier structure, but the rest of his colleagues were sufficiently persuaded by his arguments to support a two tier structure for the conurbations, with a unitary structure elsewhere. In the event it was left to Edward Heath's Conservative government, elected in 1970, to make the final decision. But the important point to note is that the need for strategic planning at a broad geographical scale, as recommended by the PAG group, was recognised, in parallel to the case for planning public transport at this level and subsidising it in the wider public interest. The phoenix of integrated land-use and public transport planning, at the level of the city region, was rising out of the ashes of the experiences of the early post-war decades. The merger of the former Ministry of Transport into the new Department of the Environment reflected this thinking at the national level and, overall, the new structures augured well for policy development and delivery.

The first significant step in the direction of combining responsibility for strategic land-use and transport planning in a single, directly elected body, came in 1970 when the GLC took over London Transport (Garbutt 1985) under the 1969 Transport (London) Act. However, it was significant that the area administered by the GLC, at 600 square miles (1554 sq km) (roughly the area contained within the metropolitan green belt), was considerably smaller than the 2,000 square miles (5180 sq km) previously administered by the LPTB. Given the extending influence of London and the fact that main line commuter services remained with BR, this was to become a significant disadvantage for strategic planning.[2]

Heath's 1972 Local Government Act produced a different structure from that envisaged by Redcliffe Maud: a two-tier system of counties and districts was created throughout England and Wales. In terms of town planning the upper tier

---

2 The former LT Country Bus and Coach Department which operated services out towards the periphery of the old London Transport area, was absorbed by the NBC, which undermined the potential for integration with rail services.

of county councils was to be responsible for producing structure plans, whereas the lower tier district authorities would produce most of the local plans. In the six major English conurbations new geographical entities, metropolitan counties, were created which became responsible for strategic land-use planning and highway planning. As in London, they took over responsibility for public transport by absorbing the PTA/PTE structure too: unlike the GLC though, the 1968 Act gave them powers to develop and finance local BR services.

The absorption by the PTEs of municipal bus fleets saw the ending of the system of Joint Operating Committees set up in the 1930s. This involvement by BR in local bus services, was replaced by the PTEs having a much more interventionist role in the planning and financing of local rail services. The bringing together of responsibility for all local transport planning under the umbrella of the metropolitan counties was a significant move towards a more integrated structure. But an important facet of it was the fact that the PTEs were legally separate organisations from their parent county councils, and often physically separate too, each being 'a body corporate with a Common Seal' (Hellewell 1996, 14). This meant that there was a significant division of labour between the PTEs which were responsible for public transport, and the county highways departments which continued to have responsibility for road planning. Therefore the institutional structure continued to provide a quite separate locus for road-oriented planning. County planning departments were usually in the same building as highways, and there was likely to be very regular contact between staff in the two departments[3] concerning matters ranging from consultations over planning applications to the production of development plans. It was clear that the structure was not as supportive of public transport oriented land-use planning as it might have looked at first glance. Also trunk road planning continued to be the responsibility of the MoT (albeit that this had notionally been amalgamated with the DoE), and proposals were developed by the Road Construction Units in a quite separate planning framework and had to be automatically incorporated into statutory land-use plans. This was further illustration of the limitations of the new structure vis-à-vis planning around rail.

The inability of the GLC (London Transport) to directly influence London commuter rail services was an issue picked up by the 1977 transport White Paper (DoT et al. 1977, 30). However the government felt that commuter services were too closely integrated with the rest of the railway network to be extracted and handed over to the GLC. But the GLC and the DoT set up a London Rail Advisory Committee to look into the improved co-ordination of rail services. In common with the GLC, and despite the city region concept, the boundaries of the new metropolitan counties were drawn relatively tightly and, by and large, they were contained *within* green belt boundaries. Given what was said in the previous chapter about the development of transport behaviour patterns which involved regular journeys *across* green

---

3   A significant development in the 1960s was the creation of separate planning departments, whereas previously planning had often been a function of surveyor's departments.

belts, these tight boundaries created significant institutional barriers to strategic planning. This problem did not occur to the same degree in Scotland where a two tier structure, with an upper tier of elected regional bodies, was created: Strathclyde region took over the PTA/PTE and as such administered an area which embraced the whole of Greater Glasgow and beyond. However the actual PTE area comprised only about an eighth of the region although, to confuse matters, the PTE acted as the region's agent on public transport matters throughout the region.

The new structure was in place by April 1974. It was striking that it reflected past trends of urbanisation in that PTA/PTEs were created in the older, industrial conurbations: other more complex urban systems such as the Leicester-Derby-Nottingham triangle, or emergent conurbations such as Portsmouth-Southampton, Bournemouth-Poole, or Bristol-Bath were not included. Even such an historic, industrially based system as Cardiff and the Valleys was excluded, despite its retention of a good local passenger network which was favoured by the area's physical geography.[4]

Although creation of the metropolitan counties and the PTA/PTE structure was positive with regard to the development of strategic land-use and transportation policy, it was more problematic with regard to local planning. Lower tier district councils were much more concerned with traditional planning issues such as the provision of housing land and urban renewal, along with developing new expertise in housing improvement area planning, derelict land reclamation and conservation of historic buildings and areas. They were generally remote from the policy interface with BR and this meant that the development of a rail-oriented culture at local planning level was unlikely. It was also significant that the districts had their own borough surveyor's departments which acted as agents on local highways matters for the county councils. This reinforced the highway oriented linkages between land-use planning and road-oriented transport planning, in contrast to the relatively remote linkages with rail oriented planning by the PTEs.

The 'shire' counties and the railway network

As will be shown in the following chapter, the mood of political optimism which marked the late 1960s changed markedly in the mid-1970s in the face of severe economic difficulties. The economy was plagued by high inflation resulting from global and domestic sources and this led to political turmoil (Sked and Cook 1993, 253-291) as Heath's government tried to cope and the unions fought back to protect real earnings and jobs. A statutory prices and incomes policy was developed which led to confrontation with the unions, and problems with oil supplies associated with the OPEC crisis were exacerbated by coal shortages caused by domestic industrial unrest. Heath introduced the three day week in the autumn of 1973, followed by other energy saving initiatives including a blanket 50

---

4   Its case was recognised in the 1977 Transport White Paper, but no action was taken.

mph speed limit on the roads. In February 1974, he called a general election on the 'who rules the country?' issue: the National Union of Miners responded by calling a national strike. Labour was returned to government without an overall majority, although this was secured in a further general election in October 1974, but the economic problems persisted.

As a reflection of this more pessimistic mood, the MoT was separated from the DoE in 1976 which arguably served to make trunk road planning even more remote from local transport planning. However, things were not altogether bleak: with the PTEs having been operating for a number of years there was a growing awareness that their administrative areas were relatively constrained and many provincial rail services served cities outside them as well as extensive rural hinterlands. The importance of the public transport work of 'shire' county councils was recognised by the 1978 Transport Act which required them to produce a five year public transport plan. This meant that, although county councils had been involved in bidding for finance from central government for road construction since the Ministry was created in 1919, it was only in 1978 that mechanisms were fully in place to empower them to plan and bid for funds for public transport developments. But, given the then current state of public finances, this was unlikely to amount to much investment in the railways in the short term.

Thatcherism and the undermining of local planning authorities

Heath's new institutional structures were only fully in place by 1974, by which time Labour was back in power. They were relatively short-lived as, following further economic difficulties leading to conflict with the unions and the 'Winter of Discontent' (Healey 1990; Sked and Cook 1993), Margaret Thatcher's 'New Right' Conservative government was elected in 1979 with a large majority in the House of Commons. The new government was committed to a break with the post-war consensus which it viewed as characterised by the mixed economy, interventionism and, since 1974, corporatism, by which was meant an overly cosy relationship between government and the unions. They were wedded to the view that it was the private sector which was the source of wealth and it had to be freed from the dead hand of state regulation. Local authorities were viewed with suspicion as, at best, a necessary evil and, at worst, profligate and subversive of the national interest. With regard to town planning and public transport therefore, the 1980–94 period was marked by a more or less continuous unwinding most of the institutional relationships which had been painstakingly built up over the previous two decades.

Town planning and urban regeneration came under the Thatcherite spotlight from the outset (Ambrose 1986; Thornley 1991). The 1980 Local Government, Planning and Land Act abolished the regional economic planning councils which survived from the 1960s and introduced 'Urban Development Areas' (UDAs). Here development control was to be taken away from local councils and, along with land ownership, investment and other interventionist powers, was vested in

Urban Development Corporations (UDCs), central government appointed bodies on the new town model (O'Toole 1996). The government acted quickly and created UDCs in the redundant dockland areas of London and Merseyside in 1981.

Another feature of the Local Government, Planning and Land Act was the power it gave to government for the creation of Enterprise Zones (EZs) in areas needing economic regeneration. These were mushrooming all over the country as a result of severe economic recession especially, but not exclusively, in the midlands and the north. Although the creation of an EZ brought a bundle of advantages to an investor, such as tax incentives and freedom from payment of local property taxes, they also created a relaxed planning regime where specified developments could take place without the need for formal planning consent. This was a further undermining of the power of local planning authorities to control patterns of land use: eleven EZs were created in 1981 with a further fourteen in 1983–84.

BR and sectorisation

The government's view of the importance of markets reflected the diagnosis of BR's ills made by Bob Reid, a career railwayman who became Chairman in 1982 and occupied the post until 1990.[5] His view was that the corporate railway had lost touch with its customers and he re-organised to create five 'business sectors', as a move towards becoming a more 'business-led' organisation. At this time there is little doubt that the primary aim was cost cutting i.e. not running trains for which there was no identified market. The passenger sectors were InterCity, London and South East (L&SE), and Provincial; Freight and Parcels (including Royal Mail and newspapers) were the other two. Bonavia (1985, 39) identified three main methods of devolution in large organisations; by function, by territory, and by product. In the early years of nationalisation, devolution was focused around function and territory; post-Beeching it focused around territory and product; creation of the sectors reinforced this trend towards product.

In order to avoid the sort of staff backlash which the post-McKinsey attempt at re-organisation had provoked, an evolutionary approach was adopted whereby the sector structure was laid over the regional structure. The regions were still responsible for running trains and maintaining the permanent way, whilst the Sectors were their 'customers'. This undoubtedly led to confusion: the Sector Directors drove the marketing function and were responsible for financial results which were produced via various internal accounting mechanisms, the first time this responsibility had been devolved below board level since the creation of BR in 1962. But, the artificiality of the financial results came in for criticism and the whole sector idea was seen, by some, as a product of; 'the desire to re-organise, to be seen to be doing *something*' (Bonavia 1985, 38). But the creation of one

---

5   His successor was also called Bob Reid, although he came from outside the railway industry.

organisation to oversee London's commuter services was something that critics had long argued for. In the provinces the creation of the Provincial sector, widely perceived as the Cinderella of the passenger businesses, potentially brought land-use planning and the railway closer together by creating a focus that had a vested interest in medium and short distance rail journeys in urban and rural areas.

Abolition of the metropolitan counties

Given its commitment to market forces and rolling back the state, the government had little enthusiasm for the sort of strategic intervention represented by structure planning and other activities of the upper tier authorities, particularly those in the conurbations. The latter were all Labour controlled anyway and were a source of effective political opposition characterised by the GLC regime led by Ken Livingstone, once Labour returned to power in London in 1981. Transport, particularly London Transport fares, became the focus for intense political conflict (Garbutt 1985, 67-76). Fundamental changes were mooted in 1983 and the GLC and the metropolitan counties were abolished in 1986 by the 1985 Local Government Act: this retrenchment did not extend to the 'shire' counties which were less directly associated with Labour. Abolition of the GLC and the metropolitan counties meant that responsibility for local transport planning fell to the highways departments of the remaining lower tier London boroughs and metropolitan district councils which had previously been acting as agents for the counties. This served to further erode the scope for integration between land-use planning in the districts and PTE driven railway planning, as any linkages usually had to be developed through, or at least in conjunction with, the highways department whose priority was the local road network.

Public transport and market forces

1986 was a seminal year as it marked the end of the attempt, begun in 1968, to integrate strategic land-use planning with the development of publicly owned public transport. From the start it was clear that the latter would be a target for Thatcherism: it was ideologically unacceptable and was viewed as being, in practice, associated with trade unions and cosy relationships with Labour controlled public bodies. This threat was reinforced when one of Thatcherisms leading ideologues, Nicholas Ridley, became Secretary of State for Transport in 1983. However, with regard to the railways there was a strong political folk memory of opposition to the Beeching closures and an awareness of the political significance to the government of the South East commuter electorate. The government therefore took a more gradualist approach to 'reform' of BR than it did with regard to its relaxation of local authority planning control or policy towards the provincial bus industry. This involved increased pressure to make BR more market oriented and to reduce its dependence on public subsidy, rather than statutory restructuring or privatisation. These pressures did indeed produce significant policy shifts within BR with regard to the ways in which the organisation was structured and run and, in terms of international comparisons, made it into a notably efficient performer amongst state-owned railways. Ironically their ideological commitment to market forces and scepticism about state-owned enterprises, made the Conservatives rather effective managers of publicly owned industries, although this was usually to make them 'leaner and fitter' in readiness for privatisation. The latter was not the case with regard to BR in the mid-1980s though.

The first statutory step with regard to public transport was the 1980 Transport Act which deregulated the inter-city coach industry. As, even under the NBC, coaches had competed with InterCity (on price), the implications of this were not particularly profound for BR, but were a shift away from transport integration nevertheless. The perceived success of this encouraged the government to extend deregulation to all stage bus services. After trials in Hereford and Worcester, and Devon (strange choices for pilot studies, given that bus services are best suited to dense urban areas) which the government saw as successful (DoT 1985), the 1985 Transport Act deregulated stage bus services and forced the various publicly owned undertakings to create 'arms length' operating companies which could run as straight commercial entities. Those services operated by the NBC were earmarked for privatisation at this stage. In April 1986 the metropolitan counties and the GLC were abolished and, in October, stage bus services were deregulated: Thatcherism was clearly making its mark in unravelling the work of 1968–72, although there was an element of caution in the strategy as bus deregulation did not extend to Greater London.

Implications for the railways

London Transport had already been replaced in 1984 by a new body, London Regional Transport, which was under the direct control of the Secretary of State for Transport. To some extent, this did improve matters for London's railways as both BR and London Underground services were then under the direct influence of the Secretary of State and he had signalled his intention to achieve better co-ordination and interchange between the two. With regard to fares, this was illustrated by introduction of the Capitalcard in 1985 which allowed travel by British Rail, Underground or bus on a zonal basis: this was a backhanded complement to the policies of Ken Livingstone.

As far as the railway network outside London was concerned, the impact of bus deregulation was felt particularly in the urban areas where buses would be free to run in competition with local rail services, and the operation of regulated, feeder services ended. However, the PTA/PTE structure survived abolition of the metropolitan counties,[6] the reason for this seems to be pragmatism, certainly not ideological commitment to integrated public transport. Much of the bus industry remained in PTE ownership and there was a need for continued administration of the funding of discounted travel for old age pensioners, children and other groups, along with the operation of a system for funding non-commercially viable bus services (tendered services – see White 2002).

Outside the conurbations the upper tier of 'shire' counties remained[7]. Since 1978 they had been preparing public transport plans and, although they did not have a statutory duty to invest in local rail services, a number of them did so, with significant results, as will be shown. A positive element of the 1985 Transport Act for the railways was Section 63, which empowered the shires to contribute revenue support to local rail services. However, the internal structure of the DoT continued to have a heavy roads bias: Bonavia (1985, 113) reported that of 16 under-secretaries, two dealt with railways and seven with roads, and of 45 assistant secretaries, four dealt with railways and 13 with roads. The DoT was poorly structured to respond to pressure from local government for investment in rail.

Further erosion of the planning system

The erosion of the powers and influence of local planning authorities continued relentlessly in the second half of the 1980s and, during the tenure of Nicholas Ridley as Secretary of State for the Environment (1986–88), reached its zenith. The 1986 Housing and Town Planning Act introduced Simplified Planning Zones (SPZs) which would enjoy the relaxed planning regimes of the EZs without the financial benefits. The first SPZ was declared in Derby in 1988 by which time there were 23 EZs. Also by that time UDCs had been created in Sheffield, the Black Country, Trafford Park, Tyne and Wear (Newcastle and Sunderland), Teeside and Cardiff, with 'mini' UDCs in Central Manchester, Leeds and Bristol. Taken together, the creation of EZs and particularly the UDAs, was a severe erosion of the influence of local planning authorities on urban regeneration, which had arguably become the most significant planning problem facing the major conurbations. In 1988 the influence of local authorities was further eroded by the replacement of grant regimes which funnelled public money through them to developers in non-UDA areas, by City Grant, which flowed directly from the DoE. By 1989 the involvement of local authorities in regeneration was so marginal that the government was criticised by its own watchdog, the Audit Commission (1989): 'The totality of government effort in the inner cities is less than the sum of its parts'. It is ironic that the concept of the development corporation which, when

---

6   The elected members coming in future from the remaining district tier of local government.

7   The balance between unitary and two tier arrangements now being the obverse of what Redcliff Maud had recommended.

used under the 1946 New Towns Act was seen as an indication of positive attitudes towards planning, should have come to be seen in the late 1980s as indicative of the contemporary government's hostility to it. The rider to this was the winding up of the new towns programme and the disposal of their assets to the private sector.

In the late 1980s, abolition of the GLC and the metropolitan counties left a vacuum at the strategic level and the government had no intention of filling it: 'The fact is this: in 1988 we start with a blank hole where strategic local government used to be' (Hall 1989, 170). However it was recognised that London, at any rate, was so large and complex that some sort of co-ordination between boroughs was required: to fill this gap, the 1985 Local Government Act created the statutory London Planning Advisory Committee (LPAC). In the provincial conurbations there was to be no such statutory body and it was left to the metropolitan districts to co-ordinate their planning activities to the extent that they saw fit. This meant that a range of post-abolition structures developed, ranging from very informal arrangements with minimal contact between authorities, to more formal structures with joint bodies at elected member and various officer levels. These changes had implications for plan making as the bodies which had produced structure plans were no longer extant. As a result a new kind of plan, the unitary development plan (UDP), was introduced which would be produced by all the remaining lower tier authorities in London and the former metropolitan counties. UDPs would have a strategic element (part one), and would also comprise a borough wide local plan (part two). Given the absence of an upper tier strategic body to fix the context for these activities, the DoE issued Regional Planning Guidance for London and each of the former metropolitan counties, but the content was brief and bland. Collectively these changes severely curtailed the potential for planning authorities to co-ordinate patterns of development with the railway network as this is dependent upon a strategic and prescriptive approach. Although the UDCs were very interventionist, the following chapter will show that, for the most part, they were not ideologically given to planning around public transport networks.

The resurgence of strategic planning

In the property boom of the second half of the 1980s the initiative for new house construction lay almost totally with the private sector. As will be seen later, this led to conflict between developers and residents in the peripheries of the city regions, especially in the South East. As this conflict was typically through the planning appeals system, it inevitably drew in the Secretary of State as arbiter, particularly where major developments were proposed, such as new settlements. Nicholas Ridley was ideologically biased towards the developers who were responding to market forces, but the opponents were frequently staunch Tories, so the conflicts were politically unfortunate for Ridley to say the least. His effigy was frequently burnt at protest rallies and his ratings reached a nadir when he was famously caught out objecting to a new development in his own 'back yard' in the Cotswolds.

These tensions resulted in his replacement in 1989 by Chris Patten who developed a significant change in the government's ideological stance towards planning, and its view of the relationship between land-use and demand for transport. Patten also saw the need to rejuvenate the regional planning process and reinforce the role of bodies such as Serplan. This was partly, perhaps, because he recognised the intellectual case for this. But also Patten saw that the voluntary involvement of local planning authorities in developing regional planning guidance meant that they would develop ownership of the policies which would reduce the risk of the Secretary of State getting mired in the sort of conflicts which had beset his predecessor. In light of such conflicts, debate developed about the lack of a statutory layer of government capable of strategic planning. With regard to greater London, Hall commented that:

> ... underneath the surface, the problems that brought the GLC into being have not gone away. On the contrary they are endemic, and if anything they have been intensified in the intervening thirty years ... We can be sure before long – perhaps by 1995, almost certainly by the year 2000 – the spectre of London government will once again rear its head (1989b, 174).

He was unduly pessimistic as debate had commenced by the early 1990s and support for some sort of strategic body to co-ordinate land development with transport infrastructure was coming from unexpected quarters, the property industry. Suggestions for a new body ranged from re-establishing a democratically elected body with an executive figurehead comparable to the mayor of Paris, to a government appointed commission which would include transport and commercial interests as well as local government representatives. However, moving the clock back in this way proved too much for the Conservatives and the existing structures remained unchanged, although reinvigorated.

The balkanisation of local government came under increasing criticism in the early 1990s, particularly with regard to urban policy. The result was an attempt by government to pull together various disparate elements into more coherent policy bundles, such as the Single Regeneration Budget, and the regional organisation of central government departments was restructured as part of this initiative. This produced regional Government Offices (GOs) in 1994 which provided a more focused approach to liaison with regional planning conferences and BR sector managers.[8]

---

8   For a summary of the changing approaches to urban regeneration from 1980 onwards see Jones and Evans 2008.

Reinforcing the sectors

It was the development boom of the late-1980s which caused the resurgence of interest in strategic planning and the boom also led to increased railway ridership and stimulated bulk freight traffic, particularly that associated with the construction industry. This generally positive economic climate reinforced the drive towards further embedding the sectorisation process which had started in the early 1980s. Economic growth was focused in the South East and its railway network had always been the most important part of the national network: this is why London and South East had been created as a separate sector. In 1986 this process moved a stage further and all London's commuter services, which had previously been operated as separate entities by the four regions with their financial results pooled for presentational purposes, were amalgamated into Network South East (NSE). Chris Green, a leader amongst that generation of managers influenced by the market orientation brought in by Beeching, was moved in from the Scottish Region as general manager. This created a single champion for London's commuter services: NSE was a sizeable business in its own right with a turnover in excess of £1 billion pa and focused management of this augured well for service development (Green 1989). The prior creation of LPAC and encouragement of Serplan meant that, surprisingly, given the government's ideological character, a very positive framework had been constructed for strategic integration between land-use planning and the development of rail services in London and the South East.

Outside London a similar improvement in institutional relationships developed. The increasing role of the 'shire' counties in rail investment has already been mentioned. The creation of the Provincial sector had produced a champion for what were third priority services, coming after InterCity and London and South East. These were a mixed bunch and included: long distance routes between major cities, such as Liverpool-Newcastle; local services in the PTE areas and around major cities; and rural services. Since 1982 the Provincial sector had developed five regional sub-sectors; Scotland, North West, North East, Central, and South Wales and West, each with its own management based in Glasgow, Manchester, York, Birmingham and Swindon respectively. In addition, the government's strict financial control over BR, and BR's growing experience with extracting money from local authorities, meant that there was growing within the industry a culture of developing and nurturing links with local government. Taken together, this meant that the institutional structures and cultures for integration between local railway planning and local authority transport and land-use planning, were stronger than at any time since 1947.

The railway side of this relationship was further strengthened when, in 1990, the Provincial sector became Regional Railways and, like NSE, took over ownership of trains and management of operating staff from the Regions. As the government's support grew for regional planning in other regions on the Serplan model, opportunities developed for closer working on policy development between the Provincial sub-sectors, regional planning conferences, and representatives from the GOs. In 1988 sectorisation was also applied to the freight business, the bulk of which post-Beeching was based on trainload traffic. The overall branding was Trainload and the subsectors were Coal, Metals, Construction and Petroleum: Freightliner was combined with the remaining UK and international[9] wagonload businesses to form the Railfreight Distribution sector, with the Royal Mail and parcels businesses comprising the final subsector.

The success of sectorisation in allowing the various railway businesses to develop their markets, encouraged BR to reinforce their role further. This process started internally in 1989 and by mid-1990 proposals had been accepted by the Board for implementation over the next few years. As in the early 1980s, there was to be progressive change on an evolutionary basis with a target completion date of 1993. The strategy was labelled 'Organising for Quality' (Ford 1991) and the aim was to make the Sectors into vertically integrated railway businesses having total ownership of infrastructure and rolling stock and to abolish the Regions. Each Sector was to be further broken down into 'profit centres' based on routes, a structure which closely resembled the Line Management approach which the Eastern region had developed in the 1950s (Bonavia 1971, 88-89). The BR Board would be responsible for setting targets, special projects such as the Channel Tunnel would be progressed by dedicated task forces, and a central services facility would remain to oversee technical work.

Just as the creation of the Sectors had been potentially beneficial to the relationship with the local planning system, their reinforcement was likely to further improve the scope for fruitful liaison. For example, the Sectors would now have 'ownership' of stations and would have a direct interest in securing passenger generating activities in and around them. NSE was quick off the mark in beginning the process of implementing Organising for Quality and publicised (Gough 1991, 6) its development of a tight/loose management philosophy. This involved having a tightly-knit central management team with responsibility for strategic planning and external liaison with bodies such as Serplan and London Transport, but would also delegate operational matters and local liaison down to each of the nine operating divisions based on specific rail corridors. This structure and management philosophy was very supportive of the development of relationships with strategic and local planning bodies and augured well for the future if the other two passenger sectors were to develop along similar lines.

Railway privatisation

In the general election of 1992 the Conservatives, under John Major's leadership, were re-elected, somewhat surprisingly in the opinion of most commentators. Eager to show that the government had lost none of the radical zeal of the Thatcher

---

9   This was quite a substantial business based on train ferries serving Harwich and Dover.

period, his ebullient Secretary of State for Transport, John MacGregor, lost no time and in July of that year published a White Paper setting out the government's intention to privatise the railways (DoT 1992). For those who thought that BR's biggest problems stemmed from intervention and manipulation by politicians for their own ends, this was the final proof of their thesis: the outcome was that just as the BRB completed the Organising for Quality initiative in April 1993 and placed all the infrastructure in the ownership of the Sectors, it was instructed to take it all away from them and place it with a new track authority, Railtrack, by April 1994. As a backhanded complement to how close the Sector structure was focused around the various rail markets, the structure of the passenger rail franchises which were eventually offered to the private sector closely followed the sub-sector structure of InterCity, NSE and Regional Railways (Harris and Godward 1997).

Conclusions

This chapter has shown that, between 1968–94, there was at the national level a high degree of continuity in the institutional structure. The BRB was in existence throughout and there was a clear leader for the industry in the form of the Chairman of the Board, with only three men occupying that role between 1971–90.[10] The DOE also remained extant throughout, although the amalgamation with Transport was short lived. However at lower levels there were substantial changes in the institutional structures for the railway network and the planning system: Figure 6.1 summarises the institutional structure and Table 6.1 summarises the thematic analysis. The period began with bringing London Transport under the control of the GLC, the creation of the PTA/PTE structure, and the re-organisation of local government. In the major provincial conurbations, this created a structure which, although it had its weaknesses, made it easier to relate railway development to strategic land-use planning and vice-versa. Outside the conurbations the 'shire' counties were also empowered to become financially involved in the development of railway services. However, this was a period when BR was characterised by a centralised or 'corporatist' approach to its management, although service delivery was still dominated by engineers and operators in the Regions. Outside the PTE areas therefore, the overall interface with local government was poor.

Although the election of the Conservatives in 1979 led, initially, to a blunting and erosion of the institutional structures for land-use planning, and looked threatening to the prospects for BR, this was not how things eventually worked out. The Bob Reid era produced very significant changes in the internal management structure of BR which sought to place it much closer to its markets and change its culture towards that of a private sector service provider, dependent on maximising sales. By the mid-1980s this structure began to engage very favourably with local authorities which became recognised and valued as both customers and partners.

---

10   Richard Marsh 1971–76, Peter Parker 1976–83, Bob Reid 1983–90.

By the late 1980s the sectors were engaging with the revived structure for regional land-use planning created in the Patten era. Overall this produced what was, arguably, the most favourable institutional structure for the relationship between the railway and land-use planning sectors of the whole post-war era. But once the government signalled its intention to restructure BR in readiness for privatisation, then the organisation entered a period where it returned to focus almost entirely on internal matters.

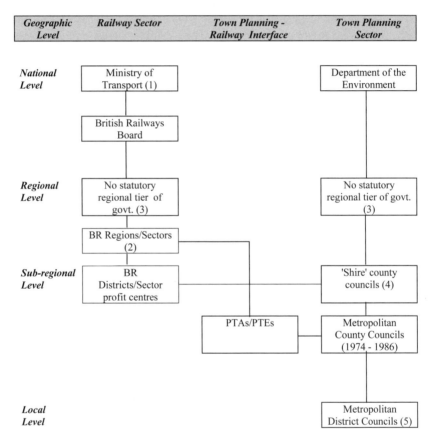

Figure 6.1 The institutional relationships between the railway and town planning sectors in England (outside London) 1969–94

*Note*s *to Figure 6.1*

1. Between 1970 and 1976 the Ministry of Transport was part of the Department of the Environment.

2. The responsibility for management of the infrastructure remained with the Regions until the Organising for Quality initiative in 1992 when infrastructure was divided between the business sectors. From 1982 onwards the sectors provided an additional interface at the regional level.

3. Regional Offices of the MoT (later DoT) and the DoE were re-opened in the 1970s. Serplan was reinvigorated in the 1980s, and similar regional planning conferences were created in the other English regions.

4. The 'shires' began to develop relationships with the regions and sectors in the early 1980s and these strengthened up to 1994.

5 .The metropolitan district councils were responsible for local planning from 1974–86, and for local and strategic planning after 1986. PTAs were made up of councillors from these authorities post-1986.

Table 6.1 Summary of thematic analysis of institutional structures 1969–94

Explanatory themes	Railway sector	Interrelationships between the two sectors	Planning sector
Politics and political ideology	Initially a centralised corporate structure, but expected to develop a close relationship with PTA/PTEs through the regional structure. Hostility by Conservatives post-1979 produced a segmented, market oriented organisation and culture, which sought linkages with the whole of local government.	Initially close in London and the PTA/PTE areas. Undermined by Conservatives in the early 1980s, but a strong resurgence in the late 1980s early 1990s which embraced the shires and regional bodies, as well as the PTA/PTEs.	Initially seen as a local public service, but with a local and *strategic* role. Hostile stance by Conservatives post-1979 saw powers transferred to other organisations or undermined. Strategic role re-emphasised in the 1990s within a culture which increasingly favoured 'partnership'.
Professions and professional ideology	Initially continuance of traditional introverted and hierarchical structures. Post-1979 development of market oriented culture which sought partnership with property interests and local government.	Initially few points of contact between professions in the two sectors, other than in London and the PTA/PTE areas. By late 1980s much more contact across a broad front, including shires and non-metropolitan districts. Presence of BR Property Board provided opportunities for project based co-operation.	Planning continued to be embedded in the same structures which were concerned with road building, and continued to look towards these primarily. Links were developed with the PTA/PTEs in the metro counties. Ideological crisis for planning in early 1980s which emphasised links with the property market, but by late 1980s planners developing links with rail sector across a broad front around the environmental agenda.

Explanatory themes	Railway sector	Interrelationships between the two sectors	Planning sector
Governance and management	Seen as a centralised, production oriented corporate body in the 1970s. Sectorisation produced a complex, devolved structure, focused on market segments, leading to valuing of links with local government.	Throughout the 1970s there was an aspiration towards linking the planning and railway sectors, especially in London and the PTA/PTE areas. Despite changes in the 1980s, the linkages remained in London, but were weakened elsewhere, only to be re-invigorated across a broad front in the late 1980s/ early 1990s.	Local government re-organisation produced a two tier structure focused on strategic/local planning. PTA/PTEs provided a linking mechanism. This was undermined in the 1980s, although the stimulus to regional planning in the 1990s created bodies which were able to re-assert the linkages in a climate where partnerships were valued.

Chapter 7
Policy: 1969–94

Introduction

This chapter will show that major investment plans for inter-city and local railway services were developed in the 1970s, but that the policy response by the planning system was limited: the main thrust was towards restricting the location of major trip generators to town and city centres which, by and large, were well served by rail. However, because of the lengthy statutory planning process, by the time these policies were formally adopted, Mrs Thatcher's government was in power and had no intention of constraining the property market in this way.

There followed a difficult period for the railway and planning sectors as the government embraced market forces and, in terms of transport and land development, their locational pull towards the road network. But from the late 1980s, owing to the growth of popular concern about the environmental impacts of road-oriented decentralisation, there began a progressive policy U-turn. Unexpectedly, this produced the most thoroughly articulated, pro-rail land-use planning policies of the whole post-war era, and a railway management which understood the importance of this and sought to build on it.

Owing to the break in the policy thread this chapter is split into two parts, broadly before and after 1979. It begins by reviewing policy at the national level to 1979, then drops down to look at London and a sample of provincial conurbations, and finally considers the rest of the country. This pattern is repeated for the 1980s, before returning to review national policy changes in the early 1990s.

The main line railways to 1979

Government concerns over the high cost of WCML electrification were finally overcome in 1970 with the decision to complete the work through to Glasgow. BR's thinking on inter-city services extended beyond conventional rail technology: building new routes was politically unacceptable so a 'tilting' train, the Advanced Passenger Train (APT), was proposed to facilitate higher speeds over the existing, sinuous main line network. It was recognised that its development would be difficult, so another train, utilising conventional technologies, was also developed: the High Speed Train (HST) which was to run at up to 125 mph (200 kmph). Prototypes of each began running in 1972.[1]

---

1   The same year that SNCF unveiled its prototype 'Train à Grand Vitesse' (TGV).

The higher priority given to rail-oriented planning was reflected in the debate around the choice of location for London's third airport: all the options included a rail link to London (see Appendix 9). Buchanan, in his Note of Dissent, favoured Foulness and he expected a new railway would be built to it (Roskill 1971, fig. 10.9): this was the most ambitious project to be countenanced since the war and was indicative of the new mood. Also, under the influence of Minister of Transport John Peyton (1970–74), a committed *tunnelista* (Gourvish 2006, 132-33), Heath's government became convinced of the viability of a cross-Channel rail tunnel: a white paper was issued in 1973, followed by a BR consultation document in 1975; completion was envisaged by 1980. The government accepted that the full benefits could only be realised if there was simultaneous construction of a new high speed rail link to London.

Despite this buoyancy with regard to the main lines, the Treasury-driven search for rationalisation continued: BR's overall mindset continued to focus around capacity, i.e. cost, reduction. Lines continued to be brought forward for closure, albeit at a reduced rate, but there was also a remorseless generation of rationalisation plans: singling of double track, removal of passing loops and sidings, closure of spurs into industrial complexes, and removal of staff from stations.

The concept of the 'railhead', an out-of-town station to which customers would drive, clearly ran the risk of inducing them to remain in their cars for the whole of their journey. However it was used positively to justify new stations, a significant innovation: Bristol Parkway, opened in 1972, was located on Bristol's periphery, close to the intersection of the M4 and M5. The concept was also used, less convincingly perhaps, to make a virtue out of necessity when, in 1973, Alfreton station was renamed 'Alfreton and Mansfield Parkway'.[2] Mansfield which is 8 miles from Alfreton, had lost its local services to Nottingham and this was intended to provide a better means of accessing long distance services than driving to Nottingham station. The parkway concept showed BR's willingness to promote the network and was indicative of an outward looking, resourceful and optimistic side to the corporate persona.

Government was willing to invest in London's commuter network and the politically important Southern Region received £220m in 1970, and further commitments to electrification followed: £35m in 1971 for the lines out of Moorgate and King's Cross to Royston (near Cambridge) via Welwyn and Hertford. However, as evidence of the restricted vision, not even London's routes were safe from closure. Despite his experience of rail-oriented strategic planning, Hall seemingly fell under the influence of the Railway Conversion League[3] and noted:

---

2   The station was in fact renamed 'Alfreton' in the 1990s, when Mansfield regained its train service.

3   A small group formed in the 1960s which argued for the closure of railways and their conversion to roads.

In some cases the motorways may use main-line railway tracks which are superfluous and no longer remunerative: the line out of Marylebone is an obvious example (1971,149).

The Public Service Obligation and rail freight grants

By the early 1970s it was clear that more support was needed for loss making passenger services than was being provided through the Section 39[4] mechanism of the 1968 Act. The economy was racked by inflation and Heath's government was using control over nationalised industries to limit rises in prices and incomes: in 1974 the BRB noted that costs rose by 33 per cent, but they were permitted to raise prices by only 16 per cent. The financial deficit continued a decade on from Beeching. A 'Rail Policy Review' was conducted by BR and the MoT and, although its conclusions were not published at the time, they were subsequently and were of great significance in setting out the principles underpinning railway policy:

a. the railway existed primarily for the purposes of the passenger system;
b. the standards and, therefore, the costs of track and signalling were determined primarily by the requirements of the passenger system;
c. in the light of a) and b), where freight shared facilities with the passenger business, it should pay only its avoidable costs;
d. on that basis, the freight business was capable (after a short transitional period) of achieving financial break-even without the aid of grant;
e. the passenger business as a whole, at anything like its then size, was incapable of breaking even;
f. the cost of the passenger system could not be reduced without service closures on a scale disproportionate to the expected savings;
g. grant should be paid for the passenger system and not on a service by service basis (DoT 1983, 8).

The 1974 Railway Act wrote-off a further £298m (1974 prices) of debt and empowered the government to pay future subsidy as a block grant. As by then the UK was a member of the European Community, the method of providing support had to conform to EEC law and took the form of a Direction imposing a 'Public Service Obligation' (PSO) which provided that:

> The British Railways Board shall, from 1 January 1975, operate their railway passenger system so as to provide a public service which is generally comparable with that provided at present ... (appendix B in DoT 1983).

---

4   This was on a short term, line by line basis.

Whereas this shows that rail freight was not a political priority, there was debate over the relative track costs of road and rail: government was sympathetic to the argument that rail was at a disadvantage and concerned about the environmental implications of growing lorry traffic. As a result, section 8 of the 1974 Act introduced 'freight facilities grants', which would be available for the development of rail infrastructure where it would transfer a measurable flow of lorry traffic to rail. An important feature of this mechanism was that it depended upon modal shift: in cases where a freight generating activity was granted planning permission and a condition was imposed limiting such movement to rail, then a grant would not be available because no modal shift could take place. Subsequently, this perverse incentive discouraged the explicit use of planning powers to facilitate modal shift.

A new transport white paper

A transport white paper was published in 1977 (DoT et al. 1977) reflecting government concerns about the rising cost of oil, erosion of the quality of life through road traffic, and the needs of non-car users. The government restated its commitment to rail[5] and identified the main line network's tasks (Table 7.1), but stated that it was not its role to be prescriptive about how different modes should be used.

Table 7.1 1977 White Paper: main tasks for the railways

a)	to continue as the major public transport carrier of long-distance passenger travel on a network of services connecting all the major centres of population;
b)	to continue and develop their function, which is essential to the industrial strategy, in carrying large flows of freight from siding to siding, especially heavy flows of bulk traffic such as coal and ores;
c)	to continue as a major carrier of people to and from work within London's vast area of work places and dormitories;
d)	to continue to provide under the Public Service Obligation and, where they are judged locally to be the right way to meet local needs, local stopping services in many parts of the country; and to provide also those services which are required under agreements with the Passenger Transport Executives within systems of public transport in the conurbations they serve. (DoT 1977, 46).

---

5   It was significant that this was still seen to be necessary.

Whereas it was expected that inter-city passenger and all freight services would be commercially viable, subsidy would be available for commuter and rural services. The most negative implications concerned freight:

> Rail can undoubtedly offer a highly competitive service on longer hauls and for movement direct from siding to siding. But it offers no real alternative for most of the goods that now go by road ... A substantial diversion of freight traffic from road to rail is not therefore immediately possible. Nor is it a sensible long-term aim (DoT et al. 1977, 39).

In order to reduce the reliance on transport, it was recognised that the basis of land development decisions would have to change:

> ... housing and employment have become increasingly separated. Larger hospitals, schools, offices and shops to serve wider areas have meant longer and often more difficult journeys (DoT et al. 1977, 7).

But this was not reinforced by commitment to more prescriptive land-use planning or by encouraging BR to capture new markets: the separation of the DoT from the DoE made this unlikely in any case. By contrast, despite the intention to reduce expenditure on road building, there was an intention to more closely integrate road planning with land-use and economic planning, and special mention was made of how institutional arrangements could facilitate this:

> The planning of road schemes must fit the wider economic and land-use plans in the regions, and it is the job of the joint Regional Offices of the Departments of Transport and the Environment to secure, with the local authorities and the Economic Planning Councils, that it does (DoT et al. 1977, 56).

The white paper identified geographical priorities for road building which contrasted significantly with the stance taken towards the railway network which was focused on underpinning existing services through subsidy, rather than improvement. The most significant references to the network were concerned with new procedures for closures which, in what appeared to be buck passing, would more closely involve local transport authorities (DoT et al. 1977, 21-23).

At this time there was also a wide ranging inquiry into lorries and their environmental impacts (Armitage 1980), which noted the effects of land-use change on demand for lorry transport:

> New industrial areas have developed with no rail access of any kind. Indeed modern industrial estates are often not linked to the railway ... There has been a bandwagon effect (Armitage 1980, 15).

The report considered a wide range of measures to ameliorate the growth of lorry traffic, one being using the planning system to influence the location of traffic generators. But there was little enthusiasm for this:

> Land use planning is a weak instrument for controlling the effects of lorries for reasons inherent in our planning system (Armitage 1980, 89).

Armitage did conclude though that structure plans and local plans[6] should consider freight transport issues, although there was no specific recommendation that this include maximising the opportunities for modal shift to rail. His recommendations with regard to rail were restricted to suggestions for widening the criteria for giving Section 8 grants.

Government planning guidance

Heath's government published a Manual on Development Plans (MHLG 1970) which emphasised that:

> In particular, the new system provides a means for the full integration of land use and transport planning throughout the process (MHLG 1970, 4).

The appendix contained indicative policies including suggestions on planning for rail: 'emphasis on rail', 'concentration of growth along rapid transit corridor', 'district shopping centre at suburban railway station', and 'facilities for modal interchange' (MHLG 1970, 71). Although this support was not reinforced by any further government publications, the importance of designing to minimise walking distances to bus stops[7] was emphasised and a quarter mile (400m) identified as a general guideline (DoE 1973). The only other significant publication with regard to neighbourhood design was a reaction against the car oriented layouts of the 1960s, but this focused on traffic calming rather than pedestrian access to public transport (DoE DoT 1977).[8]

---

6   Armitage noted that of the 1,600 or so local plans proposed by local planning authorities, work was in hand on only 350.

7   With hindsight it seems anomalous that this document did not embrace access to railway stations.

8   The other dominant planning concern in housing design at this time was poor elevational treatment by private builders and a loss of local identity: the Essex Design Guide was the precursor of many similar attempts to rectify this weakness (Essex County Council County Planning Department 1973).

Planning and the BR Property Board

During the early years of the new Property Board, planning policy was more supportive of the railway network than it had ever been, so how did the Property Board respond? The approach was termed:

> 'Optimum Management', a professionally based, prudent policy that combined sale, where it was seen to be in the best interests of the railway, with retention and development where long-term income and capital appreciation indicated a better return (Biddle 1990, 208).

Although this demonstrated strategic thinking, the underlying rationale was maximising income, not utilising the estate to promote ridership: where this happened, such as with regard to air space developments, the outcome was fortuitous. On these terms the Property Board was regarded as a success and, in 1975, became a self-accounting unit within the management structure, having yielded about £20 million a year. Lawrence realised that, without maintaining the supply of surplus land, it would be difficult to sustain this and he used his experience of the operating departments to persuade them to release property. The Board's confidence led it to launch what would eventually become its most successful project, the redevelopment of Liverpool Street station (Modern Railways 1975, 334-336).[9]

Urban regeneration: a new focus for planning policy

The economic crisis led to abandonment of the Channel Tunnel project in early 1975. In 1976, Chancellor of the Exchequer Dennis Healey made deep cuts in public spending in order to reduce the Public Sector Borrowing Requirement, and requested loans from the International Monetary Fund.[10] After years of expansion this introduced a new paradigm for the public sector; cash limits and budget cuts. The crisis had important ramifications for planning policy which had been predicated on growth. Although urban poverty had been rediscovered in the 1960s (Coates and Silburn 1970), the overriding mood had been optimistic. This changed as the economy turned down, population growth levelled off, and the shutters were brought down on public expenditure.[11] The policy focus turned towards the 'inner city problem' and what came to be known as 'urban regeneration'. Given the fact that inner city residents had typically been bus users, it was not to be expected that

---

9   It was hoped to make a start on this 25 acre (10.12 ha) mixed use scheme in 1978, although the onset of recession delayed this for nearly a decade.

10   Needlessly so he said later, with the benefit of hindsight (Healey 1990, 432-33).

11   This was initiated by Peter Shore's 'The party is over' speech in Manchester town hall (Shore 1976).

rail would feature strongly in any policy statement about the inner cities, except perhaps in London. What is more surprising is that 'Policy for the Inner Cities' (Secretary of State for the Environment et al. 1977) contained very few references at all to transport and, in the brief reference it did make, concluded that:

> The main practical requirement is likely to be for better and improved local roads and in some cases for better access to the primary road network (1977, 32).

This concerned the needs of industry rather than residents.[12]

The limits to road building: London's ringways

Buchanan inspired visions for cities began to encounter opposition once the public came to appreciate the scale of destruction necessary to accommodate the new roads and the intrusiveness of the finished product. The backlash came first in London as the draft Greater London Development Plan (GLDP) (GLC 1969) went to a public inquiry in 1970/71, chaired by Frank Layfield. As the implications of the four proposed 'ringways', which formed the core of the transport policies, became better understood, the protests grew stronger: it was estimated that 20,000 houses would have to be demolished and the total cost was put at £2 billion at 1972 prices. The opening of Westway in 1970 drew attention to the impacts: 22,000 objections to the GLDP were registered, most of them against the roads. Plowden (1972) articulated the case against 'predict and provide', pointing out that facilitating public transport had implications for land-use policy: central London was the area of maximum accessibility and activity generators should be located there, as opposed to the GLC's strategy for the development of 'strategic centres' on the ringways. The furore meant that urban transport policy moved into the glare of the political arena[13] wherein the policies of elected politicians were driven by campaigning community groups: by the 1973 GLC elections both Labour and Liberal parties were standing on an 'anti-ringway' ticket and, with a Labour victory, they were scrapped.[14]

---

12   This failure to understand the importance of access to jobs and services for deprived communities, and the failure to consider the mobility provided by public transport as a prerequisite of regeneration, came to be seen as a major policy weakness (Lawless and Gore 1999).

13   Transport 2000 was formed in 1973 as a nationally oriented anti-road building lobby group: it changed its name to Campaign for Better Transport in 2007.

14   Hall (1982, 56-86) commented on how the ringways saga characterised a fundamental shift in transport planning for London, away from the Abercrombie-Buchanan infrastructure based grand plan, towards a more complex, community driven approach: public transport and walking became more important.

This had positive implications for rail as the government set up a London Rail Study which involved the DoT, the GLC, London Transport (now under GLC control), and BR. The results, published in 1975, put forward three options for capital investment ranging from £2000 million to £2400 million, with a figure of £1400 million being the minimum for renewals. The Victoria Line had been completed through to Brixton in 1971, when work started on the proposed Fleet Line (later renamed the Jubilee Line) from Baker Street to Charing Cross, and on extension of the Piccadilly line to Heathrow.[15] The London Rail Study recommended that the Fleet Line be extended eastwards through Docklands to Thamesmead: Docklands was already in decline and the need to improve its accessibility from central London was understood. However, these aspirations were quickly forgotten in the crisis of the mid-1970s.

The planning response

The research underpinning the GLDP (GLC 1971) included a sophisticated analysis of London's railway network. This showed that: railways covered 3 per cent of Greater London's area; there was on average one route mile for every square mile; there were 566 stations on the BR and LT networks; and that less than 6 per cent of London's population lived more than a mile from a station. Maps of rail accessibility were produced along with those showing passenger interchanges and freight facilities: there was a good understanding of the strengths and weaknesses of the network and of the importance of manipulating density in both residential and employment areas. The amended GLDP utilised this to develop rail-oriented policies: as a point of departure it considered that a feature of the new structure for London:

> ... will be that a larger part of total activity, and a high proportion of all new activity, should be located in close relation to transportation facilities, particularly the underground and railway networks (GLC 1976, 11).

The Plan identified 'preferred locations' to which office and industrial developments would be steered, with rail access a significant part of their rationale. 28 strategic town centres were identified for retail development, 25 of which were also preferred office locations, and all except two were rail connected, the majority having been previously identified as rail passenger interchanges (Table 7.2). The Plan recognised the effectiveness of plot ratio[16] as a 'standard control' over development with particular relevance for transport, as well as the need to restrict private non-residential parking in major employment centres (Table 7.3). It also

---

15   It should be noted that this was not an extension to the main line system as previously envisaged by Abercrombie and British Railways.

16   The ratio of floor area to site area.

contained general policies with regard to improving rail services. Surprisingly one proposal from the ringway era survived and, unfortunately, its success came to serve as a model for others to follow:

> In addition to the Strategic Centres, Brent Cross is planned to be a large shopping centre for people who wish to use their cars for shopping (GLC 1976, 81).

Production of statutory local plans was limited nationally and, in London, only six were formally adopted by 1980 (Simmie 1994, 119): subsequently progress was swifter. With rail carrying the majority of the City's 300,000 working population, it is hardly surprising that the City of London Local Plan (Corporation of London 1986) should have been supportive of rail projects and developments at rail interchanges, along with using plot ratio to manipulate density patterns. More surprising, perhaps, is the fact that Croydon utilised plot ratio too, accepted higher values 'in the vicinity of east Croydon station and West Croydon bus and railway stations' (London Borough of Croydon 1982, 12), and adopted the GLC's recommended parking standards for shops and offices in Central Croydon. One of the most thoroughly developed rail-oriented local plans was Hammersmith and Fulham's (London Borough of Hammersmith and Fulham 1988): this sought to improve existing and create new services and stations, and there was a rail freight section too which sought to maximise the opportunities to retain/develop terminals. The plan contained an interchange strategy and used measures of public transport accessibility to underpin its land-use strategy. Together these plans showed that, despite the government's ideology, the reality in London was that road traffic growth could not be accommodated and rail access had to be developed as an alternative.

Table 7.2 Greater London Development Plan: rail accessibility and interchange facilities at preferred office locations and strategic centres

Strategic centre[1]	Rail services[2]	Strategic centre	Rail services
Barking*	BR,U, BUS	Kingsland*	BR
Bexleyheath*	BR	Kingston*	BR, BUS
Brixton*	BR,BUS[3]	Lewisham*	BR, BUS
Bromley*	BR,BUS	Peckham*	BR, BUS
Clapham Junction*	BR, BUS	Richmond*	BR, U, BUS
Croydon*	BR, BUS	Romford*	BR, BUS
Ealing Broadway*/ West Ealing	BR, U, BUS	Stratford*	BR, U
Enfield*	BR, BUS, CARP	Sutton*	BR, BUS
Hammersmith*	U, BUS	Uxbridge*	BR, BUS, CARP
Harrow*	BR, U, BUS, CARP	Walthamstow*	BR, BUS[3]
Holloway	BUS	Wembley	BR, U, BUS
Hounslow*	BR, U, BUS	Wimbledon*	BR, U, BUS, CARP
Ilford*	BR, BUS	Wood Green*	U, BUS
Kilburn	BUS	Woolwich*	BR, BUS

Notes: [1] Source – Greater London Plan 1976; [2] Source – where more than one mode is cited the information on interchanges is from Greater London Development Plan: Report of Studies 1971; [3] Brixton and Walthamstow became the termini of the Victoria line completed in 1971.
* Preferred office location

Table 7.3 Greater London Development Plan: car parking standards for office and shop developments

Area	Standard
Central area of London	1 space per 12,000 sq ft of floor space
Inner Ring	1 space per 8,000 sq ft of floor space
More important suburban centres	1 space per 5,000 sq ft of floor space
remainder of outer London	1 space per 2,000 sq ft of floor space

Source: Greater London Development Plan 1976, table 4.

The provincial conurbations

The anti-roads backlash was replicated in other conurbations, albeit more slowly, and many opponents felt public involvement in transport policy was not welcomed by the DoT: this stimulated the birth of the 'direct action' movement (Tyme 1978). Opposition to road building provided a receptive context within which to develop the case for rail: the creation of the PTA/PTEs and the new strategic metropolitan county councils provided the means through which a closer relationship between land-use and railway planning could be promoted. The result was that the road-oriented land-use/transportation planning techniques of the 1960s, were developed to include the option of investment in local railway networks.

The more structured approach to local government financial planning which had developed in the late 1960s[17] led to the introduction, through the 1972 Local Government Act, of annual submissions by county councils of Transport Policies and Programmes (TPPs). These were bidding documents specifying transport planning objectives and priorities against which central government made a financial settlement, largely through the Transport Supplementary Grant. However, because they were prepared by highway authorities, TPPs tended to reinforce the relationship between local authorities and road building, so the new structures did not guarantee pro-rail strategies. Nevertheless, there developed several distinctive relationships between the PTA/PTEs and the railway system which can be summarised using three models. The first, where there was the most extensive use of the new powers, was in Tyne and Wear. In one of its first policy statements the PTE demonstrated its awareness of the importance of land-use planning to the ability of public transport to provide for various trip requirements:

> Town Planning
> The ability of public transport to cater economically and attractively for journeys
> for all or any of these purposes depends upon:
> a) How the various centres of activity are grouped in relation to one another.
> b) The ease with which it can move directly and quickly between them.
> c) The accessibility of stopping places to either end of the journey
> (Tyneside PTE 1970, para.7.17).

A subsequent report noted the various failings of existing rail services, particularly the fact they were run-down[18] and served central Newcastle poorly (Voorhees and Buchanan 1973). Under the 1973 Tyneside Metropolitan Railway Act, the PTE proposed a light metro system linking the former north and south Tyneside networks by tunnels under Newcastle city centre. The strategy was founded on clearly identified objectives and the PTE took over ownership of the local lines

---

17   Utilising American 'Planning-Programme-Budgeting Systems' (PPBS) developed by Robert McNamara's Department of Defence for running the Vietnam war.

18   Instead of re-investing, BR had de-electrified the local routes in the 1960s.

from BR. Overall it was: 'the first truly comprehensive approach to transport provision in any major British city' (Hamilton and Potter 1985).

In the second model the PTEs relied on a co-operative relationship with BR to develop ambitious improvement plans for the BR network. In Strathclyde, before the PTA/PTE was created, reports of the Greater Glasgow Transportation Study (GGTS) (1968, 1971) had recommended that a priority should be the re-opening of the Glasgow Central Low Level route (the Argyle Line closed in 1964): the protracted development of investment cases to submit to government for the re-opening of lines closed during the Beeching era was something that came to characterise the period. However the GGTS also favoured extensive motorway building and an early version of the Study (GGTS 1968) recommended completion of inner, middle and outer ring roads around Glasgow with seven radials. Subsequent Study outputs noted that there had been a levelling off in rail ridership, despite the success of the 1960s electrification, but that:

> Greater use might be made of some existing electrified rail services, and those yet to be electrified, by the policies involving changes in land uses and location of planning projects being more integrated with the detailed usage of the rail network (GGTS 1974, iv).

The Greater Glasgow PTE, the short-lived forerunner of Strathclyde PTE, submitted a Clyderail proposal to the Scottish Office: this included the Argyle Line and another scheme (the St John's Link) to connect the line from Paisley over the Clyde into Queen Street Low Level. The investment case was broadly based being built on tackling multiple deprivation, improving central area accessibility, encouraging regeneration, and aiding the control of road traffic growth (GGPTE 1974, section 4.1).

The continuing support for rail services by Strathclyde PTE was not reflected to any great extent in planning policy. Although background work (Colin Buchanan and Partners 1974) noted that between 1965–72 £36m had been invested in the Clydeside network and ridership had increased by 5 per cent, it did not specifically address the question of how development might be managed to utilise the railway network and no special mention of Glasgow city centre was made with regard to any of its assets, let alone its accessibility by rail. The subsequent Strathclyde Structure Plan (Strathclyde Regional Council 1979) focused on economic regeneration, rehabilitation of inner areas and peripheral estates, and the supply of land for housing and industry. Whilst the role of rail in providing access to central Glasgow was recognised (p47), certain lines were earmarked for improvement and/or re-opening (Schedule 2B), and a list of urban centres was produced to which public transport access would be improved, there was no development of a more sophisticated land-use/transportation strategy of the sort used in the GLDP. The railway schemes listed in the Plan were substantially overshadowed by the plans for road construction.

Another example of the second model was Merseyside: the Merseyside Area Land Use/Transportation Study (MALTS) (City of Liverpool et al. 1969) produced by a broad grouping of interested parties,[19] recommended construction of a new road hierarchy over a 25 year period. However, it was accepted that this would not cater for all traffic needs and it was also necessary to improve public transport. Beeching had recommended closure of the Liverpool (Exchange)-Southport commuter line and this had come as a shock locally and triggered ideas for improvements as an alternative, so extension of Liverpool's underground railway system had been discussed for several years (Mugliston 1964). A Steering Committee on Merseyside Traffic and Transport had been set up in 1962 of which BR was a member. MALTS recommended investment in the 'Loop and Link' tunnelling project under Liverpool city centre. This would create a turn back loop for the Mersey railway which would also give access to Lime Street station and link the commuter routes which had terminated at Exchange and Central stations, respectively on the north and south sides of the city centre, by a link, also in tunnel, under the city centre. MALTS also had quite a lot to say about integration between land-use and public transport services, as shown in Table 7.4. This was one of the most fully articulated policy statements of the period and could have formed the basis of a sophisticated planning agenda, applicable in Liverpool and elsewhere.

The West Midlands was an example of the third PTA/PTE model where, initially, there were only very limited plans for the network. The transportation study initiated in 1963 concluded that the cost of building roads to accommodate projected traffic levels would be too high and a more balanced approach was necessary (Freeman, Fox, Wilbur Smith and Associates 1968). By 1972 the West Midlands PTE (WMPTE) had identified local rail services to be retained and developed in eight corridors, and had a strategy for improvements to station accessibility, with different proposals for those in the suburbs and town/city centres (WMPTE 1972). Analysis of traffic potential noted developments in rail corridors: in particular that the city council's housing developments at Chelmsley Wood and Kingshurst, which housed 60,000 people, were not rail accessible, but that the site proposed for the National Exhibition Centre had rail potential, as did the route to Redditch new town. This illustrated how the PTEs were committed to their *local* network and were able to consider, in *detail*, how it could be integrated with patterns of land development. By 1972 Birmingham Snow Hill station, rebuilt as a great train shed late as 1912, was already closed and, although this plan contained

---

19   As an illustration of the unwieldy institutional structure of local government before the 1972 Local Government Act came into force, these included: the City of Liverpool and the County Boroughs of Birkenhead, Bootle, and Wallasey; Cheshire and Lancashire County Councils; Bebington and Crosby Borough Councils; Huyton-with-Roby, Kirkby and Litherland Urban District Councils; Whiston Rural District Council; the Mersey Tunnel Joint Committee; the Mersey Docks and Harbour Board; the Ministry of Transport; the Ministry of Housing and Local Government; the British Railways Board; Crossville Motor Services Ltd. and Ribble Motor Services Ltd.

no specific reference to it, it did vaguely propose new tunnels under the city centre and electrification of much of the local network, although these did not emerge as serious proposals at this time.

Table 7.4 Merseyside Area Land Use/Transportation Study: the layout of communities

	In the layout of communities serious study should be given to:
a)	The inter-relationship of buildings and roads so that as many places of residence and work as possible lie within five to seven minutes walk – about five to six hundred yards – of roads suitable for the through movement of buses.
b)	The layout of through roads in a way which will not detract from the overall operating speed of buses.
c)	The need to permit as much medium and high income residential development as practical within reasonable walking distance of suburban railway stations.
d)	The importance of permitting the greatest practical concentration of employment around railway stations in areas to which it is economical to carry public transport passengers by rail.
e)	The need for entrances to railway stations to be located in a way which will place as many people as possible within convenient walking distance. In practice this could mean introducing entrances at both ends of the station.
f)	The need to make it possible for people to reach main through roads as quickly as possible; this could mean introducing "short cuts" to save time consuming walks to the end of residential streets.

Source: (City of Liverpool et al. 1969, 34).

In the West Midlands three alternative draft structure plan strategies were developed, ranging from one which was decentralised and market oriented, to one which sought to concentrate all activity into the inner city. There was a lot of internal debate about transport policies and the wisdom of relying on the private car at a time of energy shortage, despite the controlling party's commitment to cutting public transport subsidies (Struthers and Brindell, 1983, 79). Perhaps inevitably, the adopted strategy (West Midlands County Council 1982) embraced something from both extremes, a commitment to public sector investment in the inner city, along with provision of suburban sites for private sector housing and employment. Significantly there was concern that:

> Many participants (at the examination in public in 1981) considered the plan to be biased towards roads rather than public transport, particularly the railways (Struthers and Brindell 1983, 80 and 85).

Whatever its shortcomings, this plan was notable for its very specific policies for re-opening railways and safeguarding disused trackbeds[20] as set out in Table 7.5. This was a significant issue in many areas, given the growing evidence that closures had gone too far. These strategic policies were followed through by the Birmingham Central Area Local Plan (City of Birmingham Council et al. 1984) as shown in Table 7.6, and this also referred to the use of development briefs for detail planning, something which Birmingham and other authorities used very successfully, as will be shown in the next chapter. Together these policies made up a very coherent policy framework, but it is very significant that this was project based and primarily concerned with reopening a closed system, rather than furthering the utility of an existing one through a more far reaching land-use strategy.

Table 7.5 West Midlands County Structure Plan 1982: rail policies

Policy Tp 3: The restoration of the Birmingham to Stourbridge passenger services via Snow Hill will be commenced before 1991, and services now running to Moor Street station will be linked through the Snow Hill Tunnel to the Stourbridge services.
Policy Tp 4: Safeguarding of Railway Routes.
The railway formation of the former Wolverhampton Low Level line between Wolverhampton and Handsworth junction will be safeguarded for the possible re-introduction of passenger services beyond the plan period (to 1991).
Policy Tp 6: Public Transport and Development.
The design and layout of re-development or new development will ensure the maximum accessibility of homes, workplaces and shopping to public transport.
Policy H 8: Housing Densities.
New housing, including higher density development (between 35 and 45 dwellings per hectare in most cases), will in general be encouraged in appropriate locations, particularly in and close to city and town centres and close to railway stations.

---

20   The former 11 constituent strategic planning authorities of the West Midlands County had produced draft structure plans prior to 1974 and these disused trackbeds had been protected by them.

Table 7.6 Birmingham Central Area Local Plan 1984: rail policies

		Proposal 4: Development of the Snow Hill Station Site.
a)		The City Council wish to see the Snow Hill Station site developed in the following manner:
	i)	On the Colmore Row frontage: offices.
	ii)	Within the site: offices, multi-storey car parking, leisure facilities, hotel, housing and ancillary community facilities.
	iii)	Underneath the above elements: a railway station.
	iv)	To the Snow Hill-Queensway frontage, bus loading and unloading facilities.
b)		The above elements will be defined in more detail together with the arrangements for vehicular and pedestrian access in a development brief to be prepared by the City Council in conjunction with the West Midlands County Council and the West Midlands Passenger Transport Executive.
		Proposal TR 2: Passenger rail services to the city centre will be improved by:
a)		the conversion of Moor Street to a through station;
b)		the re-opening of the underground rail link between Moor street and Snow Hill;
c)		construction of a new station at Snow Hill;
d)		re-opening of the rail link between Snow Hill and Smethwick West.

Railway policy under Thatcher

An important component of what came to be called 'Thatcherism' (Thornley, 1991) was populism and one way in which this was expressed was through support for the personal freedom offered by private motoring and an underlying dislike of public transport, which was seen as the transport of last resort for those who couldn't afford to buy a car. Several of Margaret Thatcher's closest advisors were known to be hostile to BR and this included Ian Gow, who became her Parliamentary Private Secretary, and three external advisors, Professor Alan Walters, Alfred Goldman and Alfred Sherman; 'All three, with Gow, are noted for their dislike of British Rail and for their determination to minimise its role in the British economy' (Bagwell 1984, 2). An early indication of the new politics was the reference, in 1980,[21] of BR's London and South East commuter services

---

21   The Government's monetarist approach to economic management triggered a severe depression which, of course, led to a rapid decline in demand for railway transport for passengers and freight. The overall mood was sombre and Peter Parker's opening

to the Monopolies and Mergers Commission.[22] The BRB, under the chairmanship of Sir Peter Parker (1976–82), had been prescient as it produced *'The Commuter's Charter'* (BRB 1981): this marked recognition that BR had to relate directly to its customers for political support rather than relying on government ministers. The document highlighted the relatively low levels of subsidy enjoyed by BR and London Transport as compared with other countries and the fact that, if commuter services were to be improved significantly, the costs would lead to unacceptably high fare levels. The community benefits from a well used railway were cleverly described as 'invisible earnings' (BRB 1981, 1), a contemporary term being used to describe the benefits brought to GB plc by financial services in the City of London to offset concerns about the decline of manufacturing exports, and these were used to justify bridging the funding gap by subsidy. Several ways in which this could be done were highlighted: taxes on businesses, including Parisian style payroll taxes; sales taxes; tourist taxes; road user taxes; and local authority contributions. The document did not refer to taxation on betterment from property development[23] or to more focused exploitation of BR's property portfolio. Despite the hostility of government, BR had some friends in parliament: in 1981 the 'Speller amendment' to the 1962 Transport Act allowed BR to introduce service improvements on an experimental basis; if they subsequently failed to become viable they could be withdrawn without invoking the statutory closure procedures. This removed a significant disincentive to service and station development, often involving the restoration of service withdrawn post-Beeching.

The 'Review of Main Line Electrification' (DoT BR 1981) considered a range of options from a base case of ongoing schemes, through to one which included most of the network. Analysis showed that all, except the smallest, gave a rate of return of at least 11 per cent, a remarkable outcome. The report concluded that:

> ... it would take an unlikely combination of adverse factors to undermine entirely the prospect that a programme of main line electrification would be financially worthwhile; i.e. earn a return of at least 7% (DoT BRB 1981, 2).

---

comments in the 1980 annual report were: '1980 was a grim demanding year for British Rail' (BRB 1980, 7).

22   In welcoming the findings of the inquiry in the 1980 annual report, Peter Parker stated that: 'We seek closer co-operation with our operating partners in London Transport and the GLC and twelve county authorities in the area' (BRB 1980, 9). This was evidence of the growing awareness of the need for close working with local government which had positive implications for the railway-planning interface.

23   Advisedly so, as one of the first legislative actions of Mrs Thatcher's government was to rescind the 1975 Community Land Act which had been the previous Labour Government's abortive attempt at giving local authorities a lead role in the development process through land acquisition and access to betterment.

This seven per cent rate of return was picked up and applied by the DoT as a template against *all* subsequent investment: this came to be seen by critics as one of the major sources of bias against railway investment, given the use of social cost-benefit analysis to justify investment in road schemes, with the notional value of savings in drivers' time as being the prime justification for new roads. The benefits of electrification were defined as lower maintenance costs and increased ridership, but the Review referred to a submission from Transport 2000 as to the possible implications for the locational decisions of the railway's customers, and that changes producing increases in rateable values could be seen as an external benefit which should be considered. However the Review's authors considered that:

> There is insufficient evidence of the relationship between a programme of main line electrification and future land use or settlement patterns to enable a view to be taken (DoT BRB 1981, 77).

What is striking about this is that the question was not raised as to whether land-use planning should be used to deliver these. The discussion was couched in terms of the response of businesses to electrification, as though this occurred in a vacuum which public policy was unable to influence: here was evidence of the effect of the government's market led approach.

BR was affected by privatisation at this time and the hotels and Sealink passed quickly into the private sector.[24] But, for wholesale privatisation, the government's priorities were the highly profitable utilities. However, in a remarkably prescient comment, Bonavia noted that:

> ... in 1983 the railway achieved a surplus of £64 millions before interest charges, etc, after grants totalling £934 millions from central Government and local authorities, and £24 millions grants for special purposes. If – and it is a big 'if' – there was a guarantee that grants at this level would continue, might not a purchaser be interested in taking over the railway? (1985, 130).

The Serpell Report

Although privatisation was not favoured, the continued dominance of the Treasury view was illustrated in 1982 when the Secretary of State for Transport, David Howell, set up a committee with the following terms of reference:

> To examine the finances of the railway and associated operations, in the light of all relevant considerations, and to report on options for alternative policies,

---

24 As did the National Freight Corporation, the road transport company formed under the 1968 Act (McLachlan 1983).

and their related objectives, designed to secure improved financial results in an efficiently run railway in Great Britain over the next 20 years (DoT 1983, 1).

Initially the BRB welcomed this review as they expected to benefit from it, but this mood changed when the Chair was named as Sir David Serpell, a rail hawk who had served under Marples. Given the totemic status of public expenditure to the New Conservatives, Serpell's investigations looked very threatening. He considered that there was a reasonable prospect that the freight business could break even by the mid-1980s, but advised that the Board should be ready to withdraw promptly from unprofitable traffics (DoT 1983, 24). Serpell showed the rising dependence of passenger services on grant and the growing disparity between expected performance, as set out in BR plans, and outcomes. In particular the low load factor of the Provincial services was noted, 20 per cent, and reference made to the potential to make savings by bus substitution. Serpell set out what he saw as general weaknesses in the Board's financial planning (DoT 1983, 57) and considered the options for the future, illustrated by maps of much reduced networks. Predictably his major conclusion was:

> that reductions in the size of the network will be required if the level of financial support for the railway is to be lowered substantially … (1983, 85).

The shrewdness of the BRB's management strategy under Bob Reid and the positive relationship which developed between him and Nicholas Ridley, was reflected in the fact that Serpell was quickly forgotten: a significant factor was the maps which, because of the stark message they transmitted so clearly, produced a political backlash as it raised the folklore spectre of Beeching. The government stated that it was not seeking major route closures, but accelerated the rate at which the PSO grant was to be reduced,[25] and asked the Board for its views on replacement bus services. A further fillip was given by the announcement in 1984 of electrification of the ECML.[26] In the same year further approvals included extensions of existing electrified routes to Hastings, Cambridge and Norwich, a very positive outcome for the BRB.

---

25   When Nicholas Ridley became Secretary of State for Transport he brought forward the reduction of PSO from £700m to £635m from 1988 to 1986: the targets for BR implied retention of roughly the same size of railway with a 25% cut in central Government funding (BRB 1983).

26   The £306m investment was to be funded internally, so all BR had secured was permission to spend its own funds, which was indicative of how politically hamstrung it was.

The continuing drive for rationalisation of the railway network

The continuing strength of the anti-rail culture within government was reflected in publication of a report looking into the potential for conversion into roads of some of London's rail routes (Foster Posner and Sherman 1984). This considered orbital routes such as the North London Line (Richmond-Willesden-Stratford), and the Marylebone-Aylesbury radial route. The report noted the narrowness of rail alignments compared to roads and the only route subject to further consideration was the Marylebone line, as a route for National Express coaches. BR went as far as bringing Marylebone forward for closure, but the idea ran into problems over headroom limitations. The fact that such ideas received official encouragement, rather than the lines being improved as railways, highlighted the government's minimalist stance.

There was further evidence of this with regard to rural lines: bus-substitution was pursued by BR in response to Government pressure and various lines were put forward as candidates. Closures continued to be brought forward too, the most notable being the Settle-Carlisle line, one of the remaining duplicate trunk routes. This saga which began in 1981, provided volumes of evidence for conspiracy theorists who, since the days of Beeching, saw BR's senior managers as only too willing to close lines to please their political masters. However, the case also showed the changed political context of rail policy making and the potential to use the institutional structure to influence BR and Government (Towler 1990). Closure was formerly proposed in 1983 and eventually withdrawn in 1989. The final irony was that Ron Cotton, the manager briefed to run the line down, worked with local authorities, businesses, communities and pressure groups to double ridership. As part of the campaign, the local authorities formed a Joint Steering Group to develop the case for retention and practical policies to reinforce the role of the railway in its hinterland. The whole of the alignment was declared a conservation area, so that even if the line was closed, the trackbed and structures[27] would be retained: even this would be a notable advance on the closure process of the 1960s and 1970s.

The Channel Tunnel

The renewal of interest in the Channel Tunnel was a surprising development. President Mitterand and Mrs Thatcher developed a very co-operative relationship and the outcome was the 1987 Channel Tunnel Act: the political compromise was that the tunnel would only be funded by private sector finance. Thatcher's motivation was showcasing the rebirth of British entrepreneurial capitalism and she and Ridley had preferred a 'drive through' option, although this proved too

---

27   The elevated and rugged country through which the route passes means that it is characterised by having many tunnels, embankments and viaducts, typified by Ribblehead Viaduct which was adopted as a campaign logo.

risky. The political differences between Mitterand and Thatcher were reflected in their respective approaches to the rail networks which would serve the Tunnel. In France there was a rapid follow through with state commitment to build TGV-Nord from Paris to Calais, with a major interchange and associated commercial development at EuroLille. Such investment was not on the agenda in the UK: despite the potential boost to passenger services which would result from the link with European high speed systems, the government's ideological straitjacket constrained BR's scope to develop a 'vision' for the Tunnel. Harman (1989, 647) criticised the industry for this and Serplan was generally critical of the Government's failure to introduce effective regional planning for the South East and to incorporate rail planning within this:

> This opportunity must be seized: at the time this report is being prepared, there is no evidence that the Government or British Rail are showing the required foresight (Serplan 1989).

Nevertheless, section 40 of the Act which instructed BR to consult with regional bodies about Tunnel rail services, acted as a stimulus to the growing interest in rail amongst local planning authorities throughout the country, as well as private sector interests. Contemporary research showed that, with regard to freight traffic, these local interest groups were particularly concerned that:

> the requirement for a minimum 8%[28] per annum return will severely limit the implementation of regional recommendations for investment … will lessen rail's market share, and could have an adverse effect on regional economies (Farrington et al. 1990, 143).

The limitations of the UK's vertical loading gauge were becoming more apparent at this time as maritime containers were increasing in size, and the proposed link with Continental railways served to bring the issue into sharper focus. But no action was proposed as the government had made it clear that support for the Tunnel project would not translate into plans for major public investment in the domestic railway network.

Deregulation of planning and its limits: the green belt battle

The Conservative's *laissez-faire* approach to planning was reinforced by the fact that 43 per cent of their MP's had links with property interests (Healey et al. 1988). As well as initiating UDAs and EZs, the 1980 Local Government, Planning and Land Act introduced Land Registers, lists of publicly owned vacant sites, and

---

28   This was 1 per cent above the 7 per cent minimum rate of return cited in the main line electrification report, showing a further tightening of the Treasury constraints.

forced public bodies to place this land on the market. This bolstered attempts by the Property Board to dispose of land quickly and was a significant push towards utilising it for development which would yield short term financial returns, rather than securing uses which would utilise the railway network.[29] This was followed by the creation of EZs, eleven in 1981 with a further fourteen in 1983–84.

But it was not all plain sailing for the government: in 1983 they signalled their intention to relax green belt controls which provoked opposition from a united front of environmental groups and Labour and Tory controlled local government bodies. In parliament the government was opposed by over sixty Tory MPs[30] and the pressure forced them to back down and issue a revised circular re-affirming commitment to green belts, using this to demonstrate their green credentials. This was a pity as there were good planning reasons to reconsider green belt policy, not the least of which was its effect of stimulating demand for commuting by car. Green belts also sterilised land alongside railway lines, particularly around stations, which could have been developed for rail served settlements: all too often such stations had already been closed owing to lack of passengers. Despite this setback, the government pressed on with its deregulatory agenda which was embodied in the titles used for subsequent white papers: '*Lifting the Burden*' and '*Building Businesses Not Barriers*' (DoE 1985, 1986). The implications were that developers should only be refused planning permission where development 'would cause demonstrable harm to interests of acknowledged importance' (DoE 1986, 21): the policies to focus major commercial developments in town and city centres built into the first generation of structure plans were being ignored.

As the economy boomed growth was concentrated in the broader South East region, especially along motorway corridors such as the M1, M4 and the M11: 'Sunbelt Britain' (Breheny et al. 1989). This phenomenon was ascribed to four factors, one of which was:

> … a major concentration of producer services activity largely as a result of the decentralisation of activity from central London to free-standing towns and cities within a radius of about 150km of the metropolitan area (Mason et al. in Breheny et al. 1989, 57).

This suggested to the government that the markets for light industrial and office buildings were converging with firms requiring a new type of flexible, high quality building (Henneberry 1988). Debate focused on the impact of the Use Classes Order (DoE 1972) in requiring planning permission to change the use of such

---

29   The government did not take any more radical steps to create a freer market in land as suggested by Chisholm and Kivell (1987), presumably because their suggestions would impact negatively on private sector interests.

30   The total area of green belts had increased significantly since the mid-1970s as articulate residents realised it could be used to protect their environment and maintain property values: most such residents had Tory MPs (Elson 1986).

buildings and this produced a revised document which created the overarching B1 Business class (DoE 1987, 3), which formally freed large, speculative, office developments from restrictive locational policies (Haywood 1996). In the buoyant market of the late 1980s, this meant that the tremendous pressures in all the major conurbations for out-of-centre office developments were irresistible. The advantage to developers was the use of cheap land for high value development, with easy access to the major road network and abundant on-site parking as the marketing attractions. Contemporary research in the USA showed the likely outcomes (Cervero 1984a): the implications for use of the railway network were very negative.

London: the Docklands debacle and the impact of Network South East

The promotion of major urban rail projects had ended with the mid-1970s financial crisis, and the cost overrun by the Tyne and Wear Metro reminded government of the financial risks. It was surprising therefore that they should have supported the introduction of a new form of rail transport into London, namely light rail. Promotion of Docklands regeneration meant that, because its inaccessibility was seen as a barrier to private investment (LDDC 1983), it was necessary to invest in some sort of public transport system and a segregated rail system was the only practical alternative. But the government would only fund a low cost solution so, in 1982, they agreed to provide £77 million for the Docklands Light Railway (DLR), a low capacity system capable of carrying 8000 passengers per hour, which would run between Tower Bridge and the Isle of Dogs, with a link to Stratford where there would be interchange with BR's Essex commuter services and the Central Line of the Underground.

There was no overall land-use/transportation strategy for Docklands and the government had no reservations about encouraging the step change in the scale of development envisaged by the Canary Wharf scheme, associated with developers Olympia and York. This comprised 1 million square metres (10,764,000 sq ft) of development on about 30 hectares (70 acres) of land and led to the estimated number of jobs on the Isle of Dogs increasing from 25,000 to 65,000, generating a commuter flow which could not be serviced by the DLR. What followed was a gradual shift in government policy in response to the transport problems the new developments were creating. Further investment in the DLR was committed, in partnership with Olympia and York, to increase the capacity to 15,000 passengers per hour[31] and to provide a link to the City by tunnelling to Bank. Eventually, in 1993, the government approved construction of the Jubilee Line extension which could carry 24,000 passengers per hour in each direction (Willis 1997). The disregard in Docklands for integration between land development and transport was

---

31 This involved doubling train lengths and extending station platforms.

widely criticised as the most striking example of the failure of the government's *laissez-faire* approach (Brownhill 1990; Church 1990; Simmie 1994).

Rail traffic volumes closely follow the economic cycle and the late 1980s boom coincided with the development of favourable institutional arrangements as set out in Chapter 6. In addition, there was growing concern over road traffic congestion and pollution. The costs of congestion were used by the road lobby to justify further development of the trunk road network (British Roads Federation 1987) and concern was deepened by publication of revised National Road Traffic Forecasts (DoT 1989a) which projected increases in traffic over 1988 levels of between 83 and 142 per cent by 2025. The government responded by announcing a greatly expanded road building programme (DoT 1989b). Despite this, the concerns over road traffic provided an opportunity to argue the case for rail and there was widespread development of schemes to improve passenger services, which were usually incorporated within development plans and other planning policy documents.

London was a prime example: despite decentralisation, Central London's economy grew rapidly and this had profound transport impacts. Chris Green[32] (1989) demonstrated that although commuting into Central London increased by 7 per cent between 1985–88, the numbers travelling by road actually decreased, whilst those travelling by Network South East and the Underground increased by 16.7 per cent and 12.9 per cent respectively. For 14 years from 1970, rail commuting into London had declined, but the 1988 total was the highest ever recorded. The Central London Rail Study (DoT et al. 1989) was jointly produced by Network South East, London Regional Transport, London Underground and the DoT and contained a range of proposals for massive investment. These included East-West and North-South Cross Rail, and improvements to the recently introduced Thameslink system (see Chapter 8).[33] Green used estimates of employment growth to argue for massive investment which included a new generation of EMUs and DMUs, to be branded as 'Networkers', and investment in neglected routes such as those serving Marylebone[34] and the London Tilbury and Southend line. He also proposed development of services to Stansted and Heathrow airports, and major projects such as the Cross Rail routes and use of the proposed Channel Tunnel Main Line from King's Cross for express commuter services.

---

32 The transfer of Chris Green from ScotRail to become the head of Network South East put in place a politically astute manager who was alert to the impacts of property development. Like Gerald Fiennes, Green was one of the few BR managers to emerge from the anonymity of public service.

33 These schemes picked up on the themes of the wartime plans as they would enable passengers on the main line railways to reach destinations in Central London without changing to the Underground, as well as offering rapid journeys across London.

34 After years of closure threats, the Chiltern line was subject to a 'total route modernisation' plan which included new trains, new signalling and station improvements.

The provincial conurbations in the 1980s

In Glasgow, implementation of the Argyle line project, followed by upgrading of the underground system, the Subway, produced an escalation in costs for Strathclyde PTE, exacerbated by falling ridership associated with the recession. The PTE reported that revenue as a percentage of costs had fallen from 62 per cent in 1977 to 43 per cent in 1983 (Strathclyde Transport and BR Scottish Region 1983). So, even this pro-rail PTE had to introduce a cost cutting strategy which included driver-only operation, the 'Basic Modern Station' concept which replaced staff with ticket machines, closure of the Paisley Canal line, and thinning of the timetable elsewhere. The Section 20 network was in crisis and there was a need for investment and reduced operating costs: the alternative was a steady run down on all but the most highly used lines. As a symbol of its commitment to rail, even during this difficult period the PTE managed to maintain its capital programme with the proposed electrification of the route out from Paisley to Ayr. This was approved by Scottish Secretary George Younger in 1982, one of the conditions being that the PTE should obtain European Regional Development Fund (ERDF) funding, showing the widening of the funding net for the social railway and the need to demonstrate socio-economic benefits. A working group was set up in 1983, comprising members and officers, BR managers,[35] and trade union representatives,[36] which produced an investment plan coupled to reductions in manning levels: funding was to be from a combination of the PTE, the Scottish Office and the ERDF.

Approval of the original DLR investment served to stimulate interest in light rail as a tool to reduce road traffic congestion in other cities and to link this to urban regeneration. Plans usually employed a combination of street running and segregated track utilising former BR lines, and the Provincial Sector was positive in its attitude to these (Williams 1992).[37] The first proposal to crystallise as a fully costed project was in Manchester in 1985 (Knowles 1996), and this will be considered in Chapter 9. What was significant to the role of land-use planning in these proposals was that they were to be funded under section 56 of the 1968 Transport Act. Changes to the procedures governing this mechanism (DoT 1989c) meant that funding would be predicated on the expectation that schemes would provide benefits for the wider community, or 'non-users', and this could provide the basis for public subsidy. Although it was expected that the major area of non-user benefit would be reduced traffic congestion for road users, there was an expectation of regenerative effects too, including the impact on land development which would be felt near to stops on the routes. The second project

---

35   This included Chris Green before his move to NSE.

36   The inclusion of the unions to oversee acceptance of job cuts, showed their continuing influence as a constraint on BR management, despite the onset of Thatcherism.

37   The surge of interest in light rail saw 40 schemes mooted nation wide (Taylor 1993), and was likened to the Railway Mania of the 1840s.

to come to fruition was in Sheffield where parliamentary powers were in place by 1989 and government funding was committed by the Minister of Transport, Michael Portillo, in 1990. Line 1 was to be largely street running whereas Line 2, which was to run through the Lower Don Valley regeneration area to the proposed Meadowhall shopping centre, would use a route released by BR (Lawless and Dabinett 1995). The contemporary North American literature showed that a very interventionist approach was needed to ensure that property investment took place around stations on new rail systems (Heenan 1968; Knight and Trygg 1977; Cervero 1984b). Similarly, research by Hall and Hass-Klau into the impact of rail investment on city centres in the UK and Continental Europe had concluded that:

> Transport improvements by themselves can never achieve anything; they merely facilitate urban change. They have not had an obvious or marked effect on the structure and organisation of the city, even in Germany – though that may well happen in time. It will only happen, however, if other urban policies make it do so (1985, 170).

Given the government's relaxed stance towards road-oriented decentralisation, its support for light rail projects based on assumptions about property development along their routes was surprising. By the time that these schemes were entering the construction phase, local planning authorities were producing their unitary development plans (UDPs) so, theoretically, there was an opportunity to produce planning strategies to steer development to nodes on the networks. However, the government had no enthusiasm for such an interventionist approach[38] and, in any case, the areas of most intensive redevelopment in Manchester and Sheffield were being managed by UDCs, so the prospects for rail oriented planning were poor to say the least. Even in Newcastle, where the locally owned Metro was already in operation, the city planning authority's first thoughts about the content of its UDP were a depressing reflection of the hostility of the ideological context. In a document running to 169 pages, transport and its implications for planning merited only one and a half pages of vague intentions (City of Newcastle upon Tyne Planning Department 1986, 83-84).

The 'shire' counties and Provincial

The creation of the Provincial Sector facilitated development of the investment case to replace ageing Modernisation Plan rolling stock (Cornell 1993). This led to 'Sprinterisation': a second generation of mainly two-car DMUs which were

---

38   The Strategic Guidance for Greater Manchester (DoE 1989), for example, made very little mention of office development (a major trip generator), made no mention of Salford Quays (see Chapter 9), and the only mention of Manchester Airport was to state that: 'Manchester Airport will grow apace during the period of this Guidance' (para. 5).

faster and more efficient than their predecessors. These were to be used as part of a more fundamental change of operating practices whereby the running of infrequent but high capacity trains would be replaced by more frequent, faster, lower capacity Sprinter trains. The Sprinters would contain denser seating arrangements than their predecessors as the government would only authorise a 'two for three' replacement programme, which promised further cuts in operating costs.[39] By 1990 the situation for Provincial was very positive and there were no extant proposals for line closures or bus-substitution (Whitehouse 1990).

The most notable location for development of railway services through integration with 'shire' county council policies was in the Welsh Valleys, where there was a long standing culture of support within BR and the community. However, by the early 1980s, even the Valley Lines were in decline: ridership fell by 25 per cent between 1980–83 as local unemployment and fares rose. Within the 'nationalised monolith' such local systems were regarded as 'hopeless cases', with continual cost cutting as the only strategy, with inevitable consequences. However, from 1983 the Valley Lines enjoyed a remarkable renaissance (Davies and Clark 1996) as a devolved structure gave local managers their head: they developed a growth strategy which produced fares reductions, increased service frequency, plans for 20 new stations, and re-opening lines. South and especially Mid Glamorgan County Councils played a significant role by developing pro-rail policies in their respective structure plans and providing capital from their transportation budgets:

> Perhaps the most fruitful relationship ever to exist between non-metropolitan councils and a railway company in Britain was that between BR and Mid and South Glamorgan county councils in the 1980s (Davies and Clark 1996, 95).

Although the experience in the Valleys was arguably the most fruitful involvement of the shires in railway development, it was not unique: by the late 1980s Durham, North Yorkshire, Lincolnshire and Lancashire were investing heavily (Sully 1989). Nottinghamshire, Derbyshire and Leicestershire began to develop plans on the scale of the Valleys and to incorporate rail strategies into their statutory development plans. The most notable of these was the 'Robin Hood Line' scheme to reintroduce rail services between Nottingham, Mansfield and Worksop, these having been withdrawn in 1964 and part of the route closed and disposed of.[40] The project used compulsory purchase to return this to public ownership: further evidence of the over zealous closure and disposal strategy and the failure

---

39   Although this would eventually provoke a debate about space standards and passenger comfort, and the difficulties of carrying luggage and cycles in these 'cost effective' trains which have no guard's van.

40   This was in the Leen Valley where in the C19 three companies had each built a line for the coal traffic, one of the classic examples of route duplication, but all were closed and disposed of post-Beeching.

of the planning system to safeguard the alignment. The policy goals behind the project were concerned with reducing traffic congestion in greater Nottingham, and with increasing personal mobility for people in the declining Nottinghamshire/ Derbyshire coalfield. Nottinghamshire County Council was the driving force, supported by Derbyshire and the districts: together they formed a 'Robin Hood Line Steering Group', with the Provincial sector as a member. The degree of local authority commitment necessary to progress this project was reflected in the fact that, because it stood outside the PSO mechanism, they would have to supply all the capital and be prepared to underwrite any operating deficit. The local authority planning functions lent support through strategic policy development as expressed in: structure plans; case making to secure funding; and the detail of station location and development which was tied into local plans (Haywood 1992). However it is indicative of the overall state of contemporary policy development that Nottinghamshire's replacement structure plan of 1991 still did not contain prescriptive rail corridor policies. However, Leicestershire developed more innovative policies to underpin its commitment to the reintroduction of rail passenger services over two routes (Haywood 1992), which were related to a land development strategy based on 'transport choice corridors' which:

> ... are based on the railway lines in the County, along which new local railway services are proposed, and along the A6 between Leicester and Loughborough. This is the only bus route in the County which has the potential to offer, in the foreseeable future, a realistic choice of transport. Ideally, development land should be allocated in locations within walking distance of a station or proposed station or the A6 bus route. Walking distance is usually about 1 kilometre (half a mile) (Leicestershire County Council 1991, para 2.37).

National policy in the 1990s: land-use and transport integration, again

Public concern over traffic pollution, congestion and loss of countryside led to the emergence of the 'new realism' (Goodwin et al. 1991) with regard to the transportation debate: 'predict and provide' was being fundamentally challenged. The political pressures led to significant policy shifts: the fallout saw replacement of Nicholas Ridley by Chris Patten as Secretary of State for the Environment, and he introduced a more interventionist approach. This began with publication of 'This Common Inheritance' (DoE 1990): whereas this discussed the role that managing land-use and transport could have in reducing impacts on the environment, it failed to draw any conclusions:

> ... not enough is known about the relationship between choice of housing and employment location and transport mode to allow the Government to offer authoritative advice at this stage (Secretary of State for the Environment et al. 1990, 87).

Given the literature which this book has reviewed, it is clear that the reason for this was political rather than technical: a U-turn from *laissez-faire* to a more prescriptive regime would need to be gradual and carefully presented. Whatever its shortcomings though, the white paper was a crucial part of the move towards seeing the relationships between land-use and demand for transport as something which the planning system should address as part of what became the 'Strategy for Sustainable Development' (DoE 1994a). Encouraged by the evidence of policy shift, lobby groups pressurised the government with a series of reports on the transport and wider environmental crisis and the need for radical change: transport was beginning to register more strongly on the political radar (Owens 1991; Joseph 1991; Sinclair 1992; Roberts et al. 1992).

In order to develop a firm basis for policy, the DoE sponsored research (DoE DoT 1993a) which showed that, in order to promote the use of public transport, trip generating uses should be located in corridors well served by public transport, and it also identified possible areas of policy tension:

- the preservation of green belt and possible, selective urban expansion within transport corridors; and
- the safeguarding of well-accessed locations for uses 'needing' such locations and local economic or environmental considerations (1993, 65).

This was followed by research by Breheny, Gent and Lock (1993) into private sector new settlement proposals, there having been 184 of these between 1980–92 owing to government encouragement for this kind of market initiative. This evaluated five alternative development models but, although transport implications were considered in the broadest sense, particularly with regard to energy consumption and ease of providing public transport, explicit relationships with the railway network were not explored. However, the overall conclusion was significant:

> If the desire for sustainability is given great weight, then, taking all considerations in the round, new settlements of a scale approaching 10,000 dwellings (25-30,000 population) – with supporting employment and other facilities and amenities – would be the most desirable form of urban development other than urban infill (Breheny et al. 1993, 81).

Settlements of this size could be expected to support a railway service. Significantly, the report went on to draw attention to the fact that this size was comparable to that of Letchworth and Welwyn, but did not note their location on the same railway corridor or the prominent role that the station played as the focal point of their layouts. This omission showed the limitations of contemporary planning ideology.

This movement on land-use policy was paralleled by changes in transport policy, stimulated by the impact of the 'eco-warriors'. The confrontations[41] produced a political alliance between the young idealists and, much more threatening to the government, the respectable middle class. It was this which ended 'predict and provide', rather than research by consultants and academics, although this provided the intellectual justification. There was, in fact, a surge in contemporary publication which explored the concept of 'sustainable development' and its 'deep green' ramifications (Jacobs 1991; Douthwaite 1992): planning ideology became concerned with how development patterns could be manipulated to facilitate use of public transport, especially railways. This produced the concepts of the 'sustainable city' and the 'compact city' (Breheny 1992; Breheny and Rookwood 1993; Haughton and Hunter 1994): although the language was new, this was clearly a return to the ideological strands developed in the late 1960s and 1970s, which had been largely ignored since the early 1980s.[42]

The new mood produced a significant change in the TPP process: by the 1980s this had become part of the 'predict and provide' mechanism. It was recognised that transport policy needed to be co-ordinated across local authority boundaries, i.e. that transport planning has a strategic dimension, and that the TPP process needed to encourage use of transport modes other than cars.[43] This led to the introduction by government of the 'package approach' whereby authorities were encouraged to develop joint strategies, which would explicitly be in step with those in UDPs, to secure modal shift from the car. But there was no explicit steer towards promoting use of local railway networks other than to point out that:

> Public transport proposals for which the Government is able to consider resource
> allocations include new railway and bus stations, heavy and light rail schemes in
> urban areas, bus priority measures and guided busways (DoT 1993, 10).

Encouraged by the ideological swing, local transport authorities began to develop more ambitious strategies. Strathclyde pointed out the importance of the government acting to manage decentralisation more effectively:

> Resisting these pressures will require a continuation of the past strong co-
> operation between strategic and local planning authorities. It will also require
> the Government to support the planning authorities through decisions on
> development plans and planning inquiries and to implement the principles of

---

41   Battles took place at the site of the Bath Eastern By-pass, the M11 extension and the M3 extension through Twyford Down.

42   The resurgence was international too, with 'transit planning' being a part of the American 'New Urbanism' movement (Calthorpe 1993; Katz 1994).

43   There was little consideration of freight transport issues by local authorities, other than with regard to road maintenance and bridge strengthening for heavier lorries.

sustainable development set out in 'This Common Inheritance' by containing unnecessary decentralisation (Strathclyde Regional Council 1991, 52).

Authorities in the West Midlands carried out a series of Integrated Transport Studies followed by publication of a twenty year public transport strategy (WMPTE 1992): this envisaged a further cross-city rail link, electrification of local railways, improvements to the overloaded New Street station, new stations and a light rail system, the first phase of which would utilise the safeguarded trackbed between Snow Hill and Wolverhampton. The process of change was given added momentum by the arrival in 1992 of John Gummer as Secretary of State for the Environment, as he seemed to undergo a quite genuine change of outlook as a result of exposure to the sustainability debate. With regard to transport and land use, this produced the revised version of PPG13 which, in order to reduce car dependency, stated:

> ... local authorities should adopt planning and land use policies to:
> * promote development within urban areas, at locations highly accessible by means other than the private car;
> * locate major generators of travel demand in existing centres which are highly accessible by means other than the private car (DoE DoT 1994, 3).

It is important to note the generality of the language with which the support for public transport oriented planning was expressed: there were no quantitative targets for the density of development around stations, or utilisation of accessibility measures to specify the distance from stations within which major trip generators should be located. Neither were planning authorities required to produce per capita data on railway route miles or station provision of the sort produced for the GLDP. This was despite the fact that, particularly in London, planning and transport authorities had utilised public transport accessibility measures for many years, and the growing computer based technology of geographical information systems made their application easier (Kerrigan and Bull 1992).

The new PPG also endorsed the need for modal shift to rail for freight and recommended that planning authorities should designate distribution sites next to railways and safeguard rail connected, or connectable, sites for freight generating development. Support for rail freight had been present in minerals policy guidance (MPG) for several years, but MPG 10 was particularly notable in that it was the only piece of planning policy guidance which contained data about rail freight (DoE 1991):[44] stronger support for rail would have led to much wider utilisation of such data, with target setting.

---

44   It noted that the percentage of finished cement products moved by rail from production sites ranged from 61 per cent at the Hope Valley plant in Derbyshire to 0 per cent at several others, with only 7 of the 19 sites listed having rail carrying more than 10 per cent.

The scale of the policy change was reflected in the chosen alignment for the Channel Tunnel Rail Link (CTRL), which the Government had reluctantly conceded had to be built. After pressurising BR to find the cheapest and most operationally efficient route, the government, under the influence of Michael Heseltine,[45] opted for an alignment from St Pancras to Stratford, and thence through the Thames riverside area of Essex to north Kent. This high cost option with its miles of tunnel, was justified on strategic grounds because of its regenerative impacts, a strategy eventually branded as the 'Thames Gateway' (Thames Gateway Task Force 1994). Support for this project and the many other proposed rail links for London which had their roots in the Central London Rail Study, was followed through in LPAC's Strategic Planning Guidance for London (LPAC 1994). This contained a locational strategy which used Dutch 'A-B-C' policy (Sturt 1992) to develop the sorts of policies which the GLDP had contained, as shown in Table 7.7.

Table 7.7 Sustainability, Transport and Development Interaction: LPAC Locational Framework

Category A. Development proposals which generate a large number of person trips, because of the size, nature and intensity of their activities, should be located where there is high public transport accessibility and where the current or proposed public transport network has the capacity to cope with the additional trips. Parking provision would only provide for essential car trips.
Category B. development proposals which generate a more modest number of person trips could be acceptable where public transport accessibility, though still good, is complemented by the highway network which could cater for some non-essential car trips. The proportion of total person trips provided for by car could be determined by the factors identified in LPAC's Parking Advice to set parking standards for A2/B1 land uses. This approach could be extended to other land uses.
Category C. Development proposals which generate relatively few person trips could be acceptable in areas of more limited public transport accessibility, provided that the capacity of the highway network could cater for car-based trips. LPAC's Parking Advice suggests the means by which an appropriate level of parking provision could be provided. Uses within this category which would generate a large number of goods trips would be subject to other planning requirements, such as appropriate access to the Strategic Road Network and environmental considerations.

Source: LPAC, 1994, 66.

---

45   This alignment was first promoted by consultants, the Ove Arup Partnership (1990).

Conclusions

This chapter has shown that, following abandonment of urban motorway plans in the 1970s, policy swung in favour of integrating land-use policy with public transport planning, particularly in the conurbations. Professional ideologies began to change and to focus on relationships between the two sectors. This took place under Heath's Conservative government and continued under Labour, so there was a degree of consensus. However, because the implementation of these strategies depended upon sizeable investments to overcome the historic shortcomings of the railway network, the onset of recession brought this initial period of policy making to an end. Subsequently, urban land-use planning became focused around regeneration and public transport considerations slipped down the agenda, although they did comprise a clearly identifiable thread within the first round of adopted structure plans. Outside the conurbations, although the development of railway closure proposals declined, the financial losses continued. Government policy towards BR continued to be dominated by the Treasury view and any major investments had to be pursued doggedly. By the end of the 1970s, there was little likelihood of any major projects being brought forward.

After 1979 there was a rapid collapse of the supportive land-use planning policy framework, with the New Right's *laissez-faire* approach to development which favoured road transport. The ideological stance to planning, local government and nationalised industries was very hostile and, in response, professional ideologies moved away from integration. It is not an over-exaggeration to say that town planning was fighting to retain some sort of coherent ideological identity during this period (Reade 1987). However, the subsequent change in political, ideological and economic circumstances produced an unexpected combination which amounted to what became the most supportive planning policy context for rail in the whole of the post-war era:

Table 7.8 summarises the thematic analysis. With regard to the points developed at the end of Chapter 2, the railway policy agenda can be summarised as follows:

1. *rationalisation of the network*: there was a continued search for rationalisation of the network led by concerns to limit public expenditure and this produced closure plans and general reductions in line capacity; throughout the period there was a counter thrust towards re-opening closed lines, and building new light rail systems, which was becoming stronger towards the end of the period;

2. *development of railway services*: a new generation of intercity trains was planned, but restrictions on BR's ability to invest severely limited the number of schemes for improvement of the main line network to be brought forward and there was no policy to develop French style high speed routes; plans to extend electrification were brought forward periodically and in the 1980s plans were developed for second generation EMUs and DMUs;

3. *closing strategic gaps in the network*: before the crisis of 1976 several schemes were developed for new/improved railways to close strategic gaps in the network, one new London Underground railway line was planned and, after a ten year delay, plans for the Channel Tunnel were eventually developed through to implementation; towards the end of the period light rail schemes were developed as a cheaper way of providing more accessible rail projects and plans were developed for re-opening more closed cross-city routes where these had been safeguarded;

4. *development of a programme of station enhancement*: plans for the improvement of existing stations and the opening of new ones became widespread, although they were particularly associated with the PTEs; this included their proposed integration with associated development and redevelopment schemes.

With regard to town planning policy the outcome was:

5. *patterns of urban development*: before 1979 planning policy in the major conurbations in particular was supportive of rail access, although not as prescriptive as it could have been; this was followed by a marked disregard for the overall transport impacts of development policy through the 1980s which, in turn, was replaced by the return to a more supportive regime in the conurbations and many shires in the early 1990s;

6. *management of the redevelopment process in existing urban areas*: the redevelopment process was managed in ways which were predominantly concerned with road access, although in the PTE areas policies were developed to retrofit early peripheral developments through station building strategies and major developments were promoted at railway stations in many major towns and cities; planning policy generally disregarded freight except for certain bulk traffics; supportive national policy guidance was produced in 1970 and, especially, in 1994;

7. *management of the location and character of greenfield site development*: policy with regard to greenfield areas continued to be to resist their development as far as possible and, where development was proposed, the prime transport consideration was to provide access by motor vehicles: the exceptions to this trend continued to be in the new towns.

From the above it can be concluded that the overall policy context for the relationship between the railway network and land-use patterns was strong at the beginning of the period, weak during the 1980s, but with a vigorous resurgence in the early 1990s leading to what was the most mature relationship of the whole post-war period. Ironically, this came at the same time that the government committed itself to rail privatisation. It seemed that the Conservatives' new leader, John Major, wished to demonstrate that he was continuing the radical policies towards state-owned enterprises of his predecessor[46] and just as open to the advice of the Adam Smith Institute (Irvine 1988). The late Robert Adley MP, who was a Conservative friend of the railways, a frequent critic of government rail policy and Chair of the Select Committee on Transport, referred to railway privatisation as a 'poll tax on wheels'. His death in 1993 was untimely as his influence was such that subsequent events may have unfolded differently.

46   Mrs Thatcher had favoured the creation of a track authority with companies competing to run trains on it and had sponsored research into rail privatisation, but this did not come to fruition before she left office in 1990.

Table 7.8 Summary of thematic analysis of sector policy 1969–94

Explanatory themes	Railway sector	Interrelationships between the two sectors	Planning sector
Politics and political ideology	Initially a balance between the commercial and the social railway. Replaced after 1979 by a hard commercial stance: also support for rail projects if regenerative impacts and/or partnership basis. Dominance of Treasury view throughout.	Labour's vision of integrated transport embraced land use policy, but political priorities forced this down and then off the agenda. There was a strong resurgence under the Conservatives in the 1990s, as long as this could be delivered through the market and/or partnerships.	Priorities continued to be housing and countryside protection, with regeneration added post-1976. Some initial regard for rail in locational policy, but undermined post-1979, with a resurgence in late 1980s/1990s. Emphasis on re-opening projects.
Professions and professional ideology	Continuance of introverted culture focused on technical disciplines, although regional managers developed joint policies with PTEs. BR Chairmen generally more adept at PR. Post-1979 a market oriented culture which sought to develop joint projects/policies with local authorities and property developers.	Limited interface between the professions in London and the PTA/PTE areas, but a decline 1976-86. Strong recovery associated with property boom and the development of the 'New Realism' and sustainability agendas in the late 1980s/1990s.	Design oriented ideology overridden by socio-economic concerns. Limited development of ideology around planning for access by public transport, mainly through structure plans. This was eroded post-1979, but re-emerged strongly around regeneration and sustainability in late 1980s/1990s.
Governance and management	Priority to manage BR as a public corporation on business lines, minimising dependence on public funds. 1968 and 1974 Acts produced more financial transparency: rural lines at risk throughout. Post-1979 Conservatives pushed for more market oriented culture, which was responsive to/encouraged local authority/property market initiatives.	Value of the PTA/PTE structure as a link facilitating joint railway/land-use planning policy was demonstrated throughout. Post-1979 the combination of UDCs and planning deregulation produced hostile policies, but the partnership era was supportive. The Property Board played a positive role in triggering supportive policies and projects around stations.	Planning linked to the new policy agendas: the environment and then regeneration, but main transport considerations throughout continued to be around roads. Planning authorities marginalised post-1979; most UDCs not rail oriented. Resurgence of planning in the 1990s as part of the sustainability debate, in a context where public/private partnership and regionalism were encouraged.

Chapter 8

Outcomes: 1969–94

Introduction

The aim of this chapter is to review the outcomes of the interplay between the institutional structures, policies and ideologies of the railway and planning sectors in the 1969–94 period. Conclusions are drawn as to whether these were largely positive or negative with regard to the utilisation of the railway network. As in Chapter 7, this chapter is split into two halves around 1979, and the dialogue broadly follows the same pattern of reviewing national outcomes, and then dropping down to review those in London, the provincial conurbations and the areas outside.

The overriding feature of the period was the continuing increase in society's dependence on transport and the absolute dominance of the car and truck. Total passenger movement increased by 57 per cent, from 395 to 689 billion kilometres,[1] with that by car and light van increasing by 50 per cent, from 286 to 596 billion kilometres. The total by rail (BR plus all other networks) was 35 billion kilometres in 1969 and exactly the same in 1994, having reached a nadir of 31 billion kilometres in 1982 and peaked at 41 billion kilometres during the economic boom in 1988. Bus and coach travel declined by 32 per cent over the period, from 63 to 43 billion kilometres, which shows that rail continued to be relatively more successful, although its market share declined from 9 to 5 per cent. Goods lifted by all modes increased from 1964 to 2051 million tonnes, only a 4.4 per cent increase reflecting deep changes in the nature of the country's industrial base. The total lifted by rail declined by 54 per cent, from 211 to 97 million tonnes, which was a loss of market share from 10.7 to 4.6 per cent. The picture with regard to goods moved was very different, as this reflected the fundamental changes in the geography of manufacturing and distribution which, along with increasing consumerism and the introduction of just-in-time delivery schedules, became much more transport dependent: there was a large increase of 66 per cent, from 133 to 221 billion tonne kilometres.[2] Haulage by rail fell by 44 per cent, from 23 to 13 billion tonne kilometres, with a decline in market share from 17.3 to 5.9 per cent: so, by both freight measures, there was a significant relative and absolute, decline in rail freight.

---

1 All statistics in this paragraph are from DoT Transport Statistics 1995 edition.

2 The totals for goods lifted and goods moved are quite different to those for the 1948–68 period where the biggest change was in goods lifted.

The relative resilience of rail passenger traffic as compared with bus and coach traffic suggests that, although the continued growth in use of the car exerted an overwhelming influence on patterns of land development, nevertheless certain things went in rail's favour. For example, it was significant that, despite accelerated urban decentralisation between 1975–94, the percentage of households living within a seven minute walking distance of a railway station only declined from 9 per cent to 8 per cent, and the percentage living within a 7-13 minute walk remained the same at 13 per cent.[3] This chapter will show that, towards the end of the period, the interaction between the 'tail' of the interventionist policies of the 1970s and the Conservative's market-led approach was complex and, unexpectedly, produced positive outcomes. And this despite the dominance of the Treasury view, throughout, although this was the ultimate factor in deciding the network's fate.

The national network 1968–94 and main line services to 1979

Completion of WCML electrification in 1974 led to the 401 mile Euston-Glasgow journey time being reduced by 55 minutes, to just over five hours. The introduction of HSTs in 1975 was of even wider significance as they could run on any main line, not just electrified routes. They knocked 23 minutes off the London-Cardiff journey time so rail could compete effectively with the M4 motorway. London-Newcastle came down to just over 3 hours which was better than could be achieved on the M1/A1 and, in 1978, the London-Edinburgh journey came down to 5 hours. The introduction of faster trains was accompanied by steady work to improve track quality to facilitate the higher speeds: £190 million on the ECML between 1967 and 1980 for example (Semmens 1990, 191). Even on lines where speeds were restricted, as on the Midland main line between Sheffield and St Pancras where HSTs were introduced in 1982, there was ridership growth because of their positive image with the public. These improvements in inter-city services served to reinforce the traditional importance of CBDs as rail nodes.

Notwithstanding these improvements, the tendency towards retrenchment continued, but not as strongly as in the 1960s. Total length of route fell by about 3550 kilometres[4] (2206 miles) overall, from 20,080 (12,477 miles) in 1968 to 16,528 (10,270 miles) in 1994, but with less than 1000 kilometres (621 miles) lost post-1981. The length of route open to passenger traffic fell from 15,242 kilometres (9471 miles) in 1968 to a low of 14,291 (8880 miles) in 1992, but then increased to 14,357 (8921 miles) in 1994, despite the loss of some track to light rail conversions (Appendix 5). Although the number of passenger journeys on BR declined, passenger kilometres rose from 29.6 billion in 1969 to a peak of 34.3 billion in 1988/89, but then fell back in the 1990s recession to 30.4 billion in 1993/94, still above the 1968 level. Similarly ridership on London Underground

---

3   This data is from National Travel Surveys as quoted in Potter (1997).
4   All statistics in this paragraph are from DoT Transport Statistics 1994 edition.

fell from 655 million journeys in 1968 to 498 million in 1982, but then grew to 815 million in 1988/89 before falling back to 728 million by 1992/93, with a slight recovery to 735 million in 1993/94. Passenger kilometres on London Underground showed a similar pattern.

Despite the improvements, there were some significant closures (Table 8.1): even the Southern Region was not immune, with the Uckfield-Lewes line closed in 1969 being the most notable. This left no alternative route from London to Brighton should the main line be temporarily closed: this removal of diversionary routes was a typical outcome of the closure process. Also in 1969 the Carlisle-Hawick-Edinburgh 'Waverley' route was closed, despite being a 158 kilometres (98 miles) long strategic route, serving an isolated population of 100,000 in the Central Borders[5] area. By 1972 Scotland had lost 6437 kilometres (4,000 miles) of the 11, 894 route kilometres (7391 miles) it possessed at nationalisation and other strategic lines serving remote rural areas, such as Inverness to Kyle of Lochalsh, were under threat. However, as an illustration of the growth of the pro-rail lobby, there was a successful fightback against the latter, which involved MPs, local authorities and the Highlands and Islands Development Board, as well as the wider public (Thomas 1991). A central feature of the Waverley closure case was the much lower cost of alternative bus services, but opponents questioned whether, in such a remote area, these could offer anything like a comparable service. The 'bustitution' issue grew in significance and, by the 1980s, the strategy was shown to be unsuccessful (Hillman and Whalley 1980) and was challenged with increasing success by campaigning groups (Railway Development Society 1988). The Waverley closure was followed in 1970 by withdrawal of passenger services between Sheffield and Manchester on the electrified Woodhead line and their concentration on the Hope Valley route: Sheffield Victoria was closed and demolished. Despite the furore around the demolition of the Euston Arch and passage of the 1967 Civic Amenities Act[6] which promoted the protection of historic buildings and areas, many stations of great architectural quality were demolished with unseemly haste when lines were closed. With further loss of freight traffic associated with decline in coal consumption, the Woodhead route was closed completely in 1981, despite a spirited anti-closure campaign (Bain 1986).

---

5   This was despite the presence of some of Glasgow's town expansion partners being located along the route as shown in Appendix 10.

6   Interestingly this was promoted by a private member (Duncan Sandys) and not the government.

Table 8.1 Closures of main routes 1969–94

Date of closure	Route closed
1969	Uckfield-Lewes with retention of the non-electrified stub between East Croydon and Uckfield, but with loss of the role of the route as a diversionary line to Brighton
	Carlisle-Hawick-Edinburgh 'Waverley' route
1972	Exeter-Okehampton removing the remaining rail head in north west Devon
	Birmingham Moor Street-Snow Hill-Wolverhampton (former GWR main line)
1981	Manchester-Sheffield 'Woodhead' route, with retention of Manchester-Glossop/Hadfield stub for local services
1982	March-Spalding freight route and the associated Lincoln avoiding lines
1991	Leamside Line between the ECML near Durham and Newcastle via Washington New Town – freight route also used as ECML diversionary route

Closures continued at the rural extremities of the English network: Kings Lynn-Hunstanton in 1969, Barnstaple-Ilfracombe in 1970 and Exeter-Okehampton in 1972. The latter was not even in the Beeching report and was galling for those who had opposed closure of the branch lines in north Devon and Cornwall as they had been led to believe that Okehampton would remain as a railhead. This closure, along with others such as those in Northumberland, Grosmont-Pickering, Penrith-Keswick, Matlock-Chinley and Barnstaple-Ilfracombe, meant that rail access into national parks was severely eroded (see Figure 8.1 for a map of the network in 1985).

Whereas other secondary main lines remained open, often they were reduced to single line working, as with the Salisbury-Exeter line and the 'Cotswold' line between Oxford and Worcester. Main line services over the former Great Western-Great Central Joint Line through High Wycombe were withdrawn by 1973, leaving only local passenger services on the line working out of Marylebone: the link through to Banbury remained but, once again, only as single track north of Princes Risborough. Singling reduced costs but had significant effects on quality of service: a late running train would delay those running in the opposite direction, thereby reducing service quality with the result of further reductions in ridership leading, eventually perhaps, to full closure. This could lead to self-fulfilling prophesies by consciously 'managing down' a line and reflected the reductionist outlook within BR.[7] Even a strategic route such as the 'North and West' along the Welsh Marches

---

7   In its response to a government consultation prior to the 1977 White Paper, the BRB bemoaned the continuing disregard for the railway's wider role: ' … the social and

between Newport-Hereford-Shrewsbury was considered for closure, although this would have meant that all services from South Wales to the north would have had to run via Birmingham.

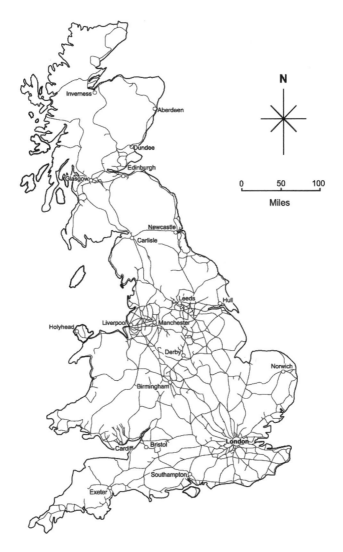

Figure 8.1 The Railway Network 1985

Source: Biddle, G. (1990), *The Railway Surveyors* (London: Ian Allan Ltd).

environmental objectives have never yet been defined in such a way that they could be injected into the network studies. This deficiency is still not made good ...' (BRB 1976, 10).

Given that closure decisions came from central government, it might have been expected that there would have been a national strategy for the protection of closed alignments for possible rail reinstatement, or as rights of way for walking and cycling. But this was not the case and it was left to local authorities to acquire disused trackbeds if they perceived a use for them and to safeguard them through policies in development plans. This occurred on an ad hoc basis, although a more coherent approach was developed in some counties, such as Derbyshire, where the Peak Park Planning Board was well placed to intervene as a body dedicated to planning the national park and it developed a good working relationship with Derbyshire County Council. Here trackbeds were acquired for recreational use and there were policies which countenanced a potential return to rail: Matlock-Chinley and the Woodhead route were protected in the structure plan. One of the most striking failures to protect a strategic alignment was that of the former Great Central main line between Sheffield and London:[8] at the very least this would have made an excellent walking and cycling route through the heart of some of England's best countryside. The promotion of access to the countryside had been part of the Attlee government's socialist agenda, proudly embodied in the 1949 National Parks and Access to the Countryside Act. With growing expectations about quality of life and growing use of the car to gain access to the countryside, the latter was under increasing pressure and the 1968 Countryside Act was intended to give local authorities powers to open up rural areas nearer the towns and cities in order to protect the 'deep' countryside, as found in the national parks. There was therefore a massive failure at national level to join up this rural strategy with the opportunities presented by railway closures.

Rail freight

Even before the introduction of Section 8 grants in 1974, the Beeching innovations were bearing fruit and bulk traffics such as coal, steel, aggregates and petroleum products were being retained. The use of 'merry-go-round' trains to deliver coal to power stations was particularly successful with 20 power stations being supplied in this way by the late 1970s (see Appendix 10) and coal haulage continued to be the most profitable part of the freight business. These large projects presented few issues for the planning system as, typically, they were associated with extant industrial complexes or those, such as power stations, which enjoyed exemption from planning control. Freightliner was having some success too and was carrying more than 5,000 containers a week by 1968. When the Swansea terminal opened in

---

8   This route was built 50 years after the other trunk routes and was constructed to a high specification as part of Watkin's aspiration for a Liverpool-Paris route. The route remained operational southwards from the landfill site at Calvert, Buckinghamshire (just to the north of Aylesbury) with a commuter service from Aylesbury to Marylebone, although even this was threatened with closure for a time.

1969 it was the twenty first: others were already to be found at Stratford, Willesden and King's Cross in London, in major conurbations such as Manchester, Glasgow, Leeds, Sheffield and Birmingham, and secondary cities such as Nottingham, Bristol and Cardiff. The provision of these terminals was straightforward, as there were plenty of surplus freight yards which could be utilised. Freightliner was having particular success with what, in the longer term, came to be its most successful market, the deep sea maritime traffic. Ports such as Southampton and Tilbury were served, along with the new port of Felixstowe which was growing rapidly as a result of containerisation and the shift towards Europe in the pattern of trade. In parallel with these developments was the closure and, in most cases, destruction of railway infrastructure built to serve the historic ports of London, Liverpool, Manchester, Glasgow and Cardiff. Despite its successes though, Freightliner lost business to road haulage and its problems undermined the finances of the National Freight Corporation: it was transferred back to BR in 1978.

There was investment in the network for freight: in 1970 access to Felixstowe Docks was improved and a new rail link was built into Foster Yeoman's Merehead quarry in Somerset. In the 1970 annual report the BRB bemoaned the lack of progress in securing planning permissions for terminals for aggregates and similar traffic (BRB 1970, 9). But concern over the environmental impact of the large volumes of lorry traffic which would be necessary to move bulk materials did lead to planning authorities including policies to encourage rail haulage in statutory plans as, for example, in the open cast coal extraction industry in Northumberland or deep coal mining in North Yorkshire. Where an operator, typically at this time the National Coal Board, did not want to apply for a rail freight grant, then planning authorities used planning conditions specifying the movement of material by rail, and even used planning agreements under section 52 of the 1971 Town and Country Planning Act to constrain lorry movements associated with the developments. The most significant example where the NCB, BR, the Departments of Energy and Environment, and local planning authorities worked together was the opening up of the Selby Coalfield. After a public inquiry this received Ministerial approval in 1975, followed by an Act of Parliament in 1978 for a new[9] 13-mile stretch of 125 mph main line to divert the ECML away from its historic alignment which would be affected by subsidence. This project was complete by 1983 and included a major rail served coal concentration facility at Gascoigne Wood, with most of the coal destined for the merry-go-round traffic to power stations.

Rail based domestic waste disposal systems involved the development by local authorities, as planning and waste authorities, of rail served waste concentration plants and remote landfill sites. The first waste trains ran in the late 1970s from Brent in North London to the London Brick Company claypits at Stewartby. By

---

9   This was the first stretch of main line built since opening of the Great Western-Great Central joint route through High Wycombe in 1906.

the early 1980s another service was running from Hillingdon to Calvert[10] and, by 1984, Avon County Council was using Calvert too. By 1984/85 Greater Manchester Council was running waste trains from four concentration depots in Manchester and Salford to a Wimpey owned disposal site at Appley Bridge near Wigan (Shannon 2008).

Despite these positive relationships between planning policy and rail freight, the general relationship was poor. It was typified by zoning land in development plans for industrial and distribution facilities which were located around the motorway network with no rail connection and no potential for one. Ironically, two of the most striking examples were at the new towns of Milton Keynes and Warrington, where the excellent strategic location on the WCML was not utilised to fix the location of extensive warehousing facilities. Although some statutory development plans, such as South Yorkshire's structure plan, contained policies supportive of rail freight, in practice most of these were ineffectual, given the steady decline of heavy industry and the fact that government was content to let road haulage dominate the rest of the freight market.

Major developments, new towns and the railway network

Across the network improvement of rail services was patchy and was most strongly associated with inter-city and commuter services in the major conurbations. It was in the major cities that there was the maximum potential for integrated land-use and transportation planning. In strategic terms the continuing focus on urban containment, after the mid-1970s in association with inner city regeneration, was in the broadest sense supportive of rail. This was because of the continuing restriction of the location of retailing and commercial services to town and city centres, rather than allowing more decentralised, road-oriented patterns of development as some developers were pressing for. Table 8.2 shows that collectively these policies were significant in terms of securing the development of a large number of schemes in rail accessible locations. As evidenced by experience in Birmingham, there was also an awareness that road building was not going to solve local transport problems and that it was important to plan for public transport too. However, as concluded in the previous chapter, there was little evidence in contemporary structure plans that this was leading to prescriptive, rail-oriented planning strategies and the number of major developments which were steered to rail accessible locations was limited, especially outside city centres.

---

10   Calvert lies to the north of Aylesbury and is a retained freight-only stub of the former Great Central main line.

Table 8.2 Major shopping malls over 46,450 sq m (500,000 sq ft) built 1969–92 and their relationship to the railway network

Location	Centre	Year Opened	Size sq m (sq ft)	Rail Access Situation
In-Town				
Doncaster	Arndale, now Frenchgate centre	1967	81,755 (880,000)	5 minute walk from station
Poole	Arndale	1969	58,622 (631,000)	5 minute walk from station
Croydon	Whitgift Centre	1970	114,828 (1,236,000)	5 minute walk from station
Luton	Arndale	1972	65,032 (700,000)	5 minute walk from station
Nottingham	Victoria Centre	1972	57,786 (622,000)	built on site of former Victoria station: 20 minutes walk from retained Midland station
Derby	Eagle Centre	1975	51,561 (555,000)	10 minute walk from station
Maidstone	Stoneborough	1976	50,353 (542,000)	5 minute walk from station
Manchester	Arndale	1976	110,462 (1,189,000)	10/15 minutes walk from Victoria/ Piccadilly: direct from Metrolink post 1992
Newcastle	Eldon Square	1976	77,110 (830,000)	10 minutes walk from Central: direct from Metro post 1984
Cardiff	St. Davids	1981	53,977 (581,000)	10 minutes walk from Queen Street and Central
Glasgow	St Enoch Centre	1989	69,677 (750,000)	on site of former St Enoch station, 5 minutes walk from Central, 15 minutes from Queen Street
Watford	The Harlequin Centre	1992	67,448 (726,000)	10 minutes from Watford Junction, 2 minutes from Watford High Street

Location	Centre	Year Opened	Size sq m (sq ft)	Rail Access Situation
New Towns				
Runcorn	Shopping City	1971	55,742 (600,000)	remote from station but accessible via the bustrack
Telford	Shopping City	1973	60,387 (650,000)	10 minute walk from Telford Central opened 1986
Redditch	Kingfisher	1973	62,802 (676,000)	5 minutes walk from station which was rebuilt 1972
Washington	The Galleries	1977	50,446 (543,000)	no station
Milton Keynes	Central MK	1979	98,942 (1,065,000)	15 minutes uphill walk after MK Central opened in 1982
Basildon	Eastgate	1980	48,031 (517,000)	10 minutes walk from station opened in 1974
Peterborough	Queensgate	1982	60,387 (650,000)	10 minutes walk – bridges over ring road
Out-of Town				
Hendon	Brent Cross	1976	70,606 (760,000)	15 minute walk from Underground stations - hostile route under elevated North Circular road
Gateshead	Metro Centre	1986	151,432 (1,630,000)	5 minutes from new station opened under Speller amendment in 1987; not on Metro system
Dudley	Merryhill	1989	130,993 (1,410,000)	not rail connected, but owners are proposing a link to the Midland Metro line as part of an expansion project
Thurrock	Lakeside	1990	106,838 (1,150,000)	not rail connected at time of opening*
Sheffield	Meadowhall	1990	102,193 (1,100,000)	new station opened 1990: accessible by Supertram post-1994

Source: Hillier Parker: British Shopping Centre Developments, various years.

Note: for centres developed in several phases, 'Size' includes all phases of development. 'Year' is that of the opening of the largest phase. * Chafford Hundred station was opened in 1995 on the Upminster-Grays line to serve the new housing scheme and a shuttle bus operates between there and Lakeside, with a connecting footbridge opening in 2000.

Although there was no further designation of new towns in the 1970s, there was evidence of their continuing association with the rail network: stations opened at Redditch in 1972, Stevenage in 1973,[11] Basildon in 1974 and Newton Aycliffe in 1978 (Appendix 10). The Stevenage and Basildon examples showed that, even in the South East, it could take 25 years to deliver a station at designated new towns. By way of contrast, expanded towns such as Basingstoke already had a town centre station at designation and, in its case, a planned retail development was complete by 1969 and there was over 162,580 square metres (1.75m square feet) of offices by 1977, all reasonably accessible from the station:

> The railway station is well sited to serve the town centre and the business area, and rail passengers arriving during the morning peak-hour produce a steady stream of pedestrians into these areas (Butler 1980, 72).

There was evidence of awareness that the rail network needed to access new activity nodes, and that the location of major set-piece developments was influenced by considerations of rail access. For example, Birmingham International station was opened in 1976 to serve both the National Exhibition Centre and the adjacent airport. A large amount of car parking was provided as the peripheral location and proximity to the motorway network was favourable for a railhead. However, despite new stations, the overall number on the network fell from 2,750 in 1967 to 2,358 in 1977 and the station planning process continued to be poorly developed:

> The location of railway passenger stations has received little attention, theoretical or practical …
> Planners have sometimes shown little appreciation of station location …
> In the past at least, British Rail has also been reluctant to provide new stations to accommodate new traffic resulting from land-use change.
> (White and Senior 1983, 113-114).

Most of the larger new towns designated in the 1960s were expansions of existing towns, like Peterborough and Northampton, and growth led to expansion of existing town centres. Completion in 1982 of the Queensgate Centre at Peterborough (Bendixson 1988) sensitively inserted a large shopping mall into a previously historic, but uninspiring, town centre. Although this was separated from the railway station by the new inner ring road, the characteristic outcome, this was bridged in a fairly satisfactory manner and the proximity made the relatively short walk a realistic proposition for rail users. Despite this reinforcing of the role of the main station, the expansion of Peterborough did not produce districts focused around new railway stations, or the re-opening of any of the area's closed lines.

---

11   The new station adjoined the new town centre and was accompanied by closure of the historic station.

New railway infrastructure was built at Milton Keynes as its development involved the creation of a city centre, on a green field site for a target city population of over 200,000: development on this scale was unprecedented. The fact that the master plan was car-oriented has already been noted but, despite this, it opted for a fairly conventional city centre with a mix of medium density office developments, a major shopping mall, community services and peripheral residential development. The focal point was the mall which was the largest of its kind to be developed outside an existing city centre at the time. As a symbol of the New Right's populism, it was opened by Margaret Thatcher in 1979. In order to take advantage of the location on the WCML a new station was planned, in association with office development, and this opened in 1982:[12] getting BR to commit itself had been a difficult task owing to its financial difficulties and the £3m cost (Bendixson and Platt 1992). The gap between railway and town planning was reflected in the fact that BR's original view had been that Milton Keynes would be served by the existing stations at Wolverton and Bletchley. It was significant too that the shopping mall was remote from the station site, being on the opposite side of the city centre, this choice being driven by aesthetic considerations.[13] This failure to plan around access to the station occurred, despite the development corporation priding itself on being a guardian of good design (Milton Keynes Development Corporation 1992). Just to underline the weakness, the shopping mall was a huge success: it was a precursor of what was to come in the 1980s and attracted shoppers from an extremely wide catchment area. The prior closure of rail links to the east and west of Milton Keynes as part of the closure of the Oxford-Cambridge through route has already been noted: the Bedford-Bletchley service survived on a stub of this but was not extended to Milton Keynes, further illustrating the weaknesses in integrating even retained rail services with planning outcomes.

Although modest in scale, the most significant (and unique) pro-rail new town development occurred at Warrington. A small shopping mall was built in the new suburb of Birchwood (Warrington New Town Development Corporation 1973, 27-30[14]) alongside the Manchester-Liverpool railway. A new station to serve the centre and the growing eastern townships opened there in 1980 and was jointly funded by BR (50 per cent), the development corporation and Cheshire County Council (50 per cent).

---

12   Birmingham International and Milton Keynes were the first major new stations on the WCML since the turn of the century.

13   The site was the highest point of the city centre and, thereby, best able to take advantage of its location along an axis oriented on the rising and setting of the sun at the midsummer solstice, a romantic but largely irrelevant basis for a master plan.

14   This document noted that BR had stated that it would be able to provide a station at this location and that talks were ongoing between BR and Merseyside and SELNEC PTEs about electrification of the Liverpool-Warrington-Manchester line although, subsequently, this did not come to pass.

The BR Property Board and surplus railway land in the 1970s

Closures led to large areas of land becoming vacant and between 1968–1973 between 2,469 hectares (6,100 acres) and 2,833 hectares (7,000 acres) were disposed of annually. By 1979 the cumulative acreage of land disposed of since 1964 was 31,970 hectares (79,000 acres).[15] The Property Board's priorities meant that income generation, not rail traffic generation, was the prime objective. However the two did sometimes overlap, especially where property was disposed of close to an operational station. Southport was one example where, in 1973, a new shopping centre was promoted as an integral part of the station: in keeping with contemporary practice it also included 400 parking spaces. A new bus-rail interchange was opened at Bradford in 1973, but this involved closing the original Exchange station and moving to a new location, 200 metres (219 yards) further out of the city centre so that the site could be redeveloped for the city's Crown Courts. A similar development took place at Fort William where the old station site was required for a ring road and was closed in 1975 on the opening of a new station, several hundred metres back up the line and outside the town centre ring road. Lines at Looe and St Ives were similarly cut back, with construction of new but more peripheral stations with minimal facilities. This marginalisation of stations continued the trend which had commenced in the 1960s and, although it produced revenue, it was clearly contrary to the railway's long term interests where convenient access to town centres would become of increasing importance as car ownership increased.

The continuing friction between the Property Board and local planning authorities, with regard to station redevelopment projects, was illustrated at Cardiff Queen Street. Adjacent parts of the city centre had become attractive to the office market but a scheme to rebuild the station, as part of a commercial development, went to appeal, with a favourable result for BR in 1970. This friction caused by planning delays was mentioned in the BRB annual reports from time to time.[16] Although hardly objective, it is suggestive of a lack of urgency by planning authorities in facilitating schemes which had obvious merits beyond income generation for the BRB.

---

15   The 1979 annual report (BRB, 1979, 33) estimated the total railway estate at 80,937 ha (200,000 acres), with 68,797 ha (170,000 acres) being operational land, with much of the remainder yielding income. There remained some 2414 km (1500 miles) of closed branch lines awaiting disposal. Disposals since 1964 had yielded a cumulative total of £226m.

16   For example, despite construction of Liverpool's Link and Loop scheme the 1979 annual report cited delays in securing planning permission for the commercial redevelopment of Central Station, which was very desirable for promoting rail access as it was to be built above a new underground station. The same report mentions continuing planning delays for a hypermarket and freight terminal at Neasden, more than five years after the project was conceived.

London and the provincial conurbations

There were many improvements to local services in London and the major conurbations and these also reinforced the role of CBDs. In London the 1970 investment in the Southern Region was mostly for modernising signalling where the intention was to operate the whole network from fourteen 'powerboxes': this brought cost savings as well as increasing capacity. Electrification of the surburban lines to Royston (near Cambridge) was completed in 1978, finally realising Howard's vision of garden cities (Letchworth and Welwyn) connected to their parent by an electric railway. Services between St Pancras and Bedford were electrified in 1982, St Pancras having survived a closure threat in the mid-1960s and becoming a Grade 1 listed building, a positive outcome influenced by the Euston arch debacle.

On the London Underground the final section of the Victoria Line opened in 1971, meaning that working class Brixton and Walthamstow had direct links to central London, as well as King's Cross/St Pancras and Euston being linked with Victoria. The Piccadilly Line extension to Heathrow was opened in 1977, just over 30 years after a rail link was first proposed by Abercrombie. In 1979 the Jubilee Line, the second of the new tube lines, was opened between Charing Cross and Baker Street, where it connected with the pre-existing Bakerloo line to Stanmore.

The Tyne and Wear Metro system was open by 1984 (Table 8.3) providing direct access to Newcastle's Central Station, the city centre and suburban town centres such as North and South Shields. The system had 43 stations including 17 new ones, one of which was the suburban office node of Regent Centre, an unusual development in the provinces. A monitoring study (Transport and Road Research Laboratory et al. 1986) reported that, although the Metro had had only a limited impact on development patterns, the stations were well located with regard to major areas of trip generation and there had been a significant increase in public transport trips, compared with decline elsewhere. Saturday was the peak day for Metro travel showing good integration with shopping and leisure trip destinations, with easy access to the new Eldon Square mall.

Table 8.3 Main post-Beeching route re-openings and new routes

Date	Length of New Track km (miles)	Location
1978	3(4.8)	Liverpool Loop and Link – opening of underground cross-city centre linkwith 3 new stations
1979	8(5)	Re-opening of Glasgow's cross city centre Argyle line with 6 new stations
1983	22.5(14)	Selby East Coast Main Line diversion to facilitate Selby coalfield
1984	51(31.7)	Opening of Tyne and Wear Metro utilising 45km of existing heavy rail suburban lines with a new 6km tunnel section under central Newcastle, 43 stations including 17 new ones
1986	16(10)	Edinburgh-Livingston-Bathgate re-opening to passenger services of former freight only route
1986	0.6(0.35)	Opening of Hazel Grove chord to south of Stockport facilitating the routing of Manchester-Sheffield services via Stockport
1987	1.2(0.75)	Re-opening of a rebuilt Birmingham Snow Hill station – service extended from Moor Street
1987	6.4(4)	Morecambe-Heysham – passenger service on former freight only line
1987	16(10)	Coventry-Nuneaton – passenger service on former freight only line
1987	8(5)	Cardiff 'City' line with 4 new stations – passenger service on former freight only line
1987	16(10)	Oxford- Bicester Town – passenger service on former freight only line
1987	11.2(7)	Abercynon-Aberdare with 6 new stations – passenger service on former freight only line
1987	8(5)	Coatbridge-Motherwell – re-opening to passenger services
1987	13(8)	Opening of first section of Docklands Light Railway between Tower Gateway and Island Gardens on the Isle of Dogs with a branch to Stratford, using part of the former heavy rail line into Fenchurch Street and other disused alignments – 13 stations
1988	0.8(0.5)	Opening of 'Windsor Link' to facilitate concentration of services at Manchester Piccadilly, including new Salford Crescent station
1988	1.6(1)	Re-opening of Snow Hill Tunnel between Farringdon and Blackfriars to create Thameslinkcross-London service between Bedford-Gatwick Airport

Date	Length of New Track km (miles)	Location
1990	9.7(6)	Glasgow – Paisley Canal re-opened to passenger services: formerly freight only
1991	5.6(3.5)	Stansted airport link opened to provide Liverpool Street-Stansted services
1992	12.9(8)	Bridgend-Maesteg line re-opened with 6 new stations
1992	31(19)	Opening of Manchester Metrolink light rail route between Bury-Manchester-Altrincham re-using former heavy rail lines with short section (3.7km/2.3 miles) of new city centre street running; 26 stops and 4 key interchanges with heavy rail stations
1993	2.4(1.5)	Manchester Airport northern chord from Manchester Piccadilly opened along with a new airport station
1993	14.5(9)	Re-opening of first section of the Robin Hood Line between Nottingham and Newstead
1994	29(19)	Opening of South Yorkshire Supertram – largely new on-street alignment but utilised former freight only heavy rail line in Lower Don Valley to access Meadowhall; 48 stops including Sheffield Station
1994	8(5)	Channel Tunnel opened – new track from portal to Dollands Moor terminal
1994	12.8(8)	Blackburn-Clitheroe 'Ribble Valley' line re-opened for passenger services with new station at Clitheroe (services withdrawn 1962)

Main line railway access to Glasgow was improved by WCML electrification. By the mid-1970s the magnificence of Glasgow's Victorian heritage, typified by Central Station, was increasingly recognised. Through the Glasgow East Area Renewal (GEAR) project came a greater awareness of the importance of the city centre and, in this respect, GEAR's launch (City of Glasgow District Council 1986) can be seen as the beginning of its renaissance. One of the PTE's early achievements was the re-opening in 1979 of the Argyle Line, linking Rutherglen in the south to Partick in the north via Central Low Level. Eight stations were opened, including Argyle Street and Central Low Level in the city centre: that at Partick provided interchange with the Subway. Surprisingly, given the closure of so many urban railways, the Subway survived into the 1970s before reaching a crisis: closure or renewal. The economy of inner Glasgow was undergoing sufficient structural change to question its raison d'être but the PTE decided on renewal. The line closed in 1977 and re-opened in 1980: ridership in the first year of operation was, at 10 million passengers, less than half that predicted,[17] and there was a significant cost overrun. Despite this, the PTE's cost cutting strategy of the early 1980s was successful and the Paisley-Ayr line was energised in 1987, further strengthening the links between central Glasgow and towns up to 35 miles distant.

In Liverpool the Loop and Link were completed in 1978 with new stations at Moorfields, Central and Lime Street to complement the long established St James. This work facilitated closure of two surface termini at Exchange and Central. Central was well located adjacent to the prime retail area and was redeveloped as a shopping centre above the new underground station, an example of integrated land-use/transportation development on a scale unusual in provincial cities. This outcome for the local network was in stark contrast to the fate of the Liverpool Overhead Railway which, owing to a requirement for major reinvestment, had been closed in 1956 and subsequently demolished.

As the public backlash against road building set in, Birmingham became notorious for the unattractiveness of its CBD. The 1960s saw considerable office development in the peripheral Five Ways area, where the station had been closed in 1944, and the growth of car commuting to it was significant. The Inner Ring Road, with 52 pedestrian subways and the associated Bull Ring scheme, was opened in 1971 with the nearby Gravelly Hill interchange on the M6 (Spaghetti Junction) opening in 1972. Following the concentration of local and inter-city services on New Street, Snow Hill station was closed in 1972 despite its proximity to the city centre office district. Although the great train shed was totally demolished, the rail alignment through the site and onwards towards Wolverhampton was protected by the City Council. It soon became apparent that road building had not solved Birmingham's traffic congestion problems: on the other hand there had been growth in ridership on the local railway network, 72 per cent on the Lichfield-New Street line between 1966–70 for example. Debate about the potential to reinvigorate railway services on the Lichfield-New Street-Longbridge 'Cross City' route led to significant investment by the PTE in 1978. This produced new stations, including one at Five Ways, improved track layouts, a DMU service of four trains per hour and six in the peak, and integration with feeder bus services. Notably, this improvement did not include electrification showing the limited funds available.[18]

The railway renaissance in the 1980s

Despite the hostile stance of the Conservatives towards public sector investment, the strength of BR's business case for electrification was demonstrated by improvements to the main line network. Electrification was extended from

---

17   The highest level of ridership was 37.3 million passengers in 1949.

18   The cross-city line gained the dubious reputation of being the most intensively operated DMU service in Europe.

Tonbridge to Hastings in 1986, to Norwich and Cambridge in 1987, to Weymouth in 1988, and Kings Lynn in 1991. Electric services on the ECML from King's Cross to Leeds, Newcastle and Edinburgh were operational by 1991. This became Britain's premier route, as the thirty year old electrification of the WCML began to show its age and cancellation of the APT[19] in 1983, owing to technical difficulties and rising costs, created an investment hiatus. Paddington and St Pancras remained as the only major London termini without electrified main line services.

The beneficial impacts of Sectorisation and the continuing ability of rail to provide competitive access to activity nodes, despite the government's policies, was demonstrated by NSE and Provincial. Between 1983 and 1989, PSO subsidy for NSE fell from £328m to £149m.[20] Although commuting into Central London grew with the economic upturn of the late 1980s, NSE was also mindful of other markets such as travel *into* centres like Reading, Croydon and Milton Keynes. These experienced significant growth in commercial floorspace and some[21] of it was located in their centres and was accessible by rail. In 1992, 19,600 commuters left Milton Keynes each workday whereas 25,000 arrived (Bendixson and Platt 1992, 269), an interesting outcome given the wartime debate over new towns and London's railway network.

Despite the buoyancy of rail travel into London and the fact that plans had been laid decades previously to improve main line penetration, none had come to pass by the mid-1980s. But, as an example of a broader phenomenon, such a cross-London link was provided very cheaply by imaginative, low cost investment. This was the Thameslink scheme which was conceived in the 1960s (Calvert 1965), but eventually came to fruition as a result of work by GLC planners, before the authority was disbanded in 1986. Opened in 1988, Thameslink utilised Snow Hill tunnel, the only cross-central London tunnel built by the Victorians on the main line network, which linked Farringdon with Blackfriars[22]. Through passenger services had been withdrawn from this line during the First World War and subsequently it had been used for inter-regional freight movements which declined to the point where the tunnel was closed in the 1970s. With services linking Bedford and Gatwick Airport and giving direct access to the City, Thameslink was an immediate success. BR took advantage of the property boom to remove the bridge at Ludgate Hill by burying the railway under a new office development financed

---

19   The sinuous character of the WCML meant that it was particularly dependent on tilt to achieve higher average speeds.

20   The BRB annual reports for 1987/88 and 1988/89 record consecutive record breaking years for passenger ridership, with InterCity recording a £57m profit in 1988/89, its first year as a fully commercial business. Government support had been cut by 51 per cent between 1983 and 1988/89.

21   Most of it was road oriented B1 office park development though.

22   This route had used the bridge over Ludgate Hill which had probably attracted even more acrimony from the aesthetic establishment than Hungerford Bridge, as it blighted the view of St Paul's Cathedral.

by Rosehaugh Stanhope, which entered into a deal with the Property Board to fund a new station too, St Paul's Thameslink (Cordner 1990). One of the most notable positive impacts of the creation of the NSE sector was Marylebone and the suburban lines out to the Chilterns. Previously threatened with closure, under Chris Green they received 'total route modernisation' with new signalling, new trains and station refurbishment in place by 1991, enabling the railway to serve the growing townships in the M40 corridor. Research by Headicar and Bixby (1992) showed how timely this was, and how the relaxed planning regime of the 1980s in association with road building, was leading to traffic congestion and other problems in the Chiltern corridor.

Despite investment in the network there was still plenty of evidence of the government's parsimony towards BR: the 1988/89 annual report recorded a series of deaths from accidents in late 1988 early 1989, 35 at Clapham, 5 at Purley, and 2 at Bellgrove. These created a sombre mood and there was widespread speculation as to whether the drive for economies, resulting in excessive overtime and the creation of rationalised 'single lead' junctions which produced conflicting train paths requiring more staff vigilance, could be contributory factors. One of the most notable examples with regard to constraints on capital investment was the Dornoch Bridge saga on the Scottish Far North Line[23] from Inverness to Wick and Thurso. Despite much effort by BR when the road bridge over the Dornoch Firth was planned, the government refused to sanction additional expenditure to incorporate a single line railway in the structure, which opened in 1991. The result is that the railway continues to meander around the various inlets on the coast and is 161 miles long, whereas the road mileage has been reduced to 100 miles. On the other hand the collapse of the railway bridge over the River Ness at Inverness in the winter of 1989/90, did not lead to closure of the whole Far North route as it might have done: the bridge was rebuilt expeditiously.

Development outcomes in the 1980s

The City of London Corporation responded to the threat posed by Canary Wharf by relaxing its strictly conservationist approach to development. Between 1988–92 nearly 2 million square metres (21 million square feet) of office development was built in the City (Corporation of London 1995) and this did produce schemes which were well integrated with the railway network. Another impact of the focus on Docklands was that it deflected attention away from more centrally located derelict areas where investment would have benefited central London's transport network, as well as the specific developments concerned. For example, the King's Cross Railway Lands, which lay in an area designated in the GLDP as a 'preferred location' for offices, and was potentially one of the biggest schemes for the Property

---

23   This had been proposed for closure by Beeching but was saved by a broad based 'MacPuff' campaign (Farr 1999).

Board, was not brought to fruition at this time. The appalling fire at King's Cross underground station in 1987 which claimed 32 lives, served to underline the air of neglect which hung over much of the Underground. Furthermore, in the King's Cross area there were extensive areas of non-operational railway land as well as a number of listed warehouses and other buildings: a proposal to redevelop the whole area for commercial development, in association with construction of an underground Channel Tunnel rail terminal, was the subject of a Parliamentary Bill promoted by BR in 1989. A scheme of this magnitude, so closely linked with rail access by Underground, suburban, inter-city and international high speed services, was a qualitative leap beyond even Broadgate (see below) and was on a par with that at Lille. But, with the focus on Docklands, the government's unwillingness to put public money into the Channel Tunnel high speed link, and then the collapse of the property market in 1990/91, the scheme was dropped.

Although the experience in Docklands was cited as evidence of the failure of the government's approach, at the end of the day because these developments took place in London where satisfactory access demanded rail infrastructure, they were eventually well served by rail. The quality of stations was generally excellent, both in terms of their visual appearance and the convenient access they provided to major developments. That at Canary Wharf was designed to a very high architectural specification and provided easy access to the commercial developments it served, as it was integrated into the building complex. This stood out as an example of what could have been achieved elsewhere, but the irony was that this resulted from private sector master planning in a situation where the statutory planning system was marginalised. The reason was that the market demanded rail access. The DLR extension to Beckton opened in 1994, running alongside the former Royal Docks. Although the collapse of the property market in 1989/90 severely delayed the redevelopment of the Royals, it is notable that this infrastructure was put in place well in advance of the market, the reverse of the government's approach in the 1980s, which was indicative of the change towards a more planning led and rail focused approach.

Investment in rail to serve new development was not the general experience in the provinces where the overall intensity of urbanisation and its associated levels of road traffic congestion were less constraining. The relaxation of planning control encouraged developers to submit planning applications for major out-of-centre regional shopping centres (those in excess of 100,000 square metres (1m square feet)) in car dependent locations with inadequate or no railway connections. Between 1982–91 there were 54 such applications: until 1987 the only example built was Brent Cross, but between 1987–92 60 per cent of retail development was out-of-centre, including several regional centres (DoE 1994a), as shown in Table 8.2. Whereas the Tyne and Wear Metro system provided excellent access to Eldon Square, the Gateshead Metro Centre, opened in 1987, was not on the Metro system although a new station was provided on the BR Newcastle-Carlisle route which adjoins the site, but this provided very inadequate access to the rest of the conurbation. In the West Midlands the Merryhill Centre at Dudley was also built with no rail connections at all. Similar large centres were still in the planning stage at this time but were going forward on the basis of not being rail accessible: these included the White Rose Centre in Leeds, Cribb's Causeway in Bristol and the Trafford Centre, Manchester. Developments of this scale outside city centres and with poor or none existent rail services, would have been unacceptable under the planning regime of the 1970s and were symptomatic of the impact of Thatcherism on the locational utility of the railway network. The development at Meadowhall was the major exception as, quite fortuitously, it was located next to a railway junction and was within the territory of the South Yorkshire PTA which was interested in promoting rail access. A £7.5 million bus-rail interchange was provided which included the terminus for the new light rail system and, arguably, Meadowhall became more accessible by public transport than Sheffield city centre (Donnison 1992).

The huge growth in suburban and peri-urban office development, typified by that in the M4 corridor such as Stockley Park, those in the Reading/Bracknell area and Aztec West at Bristol, was strongly associated with the growth of car traffic and was inaccessible by rail. Hall (in Breheny et al. 1989) considered that, although decentralisation was initially highly correlated with commuting back to London, the growth of office employment in the reception areas led to many commuters finding work nearer home. Access to this was usually by car leading to the tangle of car based journeys-to-work so common in the American urban fringe leading to the condition of what Hall, following Cervero (1986), labelled 'Suburban Gridlock'.

The accelerated rate of development experienced in Cambridge in the 1980s was a good example of a case wherein typical policies of the time collectively produced a very complex transport problem. Rationalisation of the local railway network post-Beeching had seen closure of several local branch lines, including that to the 'expanded town' of Haverhill, some 24 km (15 miles) to the south east, and the route to St Ives and Huntingdon to the north west. As a historic city, Cambridge was set within a green belt, but a large number of 'B1' developments were built within the city along with requisite car parking. The housing to accommodate the additional population attracted to the area tended to be provided in small towns and villages outside the green belt, owing to lack of space within Cambridge itself: the result was large growth in car commuting across the green belt and growing traffic congestion within Cambridge. Although the 1989 version of the Cambridgeshire structure plan had a transport section which contained bus policies, there were no rail policies, despite a long standing campaign by the RDS to re-open services between Cambridge and St Ives (Cambridgeshire County Council 1989). However the policy changes of the early 1990s were in evidence in Cambridge too, and the county council began to develop ideas about congestion charging (Tomkins 1991) and using the income generated to fund public transport projects, including a light rail system which would utilise some disused trackbeds as well as other alignments (Cambridge Traffic Planning and Liaison Select Panel 1990). However, at the end of the day because of the usual government concerns over cost, the plans eventually crystallised as a bus rapid transit system (BRT) using the former St Ives railway for part of the network.

In 1983, encouraged by the pro-developer stance of the Conservatives, ten of the country's biggest housebuilders had got together to form Consortium Developments with the aim of securing planning permission for private new settlements. These were characterised by the selection of sites not allocated for development in statutory plans[24] and the aim was to secure approval on appeal. Following the backlash against the proposed relaxation of green belts, these projects caused major political problems for the government. Although few were built, they were significant in transportation terms as their motorway oriented locations and low density designs epitomised the car-oriented nature of new housing development in this period, typified perhaps by the expansion of Reading at Lower Earley. Even where a new station was opened in association with private sector township, as at Beckton on the DLR or Chafford Hundred in Essex, the layout was not planned on the Runcorn model to secure the maxim number of residents and/or trip generators within easy walking distance.

The BR Property Board and surplus railway land in the 1980s

The dominant feature of the relationship between planning authorities and the Property Board was the reclamation, typically by means of the Derelict Land Programme, of derelict railway land: the amounts requiring reclamation were reported as 6,400 hectares (15,815 acres) in 1974, 6,000 hectares (14,826 acres) in 1982, and despite continuing reclamation works, still 5,000 hectares (12,355 acres) in 1988 (DoE 1990).[25] Other planning involvement was with facilitating the redevelopment of this land. Research by Gore (1986, 297-314) revealed that in 1985 BR had 8,119 hectares (20,050 acres) of non-operational land and that, of 13,518 km (8,400 miles) of railway line closed post-Beeching, 11,885 km (7385 miles) (88 per cent) had been sold. In addition 36,000 hectares (89,000 acres) of 'nodal' land, i.e. that formerly occupied by depots and sidings, had been disposed of. Gore looked at the types of development which had taken place on land disposed of in his South Wales case study, concluding that over a third of all sites had been used for housing, with a fifth being used for industry and warehousing, although many former 'lines' remained vacant. Unsurprisingly given the close, historic

24 The first project, Tillingham Hall in Essex, was in fact in the green belt.

25 The 1982 BRB annual report noted that 34,803 ha (86,000 acres) of land had been disposed of since 1964, reducing the size of the railway estate by one third. Some 4,856 ha (12,000 acres) of railway land, 6 per cent of the estate in England and Wales, was listed on the Registers of Vacant Land. The 1985/86 annual report noted that the length of closed lines to be disposed of dropped to less than 1,609 km (1000 miles) for the first time since 1964. The 1989/90 annual report noted that 4,909 ha (12,130 acres) of land had been removed from the statutory Land Registers since 1980.

relationship between the railway network and patterns of urbanisation in South Wales, most of these redeveloped sites were within major centres of population. But significantly, like Paul's findings in Liverpool (1980), Gore found that:

> Perhaps the most significant finding is the extent to which railway use has been replaced by roads and related purposes. As well as car parks, the latter includes new vehicle distribution centres ... car showrooms ... and bus garages ... in spite of the increased support given to railway passenger services via the Valleys Rail Strategy ... further land-use shifts from rail to road are likely in future (1986, 312).

Local planning authorities were often resistant to the proposed uses of this land which included industry and, especially, retail development including supermarkets and D-I-Y stores: sometimes housing was proposed. This was not usually because of a desire to retain the land for transport use, let alone for railway restoration, but because of 'normal' planning problems such as inadequate road access or proximity to existing none compatible uses. Because of these difficulties, the Property Board became adept at arguing that certain uses, particularly 'storage', were a continuation of the former railway use and therefore did not require planning permission with the result that:

> To the general public, one of the most noticeable signs of the railway's favoured treatment is adverse; the number of former goods yards used for what at its kindest can only be called environmentally unfriendly purposes. At how many stations, still used or not, does one see in the adjoining yard an untidy scrap dealer, road haulier or builder's merchant? (Biddle 1990, 246).

Such cases were a good illustration of how the Property Board's commercial remit worked against the needs of the operational railway because of the poor image they lent to station environs. Additionally the BRB was under particularly strong pressure from government in the early 1980s to secure income from land disposal: the 1981 annual report stated that the emphasis on cash flow would lead to the loss of long term financial benefits: transport benefits were not even on the government's agenda.

On the other hand the late 1980s boom gave the Property Board the opportunity to develop several major schemes of great commercial value which were also relevant to rail ridership and well designed. The City Corporation was particularly willing to progress such schemes so as to reinforce the City's role as London's primary office market. Schemes which gave rail an almost captive market included developments at Fenchurch Street, where the 1856 facade was retained as the frontispiece to an airspace development and, especially, the 390,193 sq m (4.2 million square feet) Broadgate Centre. This, also by Rosehaugh Stanhope (1991), involved closure and redevelopment of Broad Street Station as well as an airspace development over part of the adjoining Liverpool Street station and provided funds for refurbishment of the remaining train shed and the station concourse, producing the best quality railway interchange in the UK at that time. Elsewhere in central London, the Property Board secured development of the Plaza office and retail development at Victoria, and a particularly striking scheme by Terry Farrell and Partners at Charing Cross which projected the walkway from Hungerford Bridge into the station concourse (Architects' Journal 1986; Haywood 1997b). London Transport was able to work with London Boroughs in similar fashion and to secure developments over or adjacent to its stations which also provided money for station refurbishment: Gloucester Road, Kensington and the Broadway Centre at Hammersmith were notable examples.

Outside London the Property Board was involved in major station related commercial schemes at locations as widespread as Aberdeen (16, 723 sq m/180,000 square feet), Welwyn (the Howard Centre – 18,581 sq m/200,000 square feet), and Reading (18,581 sq m/200,000 square feet). The financial returns were impressive, with the Property Board showing growth in income from £121 million in 1985/86 to £370 million in 1989/90, and the location of major commercial facilities at rail nodes was beneficial for ridership too.

The railway renaissance in the provincial conurbations

Co-operation between the PTEs, the Provincial sector and local planning authorities produced a resurgence of integrated planning. It has been shown that, historically, the relationship between the growth of Birmingham and its railway network was weaker than in other conurbations. However, the redevelopment of New Street, the development of Birmingham International, followed by success with the Cross City line, had significantly strengthened this relationship. Subsequent events transformed the West Midlands from the third category model used in Chapter 7 to a combination of the first and second. The first major achievement was the re-opening of Snow Hill in 1987 as the terminus for local trains from the Leamington Spa and Stratford lines to the south. The planning authorities had played a significant role in this as the County and City Councils had protected the trackbed. The new station, although rather minimal and ugly architecturally, was developed as part of an office and car park development by the Property Board and served the growing number of office developments in the adjoining parts of the city centre. By 1989 the WMPTE had plans to extend rail services westwards to Worcester via Stourbridge by re-opening the closed line between Snow Hill and Smethwick, which would provide further relief to the congested New Street. This had been made worse by steady improvements in medium distance services between Birmingham and destinations such as Worcester, Cardiff, Nottingham and Cambridge as a result of 'Sprinterisation'. The Smethwick re-opening included new stations, such as The Hawthorns to serve West Bromwich Albion football ground (Boynton 1989) and was completed by 1995.

Overall in the West Midlands there was a mood of optimism about the local railway network and, reflecting this, the PTE changed its name to 'Centro', and developed a new corporate logo and train livery scheme: as with BR, the government's emphasis on market forces and entrepreneurialism was having unexpected beneficial impacts on the activities of public bodies. The optimism went further: the Cross-City line service was experiencing problems owing to worn out rolling stock and infrastructure and, in 1988, the PTE submitted an investment case to the DoT to upgrade it, including electrification. This met with the usual delays as the Department appraised the scheme and debated its rate of return, but the project was eventually approved by the Secretary of State for Transport, Cecil Parkinson, in 1990 and, by 1993, the whole improved route between Lichfield, New Street and Redditch was operational. Also Centro began to work up plans to develop a light rail route between Snow Hill and Wolverhampton on the trackbed of the former GWR main line which had been protected by the planning authorities.

During this period Birmingham City Council began to develop and implement an ambitious regeneration strategy for the city centre which involved pedestrianisation, reducing the barrier effects of the orbital ring road and promoting property led regeneration of peripheral areas outside the CBD core. Given what has been said in this book about the significance of CBD activity to demand for rail travel, this was an important change from the previous strategy which had primarily focused on areas outside the CBD: older industrial areas, the NEC and the urban periphery. By 1991 the International Convention Centre, the Symphony Hall and the Hyatt Hotel were complete and this was followed by production of the City Centre Strategy in 1992 (Birmingham City Council 1992) and the Planning and Urban Design Framework for the Convention Centre Quarter (Birmingham City Council 1994). The latter subsequently facilitated the very successful Brindley Place development which was well linked with the CBD core and incorporated plans for a new station, adjacent to the new Indoor Arena, to serve the whole of this new quarter. The combined outcome of rail improvements along with a much strengthened CBD to which access from the stations was facilitated by good urban design, was very positive in the face of what had been a very hostile context in the early 1980s. It demonstrated the underlying strengths of Birmingham's railway inheritance and the importance of the protection of closed routes following the excesses of the post-Beeching period.

This resurgence, reflecting the renewed interest in urban design amongst planners, architects and developers, was mirrored by similar developments elsewhere: Glasgow was a significant example where there was a planning-led regeneration of the Merchant's Quarter (City of Glasgow District Council Planning Department 1992). Another favourable outcome for rail travel resulted from development of the site of the former St Enoch station, closed in 1966. The great train shed and the associated hotel were demolished in 1977, a great loss architecturally, but the site was subject to a major retail redevelopment which opened in the late 1980s: its proximity to Argyle Street and Central Stations and the Underground, facilitated rail access.[26]

Despite positive outcomes in CBDs such as Birmingham and Glasgow, the underlying weakness of the overall relationship between land-use planning and rail development was highlighted by the development of the South Yorkshire Supertram. The importance to this project of securing positive impacts on the local property market has already been noted, as has the weakness of the institutional and policy contexts to deliver it. Research between 1992–96[27] utilising planning applications as indicators of development activity around the light rail route, and which also looked at comparable data around contemporary new roads in corridors parallel to Supertram, concluded that:

> ... there was little evidence of South Yorkshire Supertram regenerative impacts
> ... but that there was evidence of them clustering around the road corridor
> (Haywood 1998, 38).

This research also utilised data on land-use change within an 800 metre wide corridor around the Supertram route and similarly concluded that:

> There was little evidence of South Yorkshire Supertram having exerted a locational pull on the pattern of major developments in Sheffield, but there was evidence that the Lower Don Valley Link Road had exerted such a pull (Haywood 1998, 38).

This research produced powerful evidence to show that, even where there was an explicit policy requirement to integrate land-use and rail development, the institutional and policy contexts existing in Sheffield at the time, more or less guaranteed that this would not be the outcome. The combined effect of market forces and a *laissez-faire* planning regime meant that any new development was far more likely to be drawn towards the roads (Lawless 1999).[28]

Given that Newcastle and Liverpool had received significant investment in their local railway networks it was not to be expected that, in the political climate of the 1980s, there would be any major projects subsequently. However, Merseyside

---

26   The Buchanan Galleries retail centre was opened in 1999 on the site of the former Buchanan Street station, also closed in 1966, adjoining the extant Queen Street high and low level stations and the Subway – see Chapter 11.

27   This research went beyond the 1994 cut off date but, as Supertram was operational by 1994, it is relevant to consider the results here.

28   It is also important to note that BR used the building of Supertram as a reason to close stations at Attercliffe and Brightside in the Lower Don Valley: it is very questionable as to whether Supertram provided a satisfactory alternative and these closures looked more like a continuation of the historic trend of BR withdrawing from the local travel market in Sheffield's inner area, as in many other provincial cities.

PTE opened some new stations, with that at suburban Halewood in 1988 being the most significant as it had a 10,000 catchment within a half-mile radius (RDS 1992, 12). Tyne and Wear PTE opened an extension of the existing Metro to Newcastle Airport in 1992. It is notable though that in both cities the designated UDAs were not readily accessible by rail, with that in Newcastle being particularly poor. An analysis of travel-to-work trends using 1981–91 census data (Beatty and Haywood 1997), showed that rail ridership showed only small increases, with some decreases, except in Tyne and Wear where the impact of the Metro was obvious (Table 8.4). The 1981 figures for Merseyside show that the 1970s improvements had already had an impact.

Table 8.4 Percentage of resident working population using rail for travel-to-work 1981–91 in English PTE areas

PTE	1981	1991
Greater Manchester	2.4	2.2
Merseyside*	5.1	5.2
South Yorkshire	0.5	0.8
Tyne and Wear*	1.9	6.4
West Midlands	2.1	1.9
West Yorkshire	1.0	1.5

Note: * includes ridership classed as 'underground' in census data i.e. Liverpool Loop and Link and the Tyne and Wear Metro.

Although data compatibility problems precluded analysis of rail ridership trends for the workplace populations in the PTE areas, the percentages using rail were similar to those of the resident population in 1991, ranging from 0.8 per cent in South Yorkshire to 5.4 per cent and 5.9 per cent in Merseyside and Tyne and Wear respectively. It is notable from other data sources though that the improvement of services between provincial cities through Sectorisation and Sprinterisation, coupled to the renaissance of their CBDs, did lead to increased ridership on CBD to CBD services: for example that between Manchester and Leeds was reported as increasing by 55 per cent between 1986/87 and 1991/92 (Abbott 1992).

Railway renaissance: the 'shires'

The strategy for the Valley Lines developed jointly by local managers in the Provincial sector and the county councils produced what has been claimed to be the best local rail service of its type in Europe: annual passenger journeys increased from 4.7 million in 1982 to reach a peak of 9.5 million in 1990/91 with 30,000 daily passengers. Historically the Valley Lines had served towns, such as Pontypridd and Caerphilly, where stations were conveniently located for passengers travelling in from surrounding areas. However, the major asset of the network was Cardiff Queen Street station which had long provided a convenient access to the city centre and was the busiest station in Wales.[29] During the 1970s the Valley Lines benefited from a £0.75M improvement scheme which included works to most of the 46 stations on the network at that time and the redevelopment of Queen Street was completed in 1975.[30] In the 1980s, the planning process facilitated further office development around Queen Street and the central retail area saw major investment too, including a new mall and extensive pedestrianisation. The support from the county councils and the Welsh Development Agency for station building and line re-opening produced a remarkable improvement in rail accessibility with the first new station opening at Cathays in 1983, followed by a further fifteen new stations involving the re-opening of passenger services along the Cardiff 'City' line in 1985, to Aberdare in 1988, and to Maesteg in 1993 (Railway Development Society 1992; Davies and Clark 1996). A novel feature of the Valleys renaissance was the use of dedicated feeder bus services which appeared in the railway timetable and provided a rail link into the wider community.

The creation of the Cardiff Bay Development Corporation (CBDC) in 1988 presented a significant transport problem as it wanted to promote the former dock area, located to the south of the city centre, for developments which would have a significant impact on passenger trip generation. There was a rail link into the dock area, the Bute Town branch, but this ran on an embankment along an alignment where CBDC wished to build a road link to the city centre. CBDC floated plans to demolish this and replace it by street running light rail which would link into the Valleys Network, which would be partially converted to light rail on the core routes. This ambitious plan did not come to fruition and there was no significant improvement in rail services into the UDA, although there was major investment in new roads (Davies and Clark 1996, 65). This outcome in Cardiff was further evidence of the failure of the UDA mechanism, outside London, to integrate land development with local railway networks.[31]

---

29   Cardiff Central, on the Great Western main line, is very accessible to the city centre too.

30   The largest of the associated office developments, Brunel House, became HQ for the Western Region. Similar offices for regional managements were opened in the 1960s and 1970s at Manchester Piccadilly, Sheffield Midland, Plymouth and East Croydon. Although convenient for railway staff, the fact that they all travelled free meant that commercially this was a questionable use of such valuable rail accessible developments.

31   Gore (1986, 323) showed that the projected investment in the Valleys Rail Strategy, £17M over five years, was very modest compared with investment in new

In Nottinghamshire the first phase of the Robin Hood project between Nottingham and Newstead opened in 1993 and the route through to Mansfield was open by early 1995; overall this involved the construction of seven new stations (Sully 1995). Given organisational problems and rising costs associated with impending privatisation, this project stands as a remarkable monument to the strength of the relationship that was developed between Regional Railways and the local authorities, particularly the counties, and the town planning process was a significant element of this[32] (Haywood 1992).

Partnerships between the shires and various BR bodies were also formed to achieve more modest goals. For example, there was one established in 1983 between Hampshire County Council, NSE, and BR's Community Unit, which worked to improve existing stations and their settings, bridges, and the linesides (Hampshire County Council et al. 1993). The visual attractiveness of the station schemes gave the railway a positive and re-assuring image, a factor which was increasingly recognised as important in facilitating ridership as BR became more 'customer aware'. Other partnerships, such as that in Devon and Cornwall, worked to promote ridership on rural lines. This was by: producing promotional material; encouraging tourist facilities to locate on or near stations; developing footpaths and cycle routes linked to stations; and including supportive policies in relevant statutory land-use plans (Regional Railways et al. 1993). This work went well beyond land-use planning and was indicative of just how sophisticated and supportive the relationship between BR and local authorities had become, based on an holistic view of how the railway could be used for maximum benefit to the community and BR.

Rail freight: mixed fortunes

For the reasons discussed previously, with the additional factor that most of the national motorway network was built by 1980, rail freight traffic continued to decline, leading to closures and disposal of land. For example, in Sheffield, Tinsley Yard became redundant and the Freightliner terminal closed.[33] This was followed by closure of nine other Freightliner terminals in 1987, including those at Edinburgh, Newcastle and Nottingham which left them, along with most other medium sized cities, with no rail freight facility at all. The rundown of the mining industry which provoked the desperate miner's strike of 1984–85, was a major threat to the coal traffic which, despite all the new business developed post-Beeching, continued

---

roads in Mid and South Glamorgan in 1981–86 of £128.5 million, this being followed by construction of the Cardiff Peripheral Distributor Road at a projected cost of £165 million.

32   The line subsequently opened through to Worksop in 1997 with construction of a further four new stations.

33   The only rail freight left in this archetypal railway age city, was a couple of spurs into steel works.

to be the mainstay of the rail freight industry. Surprisingly, in the late 1980s rail haulage of coal increased as British Coal persuaded a number of major industrial concerns to switch their energy source from oil to coal and Trainload Coal was very focused in its pursuit of business. Lower cost opencast coal was increasingly attractive to British Coal and growth of this drew planning authorities into greater contact with the industry: they usually demanded rail transport as a requirement of planning consent. Durham and Northumberland County Councils became particularly involved with the development of rail connected concentration and disposal points at Wardley and Haltwhistle respectively (Allen 1990).

The 1980s property boom and, ironically, the government's road building programme, also stimulated the rail freight market because of the demand for aggregates and Trainload Construction was well placed to take advantage of this. With the boom focused in the South East and the primary aggregate sources being in other regions, typically the Mendips and Charnwood Forest, rail haulage made good economic sense. This was also desirable from the minerals planning authorities' points of view too. This traffic was so significant as to provide sufficient incentive for one of the Mendips quarry operators, Foster Yeoman, to acquire a fleet of five locomotives to haul[34] their own wagons which had previously been hauled by BR locomotives. Customers often had their own wagons but to acquire locomotives was unprecedented and was held up as evidence of BR's customer focus and flexibility. ARC followed suit a few years later and Redlands also invested in a train of 'self-discharging' wagons to give greater flexibility in delivery. These investments reflected the government's market-led minerals planning regime which recognised the need to import construction materials into the South East, and the suitability of rail for this work.

The buoyancy of the traditional traffics, whilst Freightliner was struggling, underlined the dominance of road haulage. All modes freight tonne-kilometres increased by 27 per cent between 1980–89, but rail's market share declined. From a land development perspective this marginalisation was illustrated by the fact that, even where major new manufacturing complexes were developed, such as by Nissan at Sunderland and Toyota near Derby, the plants were not rail connected. This was despite their proximity to railways and BR's experience elsewhere in serving the automotive industry. The ideological context was not one where the local planning authorities felt that they should, or could, demand rail haulage to reduce the environmental impact of these politically sensitive developments by inward investors.

The wagonload business suffered from the Sectorisation of the rail freight industry as the Sectors were reluctant to let another cost centre handle their traffic. Eventually this, and the difficult underlying economics of the wagonload business, provoked a crisis for Speedlink and, after a review, BR abandoned the business in 1991 and more yards were declared surplus to requirements (Shannon and Rhodes 1991). In the run up to privatisation, BR was forced to rationalise its operations in

---

34   These were operated by BR drivers.

order to maximise the profitability of its various businesses and this led to various 'marginal' flows being deliberately priced off the network and more customers[35] closed their rail links. The closure of the Ravenscraig steel plant at Motherwell in 1992, was further evidence of the decline of the traditional market. By 1995 rail freight's market share had declined to 6 per cent.

But construction of the Channel Tunnel provided an historic opportunity for rail to compete more effectively for international traffic where, theoretically at any rate, it should be able to offer faster delivery times than road at competitive rates. Prior to the opening of the Tunnel, rail could only offer a limited international service using purpose-built ferries. To develop the Tunnel traffic a network of inter-modal terminals and freight villages was developed. Railfreight Distribution took the lead, but private developers and local authorities were involved too. Some of the schemes involved the intensification of the use of existing 'stand-alone' terminals such as Manchester's Trafford Park, and these did not require planning consent. But the development of terminals and freight villages at Daventry, Hams Hall and Wakefield was historic in the sense that it involved the development of land not previously used for general rail freight. They also brought with them some significant planning policy issues as they showed that commercial developers had become aware of the potential to use rail access to proposed major freight distribution developments as a counter to planning policy concerns about the appropriateness of such development. For example, Wakefield Europort was jointly promoted by Wakefield Metropolitan District Council, Railfreight Distribution, and a private company, AMEC Developments, on a site adjoining junction 31 of the M62 and an existing industrial estate. The rail terminal was only a small part of the overall 140 hectares (350 acres) of land to be developed, most of which was green belt. The project was contrary to planning policy and was evidence of a failure to incorporate these new demands within the planning process. The development was subject to a public inquiry and was only granted planning permission by the Secretary of State, John Gummer, because of the exceptional and strategic significance of the rail freight facility. Significantly and wisely, the planning permission required the terminal to be built before any subsequent development of the site. A similar outcome occurred at Hams Hall, which was also a green belt site. In both cases the lasting impression was that they received planning permission despite the planning system, not as a product of it (Haywood 1999). In fact a similar project at Toton Sidings near Nottingham was the subject of two planning applications which were withdrawn in 1990 and a third, submitted in 1994, was refused consent in 1995 (Greensmith and Haywood 1999): no appeal was lodged. A further negative outcome occurred at what was the largest distribution development of the early 1990s, Magna Park off Junction 20 of the M1 near Lutterworth in Leicestershire. This was permitted by the planning process, with no rail access, and sat uncomfortably with the county's pro-

---

35 A significant example was the Castle cement works near Clitheroe: the cement industry had been a major BR customer for years but the traffic fell away rapidly. Smaller ports such as Boston, Goole and Kings Lynn also closed their links.

rail strategies: ironically the disused alignment of the former Great Central runs close by.

The Daventry scheme was the exception as its origins can be traced back through the planning process. Although located on what was open countryside, this was not green belt, and the strategic significance of the location was identified in supportive regional planning guidance: this site lies within an area known in the logistics industry as the 'golden triangle' as it is relatively close to very large centres of population and has excellent motorway connections to them. Subsequently the statutory local plan for the area was amended to incorporate the terminal and freight village (Daventry District Council 1993). This preparation meant that, when the planning application was submitted, it had a relatively smooth ride: local councillors were supportive of the economic benefits and approved the scheme, which was not 'called in'.

The overall outcome of the Channel Tunnel initiative (Tables 8.5 and 8.6) showed the difficulties in delivering a balanced strategy whilst depending upon the vagaries of the property market and the reactive development control process to deliver sites and funding. For example, terminals were developed very close to each other at Doncaster and Wakefield, and at Hams Hall and Daventry, whereas no new terminals and freight villages were delivered anywhere in the South East. Similarly, as shown in Table 8.5, the exclusion of Freightliner from the process left this business on historic and somewhat constrained sites, with that at Coatbridge being the worst example.

Table 8.5 BR Terminals developed for the Channel Tunnel and their relationship with the nearest Freightliner terminal

Location	Channel Tunnel traffic	Freightliner
Birmingham	Originally to be with Freightliner at Landor Street pending development of out-of-town site (this became Hams Hall – see Table 8.4)	Landor Street – established city centre site
Cardiff	To share Pengam with Freightliner	Pengam – established city centre site, since replaced by new terminal at Wentloog
Glasgow	Development of Mossend Euroterminal on largely greenfield site in association with industrial/warehousing development by Lanarkshire Development Agency	Terminal on cramped, established site with poor access to the motorway network a few miles to the north at Coatbridge
Liverpool	Development on existing rail site within the port area at Seaforth – no freight village	Garston – established site
London	Development of existing Freightliner facilities at Willesden and Stratford (latter not progressed)	Barking – established site
Manchester	New Euroterminal on BR land in Trafford Park – no freight village	Separate established site next to the Euroterminal
Wakefield	Europort – new development on green belt in assocation with industrial/warehousing development	Leeds (Stourton) on established site
Middlesbrough	To share Freightliner terminal – not developed as a Tunnel terminal	Freightliner continue to operate the established site

Table 8.6 Channel Tunnel terminals promoted by parties other than BR

Location	Developer
Daventry	Promoted by private sector on green field site in association with freight village
Doncaster	Promoted by Doncaster MBC on industrial land adjacent to longstanding BR freight facilities – no freight village
Hams Hall	Promoted by privatised electricity generator on former power station site in green belt in association with industrial/warehousing development
Toton	Promoted by private landowner in association with RfD on green belt land adjoining long established sidings area: planning permission refused, no appeal

Conclusions

The analysis of the 1968–94 period has showed that, as part of a second ideological swing towards integrated public transport, there was support for greater intervention in the railway industry to limit the impact of the commercialism of the early 1960s. By the mid-1970s, the fundamental questioning and rationalisation was over and the balance of power in the political debate over transport constrained the Treasury view. Nevertheless, the tensions between the commercial and social railways remained, with continuous pressure from all governments to cut costs. The interplay between ideology, institutional structures and policy was very complex over the period but at no time did they all fall into place in the railway sector's favour. The overriding outcome was that, despite all the positive outcomes reviewed above, rail passenger ridership did not change significantly over the period, despite a large overall increase in society's mobility: rail freight fared much worse and virtually collapsed.

The severe economic crisis of the early 1970s meant that, whatever its successes, the BRB's costs escalated and government intervention limited its ability to raise prices accordingly. The solution of 1968 provided only a temporary respite. The economic downturn post-1976 further compounded the problems and, by the late 1970s, the railway network was characterised by under-investment and what Peter Parker called 'the crumbling edge of quality'. On the other hand the achievements of the PTEs were a notable success with significant improvements in railway planning and investment, until the downturn post-1976. The presence of the PTEs, the GLC, the metropolitan and 'shire' counties and the creation of the BR Property Board, put in place institutional arrangements which could deliver pro-rail outputs, if the economic context was favourable and policy makers sought to use the structures favourably.

The major shifts in planning ideology in the late 1960s impacted at the local and strategic levels. At the local level came the pressures to democratise the planning process associated, particularly, with the change in housing policy from clearance to rehabilitation. At the strategic level came structure planning where there was a link with the emergence of the pro-rail stance in urban transport planning. Public involvement with planning spread to resistance to urban road building. This mix of institutional and ideological change was very favourable for the relationship between planning and the railways as compared with the situation post-1948, and there were some notably successful outcomes in the 1970s. The pro-public transport ideology which underpinned transport and land-use planning ensured that many major developments, particularly office and retail schemes, were restricted to city and town centres and were thus, broadly speaking, located favourably with regard to the railway network, often in association with improvement of the latter. But by the time the new local government system was beginning to bed down in the late 1970s, new planning issues had arisen which tended to push transport considerations down the agenda.

The economic downturn of the late 1970s, followed by Thatcherism, initially produced a very hostile policy context for the planning-railway interface. The BRB responded positively and the new emphasis on customers and markets under Robert Reid produced a break up of the monolithic 'corporate railway' and creation of the sectors. This led to a re-conceptualisation of the relationship with national and local government and to them being perceived as 'customers'. The BRB encouraged managers to pursue partnerships with local government, which extended to liaison over strategic and, to a lesser extent local, land-use planning policy development. The pressure from government to reduce dependency on the public purse, also forced the Property Board to become more aggressive in its land development activities. Although, on the one hand this led to short termism, on the other it produced high density, commercial developments around a number of major stations and countered the general market trend of car-oriented decentralisation, the archetypal development form of the 1980s. Overall the 1980s turned out to be a good decade for the railway industry and commentators referred to a 'railway renaissance'.

Town planning had much more difficulty in finding a response to Thatcherism. By the early 1980s when statutory land-use plans were adopted which sought to restrict major activity generators to rail accessible nodes, the government showed that it had no intention of constraining road oriented urban decentralisation: it saw virtue in encouraging it in fact. With so much emphasis on the primacy of market forces and the active encouragement of developments which ran counter to existing strategic policies, the very existence of planning was called into question. Initially, it was only through the work of the Property Board, and in situations such as Docklands, the City of London or the development of the Channel Tunnel terminals where the market happened to favour rail, that developments of any significance around rail nodes were achieved. But the successes were notable and, to varying degrees, did arise from positive engagement between the planning and railway sectors. In fact, the positive products of the market led trends produced a further shift in ideology, back towards pro-actively co-ordinating the sectors. These trends produced an unexpected ideological convergence around rail in the late 1980s, as the government began to pull back from its extreme deregulatory stance towards land-use planning. This period saw pro-rail policies coming to fruition across a wider front with re-opening of stations and lines, and the completion of development schemes which were rail accessible, including high quality schemes around stations. However, a thread running throughout the period was that the most rail-focused planning activity was safeguarding disused trackbeds and developing re-opening strategies in partnership with BR (and the PTAs/PTEs where appropriate): in other words putting back what BR and central government had previously taken away. This and the heavy reliance on a market-favoured approach to rail-oriented development, tended to give a geographically constrained, project-level bias to implementation, rather than more widespread activity to maximise accessibility across the network as a whole.

Despite the economic downturn in 1989–90, the ideology around integrated land-use planning around railways continued to strengthen. Several factors combined to produce this trend: these included the reaction against the development pressures of the previous few years; the perceived regenerative potential of rail schemes; and the general rise of environmental consciousness which focused increasingly on the negative aspects of road traffic growth. Changes in planning ideology produced the amended PPG13 in 1994 which showed an expectation that these trends would continue. This, for the first time since 1947, was an official planning policy document which set out how land-use policy should produce patterns of urban development which would facilitate utilisation of the railway network for passenger and freight purposes. It had taken nearly 50 years to arrive at that point. It seems remarkable that this innovation should have been produced by a government which took its ideological inspiration from Thatcherism. There has been much debate as to why the Conservatives used planning to lead their policy thrust towards environmentalism, and sceptics saw the reasons as being that it would have least impact on constraining business, whilst having a high public profile. Nevertheless, the experiences of the 1980s showed that there was real potential to skew land development patterns towards rail and that, in congested urban areas at least, there was an identifiable market trend towards that and planning could be used to encourage it.

A summary of the thematic analysis is shown in Table 8.7 and with regard to the list of points developed at the end of Chapter 2, the following summarises the overall outcome for the period with regard to the rail network:

1. *rationalisation of the network*: although much reduced, the process of rationalisation continued, but there was a counter thrust which saw re-opening of closed stations and lines in major conurbations and their hinterlands, demonstrating that the process of rationalisation had been taken too far;
2. *development of railway services*: significant improvements in the main line network were made to allow faster speeds, with completion of London-Scotland electrification on both main lines; electrification of local and semi-fast services on routes outside the South East was limited; at their best the quality of passenger services improved significantly with regard to speed, comfort and frequency for inter-city, regional and local services, but quality was patchy and, at the margins, cramped, squalid and unreliable. Similarly with regard to freight, core services with regard to bulk traffics were reliable and competitive, but the railway just did not try to compete for most traffic, although the advent of the Channel Tunnel brought better prospects for international intermodal services;
3. *closing strategic gaps in the network*: there were significant strategic improvements to the network including cross-CBD tunnelling/tunnel re-opening, LRT street running, building of new railway/light railway routes into major developments/regeneration areas, construction of one new London tube route, and opening of the Channel Tunnel;
4. *development of a programme of station enhancement*: although some stations were closed, the balance was heavily in favour of station openings, and there were some notable examples of major mixed use redevelopment projects in major towns and cities around stations;

The following summarises the outcome with regard to the operation of the planning system:

5. *patterns of urban development*: planning practice in the 1970s steered major trip generating uses to CBDs and there were some supportive developments in the new towns too which produced positive outcomes for inter-city and commuter services, but this was severely undermined in the 1980s, apart from special cases strongly favoured by the property market;
6. *management of the redevelopment process in existing urban areas*: planning practice in the 1970s steered development to locations in CBDs which were accessible to stations with generally a much weaker relationship in suburban developments, but even the CBD focus was undermined in the 1980s when development de-centralised, largely to rail inaccessible locations; during the 1970s the detail design of this relationship was generally poorly handled, but this was exceptionally well handled in those cases in the 1980s where development at and/or around stations was favoured by the property market; the closure and disposal of freight facilities continued throughout the period, although developments in mineral extraction and waste disposal

and construction of Channel Tunnel terminals brought some engagement with the planning process;

7. *management of the location and character of greenfield site development*: planning practice throughout the period with regard to greenfield areas continued to be to resist their development as far as possible and, where development took place, the prime transport consideration was to provide access by road: the exceptions to this trend continued to be in the new towns although the pace of development in most of them slackened considerably in the 1980s and, even where development continued, its relationship to the railway network was weaker than previously.

Table 8.7 Summary of thematic analysis of outcomes: 1969–94

Explanatory themes	Railway sector	Interrelationships between the two sectors	Planning sector
Politics and political ideology	Supportive context produced significant improvements to main line and local services to mid-1970s. Stagnation, followed by government hostility made it difficult to invest. But combination of market orientation and partnerships produced limited but significant benefits, despite this.	Positive outcomes in 1970s in London, some new towns and PTA/PTE areas, followed by stagnation. Recovery in late 1980s associated with sectorisation and urban regeneration in some areas, plus some shires. Continuing emphasis in rural areas on holding on to existing services, with some supportive developments.	The supportive context delivered some relevant developments in new towns and some CBDs to mid-1970s. Stagnation subsequently, followed by a flood of road oriented decentralisation in 1980s. Market oriented planning produced some relevant development, particularly in CBDs.

Explanatory themes	Railway sector	Interrelationships between the two sectors	Planning sector
Professions and professional ideology	In the 1970s the continued dominance of the technical professions improved inter-city and London commuter services: relationships with the PTEs influenced regional managers and delivered improved local services. Sectorisation reinforced the outward facing customer oriented role, which produced effective liaison with planning authorities.	A limited engagement in the 1970s which was of most significance in delivering macro co-locational outcomes in CBDs. Positive outcomes post-1979 were initially limited to locations favoured by the market, but growing liaison between the sectors developed wider benefits throughout the range of local authority areas.	Structure planning had a limited effect in restricting trip generators to CBDs, but the detail of development produced poor integration with stations. The largest and best designed pro-rail developments of the 1980s were largely market driven, although pro-rail planning ideology delivered significant re-openings and other benefits towards 1994.
Governance and management	The BR corporate period made liaison with planning authorities difficult, although the PTEs bridged the gap to a degree. Sectorisation revealed the benefits to be gained from working with the full range of planning bodies and delivered significant outcomes.	The creation of strategic local authority bodies in the 1970s helped relationships between the sectors, but by the time sectorisation produced a more receptive BR, government support for strategic planning had waned. The recovery towards the end of the period was delivering significant outcomes.	Many upper tier authorities pursued effective pro-rail strategies and the PTA/PTEs served as an effective bridge. Hostility to local government undermined planning's role in the 1980s, but the return to a more supportive government attitude produced a significant recovery with notable achievements by 1994.

Chapter 9

Case Study:
The Manchester City Region 1830–1994

It will be recalled from Chapter 1 that Manchester was selected as a case study as it can be seen as a model conurbation to demonstrate how the complex interplay of institutional structures and policy played out within a single city region. This is because it developed a complex railway network and the city radiated out along it in all directions on the level plain of the Manchester Embayment. It will be shown that the network exhibited prototypical strengths and weaknesses and played a significant role in urban decentralisation. In the 1948–94 period there was a great deal of change to this network, of both a positive and negative kind; this took place in the context of extensive land-use planning activity which had identifiable impacts upon patterns of urban development.

The chapter begins by briefly reviewing the history of the area's railway network, its relationship with patterns of urban development and the stance of land-use planning towards this, in order to define a benchmark to serve as a point of departure for the post-1947 analysis. The latter is structured using a spatially hierarchical approach comprising, firstly, an analysis of the impact of national policies on the broad geography of the Manchester railway system and its relationships with the growth patterns of the conurbation. Secondly, the analysis moves on to consider how regional, and particularly sub-regional, considerations impacted on the development of the railway network serving Manchester's CBD and its relationship to the development of that CBD, especially with regard to patterns of development close to stations. The third element considers two matters at the local level: detail patterns of development in a high growth area on the outer fringe of the conurbation and the re-use of surplus railway land.

Manchester 1947: the inherited relationship between the railway network, urban form and planning

Laissez-faire produced a network wherein east-west trans-Pennine routes criss-crossed north-south routes to London (Patmore 1964). One of the major companies, the Lancashire and Yorkshire, only served provincial markets on the east-west axis whereas the Midland and, particularly, the London and North Western, had trunk routes to London. The Manchester Sheffield and Lincolnshire Railway started life as a trans-Pennine company but developed into the Great Central, with its main line to Marylebone. Manchester was provided with several major stations

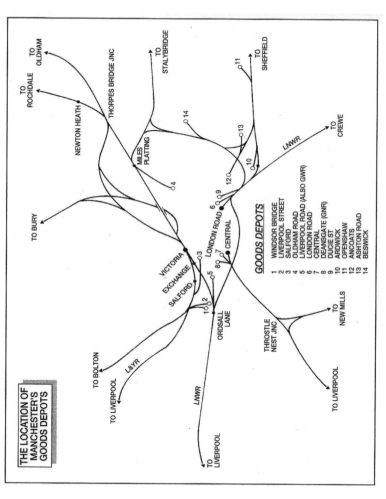

Figure 9.1 Lines, stations and goods depots around central Manchester: 1914

Source: Hall, S. (1995), *Rail Centres: Manchester* (London: Ian Allan Ltd).

and goods facilities around the periphery of the CBD (Figure 9.1), and there were many areas of extensive sidings on the various approaches.[1] Although the network was complex, basically it comprised two separate sub-systems, one to the north of the city and the other to the south. London Road, Oxford Road, and Central stations became the focal points of the southern network, and Victoria, Exchange and Salford were their counterparts to the north.

From the 1860s Manchester developed middle class railway suburbs, largely outside the City's administrative boundary; these included Prestwich to the north, Heaton Moor, Wilmslow, and Alderley Edge to the south, and Urmston, Flixton, Sale and Altrincham[2] to the west. In response to competition from street tramways, the railway companies invested in services to the outer suburbs; in 1909 the London Road-Wilmslow via Styal (the Styal line) was opened,[3] and in 1916 the steeply graded Victoria-Bury line was electrified. Although these brought rail access to growing suburbs, most of Manchester's inner suburbs, and certainly its most notable planned suburbs, Chorltonville and Burnage, were more readily accessible by street tram (Sutcliffe 1981).

The development of middle class suburbs was strongly related to the transformation of central Manchester from a residential and industrial area into a CBD with ample employment in various white collar jobs as housing and industry decentralised. The core of the CBD was most readily accessible from Exchange and Victoria stations. However the main area of grand warehouse development, which was Manchester's most distinctive contribution to Victorian architecture, lay along the Portland Street axis and was much closer to London Road;

> which provided the impetus for such lavish buildings, for it was the line to Euston that brought important clients up from London (Parkinson-Bailey 2000, 73).[4]

Manchester's network was largely owned by the LMS during the period of the 'Big Four'. Little rationalisation occurred and the only significant improvement was electrification of the Manchester-Altrincham line in 1931, which allowed the railway to compete more effectively with trams and buses for the traffic from the growing suburbs along this important axis: two new stations were opened

---

1   Many of these were associated with various industrial complexes such as breweries, collieries, gas plants, steel works and engineering works, but others were 'exchange' sidings necessitated by the interfaces between the various company networks.

2   Patmore (1964, 167) commented that the Manchester South Junction and Altrincham Railway opened in 1849 was: 'purely suburban in function but from its opening had an intensive passenger service and did much to develop the south-western outskirts of Manchester as a residential area'.

3   This included the opening of Mayfield as a major extension to London Road in the city centre.

4   In the following sections various major developments and their chronology are referred to, and unless otherwise stated, this publication is the source.

at Navigation Road and Dane Road. On the Manchester-Irlam-Liverpool line[5] stations were also opened at Chassen Road near Flixton and at Old Trafford (on the instigation of Manchester United football club). Despite recession in the cotton industry, there were further commercial developments in the core of the CBD which maintained demand for rail travel. These included major office developments along King Street such as Ship Canal House and the Midland Bank, Arkwright House in St Mary's Parsonage, and the Rylands and Kendal Milne's department stores.

Post-1919, Manchester City Council tackled its slum problem but shortage of land forced it to look outside the City boundary. It was successful in 1926 in what was then north Cheshire where it decided to build a garden city, Wythenshawe, with a projected population of over 100,000 (Her Majesty's Stationery Office 1995). However, despite this size, the peripheral location and proximity to railway lines, this was not focused around a rapid rail link to the mother city: municipal bus services to the tram terminus in south Manchester were used instead, a rather tenuous link.

As in other cities a plan to guide reconstruction was produced during the Second World War, the Nicholas plan (Nicholas 1945). This only related to the administrative area of the City of Manchester and so could not address the strategic development of the wider conurbation. It incorporated extensive proposals for orbital roads, but had little to say about integration between the railway network and outer suburban growth. However, Roy Hughes of the LMS assisted with the plan and, as a result, it recognised the need for better rail access to Wythenshawe and links across the city centre. However it rejected the idea of a connecting tunnel as too costly and proposed an elevated loop line around the periphery of the CBD with rationalisation of the city centre stations.

The important points about Manchester's railway network and its relationship with the area's urban geography which would influence the post-1947 period were:

- there was duplication of lines, stations and goods facilities;
- there was a tradition of rail served outer suburban growth, but this was overlooked in the development of Wythenshawe;
- the north and south networks were poorly linked;
- penetration of Manchester's CBD was poor;
- electrification was limited to two suburban routes;
- local authority transport and land-use planning for the wider area was dominated by municipal engineers and road building.

---

5   This line was operated by the Cheshire Lines Committee (CLC), created by the Manchester Sheffield and Lincolnshire Railway, the Great Northern and the Midland. The CLC was created to break into the territory of the London and North Western: like some other 'joint lines' it remained outside the Grouping but became part of BR's London Midland Region on nationalisation (Dyckhoff 1999).

The impact of national policies across the city region: rail policy 1947–94

For most of the period the BR regional structure placed Manchester in the London Midland Region: although there was a local management presence in Manchester this was largely concerned with operating matters and the big decisions were taken in London. One of the few early strategic investments was electrification of the Manchester (London Road)-Sheffield via Woodhead route, completed in 1954. Although the rationale for this was interregional freight haulage, particularly coal, it facilitated electric haulage of express passenger services,[6] as well suburban services to Glossop and Hadfield.[7] The Modernisation Plan led to electrification of the WCML to London, including the spurs to Manchester via both Crewe/Wilmslow[8] and Stoke-on-Trent/Macclesfield (these routes joining up at Stockport to the south of Manchester), with a significant reduction in journey times and growth of passenger traffic. London Road was modernised and renamed Manchester Piccadilly in 1960 becoming a flagship station for the modernised railway. By 1968, local electric trains worked to Stoke and Crewe and station rebuilding in the new, functional style took place at Cheadle Hulme, Handforth and Macclesfield. Because electrification was restricted to the London trunk routes, there were significant gaps with regard to strategic routes serving Manchester, particularly the two Manchester-Liverpool routes and Manchester-Bolton-Preston-Blackpool.

Despite the improvements to the London routes there was simultaneous rationalisation of other parts of the network. Central Station with its great arched roof was closed, although the building was retained and subsequently listed, and the retained services were diverted to Piccadilly and Oxford Road, the latter also being rebuilt.[9] Exchange was demolished, like Central the site became a car park, and services were diverted to Victoria. Generally the network to the north of the city centre began a long period of relative decline owing, to a significant degree, to the fact that it was not part of a trunk route to London.[10]

Trunk route rationalisation post-Beeching, brought complete closure of the Chinley-Bakewell-Matlock section of the trunk route from Central to London (St Pancras) via Derby, and ending of passenger services on the Woodhead line to

---

6   Services beyond Sheffield required a change of traction to steam haulage at Sheffield Victoria.

7   This was on the 1500volts DC model which was quickly rendered obsolete by the introduction of 25kv AC model for all subsequent electrification on British Railways.

8   The new premier electric service to London, the Manchester Pullman, stopped at Wilmslow as well as Stockport, and from this time Wilmslow can be regarded as a de facto parkway station for south Manchester/north Cheshire. Macclesfield which lies just outside the conurbation, took on a similar role.

9   Followed in 1971 by conversion of the electric service to Altrincham to 25kv AC, the same as the WCML, which facilitated running through trains between Crewe, Piccadilly and Altrincham.

10   Although east-west rail routes were not modernised, the M62 motorway made road travel quick and convenient across the Pennines to the north of Manchester.

Sheffield. These significantly reduced the potential for rail access to and from the Peak National Park and greatly reduced the convenience of rail for journeys between the North West and the East Midlands which thence forward were routed via Sheffield, a lengthy diversion. Services to Sheffield, South Yorkshire and the East Midlands were concentrated on the Hope Valley line which saw minimal investment, retaining its Victorian semaphore signalling system throughout the period.

Completion of WCML electrification was largely the end of the story as far as the positive impact of national railway network policy was concerned: the most significant factors subsequently were negative. Despite the Crewe-Piccadilly-Preston route being an important diversionary route for Anglo-Scottish services, the section between Manchester and Preston was not electrified. The Woodhead route was closed completely in 1981. The introduction of the APT, which had held so much promise for accelerated services between Manchester and London, was abandoned in 1986.[11] Without it, the best that could be achieved on the sinuous WCML was a 110mph line speed. In the early 1990s plans were developed for new trains and investment in the ageing infrastructure, but these were abandoned as a result of the recession and the preparation for privatisation. In 1994 the journey time to London at 2 hours 35 minutes, was slightly longer than the 2 hour 30 minutes in 1966 when electric services were first introduced.

With regard to local services, south Manchester experienced loss of railway passenger services in 1958 when those on the orbital route from Gorton/Fairfield on the Woodhead line to Manchester Central via Levenshulme and Fallowfield were withdrawn. Longsight station on the main line to London Road was closed at the same time. There were extensive proposals in the Reshaping Report for closure of local lines, including those out to Glossop,[12] Buxton and Bury, but there was widespread and successful opposition to these. The most significant losses in the conurbation core were associated with severing of the trunk route to St Pancras: the line from Cheadle to Central via Didsbury, Chorlton-cum-Hardy and Trafford Bar, reflecting BR's withdrawal from the inner suburban market. Further out, the orbital Marple-Stockport-Altrincham-Irlam/Warrington axis and Rochdale-Bury-Bolton lines were closed too: these were parts of duplicate main lines to Liverpool. The local railway network was paired back to its core of radial routes serving the bulk commuter flows on axes leading to central Manchester, with major investment only taking place on the back of WCML electrification. Analysis showed that sixty-four stations were closed in the area (Table 9.1, Figure 9.2), with 49 (79 per cent) as a product of complete line closures. The relative decline of the northern network was shown by the fact that it received 61 per cent (39) of the closures, and Oldham, Bury and Bolton lost much of their local networks. All the

---

11   The long development process for the APT, culminating in failure, was in stark contrast to the rapidity with which Boeing got the 737 into service for British Airways on competing shuttle services between Manchester and Heathrow (Modern Railways 1982, 99).

12   After closure of the Woodhead route local passenger services were retained to Glossop and Hadfield on the remaining stub.

general merchandise facilities around Manchester city centre, as well as those in surrounding towns, were closed, along with numerous areas of sidings. Freightliner terminals were opened on existing operational railway land at Longsight and Trafford Park.[13] By the mid-1970s Manchester Docks were running down and closed in 1985 and the internal railway network became redundant. Although the Trafford Park estate experienced large job losses, such as the ten thousand that went when AEI and English Electric merged to form GEC, its internal railway network survived although much reduced and used sporadically.

It is notable that station closures, other than those already in the pipeline, stopped as soon as the Greater Manchester PTE (GMPTE) was created. The extent of previous closures suggests that this was largely because all those that BR was pressing for had already been made. For the future, the biggest strategic issue facing GMPTE was the separation of the northern and southern networks. The first solution[14] proposed was a tunnel linking suburban services previously terminating at Piccadilly and Victoria, which would pass under the core of the CBD, a scheme known as Picc-Vic. This scheme was abandoned when public expenditure was capped in the mid-1970s and policy for the local network was plunged into crisis. As a result, the PTE's achievements were modest: the most notable were bus-rail interchanges at Bury and Altrincham. The former included a short diversion of the railway away from Bolton Street station to a new location adjoining the retail core, whereas the latter involved bus facilities in the station forecourt, as the existing station was already conveniently located for the town centre. These schemes were followed by the opening of 20 new stations which were intended to improve access to rail as they were adjacent to new housing areas, including overspill estates, as shown in Table 9.2. Analysis shows that all the new stations, except for Manchester Airport, were for local as opposed to inter-regional or inter-city services. Excluding those stations built in the city centre for Metrolink (see below), seven new stations were on the northern network and eight on the southern (Figure 9.3), showing again that the northern network was at a disadvantage, albeit slight.

---

13   Longsight was for London traffic and Trafford Park for Glasgow: owing to low traffic volumes, Longsight was subsequently closed and business was concentrated at Trafford Park.

14   The development of this proposal for the heavy rail network had been delayed until 1971 whilst a feasibility study was carried out in the late 1960s for a north-south rapid transit railway (White 1980).

Table 9.1 Stations closed in the Manchester conurbation 1948–94

Number on fig. 9.2	Station	Route	Date of Closure
*	Barton Moss	Mcr Victoria-Liverpool	1929
*	Molyneux Brow	Bury-Clifton Jcn	1931
*	Weaste	Mcr Victoria-Liverpool	1942
1	Darcy Lever	Bolton-Bury-Rochdale	1951
2	Holcombe Brook	Holcombe Brook-Bury	1952
3	Greenmount	Holcombe Brook-Bury	1952
4	Tottington	Holcombe Brook-Bury	1952
5	Woolfold	Holcombe Brook-Bury	1952
6	Brandlesholme Road	Holcombe Brook-Bury	1952
7	Bradley Fold	Bradley Fold-Radcliffe (spur off Bolton-Bury)	1953
8	Ringley Road	Bury-Clifton Jcn	1953
9	Bolton Great Moor Street	Bolton-Worsley-Eccles	1954
10	Plodder Lane	Bolton-Worsley-Eccles	1954
11	Little Hulton	Bolton-Worsley-Eccles	1954
12	Walkden Low Level	Bolton-Worsley-Eccles	1954
13	Worsley	Bolton-Worsley-Eccles	1954
14	Monton	Bolton-Worsley-Eccles	1954
15	Delph	Moorgate-Delph	1955
16	Dobcross	Moorgate-Delph	1955
17	Moorgate	Moorgate-Delph	1955
18	Grasscroft	Greenfield-Oldham (Clegg St.)	1955
19	Grotton	Greenfield-Oldham (Clegg St.)	1955
20	Lees	Greenfield-Oldham (Clegg St.)	1955
21	Glodwick Road	Greenfield-Oldham (Clegg St.)	1955
22	Ashton-Under Lyne (Park Parade)	Guide Bridge-Oldham (Clegg St.)	1956
23	Seedley	Mcr Victoria-Liverpool	1956
24	Irlams-o'th'Heights	Mcr Victoria-Wigan	1956
25	Radcliffe Bridge	Bury-Clifton Jcn	1958
26	Fallowfield	Fairfield-Mcr Central	1958
27	Hyde Road	Fairfield-Mcr Central	1958
28	Levenshulme	Fairfield-Mcr Central	1958
29	Wilbraham Road	Fairfield-Mcr Central	1958
30	Longsight	Mcr London Road-Stockport	1958
31	Oldham (Clegg Street)	Guide Bridge-Oldham (Clegg St.)	1959
32	Cross Lane	Mcr Victoria-Liverpool	1959
33	Pendlebury	Mcr Victoria-Wigan	1960
34	Heaton Mersey	Mcr Central-Cheadle Heath	1961

35	Withington & West Didsbury	Mcr Central-Cheadle Heath	1961
36	Dunham Massey	Timperley-Warrington	1962
37	Broadheath	Timperley-Warrington	1962
38	Stockport Tiviot Dale	Stockport-Woodley	1962
39	Lowton St Marys	Wigan-Glazebrook	1964
40	Tyldesley	Wigan-Tyldesley	1964
41	Baguley	Stockport Tiviot Dale-Glazebrook	1964
42	Cadishead	Stockport Tiviot Dale-Glazebrook	1964
43	Cheadle CLC	Stockport Tiviot Dale-Glazebrook	1964
44	Northenden	Stockport Tiviot Dale-Glazebrook	1964
45	Partington	Stockport Tiviot Dale-Glazebrook	1964
46	West Timperley	Stockport Tiviot Dale-Glazebrook	1964
47	Middleton	Middleton-Middleton Jcn	1964
48	Middleton Jcn	Middleton Jcn-Oldham Werneth	1966
49	Ramsbottom	Bury-Accrington	1966
50	Newton Heath	Mcr Victoria-Rochdale	1966
51	Royton	Royton Junction-Royton (Oldham)	1966
52	Oldham Central	Mumps-Werneth-Mcr Victoria	1966
53	Cheadle Heath	Mcr Central-Cheadle Heath	1967
54	Chorlton-cum-Hardy	Mcr Centra-Cheadle Heath	1967
55	Didsbury	Mcr Central-Cheadle Heath	1967
56	Clayton Bridge	Mcr Victoria-Stalybridge	1968
57	Droylsden	Mcr Victoria-Stalybridge	1968
58	Manchester Exchange	Liverpool-Mcr-Halifax-Leeds	1969
59	Manchester Central	Central-Cheadle Heath	1969
60	Bury(Knowlsey Street)	Bolton-Bury-Rochdale	1970
61	Bollington	Marple Rose Hill-Macclesfield	1970
62	High Lane	Marple Rose Hill-Macclesfield	1970
63	Higher Poynton	Marple Rose Hill-Macclesfield	1970
64	Royton Junction	Mcr Victoria-Oldham-Rochdale	1987
*	Miles Platting	Mcr Victoria-Oldham/Rochdale/&Stalybridge	1995
*	Godley East	Mcr Piccadilly-Glossop/Hadfield	1995
*	Park	Mcr Victoria-Stalybridge	1995
*	Pendleton	Mcr Victoria-Bolton	1999

Note: * Closures which pre or post-date public ownership of BR.

Source: Daniels and Dench 1980, Jowett 2000 and OS maps.

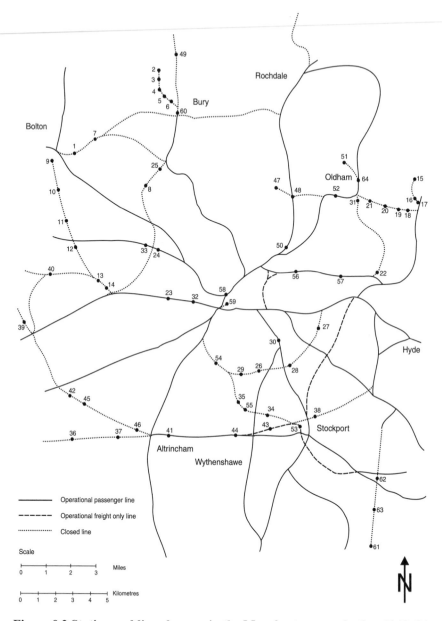

Figure 9.2 Station and line closures in the Manchester conurbation 1948–94

Table 9.2 New stations in the Manchester conurbation 1968–94

Number on fig. 9.3	Location	Route	Date of opening	Comment
1	Brinnington	Piccadilly-New Mills	1977	Serving council estate
2	Hattersley	Piccadilly-Glossop	1978	Serving council estate
3	Humphrey Park	Piccadilly-Warrington	1984	Outer Manchester suburb
4	Mills Hill	Victoria-Rochdale	1985	To serve Middleton – original station closed 1964
5	Derker	Victoria-Oldham-Rochdale	1985	To replace Royton Junction
6	Flowery Field	Piccadilly-Glossop	1985	Hyde suburb
7	Ryder Brow	Piccadilly-New Mills	1985	To serve south Gorton, mostly council housing
8	Smithy Bridge	Victoria-Rochdale-Halifax	1985	Re-opening
9	Godley	Piccadilly-Glossop	1986	To replace Godley East
10	Hall i'th Wood	Victoria-Bolton-Blackburn	1986	Bolton suburb
11	Salford Crescent	Piccadilly/Victoria-Bolton/Wigan	1987	In association with concentration of E-W services on Piccadilly
12	Hag Fold	Victoria-Wigan	1987	To serve Atherton
13	Lostock Parkway	Piccadilly/Victoria-Preston	1988	To serve Bolton suburbs
14	Woodsmoor	Piccadilly-Hazel Grove	1990	Stockport suburb
15	Market Street	Bury-Manchester-Altrincham	1992	Metrolink-Manchester city centre
16	Piccadilly Gardens	Bury-Manchester-Altrincham	1992	Metrolink-Manchester city centre
17	Mosley Street	Bury-Manchester-Altrincham	1992	Metrolink-Manchester city centre
18	St Peter's Square	Bury-Manchester-Altrincham	1992	Metrolink-Manchester city centre
19	GMEX	Bury-Manchester-Altrincham	1992	Metrolink-Manchester city centre
20	Manchester Airport	Piccadilly-Airport	1993	In association with new line to serve the airport

*Source*s: Hall 1995, Railway Development Society 1992, 1994.

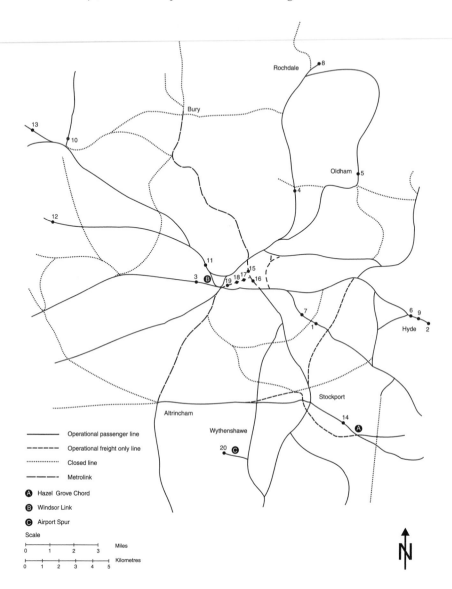

Figure 9.3 New stations and lines in the Manchester conurbation 1968–94

Despite the hostility of Thatcherism, there were some significant, though modest, improvements to the local network as a result of promotion by the PTA/PTE. In 1986 the Hazel Grove Chord was opened allowing Sheffield-Manchester-Liverpool trains to run via Stockport, which was important to the latter's development as a rail hub. In 1988 the Windsor Link was opened to the west of central Manchester connecting the north and south networks and facilitating concentration of trans-Pennine and local services on Piccadilly. Salford Crescent station was opened to facilitate interchange, but although this was well located for Salford University it did not improve access to Salford Precinct,[15] as this was remote from the network. Concentration of services on Piccadilly reinforced its role as Manchester's principal station, but also facilitated downsizing at Victoria which released land for development.

A significant example of commitment to the network was the opening, in 1993, of a spur to Manchester International Airport (MIA), which was thereby accessible via Piccadilly from Liverpool, Preston, Blackpool, Huddersfield, Leeds, York and Sheffield. Initially this station was not accessible to trains from the Crewe direction, but a south chord, opened in late 1995,[16] facilitated this. Although more concerned with medium and long-distance than local traffic, the airport link was successful but has already experienced capacity problems, as well as being criticised for poor links with areas to the west in Cheshire and North Wales. This illustrates the inability of the agencies involved to plan sufficiently expansively, because of the difficulties involved in securing funding.

The impact of Sectorisation was positive with regard to interregional services: its focus on CBD-to-CBD routes, especially Liverpool-Manchester-Leeds-Newcastle, was very beneficial with increases in service frequency as a result of Sprinterisation which produced increases in ridership: it is notable though that this very important route[17] was not electrified although, like Manchester-Preston-Blackpool, this was mooted on many occasions but always turned down owing to the restrictive Treasury inspired investment criteria. The impact of Sectorisation on local services was muted; for example, routes serving Victoria, typified by the Manchester-Oldham-Rochdale service, became very basic railways using rail buses and unstaffed stations. The area did not experience the reopening of closed routes.

---

15   This was a Salford City Council promoted development at the heart of a large housing CDA.

16   As an illustration of the difficulties in securing funding for rail projects, BR was a sponsor of the first link but not the second, whereas Manchester Airport funded the second but not the first: only GMPTE was involved in both showing the significance of the PTE role.

17   Known as 'North Trans-Pennine' it is the most important trans-Pennine route – with the benefit of hindsight it can be seen that the BTC electrified the wrong route when Woodhead was selected in the early 1950s.

The abandonment of Picc-Vic had left two significant problems with regard to the local network: poor penetration of the regional CBD and the need to modernise the area's most significant commuter routes – those to Altrincham and, especially, Bury. These were converted into Metrolink,[18] light rail lines connected by a short street running section across the city centre providing an imaginative, though partial, solution to the penetration problem and the separation of the north and south networks. It is notable that this came 20 years after the PTA/PTE were created, with Metrolink becoming operational in 1992. Outside the city centre the tram stops were former railway stations and were, generally, well located with regard to journey patterns because of the historic role of the commuter lines. However, no funds were available for station rebuilding, only for the installation of lifts to provide easier access for disabled people, and this forced the system to utilise high-floor trams which necessitated construction of intrusive, high platforms in the city centre. At the time of its inception the Bury-Altrincham line was seen as part of a wider network which would involve further conversions of parts of the heavy rail network, as well as new alignments, but none were committed before 1994.

The impact of national policies across the city region: town planning 1947–94

Housing renewal and associated land supply issues were the most significant strategic planning problems in the early post-war period. Initially, Manchester's favoured policy was dispersal to new towns in north Cheshire and south east Lancashire: Mobberley, Lymm, Risley, Westhoughton and Winsford were considered but rejected, largely as a result of resistance by the county councils (Hall et al. 1973a, Robson 1980). The institutional arrangements for planning, whereby the areas administered by Cheshire and Lancashire County Councils extended deep into the conurbation, mitigated against a strategic approach and central Government did not intervene: the national priorities were London, Glasgow and the Durham coalfield. In the 1950s and early 1960s the exporting authorities, mainly Manchester and Salford, therefore had to utilise overspill estates on whatever sites they could persuade their neighbouring authorities to release, which undermined consideration of transport links. The resistance by the county councils was reinforced by their development of draft green belts, the effectiveness of which was not undermined by the fact that it took many years for them to become formally adopted, 1984 in the case of Greater Manchester (GMC 1984). As a result, dispersal was largely to overspill estates where between 1955 and 1973 the biggest exporter, Manchester,

---

18   GMPTE worked Metrolink into a firm proposal in 1983 and won funding in 1989: the delay was caused by the DoT considering Metrolink's impact on bus deregulation and by introduction of new assumptions to underpin the section 56 funding mechanism as described previously.

built approximately 22,000 council houses (Manchester City Planning Department 1981). Most of these were in locations with poor access to the rail network or, even where they were in a settlement that nominally enjoyed a railway service, such as Wilmslow or Knutsford, they were located on their periphery, well outside a ten minute walking distance from the nearest station. At this time even where estates were alongside the railway, no thought was given to opening a new station. Many sites within the city were redeveloped, but rail access was not a consideration for these either. A prime example was the redevelopment of huge sites previously occupied by the BR owned Gorton Works and the nearby Beyer Peacock's locomotive works: although within walking distance of Gorton station these were developed by the City Council for non-housing purposes.

With the growth of the private housing market, suburbs developed outside the draft green belts, primarily in the south east in areas like Macclesfield, Wilmslow, and Knutsford, but also in the northern outskirts of Bolton and Bury (Robson 1980). They were associated with car commuting and the development of the regional trunk road network. As part of the latter, the City of Manchester Development Plan[19] contained extensive proposals for road building within the city derived from the Nicholas Plan, exemplified by completion in 1966 of the Mancunian Way, an elevated motorway running orbitally around the southern edge of the CBD, which was intended to become the inner of three rings. Although these plans were scaled back, the M62, M63 and M56 were open by the early 1970s. The general lack of policy towards the railway network was illustrated by the fact that Manchester's Development Plan contained only one reference to it;

> Railways.
> No proposals are envisaged by the British Railways involving changes in land use and the Development Plan is based on the retention of railway facilities in their present form (City of Manchester 1961, 14).

The difficulties in securing a new town to take decentralisation from Manchester were eventually overcome when Warrington was designated in 1968: this had existing stations on the Manchester-Liverpool railway and the WCML, and an additional station was subsequently opened at Birchwood, as outlined in Chapter 8.

As well as closure of BR's general merchandise facilities, the national decline in rail freight was exemplified by East Manchester, an archetypal nineteenth century, rail served industrial area. The 1960s saw the end of locomotive building with closure of Gorton Works and Beyer-Peacock's, along with closure of Bradford Colliery. These were followed in the early 1970s by closure of the rail served English Steel works,[20] Bradford Gas Works and Stuart Street Power station.

---

19   This was belatedly approved by the Minister of Housing and Local Government in 1961 after submission in 1951.

20   Following abandonment of high rise and overspill, Manchester City Council launched a search for 1000 housing sites within the city in the early 1970s which led to

Regeneration of the area came to be seen as dependent on significant improvements to the strategic road network, improvements to which had been already made, as outlined above (Manchester City Planning Department 1983). The planning system allocated sites for industry in East Manchester, but rail access was not sought by developers or BR, and was not incorporated into the redevelopment process.

But there were more favourable outcomes for freight elsewhere. These included development of waste compaction and rail loading facilities at Northenden (south Manchester), Brindle Heath (Salford), Dean Lane (east Manchester) and Bredbury (Stockport), the retention of several stone terminals, the rehabilitation of the lines into Trafford Park by Trafford Park Development Corporation (TPDC) and, in the 1990s, development of the Euroterminal. The latter was permitted development[21] and, generally, the role of the planning system in the provision of these freight facilities was reactive.

By the mid-1960s more new jobs were being created in the service sector in association with commercial redevelopment schemes, than in industry. The outcome in Manchester was that the city centre and certain suburban centres came to be seen by the market as attractive locations for office development and this was encouraged by local planning policy. Outside central Manchester, demand for office space was strongest to the south and south west of the city and planning policy steered development to locations such as Trafford Bar, the biggest concentration, situated alongside the Manchester-Altrincham railway. Other concentrations were in or near suburban town centres: these included Sale and Atrincham with 88,255 square metres (950,000 square feet) and Stockport, where more than 74,000 square metres (800,000 square feet) was built between 1965–76, including a secondary node adjacent to Cheadle Hulme station, a long standing source of commuter traffic. Further out Wilmslow developed into a successful office location where rents rivalled those in central Manchester and all the developments were in the town centres and nominally accessible by rail. Several suburban town centres also saw significant redevelopment of their retail areas: Stockport, Sale, Bolton and Altrincham were the most notable: disposals by BR in the 1960s produced small retail developments close to stations at Urmston and Alderley Edge. Undoubtedly, office decentralisation and town centre redevelopment were strongly associated

---

some controversial developments. Openshaw Village on the site of the former English Steel works was one such site: it was isolated, inaccessible by public transport, and adjacent to noxious industrial premises. This development reinforced the missed opportunities to provide housing on more accessible sites such as those in Gorton mentioned previously.

21   To underline subsequent controversy around the extent of permitted development rights enjoyed by the railway industry (Greensmith and Haywood 1999), the operation of this terminal, which included night time working, triggered complaints from local residents and Trafford MBC environmental services department demanded the installation of noise attenuation measures.

with use of the car, nevertheless the suburban centres were generally well located for rail access and this facilitated utilisation of local services.

By the late 1970s the Greater Manchester Council (GMC) had produced a Structure Plan which had four major themes;

> urban concentration, redirection to the inner core, maintenance of the regional centre, resource and amenity conservation (GMC 1982, 1).

The stance towards commercial development was typified by office policy:

> Office developments will normally be expected to locate in or adjacent to town centres or in Trafford Bar office centre (GMC 1986, 4[22]).

The resistance to the decentralisation of such trip generating uses was, in the broadest sense, supportive of the railway network.

The Manchester-Salford Inner City Partnership was created in 1978 and the initial strategies were focused on housing schemes, community projects, industrial developments and the environment, particularly the reclamation of derelict land. Whereas there was an awareness that the regional centre was of crucial importance to the well-being of inner city residents (Manchester City Council 1983), it took a while for this to crystallise into a city centre strategy as such. When this occurred, a significant feature which was seen as essential to competition with suburban town centres, but which was inimical to the utilisation of the railway network, was the promotion of short stay car parking. An eight per cent increase was reported in 1985 (Manchester City Council 1986, as cited in Healey et al. 1988). It was recognised that there was a need to improve the railway network's penetration of the city centre, but;

> The fact that the railway network converges on termini on opposite sides of the City Centre coupled with the relative scarcity of stations in the Inner Area means that the railway is little used by Inner Area residents. However the County Council are considering proposals for linking together the two networks and converting some existing railway lines to a light rapid transit system. This will increase frequencies and may involve a greater number of Inner Area stations. All these factors should increase the attractiveness of the network to inner area residents ... (Manchester City Council 1983, 49).

Manchester City Council was hostile to the Thatcher Government but Salford was more pragmatic and lobbied for EZ status for 150 hectares (370 acres) of the derelict docks area, which was granted in 1981. The Council took the lead in developing a market-oriented planning and regeneration strategy for the area,

---

22 This was the final version of the structure plan produced just before abolition of the GMC.

branded as Salford Quays. The Conservative controlled Trafford Council similarly lobbied for EZ status for the declining Trafford Park industrial estate, which was also granted in 1981: in 1987 regeneration of the area was handed over to Trafford Park Development Corporation (TPDC).

Despite the various initiatives, employment in inner Manchester declined by six per cent between 1984–91 (DoE 1996a, 44) whereas there was a 41 per cent increase in outer Manchester, and between 1981–96 there was a 62 per cent decrease in manufacturing jobs in the city, a seven per cent decrease in public services and a two per cent decline in private services (Power and Mumford 1999). These trends were suggestive of a continuing weakening of demand for traditional radial rail commuter services. The impact of Thatcherism was significant with abandonment of the restraint on office decentralisation being the outcome.[23] Research (Haywood 1996) showed that deregulation of planning control influenced the location of office developments and that the total floorspace completed outside the city centre during the 1989–1991 boom, was considerably greater than that within it. The locations outside the city centre were suburban, free standing and poorly located for rail access. Even where they were reasonably close, such as around the Airport rail link, the details discouraged rail access: although an excellent station was built to serve the airport, there was no Docklands style vision of a high density, rail served development node. Even at Salford Quays, where there was no prior passenger rail access, none was built, despite the area being developed as a major office node containing over 185,000 square metres (approx. 2m square feet) of floorspace (Law and Dundon-Smith 1994), in association with housing and leisure uses. This failure to integrate the development of such a major growth pole with the local rail network was typical of the 1980s approach outside London as, in the absence of a transit oriented planning vision, the property market was car oriented: multi-storey car parks were built to serve the development.[24]

In the wider conurbation, despite the shifts in national planning policy in the early 1990s, the long lead time of major developments meant that several schemes which contravened the new policies were completed after the changes, or were still in the pipeline in 1994. The major out-of-centre shopping schemes alongside the A34 by-pass were notable examples: although relatively close to Handforth station on the Manchester-Crewe line, they were not readily accessible from it and were wholly focused on the new road, which they partially funded through

---

23   An early indicator of the new policy context for office development was the movement in 1985 of the Refuge Assurance Company from its Edwardian, purpose built premises adjacent to Oxford Road station to new purpose built premises in the green belt to the south of Wilmslow on a site not within convenient walking distance of Wilmslow station.

24   The first Metrolink extension, to Eccles via Salford Quays, did not open until 1999 and was funded largely from the £77m premium obtained from refranchising Phase 1 with the Phase 2 (Eccles extension) contract. About £25 million of the £42 million received from privatising Greater Manchester Buses was also invested in phase 2.

planning gain (Haywood 1997). To the west of Manchester, the new regional shopping centre at Dumplington,[25] comprising approximately 93,500 square metres (approx. 1m square feet) with 10,000 parking spaces, was supported by central Government in a complex legal battle[26] going to the House of Lords in 1995 (EGi Legal 1995), despite it contravening the new policies and being fiercely resisted by local planning authorities in Greater Manchester. It is not accessible by rail. The retail and leisure developments on the former railway land adjoining Stockport station were one of the few examples of rail accessible major developments built in the conurbation in the 1980s, although the detail of this detracted from the accessibility of the station, which itself received no investment at the time.

National policies: conclusions

The emphasis on main line investment led to: piecemeal improvement in railway services with priority for those on trunk routes to London; removal of some services on secondary and branch lines and stagnation of others. There was a significant difference between the northern and southern networks and it was the latter, focused on Piccadilly and the WCML, which received most investment. In particular there was only one closure on the retained radial routes to Oxford Road/Piccadilly (i.e. Longsight) and that predated electrification. By managing decentralisation, planning policy was broadly supportive of passenger rail use, particularly during the 1960s and 1970s, but not specifically rail oriented. There was evidence of significant dislocation in the early years with regard to the location of overspill, and especially in the later period as a result of Thatcherite *laissez-faire*. The overall relationship between land-use planning and Manchester's network can be characterised as partial and inconsistent.

The impact of national and local policies on rail access to central Manchester and access to rail in central Manchester

It has been shown that Manchester inherited a major problem with regard to rail access to the CBD. Despite the Nicholas plan there was no improvement before 1968, although inter-city and local services into Piccadilly were significantly improved. Closure of Central removed what was arguably the best located station for city

---

25   Renamed the Trafford Centre, this scheme opened in late 1998.

26   The original outline planning permission was granted by the Secretary of State in 1986 but this was followed by two public inquiries, the second one focused on concerns over traffic congestion on the adjacent M63 (now M60) motorway. The basis of the submission to the House of Lords by the opposing local authorities was that the Secretary of State had ignored changes in retail policy and was perverse: the Secretary of State's decision was upheld and full planning permission granted.

centre access, although retention of Piccadilly, Oxford Road, Deansgate, Victoria and Salford left stations at significant, if peripheral, locations.

The general vitality of Manchester's CBD and the encouragement of commercial redevelopment by the City Council through the use of the CDA mechanism, was exemplified by completion of the Co-operative Insurance Society building in Miller Street in 1962, which was very accessible to Victoria. The even bigger Piccadilly Plaza scheme, completed in 1965, was on a war damaged site and was also the subject of a CDA plan, along with other office development sites on nearby Portland Street. London Road station was within 400 metres (437 yards) of Piccadilly and it is instructive that BR chose that name to rebrand the station in the modernisation process. In 1961 the BTC completed the development of Rail House, a ten-storey office building adjoining Piccadilly station. Other large office developments were completed in the vicinity suggesting that railway modernisation and property initiatives by BR, had served to boost the market here and the planning process had facilitated this: the seven-storey Gateway House on the site of the former LNWR goods depot on the station approach was the most notable scheme, completed in 1969.

Following publication of the Buchanan Report the encouragement of large, multi-storey, mixed-use redevelopment schemes impacted in Manchester with the working up of the Arndale redevelopment through a CDA based partnership between the City Council and Town and City Properties. Although not completed until the mid-1970s, this 100,000 square metres (1.2 million square feet) development, and the adjoining Market Place scheme, served to reinforce the attractiveness of the city centre in the face of intense competition from suburban centres. The late 1970s also saw pedestrianisation of Market Street and St Anne's Square which linked with these precinct developments. Other significant office developments were completed in the early 1970s, mainly in the financial core around King Street, an area that became known as the 'square half mile'. To the extent that employees and customers used rail for access to the city centre, these schemes were beneficial to the rail network, despite the peripheral location of stations: the PTE's station minibus service, introduced in the early 1970s, provided some sort of link. Taken together, these developments in the 1960s and early 1970s showed how, in the most general sense, planning reinforced the importance of Manchester's CBD, which was crucial to ridership on the local rail network. However, despite modernisation of Piccadilly and Oxford Road stations, no steps were taken to facilitate pedestrian access to them from the core of the CBD: this was not perceived as a planning issue.

During the second half of the 1970s, Manchester's CBD entered a period of relative decline. This was partly a result of a contraction of the commercial core, which was strongly associated with closure of railway freight facilities,[27] but it also

---

27   Warehousing activities became road served and moved out to locations on the motorway network, typified by Warrington new town at the intersection of the M6 and M62.

arose from competition from suburban town centres and the economic recession. In response, Manchester City Council produced the City Centre Local Plan which was a new kind of statutory plan with a conscious, promotional role. For example, it recognised the importance of office development to the centre and argued that:

> Office activity is a major and vital part of the Regional Centre, providing substantial, wide-ranging employment opportunities and helping to sustain, both directly and indirectly, a wide variety of other uses and activities (Manchester City Council 1984, 43).

The importance of transportation was recognised, particularly public transport, as central to the goal of attracting more activity to the city centre. The abandonment of Picc-Vic was a serious blow for city centre rail access and for several years the best the PTE could do was the mini-bus shuttle service between Piccadilly and Victoria via the CBD. The concentration of trans-Pennine and local services on Piccadilly in 1988 further reinforced its primacy as the city's main station, but triggered further running down of Victoria. The opening of Metrolink in 1992, with its street running penetration of the city centre, provided an imaginative and cost-effective solution in a very hostile political context. The city centre section runs through both Victoria and Piccadilly and passes close to the main retail, office and leisure areas.

Despite the surge in out-of-centre office development in the late 1980s, the CBD remained an attractive location (Figure 9.4). However, the accessibility of office developments to the rail network was variable. For example, the square half mile continued to be a favoured location and, whereas it was reasonably accessible by Metrolink, it was not close to the heavy rail stations. The pattern of office developments outside the square half mile, particularly those in the Oxford Road/ Mosley Street area, was more favourable with regard to heavy rail access. What is clear however is that, unlike the 1960s, the areas around Victoria and Piccadilly were not attractive to significant office development during the 1980s boom.

The popular backlash against the large scale urban redevelopment of the 1960s and 1970s came to have positive impacts on planning policy for central Manchester, which in turn had positive implications for development and, thereby, demand for rail travel. Despite the blitz and redevelopment, many buildings from the Victorian and Edwardian periods remained in the early 1970s and, progressively, these were listed and incorporated into conservation areas (Manchester City Council 1984, 30). Lower King Street had a significant concentration and, owing to its proximity to the prime retail area, it was pedestrianised. However, the conservation areas also included the peripheral Castlefield and Whitworth Street areas, and such notable buildings as Liverpool Road station and goods buildings, Central Station and the Great Northern goods building. Although the City Council had sought to promote the regeneration of these large areas, progress had been modest: significant successes included conversion of Central Station into the GMEX centre and creation of the Museum of Science and Industry in the historic railway

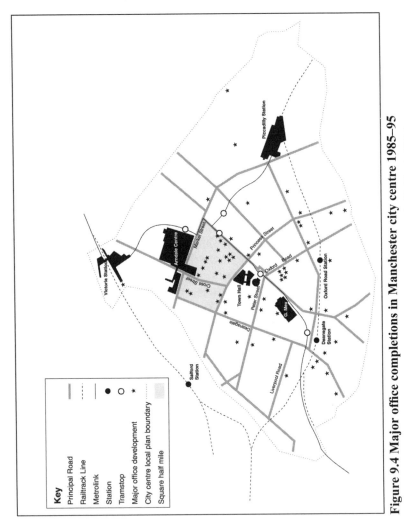

Figure 9.4 Major office completions in Manchester city centre 1985–95

Source: This figure first appeared in *Town Planning Review*, vol. 67, No. 1, 1996.

buildings on Liverpool Road. In order to further stimulate the market, in 1988 the Government handed regeneration of the area stretching along the Rochdale Canal from Castlefield to Piccadilly Station to the Central Manchester Development Corporation (CMDC): the railway running peripherally around the city centre from Castlefield to Piccadilly ran parallel to this regeneration area, with Oxford Road station located at the half-way point. Intervention by CMDC (CMDC 1990), and the increasing attractiveness of Manchester to developers in light of the favourable image projected through the Olympic bidding process (Kitchen 1993) and a growing reputation as a centre for music, art and culture, boosted property market interest. The result was significant investment in the CMDC area in historic buildings and new build, including the Bridgewater Hall and the Great Bridgewater office development (20,460 sq. m/220,000 sq ft.).[28] All of this was accessible from Piccadilly and, especially, Oxford Road and Deansgate stations, as well as Metrolink stops at GMEX and St Peter's Square. On the other side of the CBD, there was development of the Arena concert venue which incorporated the rationalisation of tracks through Victoria Station and partial rebuilding of the station underneath the Arena. This was a very significant development as it was the first attempt in Manchester to produce an airspace development[29] but, despite this, the Arena also contained 1000 new parking spaces. The presence of around 20,000 long stay parking spaces in the city centre as a whole (Kitchen 1995), particularly the large number of private and contract spaces, undermined utilisation of rail for CBD access.

Census data shows that between 1981–91 the proportion of journeys-to-work by rail fell from 2.4 per cent to 2.2 per cent in Greater Manchester (Beatty and Haywood 1997) and, although this does not tell the full story with regard to rail utilisation for access to the CBD, it is indicative of the overall situation. Although it is necessary to go beyond the 1994 cut-off to develop an understanding of the impact of Metrolink, by 1996 this was carrying more passengers than the local heavy rail network, showing the positive effects of frequent, high quality services and improved CBD penetration (GMPTE 1996). These attributes were, of course, missing from the heavy rail network.

The impact of national and local policies on rail access to central Manchester and access to rail in central Manchester: conclusions

Rail access to the regional CBD was rationalised with priority for routes associated with the WCML electrification. Manchester lost two of its four main city centre stations and investment at Piccadilly far outweighed that at Victoria which, despite

---

28   Although not completed until 1995–96 these developments were underway by April 1994.

29   It was also notable that, apart from Metrolink, local services using the new station were largely operated by low quality rail buses produced in the 1980s.

partial rebuilding at the end of the period, enjoyed a worsening 'main line' rail service with no electrification, apart from Metrolink. Manchester experienced massive delay in securing improved rail penetration of the CBD and, when delivered, this was via light rail and only benefited local services on the Bury-Altrincham axis. There was no benefit for heavy rail users without them changing onto Metrolink.[30] By steering development to the CBD, planning policy was generally supportive in the 1960s and 1970s, although the experience in the 1960s in securing major trip generators near to Victoria and Piccadilly was not repeated in the 1970s. Subsequently circumstances forced a concentration of planning activity on the core of the CBD and it was not until the late 1980s/early 1990s that significant development activity was taking place in the peripheral areas nearer to/at the main stations. There was not sufficient momentum for this to produce urban design improvements in the public domain to facilitate access to the main stations and their environs.

The impact of national and local policy at the local level: suburban corridors and redundant railway land

The research for this part of the case study focused on the south eastern part of the conurbation where the southern parts of Manchester and Stockport merge with north Cheshire. This area was chosen as it had experienced significant suburban growth and retained five radial rail corridors. One secondary radial line was closed, the Marple-Bollington-Macclesfield route, although the northern stub of this between Marple and Rose Hill (and thence to Piccadilly) remained open. Other orbital routes and routes linking south Manchester with Central Station were closed as reviewed above. As a result of the WCML electrification, three of the routes radiating from Manchester Piccadilly were electrified: the Styal line (to Wilmslow), Stockport-Cheadle Hulme-Wilmslow-Alderley Edge (for London via Crewe) and Stockport-Cheadle Hulme-Bramhall-Poynton-Macclesfield (for London via Stoke-on-Trent). The original Metrolink project envisaged conversion to light rail of the Manchester-Marple/Rose Hill route, but this did not take place.

The research entailed tracking the chronological and geographical pattern of suburban growth by superimposing tracings from sequential Ordnance Survey maps of the area, as reproduced in Figure 9.5. This shows development before 1939, between 1945–68, and between 1969–97: the latter post-dates the end point of the research but was the only map version available. Inspection of the map shows that development fell broadly into two geographical categories: the mass of the continuous built-up area in the north, and the discrete settlements to the south which, broadly, sit astride the rail corridors as 'beads on a string'. It is the latter which the research was particularly concerned with, especially in the electrified rail corridors. As outlined earlier, the core of these developed as rail commuter

---

30   The city centre minibus continued post-Metrolink from Piccadilly.

settlements before 1914, but there has been significant expansion subsequently as shown. In the most general sense, because of the broad association with the rail corridors, the map provides evidence that the planning system managed decentralisation in ways which were favourable to the utility of the railway network. The main tools used to achieve this were the power to prevent development in certain areas, typically through use of green belts, and to release other specific areas of land for development.

However, on closer examination, the outcome can be seen to be not as favourable for rail as it might have been. There is a limit as to how far people are prepared to walk to a public transport stop, typically around 400 metres. What is clear from the map is that, generally, expansion of the settlements was permitted to take place incrementally on their *outer* peripheries, at increasing distances from their centres: the westward expansion of Wilmslow was a good example. This progressively reduced the likelihood of residents walking to the station. Alternative means of transport to link housing areas with the station could have been provided, either bus services, cycle facilities or car parks. The latter has been provided at Wilmslow,[31] but the typical outcome is that commuters have opted to use their cars for the whole of their journey, rather than a short trip to the station.

Two main factors have encouraged this. One was the development of the trunk road network: the radial M56 (and its extension into Manchester via the improved Princess Parkway) and part of the orbital M62/63[32] (now the M60) were open by the mid-1970s. Construction of the A34 by-pass had commenced before 1994 and would reinforce the role of the A34/Kingsway axis as a commuter route into Manchester (this project was completed in 1995). The second factor was the decentralisation of employment and other trip generators to suburban locations, not readily accessible by rail. It will be recalled that by 1975 Cheadle Hulme had emerged as a rail accessible suburban employment node: it is notable that office and retail development in these corridors in the late 1980s was road oriented. Taken together, the difficulties at both ends of the journey made rail very unattractive to most of those who had access to a car.

---

31   Wilmslow is an intercity service station and most car park users are likely to be travelling to London. This contrasts with the situation at Hazel Grove where there is a large car park and only a local train service to Stockport and Manchester. Hazel Grove was promoted for park-and-ride by GMPTE whereas Wilmslow is outside the PTE area.

32   The final north eastern quadrant of this orbital motorway between Denton and Heaton Park did not open until 2000.

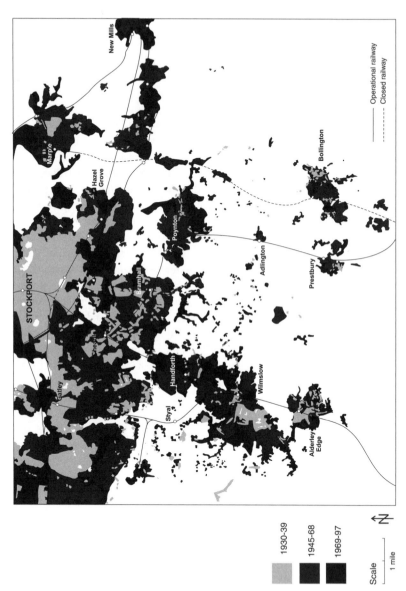

Figure 9.5 The railway network and suburban growth in South Manchester 1930–97

Operational railway
Closed railway

1930-39
1945-68
1969-97

Scale
1 mile

N

The impact of green belt policy can also be seen to have had negative impacts in that there are long lengths of expensively maintained railway which pass through open countryside with no stations. In other cases there are extant stations, but little development has been permitted around them: Styal and Adlington are key examples in the area studied. Traffic at Styal became so limited that, whereas until the mid-1980s it had a half hourly service to Manchester, the service had become so sparse by 1994 as to be virtually unusable. The service at Adlington was minimal but useable: half hourly at the peak and hourly off-peak.

This mapping exercise revealed the sorts of outcomes from the planning process recorded by Hall in the 1960s, with the additional impacts of the accelerated road-oriented decentralisation of the 1980s. The map clearly shows the power of the planning system to manage the land development process, but it also shows that this has not been used in ways to maximise utilisation of rail services.

The second element of this part of the case study comprised analysis of the re-use of redundant railway land. This related to land in the City of Manchester and utilised records of all disused land held by the City Planning Department from the mid-1970s, to inform the inter-departmental Sites Appraisal Group (SAG). The initial trigger for this had been the need to find sites for council housing, once both high rise and overspill developments were abandoned, but the mechanism became used as part of the general regeneration process. As the BR Property Board made sites available for development, they were entered into the SAG system. The vast majority of the sites were areas of sidings, or small goods yards, which became redundant as a result of the collapse of the wagonload business and the closure of rail served industries. Although it has not been possible to quantify the proportion of all redundant railway land in the wider conurbation which entered the SAG system, it is fair to say that because the City of Manchester lies at the heart of the area's railway network, the sites studied were very representative.

The research identified 50 sites with a total area of approximately 162 hectares (400 acres) as shown in Table 9.3. Tracking the subsequent use of the sites through field work (carried out in 1999–2000) showed that the largest category of after use was industrial, with 48.2 hectares (119 acres), 29.7 per cent of the total. Typically this comprised small units and none of it was rail connected, although there was a theoretical potential for use of Freightliner truck services to move containers in and out. Vacant land was the second largest category at 39.6 hectares (97.8 acres), or 24.4 per cent of the total: this reflected the problematic nature of much disused railway land which was, typically, elongated and inaccessible. Nearly all of it was in East Manchester too, formerly an area of heavy industry where the property market was extremely weak. If landscaped sites from the 'other' category are added in, vacant and landscaped land comprised almost 46 hectares (113 acres), almost as large as the industrial category: landscaped land such as the Irk Valley is very little used, acting as an informal greenspace. Approximately 11.5 per cent of the land was used for transport purposes, with one site partially in use as a rail-served stone terminal and another site being used for the Metrolink depot: the largest site was the former main line to Manchester Central between Didsbury and Chorlton-cum-Hardy which is a linear walkway, although it is safeguarded for use as an extension to Metrolink. Where sites were redeveloped for retail or residential use, their potential impact on rail ridership would have depended upon their proximity to a station and, in the case of retail, on the propensity of customers to use rail to access the particular kind of outlets concerned. The two largest residential sites were close to Dean Lane and Moston stations respectively, but the retail uses were supermarkets or D-I-Y stores and were not likely to generate rail traffic, although the latter adjoined Mauldeth Road station. One large site in the 'other' category was a distribution facility, a new road-only Royal Mail[33] depot on Rochdale Road.

Table 9.3 Summary of analysis of the use of redundant railway land in the City of Manchester

Industry		Transport		Retail		Residential		Vacant		Other		Total	
Ha (acres)	%	Ha (acres)	%	Ha (acres)	%	Ha (acres)	%	Ha (acres)	%	Ha (acres)	%	HA (acres)	%
48.2 (119)	29.7	18.5 (45.8)	11.4	4.1 (10.1)	2.5	17.6 (43.5)	10.9	39.6 (97.8)	24.4	33.9 (83.7)	20.9	162 (400)	100

Source: City of Manchester Planning Department, Sites Appraisal Group records.

It was in the city centre that redevelopment had the largest potential for promoting rail ridership, albeit indirectly. The use of the former Liverpool Road station and goods buildings for the Museum of Science and Industry created a rail accessible tourist facility, and the Nynex Arena project was an airspace development over Victoria station. Central Station did not become a SAG site, but its use as the GMEX exhibition centre had positive implications too. However, the Arena and GMEX also provided large numbers of car parking spaces; 1656 between them. Three other redundant railway sites which did not enter the SAG system were the sites of the former Exchange Station, the Great Northern[34]

---

33   As part of a major restructuring of Royal Mail's use of the railway network in the mid-1990s, all rail usage in the Liverpool-Manchester belt was concentrated at Warrington which is accessed by road from the two cities. Previously the disused Mayfield Station and an adjacent large building erected in the 1960s had been used by Royal Mail for the rail parts of their Manchester business.

34   This was a 'state of the art' integrated goods building when erected in the late nineteenth century: it is now listed and has been converted to a retail and leisure centre. Controversially, the structures which carried the approach lines have been demolished. The viaducts over the Castlefield basin which gave access to this building were listed but unused for many years until re-utilised for Metrolink.

goods building adjoining Central, and most of the former goods yard[35] adjoining Piccadilly Station. These had been in long term use as car parks with 1440 spaces in total. Additional parking space adjoining Piccadilly was retained by BR for Intercity users.

The impact of national and local policy at the local level: suburban corridors and redundant railway land: conclusions

Land-use planning was rail oriented in the corridors studied, but only in the most macro-geographical sense. Even before the onset of Thatcherite *laissez-faire*, new development in rail corridors was, in detail, poorly located for rail access, and during the 1980s the rail corridors and their stations were largely ignored as locational factors. Although some new stations were built in the area studied, it is significant that none were built on the main electrified corridors. Generally stations were not utilised as the focal points for new suburban nodes, despite some fairly large developments in the corridor. Rather than being higher density and designed around pedestrian access from stations, the norm for commercial development was low density schemes along roads. The Airport rail link was the exception, but even this failed to provide easy access to the many office developments built in the locality.

Outside central Manchester redundant railway land has not been redeveloped in ways likely to promote rail utilisation, except in a minority of cases with two housing sites being the most notable. The major qualification to this was the fact that there were several key sites/railway structures in the city centre where significant re-use or redevelopment was likely to have promoted rail utilisation, owing to the nature of the end use and proximity to stations. However even these developments comprised generous car parking facilities and the overall effect is likely to have been to stimulate access by car more than access by rail.

Overall conclusions from the case study

The main conclusions from the Manchester case study are: the importance of the creation of the PTA/PTE structure to champion the local rail network; the continuing importance of Manchester's CBD to the passenger rail system; and the inordinate length of time it took to deliver even a partial solution to the problem of poor rail penetration of the CBD. The planning system was broadly supportive of promoting rail access to the CBD throughout much of the period, although it was never single-mindedly focused on delivering high density development around stations, except at the Arena at the end of the period. Generally speaking, suburban

---

35   The former Great Central goods building was listed and remained vacant until late 1999 after which it was converted to residential use.

planning delivered little for the rail system outside of restraining the excesses of housing decentralisation and limiting commercial developments to town centres or other rail accessible locations, although even the latter was abandoned in the 1980s. Outside the city centre, the redevelopment of redundant railway land had minimal impacts on demand for rail services.

Chapter 10

The Post-Privatisation Period 1994–2008: Institutional Relationships

Introduction

It is generally accepted that the motivations behind the privatisation of BR were the desire of the Major government to be perceived as continuing the Thatcherite agenda of the successful disposal of state utilities and the medium term goal of reducing the financial burden on the Treasury. The expectation was that traffic levels would continue at more or less the same volumes which, because of the continuing increase in road traffic, implied further relative decline which would facilitate a relatively smooth handover to the private sector with government increasingly taking a back seat. However the outcomes have been quite different. There have been major problems with regard to the management and operation of the railway network, passenger and freight traffic have grown very significantly and lack of network capacity has become a major issue. The operational issues have led, amongst other things, to a significant increase in the costs of running the railways with much greater calls on the public purse than those enjoyed by BR. Far from getting the railways off the government's hands and out of the political arena, privatisation has been accompanied by a process of almost continuous government interventions with persistent, sometimes very hostile, media commentary.

This has also been a period of rapid change in institutional arrangements for planning and in planning policy, so overall there has been a great deal of change in the relationships between the two sectors. To maintain continuity, this chapter reviews changes in institutional structures, Chapter 11 moves on to review policy developments and Chapter 12 analyses the outcomes and draws conclusions.

Institutional arrangements: the railway industry

There were several alternative models that could have been selected for railway privatisation. The whole industry could have been sold off as a single entity, BR plc, or the network could have been broken down into a number of regional chunks on the Big Four model. Either of these two approaches would have preserved the historic, vertically integrated structure of common ownership of track and trains. However the government wanted to promote internal competition whereby more than one operator could run trains on the same route and therefore opted to separate track and train ownership: the 'track authority' model (DoT 1992). In this, management of the fixed infrastructure is in the hands of a quite separate organisation to those which run the trains and interface with the industry's customers. This is major break with traditional railway practice and the intention was that internal competition would unleash private sector initiative and, thereby, improve services, raise revenue, drive down costs and reduce the need for public subsidy.

Privatisation on this basis, under the 1993 Railways Act, was rushed through by early 1997 in order to be complete before an impending general election. It created a complex institutional structure with over 100 hundred separate railway organisations of one kind or another with a relaxation of centralised management and no single 'controlling mind', as embodied previously by the Chairman of BR. In order to facilitate the desired competition between train operating companies (TOCs), the fixed infrastructure was sold off, in 1996, to a track authority (originally a private limited company called Railtrack, subsequently replaced by a 'not-for-dividend' trust called Network Rail – see below). Passenger TOCs secured the right to operate trains through a competitive bidding process for 25 time-limited franchises[1] from the Office for Passenger Rail Franchising[2] (OPRAF) (Harris and Godward 1997; Freeman and Shaw 2000). Franchises are awarded on the basis of minimising the amount of subsidy required by operators or, where circumstances are favourable, maximising the premium to be returned to the public purse. Most of the franchises, wherein there is little scope for competition from other operators once the franchise has been awarded,[3] have been won by the small group of large companies which have come to dominate the bus market following its deregulation and privatisation, an interesting reversal of the situation in the 1930s when the private sector bus market was dominated by the Big Four. These companies include Stagecoach, National Express, First Group, Arriva and Go-Ahead. Other TOCs have been controlled by Virgin Group and Sea Containers (the now defunct Great North Eastern Railway) and, more recently, several foreign railway companies have moved into the market too (see Table 10.1). Privatisation has created particular problems with regard to planning at and around stations as, although all stations are now owned by Network Rail, it only manages seventeen itself, the major stations, ten of them in London. Day-by-day management of the

1   EU Directive 91/440 requires separate accounting systems for the fixed infrastructure and train operation; British railway privatisation can be seen as a very literal interpretation of this and is in stark contrast to the approach in other EU countries where national railways currently remain as publicly owned industries, with operational structures and accounting procedures adapted to meet EU requirements. In Japan where the state railways were privatised in the 1980s, this was as vertically integrated companies and in the USA where most railways are privately owned, they are vertically integrated too.

2   This reflects the fact that, although the railway network itself and the rolling stock were privatised, the right to run passenger trains on it was not, it is merely franchised off for specific periods of time.

3   There are a few 'open access' operators providing services for niche markets, such as Hull-London but, although such services are valued locally, the volume of passengers carried is insignificant nationally.

majority of stations is taken on by TOCs as part of their franchises. Although several TOCs may use a station only one takes on the management role, becoming the 'station facility operator' (SFO).

Table 10.1 Passenger Rail Franchises: Spring 2008

Franchise	Type of operator	Parent company(ies)	Period of franchise (rounded to years)	Franchise running from
Arriva Trains Wales	Regional	Arriva	15	2003
Arriva Cross Country	Long distance	Arriva	8	2007
Chiltern Railways	London and South East	Deutsche Bahn AG	20	2002
East Midland Trains	Regional	Stagecoach	8	2007
First Capital Connect (Thameslink)	London and South East	First Group	9	2006
First Great Western	Long distance	First Group	10	2006
First Scotrail	Regional	First Group	7 extended to 10	2004
Gatwick Express	London and South East	National Express Group	12 absorbed by Southern in 2008	1996
Grand Central	open access operator Sunderland-London	private	n/a	service commenced 2007
Hull Trains	open access operator Hull-London	First Group (80%) and Renaissance Trains	n/a	service commenced 2007
Island Line (Isle of Wight)	Regional	Stagecoach	see South West Trains	

Franchise	Type of operator	Parent company(ies)	Period of franchise (rounded to years)	Franchise running from
London Midland	Regional	Govia	8	2007
London Rail (London Overground)	London and South East	MTR (Hong Kong) Laing	7	2007
Merseyrail	Regional	Serco & Ned Rail (Nederlandse Spoorwegen)	25	2003
National Express East Anglia	London and South East	National Express Group	7	2004
National Express East Coast	Long distance	National Express Group	8	2007
Northern Rail	Regional	Serco & Ned Rail (Nederlandse Spoorwegen)	9	2004
Southeastern	London and South East	Govia	8	2006
Southern	London and South East	Govia	4	2005
South West Trains	London and South East	Stagecoach	10	2007
TransPennine Express	Regional	First Group (55%) and Keolis (45%)	8	2004
Virgin West Coast	Long distance	Virgin (51%) and Stagecoach (49%)	15	1997 with subsequent reviews

Note: Heathrow Express, operated by British Airports Authority (Ferrovial), is not part of the national rail system and is not a franchise.

There is further complexity as locomotives and passenger rolling stock were sold off to leasing companies, of which financial institutions have been the main owners, and the maintenance and renewal of the track and signalling was initially outsourced by Railtrack to private contractors too. Most of the freight businesses and their associated rolling stock were sold outright (not franchised), to a company which became known as English Welsh and Scottish Railway (EWS). EWS was originally American owned but is now part of a growing Europe-wide rail freight operation owned by the German state railway operator, Deutsche Bahn. The Freightliner business, so strongly associated with the more positive side of Beeching's vision, was sold separately and the name lives on, although the company is now owned by Bahrain based Arcapita. Subsequently, there have been several new freight operating companies (FOCs) entering the market too, so in this case privatisation has produced on-track competition.[4] Ownership of rail freight facilities was complex in BR days as some were railway owned but others, such as quarries, ports and new regional distribution centres such as Daventry, were not. Post privatisation the development of rail freight facilities, always more difficult than developing a purely road served freight facility, has become more complicated owing to the greater number of potential operators and the division between them and the track authority.

The overall thrust of these changes was to replace the monolithic command relationships which existed between the various parts of BR with contractual relationships between a large number of free-standing autonomous bodies (Tyrrall 2006). To ensure transparency and fairness in these complex contractual relationships, the industry is overseen by the Office of Rail Regulation (this role was initially carried out by the Rail Regulator), as shown in Figure 10.1 and one of its main duties is to set the level of track access charges paid by TOCs to the track authority. A strange product of the whole process is that the passenger TOCs, which actually run the trains, own very little: their operational staff is their major asset.

Concerned about the shortcomings of Railtrack with regard to long term planning, Tony Blair's New Labour government, elected in 1997, created the Strategic Rail Authority (SRA) under the Transport Act 2000 to develop a strategic vision for the network, promote integration and interchange and take over management of the franchising operation to more effectively secure public benefits. Sir Alastair Morton, formerly of Eurotunnel, was the first Chairman and it was hoped that his financial expertise would be used to encourage TOCs to develop franchise bids containing capacity enhancement projects to be externally funded by mechanisms he termed Special Purpose Vehicles (SPVs). However, unintended effects of privatisation caused operational problems which led to an erosion of public confidence in railway safety, turned the industry's gaze inwards and caused the whole rationale for privatisation to be seriously questioned (Wolmar 2001).

---

4   The rail freight industry was one of the strongest supporters of the track authority model for privatisation.

These problems included a series of fatal accidents which attracted very hostile media attention: at Southall in 1997, Ladbroke Grove in 1999, Hatfield in 2000 and Potters Bar in 2002. Hatfield, caused by the catastrophic failure of a broken rail, highlighted fundamental flaws in the institutional structure of the industry whereby management of the fixed infrastructure had broken down. Subsequent imposition of speed restrictions by Railtrack[5] to prevent similar accidents, led to the collapse of the network timetable, something unthinkable in BR days.

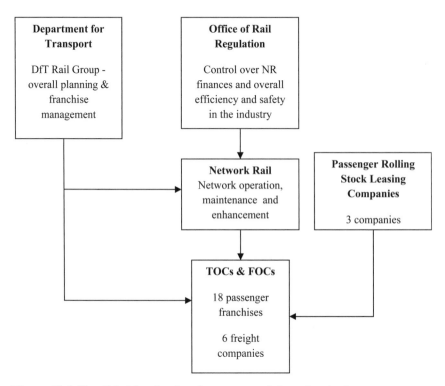

Figure 10.1 Simplified institutional structure of the privatised railway industry: 2008

---

5   The general response of rail companies to accidents was to deny responsibility in order to limit the financial consequences. Railtrack protected itself post-Hatfield by the widespread imposition of 20mph speed restrictions wherever cracked rails were detected. This transferred the risk to rail passengers who, because of the consequent service collapse, transferred to other modes, especially cars, with higher accident risks than rail.

In addition there has been a large escalation in the costs of maintenance and renewals and this became critical on the WCML upgrade. This project, which was long overdue being originally considered by BR in the 1980s in association with the APT, was initially heralded as a success for privatisation. However it will have outturn costs of around £8bn, as against an original projected cost of £2.2bn, will be several years late and to a lower specification than originally envisaged. Concerns over this, on the back of the Hatfield debacle, led to Railtrack's bankruptcy being, controversially, precipitated by the then Secretary of State for Transport Stephen Byers in October 2001 and it was replaced by Network Rail, a 'not for dividend' trust, with a focus on engineering matters. By 2004 Network Rail had taken back 'in house' 15,000 maintenance staff previously working for private contractors and subsequently developed an internal structure built around 26 long distance routes (which are really areas), each with its own route director. Many commentators saw the creation of Network Rail, on the back of the creation of the SRA which had taken control of planning and financing network enhancements, as tantamount to re-nationalisation, although the government denied this, not wishing to be associated with 'Old Labour' ideology. This is despite the strong opposition by the Labour Party to privatisation at the time that it was taking place.

There have been difficulties too with franchising as a pattern developed wherein TOCs were given higher subsidies in loss making situations, provoking debate about who is taking the risk and what the aims of franchising are. Richard Bowker (formerly of Virgin Trains) replaced Morton as head of the SRA in 2002 and the approach to franchising changed, with an emphasis on shorter time scales tied to more rigorous service delivery targets, with minimal TOC investment in the fixed infrastructure. With most franchises now running for around 7 years (Table 10.1), a relatively short period in planning terms, there are very real problems with regard to how much priority TOCs can give to long term matters such as engaging with local planning and transport authorities to develop rail-oriented policy in station catchment areas. Bowker also pursued a strategy of reducing the number of TOCs, with, for example, having all services in major London termini controlled by one operator.[6] This is further evidence that one of the central goals of privatisation, securing on line competition between TOCs, has been dropped, although this does have the positive effect of reducing the number of railway industry players involved in external liaison around station planning.

Creation of the SRA meant that it became even more unclear as to who was 'running the railway' as power was spread between the Secretary of State for Transport, the SRA, the Rail Regulator and Network Rail, with the daily operation of passenger and freight services being in the hands of private company executives. Concern over the government's inability to control the flow of taxpayers' money into the industry, led to a further industry review in 2004 by the then Secretary

---

6 In addition management of the largely self-contained Merseyrail network was handed over to the local PTA in 2003, with Network Rail responsible for maintenance and with train services being provided through a new franchise.

of State, Alistair Darling, who had replaced Byers in 2002 with a brief to take transport out of the headlines, something for which his bland manner well suited him. This review resulted from prior conflict between the Rail Regulator, the SRA and government over how much money Railtrack needed to maintain and develop the network in 'Control Period 3' (2004–09): five year Control Periods have been the norm for regulatory management of the industry's finances. In the absence of any clear guidance to the contrary from the SRA or the government, the Regulator had endorsed a level of spend that would require a significant increase in public funding and the government, especially the Treasury, was far from amused by this exercise of regulatory independence (see Winsor 2004 for the Regulator's side of the story). In the government's view, something had to be done to restore its control through a less complex managerial and regulatory regime. As there would be a continuing need for regulation of the relationships between the various players because the government had no intention of re-integrating the railway (into either public or private hands), the SRA became the sacrificial victim. Its abolition after so short a life illustrated the continuing institutional instability and the absence of a shared, long term view within government as to how the railway should be managed. The passenger franchising, freight grant and strategic planning functions were absorbed into a new Railway Directorate within the recently reconstituted (see below) Department for Transport (DfT), with Network Rail as the lead operational body. The latter was rather perverse, given New Labour's market oriented ideology, as Network Rail has no direct contact with the industry's customers, this being handled by the TOCs and FOCs. With the strategic management of the industry largely in the hands of DfT civil servants and a company with no shareholders and its debts underwritten by the government, this is a rather perverse outcome to the privatisation process, given the initial aims. For example, the DfT has been involved in the minutiae of timetable planning, managing the transfer of rolling stock between TOCs and the design of a new generation of high speed trains (the Inter City Express project). This is a much higher level of civil service involvement in the day to day running of the railway than in BR days and flies in the face of the Blairite modernising agenda wherein there has been an increasing tendency to reduce public sector delivery of many public services. This high level of control leaves very little room for the much vaunted private sector initiative. Also it is difficult to envision the DfT acting as an independent and creative champion of the railway in the way that the former BR Board or the SRA did. The fear is that this is, in effect, a return to an even more constraining form of Treasury control, engendered by the crisis over costs, but with a greater risk of civil service and political interference in operational matters. The financial pressures have impacted on franchising too with strong emphasis on the short term, minimising subsidy and maximising premiums.

Given that these problems with management of the main line railway network can largely be attributed to the form of privatisation which was adopted and the speed with which such a massive upheaval was introduced, it is surprising that running in parallel the government opted for a very complex part privatisation of the London Underground, this process being led by then Chancellor of the Exchequer, Gordon Brown. Here the model adopted was a Public-Private Partnership (PPP) and in 2002, after protracted negotiations, London Regional Transport entered into three agreements with private sector partners whereby they would take over maintenance, renewals and development of the fixed infrastructure for 30 years, receiving payment from the public sector based on a very complex performance regime (Wolmar 2002). Operation of the Underground would remain with the public sector. A consortium known as Tube Lines took over one group of lines but a second consortium, Metronet, took over two groups which, together, comprised two thirds of the network. This deal was being driven through during the process of the creation of a mayor for London with extensive planning and transport powers (see below) and the new mayor, Ken Livingstone, was hostile to this approach. However he eventually acquiesced as part of a deal to secure his re-entry to the Labour party and secure government funding for his various strategies for London. In 2003 London Underground was transferred from London Regional Transport to the new transport body for London, Transport for London, which then took over operation of the network and management of the PPPs. In 2004 the National Audit Office (NAO) produced a report (NAO 2004) which estimated the cost of setting up the PPPs at £455m. If this was not bad enough, in mid 2007 Metronet called in the administrators owing to a funding gap of £2bn caused by cost overruns and what it claimed were inadequate payments. Obviously this caused a further political furore, given the arguments when the PPPs were created and the demise of Railtrack. Metronet was eventually transferred to TfL in May 2008, cementing another failed privatisation in the railway industry.

National and local government

On its election the New Labour government, under the influence of Deputy Prime Minister John Prescott, had combined the former Departments of the Environment and Transport into a new 'super department', the Department of the Environment Transport and the Regions (DETR), reflecting a high priority for integrated transport, a strategy with which Prescott was strongly associated. However 'environment' was soon moved to the Department for Environment Food and Rural Affairs in 2001, suggesting a reduced emphasis on environmental matters. In a depressing replay of events in the 1970s, the deconstruction of DETR continued in 2002, when a perceived failure to make progress on the transport agenda, led to it being moved back into a separate Department for Transport. This left local government, planning, urban regeneration and regional planning policy in a new and rather pompous sounding, Office of the Deputy Prime Minister (ODPM). With the withdrawal of John Prescott from governmental activity following a scandal about his private life in 2006, the ODPM became the Department for Communities and Local Government (DCLG). This further name change reflected the continuing down-playing of environmental concerns by the Blair government (despite rhetoric to the contrary), and the emphasis on the 'modernising' and customer/community care agendas for local government. These changes have been seen as resulting from a desire to emphasise the benefits of bringing private sector attributes into public services rather than emphasising the need for more effective state regulation of aspects of the market to secure the environmental elements of the 'sustainable development' (see Chapter 11) agenda (Batchelor and Patterson 2007).

A further complication in public governance which impacts on rail planning has arisen from Welsh and Scottish devolution, the Scottish Parliament and the Welsh Assembly Government having their first meetings in 1999. From the outset these showed interest in railway matters, although their statutory powers and duties were not formalised until enactment of the Transport (Scotland) Act 2005 and the Transport (Wales) Act 2006. ScotRail, having been created by BR in 1983, was one of the original franchises and, subsequently, a redrawing of the franchise map by the SRA created a Welsh franchise in 2003 which created a very clear relationship between the devolved bodies and the passenger businesses.[7] So devolution has led to marked differences between Scotland and Wales on the one hand, and the English regions on the other, where there have been many changes but with rather different outcomes vis-à-vis railway planning.

The 1998 Regional Development Agency Act created statutory Regional Development Agencies (RDAs) in the eight English standard regions with duties and powers to promote economic development, regeneration and sustainable development which include the capacity to invest in regional transport networks. RDA's membership is appointed by government and they reported to the Department of Trade and Industry (not the ODPM) now replaced, in yet another renaming, by the snappily titled Department of Business, Enterprise and Regulatory Reform. At the same time that the RDAs were created, the ODPM encouraged the creation of eight non-statutory regional assemblies, or regional planning bodies, to scrutinise their work and produce regional land-use and transport planning strategies. The previous Conservative government had combined the regional offices of key government departments into integrated and spatial planning oriented Government Offices (GOs) in 1994, and these were retained by New Labour to complete this rather complex structure of regional governance.[8] This book has shown the significance of the regional dimension to the relationship between the planning and railway sectors so its reinforcement was, potentially, a good thing for rail-

---

7   Most of Scotland's rail services run internally within Scotland but that is not the case in Wales with the main routes in South and North Wales being at the end of east-west routes originating in England. The case for a Welsh franchise is therefore, arguably, political rather than operational.

8   There was an aspiration for the creation of elected regional bodies in England to complement those created in Wales and Scotland, and this strategy was strongly associated with John Prescott. However the process came to an abrupt halt when the first referendum, in the North East, an area with a very strong regional identity, very firmly rejected the proposal in November 2004.

oriented planning, although the boundaries of the standard regions don't sit very comfortably with Network Rail's 26 routes. Also the crucial difference between England and the Welsh and Scottish devolved bodies,[9] is that the English regional planning bodies are non-statutory, with no powers and no budgets.

Following more changes in the structure of English local government (see chapter 3 in Cullingworth and Nadin 2006) there are complexities on that level too, with some parts of England administered by a two tier structure of county and district councils and others administered by a single tier of unitary authorities. In addition to the 36 unitaries created in 1986 when the former metropolitan county councils were abolished by Mrs Thatcher's government, a further 46 have been created subsequently in the 'shire' counties. This has meant that the areas administered by the counties, some of which it will be recalled have been very active in rail promotion, have been significantly reduced in size and some, such as Cheshire County Council, are to disappear altogether: as a result some of the smaller, new unitaries have struggled with their transport portfolios. Welcome continuity in institutional arrangements arises in the former metropolitan counties where the PTAs/PTEs continue to play a crucial role in planning and funding local rail services, although their powers with regard to the latter have been eroded. However, despite the continued growth of other conurbations such as Bristol-Bath, Portsmouth-Southampton or greater Cardiff, no new PTAs/PTEs have been created.

Developments in London have produced more positive outcomes. In 1998 a public referendum voted in favour of the creation of an elected strategic authority (the GLC it will be recalled was also abolished in 1986) and this led to the creation in 2000 of the Greater London Authority (GLA) with a directly elected mayor with real executive power on the French and American models. The GLA has a duty to produce an integrated transport strategy and a new executive agency, Transport for London (TfL), was created to deliver it. TfL has responsibility for the Underground, light rail and bus service planning (buses were not deregulated in London, although bus ownership was privatised – see White 2002) and in 2007, became responsible for the administration of certain main line commuter rail franchises, these being part of a developing 'Overground' brand. The mayor has a duty to develop strategic planning policy in the form of a Spatial Development Strategy which embraces economic development, regeneration, transport and land use. Notwithstanding the general complexity of the railway industry, this combining of power to strategically plan rail and land development activities in a single agency is a significant change and stands in stark contrast to the situation in other major British cities.

---

9   And regional bodies in many other European countries – see Haywood 1998.

Statutory development plans

During the Thatcher era planning was under threat and there was retrenchment by local planning authorities into the basic statutory requirements of producing development plans and development control. Owing to the lengthy nature of the plan making process, development plans always had difficulty in keeping in step with the property market. But from the 1980s owing to emergence of the politically important and fast moving world of urban regeneration, they came to be seen as, at best, out of date and largely irrelevant or, at worst, barriers to regeneration. It was therefore development control which tended to become the more visible part of planning and, as this can be a re-active and merely regulatory process, this also called into question the role and relevance of planning.[10] However, the New Labour government re-affirmed its commitment to planning but was concerned about the suitability of the extant development plan schema, as well as other aspects of the statutory system and its delivery. It therefore initiated a debate about 'Modernising Planning' with a Green Paper in 2001 (Byers 2001). Eventually and controversially, this led to significant changes in the English[11] statutory development plan system under the Planning and Compulsory Purchase Act 2004. This system now comprises an upper tier of statutory Regional Spatial Strategies, which incorporate Regional Transport Strategies and replace county level structure plans (ODPM, 2004a). These regional plans are currently produced by the non-statutory regional planning bodies. Lower tier Local Plans are being replaced by Local Development Frameworks (LDFs), as shown in Figure 10.2, and these are produced at district level. Although intended to simplify and accelerate the production of development plans, government requirements with regard to the procedures for their production and content has called the validity of the reforms into question. Also the Blairite emphasis on stakeholders and partnerships has led to labyrinthine structures at the local level wherein local authorities are interlinked with complex groupings of public, private and voluntary sector bodies with various 'branded' regeneration initiatives and this has served to dilute the role of local authorities in general and planning in particular.

---

10   See Kitchen 1997 for some all too rare reflections on the world of the planning practitioner during this period.

11   There have been changes in Wales and Scotland too: see Cullingworth and Nadin 2006.

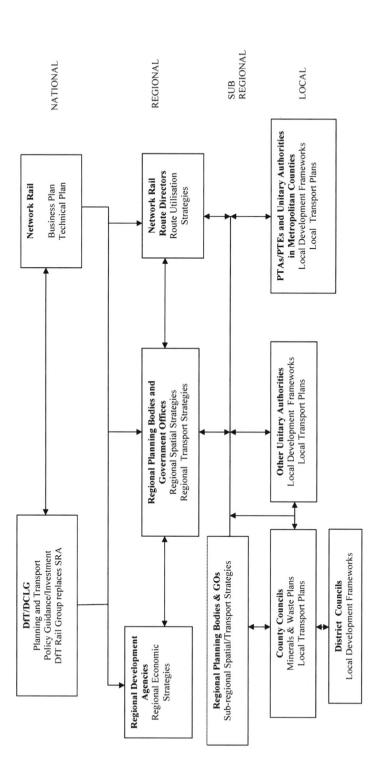

Figure 10.2 The Institutional Framework for Integrated Planning Around Rail (at December 2006)

Statutory Local Transport Plans (LTPs) were introduced under the Transport Act 2000 as one of the vehicles for delivering the new transport policy agenda but, although one of their roles is to integrate local transport planning with land-use planning, their relationship with the new statutory land-use planning system is rather mixed. This is because it is the county councils and *unitary* districts which produce LTPs. It is only in the case of the unitary districts where LTPs and LDFs are produced by the same authority. In non-unitary districts the LTP is produced by the county council, so a co-operative spirit is necessary to make the relationship between transport and land-use work. The removal of the duty on county councils to produce structure plans seriously threatens the relationship between strategic land-use and rail planning (and other aspects of transport planning) at that level, which many county councils have co-ordinated with some success.

Conclusions

Whereas there was a high degree of institutional stability at the national level between 1970–94 with the BRB and the DOE extant throughout, there has been almost continuous change since 1994. There has been much change at lower levels too, with short rail franchises, changes in the field organisation of Railtrack and Network Rail and changes arising from devolution and local government re-organisation, added to which there have been significant changes in statutory development plan making. So the interface between railway interests and local authorities for integrating rail planning with local land-use and transport planning is complex, ill-defined and has been subject to a great deal of churn. Table 10.2 summarises the analysis of this utilising the three core themes.

This complexity creates difficulties in securing mutual understanding and confidence, and in aligning policy and funding between the organisations concerned. There are mechanisms created by the Railway Act to try and overcome any conflicts within the railway industry, but the many interfaces between the various players involved in securing integration between railway and land-use planning create 'friction' in decision making processes and confusion as to who is doing what and who should lead, with the net result that innovation is likely to be held back. The complexity also raises transaction costs and the viability threshold is raised. The SRA was developing a land-use planning capacity to work at this interface and its loss has created a vacuum which has only partially been filled by developments in Scotland, Wales and London.

Table 10.2 Summary of thematic analysis of institutional structures 1994–2008

Explanatory themes	Railway sector	Interrelationships between the two sectors	Planning sector
Politics and political ideology	Initially seen as increasingly a matter for the private sector but the state was steadily drawn back into a controlling role; strenuous efforts were made to ensure that this could not be seen as renationalisation to create a state monopoly, so the structure has remained complex with many players; structures simpler in Scotland and Wales.	The pre-privatisation structures have been seriously undermined; the desire for effective planning is in conflict with the wish to be seen as supportive of free markets.	Commitment to planning re-affirmed but reform created more unitary district councils and the strategic role of the counties was eroded; development plan schema reformed with the intention of becoming more property market oriented, but new processes are bureaucratic and time consuming; introduction of LTPs created a vehicle for land-use transport integration.
Professions and professional ideology	The collapse of Railtrack led to a more internally focused, engineering led approach by Network Rail. This and concerns over cost control meant that, despite the stated commitment to the market, the train companies are heavily constrained and there is limited scope for activity other than a focus on their daily customers.	Few points of contact between professions in the two sectors and the knowledge of each other built up in the immediate pre-privatisation period has been lost.	The importance of planning has been recognised and much effort has gone into reforming the structures which deliver it and into making the development plan system more robust. However the links with railway planning have tended to become more tenuous, especially since the demise of the SRA.
Governance and management	A tension between perceived needs for centralised control over financial and engineering matters and a desire to be customer oriented has led to the retention of an overly complex structure.	The creation of relatively simple and effective structures to facilitate integration between railway and land-use planning has not been a priority, other than during the brief life of the SRA.	A great deal of churn with planning being associated with three different central government departments; further change at local government level as a result of the modernising agenda.

Chapter 11

The Post-Privatisation Period 1994–2008: Policy

Introduction

The decade or so since privatisation has shown that, although there was an expectation that the private sector would take the initiative in the development of the railway network, this has been far from how things have worked out. Instead there has been the most intensive period of public policy development with regard to the railways for many years, partly as a result of attempts by New Labour to secure integrated transport, although this tended to be overshadowed by actions necessary to address problems arising from privatisation. The general re-affirmation of commitment to planning, firstly by the Conservatives and then by New Labour, has also involved increased commitment to rail oriented planning, thereby continuing the trends of the early 1990s. But the problems caused by privatisation have led to imbalance in the policy process whereby expectations with regard to the railway network arising from planning and transport policy, have not been met.

Rail policy

Although the privatisation process dominated rail policy in the last years of John Major's government, significant decisions were made with regard to the promotion of a high speed rail link to the Channel Tunnel. In 1994, after prolonged dithering in the early 1990s over route options and funding issues, the government finally opted for a relatively high cost route which involved a tunnel under the Thames and more tunnelling to gain access to east London and the terminus at St Pancras Station (Gourvish 2006). This decision was heavily influenced by the then Deputy Prime Minister Michael Heseltine's desire to use the investment to promote the regeneration of the Thames Gateway, this being a strategy aimed at deflecting some of the growth pressures from the economically buoyant west of London to an area to the east, from Docklands to the Essex Marshes and north Kent (DOE 1995). In 1996 London and Continental railways was selected to undertake construction of the line. However financial problems arose in 1998 and 2002, and it was only as a result of firm support by John Prescott, and some complex financial manoeuvring, that commitment to construction of the north Thameside part of the route was maintained, otherwise the project could have been terminated after completion of phase 1 from the Tunnel to north Kent.

With regard to transport policy in general, after a consultation exercise (DETR 1997), the New Labour government published a transport white paper[1] with a focus on a complex interpretation of 'integration', the first time this had featured so centrally in transport policy since the late 1960s:

Integration of Transport policy

An integrated transport policy means:

- integration within and between different types of transport – so that each contributes its full potential and people can move easily between them
- integration with the environment – so that our transport choices support a better environment
- integration with land use planning – at national, regional and local level, so that transport and planning work together to support more sustainable travel choices and reduce the need to travel
- integration with our policies for education, health and wealth creation – so that transport helps to make a fairer, more inclusive society (DETR 1998, 8)

The white paper contained an ambitious strategy, very much associated with the aspirations of John Prescott, which was a continuation of how transport policy had been developing under the Conservatives (Docherty and Shaw 2003). It sought to reduce road traffic congestion through a combination of policies which included 'hard' options, such as congestion and parking charges with hypothecation of the funds raised to transport projects, and 'soft' options, which included promoting modal shift to public transport and providing 'more and better … trains'. These policies were related to global environmental goals requiring reductions in greenhouse gas emissions, as agreed by Prescott under the Kyoto Agreement of 1997. The intention to create the SRA was declared, as was the setting up of a Commission for Integrated Transport to advise on transport policy, and the introduction of statutory Local Transport Plans to secure delivery. This was followed by publication of a 'daughter' document on sustainable distribution (DETR 1999) which endorsed the ambitious growth targets then being espoused by the private rail freight industry.[2] This promised development of a national policy framework for major freight interchanges and more grants to encourage modal shift.

---

1   This was the first transport white paper since 1977 and contained some interesting parallels with the content of that document which also expressed concern over continuing increases in road traffic and the impact of land use change in stimulating demand for transport.

2   EWS aimed to triple its traffic over 10 years and Freightliner aimed to increase the volume of containers carried by 50 per cent over 5 years.

Next an ambitious Ten Year Plan (DETR 2000a) was produced which envisaged a 50 per cent growth in rail passenger traffic and an 80 per cent growth in rail freight. The Plan was an attempt to overcome the short termism which had been seen to dog transport investment for many years and to stymie critical comment of the government, and Prescott in particular, who was portrayed as developing policy with little action on the ground. As far as heavy rail is concerned, the commitment to deliver a broad package of improvements by 2010 included: modernisation and increased capacity on the WCML and ECML; the high speed Channel Tunnel Rail Link serving Kent and the Thames Gateway; improved commuter services into London and other cities; upgrading of freight routes to major ports; and better integration with other modes. For London a new east-west link was promised along with Thameslink 2000 and the East London Line. There was also an expectation of up to 25 new light rail schemes in major cities and conurbations, holding out the promise of integration with main line services on the European model.

These high level plans were being developed during the Railtrack era when the company produced annual Network Management Statements. Over the years these did get better in terms of giving overviews about network capacity, identifying possible enhancements and bringing forward station enhancement schemes, particularly at major stations. But the proposed network enhancements were mainly just wish lists and Railtrack tended to look to other organisations, such as the TOCs or local authorities, to actually do the investing. This lack of commitment to strategic investment in the network was part of the government's rationale for the creation of the SRA.

One of the first strategic documents to be produced by the SRA was the Freight Strategy (SRA 2001a) which sought to carry forward the commitment to increase rail freight by 80 per cent which, it was pointed out, would only increase rail's market share from 7 to 10 per cent, showing how far rail's share had declined. The Ten Year Plan promised £4bn for rail freight over the plan period and the SRA strategy envisioned spending this on: diversionary routes, so freight could get through when primary routes were closed for some reason; infill electrification; gauge enhancement to take larger containers; increased grant aid to secure modal shift; and promoting the development of freight terminals. In order to secure a step change in the modal share of rail freight a private company, Central Railway, developed a proposal for a privately funded high gauge railway from the north west of England to the Channel Tunnel via London. This would allow the Channel Tunnel's piggy-back[3] operation to run to locations north of London, thereby relieving the south east's motorways of much heavy truck traffic, in the same way that trans-Alpine truck traffic is diverted to rail in Austria and Switzerland. This ambitious project would utilise some existing railways, but would also see a new railway along part of the disused trackbed of the former Great Central railway between Leicester and north London. It required parliamentary powers but, in

---

3 Piggy-back involves carrying lorry trailers and tractor units on rail wagons, not just intermodal containers, and therefore requires a high loading gauge.

2004, the government refused to support this because of fears that it may need public moneys and the project collapsed. The CTRL will have capacity for freight, but an issue is the lack of sites for large scale intermodal distribution hubs along the route, the poor provision for which is a significant shortcoming of planning around greater London.

Things soon began to go wrong with the integrated transport strategy as in September 2000, the government caved in to the 'fuel tax revolt' led by hauliers and farmers and abandoned the politically ambitious automatic fuel duty escalator,[4] introduced by the previous Conservative government. The government, and in particular the prime minister, subsequently worked hard at not being perceived as 'anti-car' so as not to alienate the electorate and this tended to undermine commitment to strategies focused on modal shift. Following the post-Hatfield crisis in the rail industry, the SRA began managing the network on the less optimistic assumptions of a 20 to 30 per cent growth in passenger kilometres and similar growth in freight tonne kilometres between 2001/2 and 2010/11 (SRA 2003a). Accidents, cost overruns and falling reliability were the background to the SRA taking control of the strategic management of the network through a complex sequence of initiatives as shown in Table 11.1: the network was placed firmly under public sector control. But as well as getting a grip on management of the railway in order to restore its credibility, the SRA recognised that, in difficult times, it had to be its champion and therefore published 'the Case for Rail' (SRA 2003f). In a press release, Bowker claimed that 'this is the best argued case for the development of Britain's railway that has been produced for a very long time'(SRA 2003g) and, indeed, the balkanised post-privatisation structure had led to a lack of leadership. The case made was broad based ranging from the importance of rail to London and the South East and other major cities, through the reduction in road traffic congestion and limitation of urban sprawl, to urban regeneration, countryside protection and electricity generation. The new financial climate for the railway was harsh, but Bowker said:

> … I am not going to propose simply what I think the treasury might be prepared to live with. The task is to present the right number for the right network that focuses on what rail does well (SRA 2003g).

The SRA prioritised early completion of the WCML project whilst reining back costs, replacement of all the 'slam door' 1950s/60s rolling stock on the south London commuter lines[5] which was seen as unsafe for passengers, and supporting

---

4   This was introduced by the Conservatives in 1993 with the aim of constraining road traffic growth and was set at an annual increase of 3 per cent ahead of inflation, later rising to 5 per cent. Under New Labour the rate of increase was raised to 6 per cent per year.

5   This involved some heavy investment in electricity supply infrastructure as the new rolling stock ordered by the TOCs draws more power than its predecessor which the system could not supply. This problem was not foreseen by Railtrack, illustrating the lack

Network Rail in containing costs and taking a firmer lead on operational matters. The policies on route capacity, the Route Utilisation Strategies (RUS), were concerned with resolving conflicts between various kinds of traffic on the routes under study so that use of existing capacity could be optimised with no need for major investment, as this was unlikely to be forthcoming. This led, in particular, to conflicts between local services and long distance services and concerns about capacity for freight. The positive side of the financial crisis was that it highlighted the benefits of small scale capacity improvements of the sort funded by one of the TOCs (Chiltern Trains), the SRA and, following its abolition, Network Rail. These included things like the redoubling of routes which had been reduced to single track and were a sort of mirror image of the long sequence of capacity rationalisations forced on BR under the iron grip of Treasury control, following the initial post-Beeching full line closures.

Table 11.1 SRA rail network capacity management initiatives

Title of publication	Date	Reference
Capacity Utilisation Policy: Network Utilisation Strategy	2003	SRA 2003a
Appraisal Criteria: A Guide to the Appraisal of Support for Passenger and Freight Services	2003	SRA 2003b
Specification of Network Outputs	2003	SRA 2003c
Strategy for the West Coast Main Line	2003	SRA 2003d
Midland Main Line Route Utilisation Strategy	2003	SRA 2003e
Brighton Line Route Utilisation Strategy	2004	SRA 2004a
West Coast Main Line: Progress Report	2004	SRA 2004b
Great Western Route Utilisation Strategy	2005	SRA 2005

In this harsh financial climate the SRA began to express concerns about the costs of supporting some lightly used rural lines and the spectres of Beeching and Serpell stirred. However, in late 2004, the SRA published the Community Rail Development Strategy (SRA 2004c) which focused on these routes. Although widely perceived in the national press as a veiled closure threat, this strategy sought to draw local authorities and communities into the promotion of rural lines in order to secure their retention and this created a basis for optimism around this initiative and the work of the non-statutory Community Rail Partnerships (see

---

of liaison with the TOCs on essential operational matters, and the SRA had to step in and drive through a programme of works.

Chapter 12). It was in fact an intention to carry on with the approach of the former Regional Railways.

The long standing mechanism of freight facilities grants and a new Rail Passenger Partnership Fund introduced by the SRA had been very successful in levering external finance from the private sector (mainly for freight), local authorities and other public bodies, to secure new services and network benefits. But after an initial surge post 1997, funding for the former was halted in England in 2003 and the latter was scrapped. However the devolved bodies in Wales and Scotland have been able to maintain a higher level of commitment to enhancing their networks than has been the case in England and continued paying freight grants and a number of passenger re-opening projects have been developed through to fruition, as will be shown in the next chapter.

More optimistically, the SRA developed a wider planning capacity which could interface with the devolved governments, regional and, to a certain degree, local planning bodies with regard to strategic land-use, transport and economic policy. The Freight Strategy, for example, had displayed good awareness of the need for the planning system to deliver more terminals if modal shift to rail was to take place and the SRA began to intervene in the planning process to support projects such as rail served regional distribution centres. An important example of the latter was its support for the proposed London International Freight Exchange (LIFE) in the green belt near Heathrow airport: it was considered that three or four such facilities would be required around greater London. As well as producing general town planning policy advice (SRA 2001b and c), the first time ever that the railway industry had done this, it had also begun to produce Regional Planning Assessments (SRA 2003h) to engage with regional spatial policy making and provide the wider context for the RUS, and issued specific guidance re station (SRA 2004d) and freight terminal development (SRA 2004e). This was also the first time that such documents had been published to guide third parties interested in promoting rail utilisation. But these positive steps were cut short by the untimely abolition of the SRA. However, on the back of a better understanding of the state of the network under its management, Network Rail has continued to issue Route Utilisation Strategies and, although still heavily constrained financially and still falling short of local authority expectations, these have been seen as more focused on increasing capacity and facilitating growth in rail traffic volumes through small scale enhancements. But Network Rail has not maintained the pro-active stance of the SRA towards the promotion of rail accessible development through the planning system and has been content to limit its role to reacting to local authority initiatives, promoting development projects at its major stations, such as Euston, and promoting increases in station car parking, as along the WCML.

In 2004 the government produced another transport white paper, 'The Future of Transport: a Network for 2030' (DfT 2004a). Despite its title and coming so soon after the 1998 white paper, this played down the mantra of 'integrated transport' and did not contain a vision as to what the railway network might look like much beyond 2012. It was primarily concerned with getting rid of the SRA, emphasising the importance of financial realism and cost control in developing all transport projects, and quietly burying many of the ambitious targets from the 10 Year Plan. The gloom surrounding the downbeat Secretary of State Alistair Darling, was further darkened when he announced that light rail projects at Manchester, Leeds, Liverpool, Blackpool and South Hampshire would not be going forward. At the same time a rail specific white paper, 'The Future of Rail' (DfT 2004b) and the subsequent Railways Act 2005, introduced a new mechanism to ensure that the DfT and ORR keep in step with regard to rail funding. This involves the government producing a 'High Level Output Specification' (HLOS) of what it wants Network Rail to deliver and a 'Statement of Funds Available' (SoFA) to finance it. Network Rail is then required to respond by stating whether these funds are adequate to meet the government's requirements, with the ORR acting as referee when the two are not in balance, as is likely. Like much in the privatised rail industry, this is a very complex, labour intensive and expensive decision making process involving the employment of teams of specialist consultants by each of the players, in sharp contrast to the way in which these things were done in BR days. However, it is transparent and makes clear what kind of railway the government wants and how much taxpayers' money it is prepared to commit to pay for it. In what looked like an invitation to consider rail closures, this white paper also contained a proposal that PTEs would no longer to have an automatic right to co-sign passenger franchises and they will have to bear the full cost of any improvements above the DfT specified 'base service provision and budget'. However they would be allowed to propose rail service reductions or closures and to divert finance into replacement bus Quality Contracts.

The Treasury's Comprehensive Spending review of 2007 along with requirements to produce the HLOS and SoFA, led to production by Ruth Kelly, as a new incumbent to the post of Secretary of State for Transport, of another white paper, 'Delivering a Sustainable Railway' (DfT 2007a). This title reflected the shift in emphasis in transport policy away from 'integration' towards promoting 'sustainable transport' which should address the economic, social and environmental agendas as well, perhaps, as being financially viable and politically deliverable. The context for this had also been influenced by production, in late 2006, of two reports sponsored by the Treasury (Gordon Brown, who had been Chancellor of the Exchequer since 1997, was flexing his political muscles prior to becoming prime minister in mid-2007, when Tony Blair eventually stepped down). These were the Stern Report (Stern 2006) on the economics of climate change and the Eddington Report (Eddington 2006) on the links between transport and economic productivity. The key implications for transport of the former were recognition that it accounts for 14 per cent of global green house gas emissions but that deep cuts in the sector were seen as unlikely before 2050, because the costs of securing cuts are higher than in other sectors. Nevertheless, the climate change problem was seen as an urgent international priority and countries were seen as able to take action to reduce the impacts with three policy priorities: carbon pricing and trading, support for low carbon technologies, and action to promote behavioural change. The key points of the Eddington Report were that, overall the UK's transport system is quite good in its ability to link up the key nodes of economic activity but there is a need to relieve congestion in priority areas. These are growing urban areas, airports, ports and some inter-urban corridors; the priority is to make existing networks work more efficiently. The report endorsed road pricing as an alternative to building more road capacity and, recognising the emissions problem, stated that all modes should pay for their external costs. It highlighted the economic benefits of targeted, small scale projects and came out against 'large projects with speculative benefits and relying on untested technologies' which, in the rail industry, was interpreted as discouraging new routes using magnetic levitation or MAGLEV. Subsequently, Eddington said he thought high speed rail using established technology had a key role to play. There was particular concern expressed about the time scales involved in delivering major transport projects and the complex problem of overlapping consent regimes: 'the Thameslink 2000 scheme required over 30 consents under four different Acts and took over eight years'[6] (Eddington 2006, 7). There was therefore a call to speed up the planning process with the creation of an Independent Planning Commission to take decisions on projects of strategic importance.

In some respects the 2007 white paper was the most optimistic and broad ranging view of rail development since the 1955 Modernisation Plan, with planning based on an expected increase of 22.5 per cent in passenger demand by 2014 and a long-term goal of doubling the level of demand that rail can accommodate. It sought to take policy beyond the internal concerns of recent years:

> For too much of the past decade, policy on rail has been about repairing the problems of a flawed privatisation. The government rightly focused on reversing decades of under-investment and putting the industry on a stable footing (DfT 2007a, 5).

£15bn of investment was committed over the next seven years with £5.5bn for Thameslink, funding for Birmingham New Street and Reading station upgrades (two strategically important rail nodes), more passenger rolling stock,[7] minor upgrades and £200m to develop the strategic freight network. The latter has subsequently been followed by Network Rail's publication of a policy document for development of the 'Strategic Freight Network' which includes proposals for

---

6   At the time of the publication of Eddington, no funding was committed for Thameslink and commentators have seen the reluctance of government to fund major rail projects as a bigger factor leading to delay than problems with the planning process.

7   The white paper gave a commitment that the government would produce a Rolling Stock Plan which was duly delivered by the DfT (DfT 2008) in early 2008, with proposals for 1300 new carriages. However there has been critical commentary on the detail of this in the railway press and concern expressed about a government department becoming so involved in detailed operational matters.

gauge enhancement and diversionary routes (Network Rail 2008). The white paper also envisaged no closures but, on the other hand there was a distinct lack of a long term view beyond 2014 with no main line upgrades, no electrification programme (seen as essential by critics if rail is going to be able to draw power from non-carbon producing sources and make use of regenerative braking[8] (see Givoni et al., forthcoming)), no route re-openings (in England), no firm commitment to Crossrail, and no commitment to extending the Channel Tunnel high speed railway north of London.[9] On the financial side concern was expressed at the growing burden of cost to the taxpayer, with the pattern of 25-35 per cent subsidy in the late 1990s increasing to 40-50 per cent since 2000 and 51 per cent in 2005–6: this amounted to some £4.5bn, or four times the amount of subsidy typically received by BR. An intention was therefore expressed to move the figure back towards what was vaguely termed as 'historic levels', with farebox income rising from £5bn to £9bn by 2014 with the inevitable result that, despite more revenue from additional passengers, rail fares would increase above the rate of inflation. Critics saw this as the government continuing to send out the wrong price signals if it was serious about reducing road traffic congestion and emissions.

In what is a dizzying production line of policy documents compared with railway politics in the BR era, yet another transport white paper with rail and land-use planning content was published in October 2007, 'Towards a Sustainable Transport System: Supporting Economic Growth in a Low Carbon World' (DfT 2007b). This was the government's response to Stern and Eddington and set out five broad policy goals: maximising the overall competitiveness and productivity of the economy; reducing transport greenhouse emissions; contributing to better health; improving quality of life; and equality of transport opportunity. In what is a discussion document, there is a strong commitment to promoting economic growth whilst reducing $CO2$ emissions (the smart growth agenda), re-affirmation of the rail proposals in the earlier white paper, commitment to working with DCLG to deliver the housing target in a sustainable way (see later re the Sustainable Communities Strategy) and to encouraging modal shift in urban areas through land-use planning. In addition there is specific reference to conclusion of the deal to fund the £16bn Crossrail project and to transforming the rail network around Manchester (see later re the Northern Way Initiative). Finally there is a commitment to a further all modes white paper in 2008–9.

A significant by-product of the Stern and Eddington reports has been to promote debate within the rail industry about the environmental case for rail. On the engineering side there has been a realisation that, whereas the environmental footprint of road vehicles has improved considerably, there are grounds for concern

---

8   With electric traction the energy produced when braking can be in the form of current returned to the grid, rather than just being dissipated as waste heat.

9   An industry based lobby group, Greengauge 21, had been formed in 2006 to campaign for government commitment to new high speed rail links between London and major provincial cities.

about rail vehicles as they have tended to become heavier (more powerful traction equipment for higher speeds and to drive on board 'hotel' functions) and thereby less energy efficient. Although historically it would have been the Chairman of the BRB who would have driven through a response to this, or more recently the Chairman of the SRA, it is the rather faceless (in terms of a profile with the world beyond the railway) ORR which produced a response (ORR 2007). Quite rightly, this prioritised engineering matters which are outside the scope of this book, but it did note that Network Rail should address sustainable development issues in its Route Utilisation Strategies and there should be more discussion as to the implications of this. Although broadly encouraging in terms of the relationship between the railways and the planning system, the blandness of this was indicative of the ground which has been lost since the demise of the SRA.

Town planning policy

Chapter 7 identified developments in the wider literature in the early 1990s which emphasised the growing importance of rail-oriented planning, as part of the debate around sustainable development and compact cities. This continued subsequently, with international and UK threads. For example, in north America a developing critique of low density, automobile-oriented suburban sprawl (see for example Langdon 1994) crystallised into the 'New Urbanism' movement and an important dimension to that was awareness that planning to promote Transit Oriented Development (TOD) was essential for the development of more urban, higher density suburbs, especially for areas within a 'comfortable walking distance' of a transit stop (usually defined as within approximately 10 minutes walking time). Calthorpe (1993, 43) articulated a set of urban design principles for TOD as shown in Table 11.2 and there is a growing awareness of how to break the barriers holding back this form of development (Dittmar and Ohland 2004).

In continental Europe there has been more development of heavy and light rail networks than in the UK, including the development of high speed rail routes with stations providing a focal point in larger development schemes, as in Lille for example. Bertolini and Spit (1998) developed theoretical perspectives to underpin their wide ranging review of European station projects, summarising the roles of stations as a 'node', a point of interchange between various transport modes, and as a 'place', a specific locality within the urban realm which acts as a gateway between transport systems and the wider city. They had some interesting comments on the British situation too:

> ... Britain has had no clear overarching framework at the national level to integrate, at least conceptually, individual initiatives. There was no plan for expansion of a national HST network, as in France. There were no national or regional policies promoting development at public transport interchanges, as in the Netherlands and Switzerland. And there was no national integrated transport

and property strategy of the railway company, as in Sweden. Furthermore the role of local authorities seems to be much more limited than elsewhere (Bertolini and Spit 1998, 181).

Table 11.2 Calthorpe's urban design principles for TOD

- organise growth on a regional level to be compact and transit-supportive;

- place commercial, housing, jobs parks, and civic uses within walking distance of transit stops;

- create pedestrian-friendly street networks that directly connect local destinations;

- provide a mix of housing types, densities and costs;

- preserve sensitive habitat, riparian zones, and high-quality open space;

- make public spaces the focus of building orientation and neighbourhood activity;

- encourage infill and redevelopment along transit corridors within existing neighbourhoods.

Subsequently Bertolini (1999) demonstrated how various pieces of quantitative data could be utilised to develop measures of node and place and the balance, or imbalance, between them to be found at particular stations. Further work has explored these concepts and refined the understanding of the implications for planning and urban design around high quality public transport, with a developing portfolio of good practice (see European Commission, 2005a and b for example). British authors have contributed to this growing literature too: Edwards (1997) explored the principles of station architecture and developed a useful typology of stations and this was followed by Ross (2000) with a more detailed architectural consideration of the operational, commercial and aesthetic principles underpinning station design. With regard to broader planning around railways, Hall and Ward (1998) produced an updated version of Howard's garden city vision with new settlements distributed along rail lines serving London.

These developments in the academic literature were accompanied by official policy changes embodied in the revisions to PPG13, as outlined in Chapter 7. This was followed up by 'PPG13: A Guide to Better Practice (DOE, DoT,

1995), a "practical users" manual'. For the first time in many years in an official document this set out planning principles with regard to relationships between public transport and settlement size and used concepts such as corridors, nodes, catchment areas and the 'walk radius'. It included several UK and international examples of integrated planning around heavy and light rail.

In a further policy U-turn for the Conservatives, Environment Secretary John Gummer produced a revision to the policy guidance (PPG 6) on 'Town centres and retail developments' (DOE 1996b). This recognised that city and town centres were in bad shape (DOE 1994a) and that it was time to call a halt to the decentralisation of retail, leisure and employment generating activities to out-of-centre sites. Subsequently there was to be a sequential approach to site selection with priority for town centre and then edge of town centre locations. Local planning authorities were also called upon to plan 'positively' to promote town centres in local plans and other documents in ways consistent with the policies set out in PPG13. There was encouragement for mixed use developments, coherent parking strategies and the use of good urban design. As travel to city and town centres is so significant to rail utilisation, this commitment to steering trip generating developments to town centres was a welcome development, albeit one which addressed problems exacerbated by previous Conservative policy.

Following Gummer's lead on promoting urban quality (DOE 1994b), in 1998 John Prescott set up an Urban Task Force, chaired by Richard Rogers, to establish a vision for the cities founded on the principles of design excellence, social wellbeing and environmental responsibility. In articulating a vision for compact urban areas, the Final Report contained perhaps the most thorough reworking of the principles of planning around urban public transport corridors in a quasi-official document for several decades (Urban Task Force 1999). The 'Core Cities Group' embracing Birmingham, Leeds, Liverpool, Manchester, Newcastle, Nottingham and Sheffield was created in 1995 to promote economic growth and regeneration in the cities and their surrounding regions and this group was promoted by New Labour to pursue the Rogers inspired vision.

The continuing economic boom of the late 1990s fuelled the demand for housing and the New Labour government came under the same pressure as its predecessor to restrict the rate of consumption of greenfield sites. This resulted in a commitment to ensure that at least 60 per cent of new housing should be built on previously developed land (brownfield sites) and revisions to the relevant planning policy guidance (DETR 2000b) extended the use of sequential testing into the housing arena. The guidance required local planning authorities to:

> seek to reduce car dependence by facilitating more walking and cycling, by improving linkages by public transport between housing, jobs, local services and local amenity, and by planning for mixed use (DETR 2000b, 6).

Table 11.3 Sample of pro-rail policies in PPG 13 (2001)

Linking Planning and Transport

Local authorities should seek to ensure that strategies in the development plan and the local transport plan are complementary: consideration of development plan allocations and local transport priorities and investment should be closely linked. Local authorities should also ensure that their strategies on parking, traffic and demand management are consistent with their overall strategy on planning and transport. In developing the overall strategy, local authorities should:

- focus land uses which are major generators of travel demand in city, town and district centres and near to major public transport interchanges. City, town and district centres should generally be preferred over out of centre transport interchanges …

- actively manage the pattern of urban growth and the location of major travel generating developments to make the fullest use of public transport …

- allocate or re-allocate sites which are (or will be) highly accessible by public transport for travel intensive uses …

- ensure that interchange points are well related to travel generating uses, and that the design, layout and access arrangements of surrounding development and interchanges are safe and convenient so as to maximise the walking and cycling catchment population for public transport services

- identify interchange improvement that need to be made, and seek funding through local transport plans, public-private partnerships and planning agreements

- consider the case for parking facilities at urban and suburban rail stations, and the treatment of on-street parking near to stations within the context of their local transport plan

Freight

While road transport is likely to remain the main mode for many freight movements, land use planning can help to promote sustainable distribution, including where feasible, the movement of freight by rail and water. In preparing their development plans and in determining planning applications, local authorities should:

- identify and, where appropriate, protect sites and routes, both existing and potential, which could be critical in developing infrastructure for the movement of freight (such as major freight interchanges including facilities allowing road to rail transfer or for water transport) and ensure that any such disused transport sites and routes are not unnecessarily severed by new developments or transport infrastructure. In relation to rail use, this should be done in liaison with the SRA which is best placed to advise on the sites and routes that are important to delivering wider transport objectives;

- … promote opportunities for freight generating development to be served by rail or waterways by influencing the location of development and by identifying and where appropriate protecting realistic opportunities for rail or waterway connections to existing manufacturing, distribution and warehousing sites adjacent or close to the rail network, waterways or coastal/estuarial ports; and

- on disused transport sites consider uses related to sustainable transport first, before other uses.

Source: Crown copyright.

PPG13 was further amended under Prescott and this (DETR 2001) continued with the broad thrust of its predecessor, but with a sharper focus around the drive to promote integrated transport. It continued to have a generic focus on public transport as a whole referring to 'interchanges' rather than railway stations per se, although it was supportive of rail in the most general sense as shown in Table 11.3, for freight as well as passenger transport. The revision also required developers to submit Transport Assessments with their planning applications to demonstrate how they intended to promote use of modes other than the car, although it was several years before guidance on this was produced by the Department for Transport (DfT 2007c).

The Guidance to local transport authorities on production of the new Local Transport Plans (DETR 2000c) had limited commentary on station policy and this also tended to be fairly generalised, focusing on 'interchange facilities' rather than specifically 'railway stations'. However, making interchange more convenient was encouraged as was, specifically, promoting access to stations by foot. The Guidance reiterated the land-use planning policies relevant to public transport interchanges set out in PPG13, further illustrating the attempt at integrating land-use and transport policy. The Guidance included in annex D criteria which would be used to evaluate the quality of LTPs and table 27 of this showed the degree of sophistication expected with regard to the promotion of sustainable distribution: this was perhaps the most encouraging promotion of rail freight ever set out in an official document and is reproduced as Table 11.4. It is notable that this level of detail was removed from the subsequent LTP guidance produced under Alistair Darling when the priorities were focused around greater realism on costs, securing value for money in the planning process and new policy priorities such as the promotion of social inclusion (DfT 2004c).

Given their role with regard to the promotion of public transport and their lead role in co-ordinating the production of LTPs in metropolitan areas, PTA/PTEs were able to take a strong lead in promoting integration between land-use and transport planning. The Planning Green Paper (Byers 2001) had encouraged the production of 'standing guidance' by non-statutory consultees which, surprisingly, is what PTEs are. An example of what can be done is Greater Manchester PTE's Land Use Planning Guide which sets out principles with regard to the location, type and design of development which will promote the use of public transport, as shown in Figure 11.5. This Guide specifically develops the concept of designating 'station development zones',

> ... where authorities will develop coordinated proposals to better link stations and the areas they serve, identifying improvements to local roads (including pedestrian crossings), walking routes, cycling, car parking, local signage, information boards and landscaping (GMPTE 2006).

**Table 11.4 DETR Guidance on Full Local Transport Plans:
Sustainable Distribution**

Minimum requirements

- Description of policy for the development of an integrated, sustainable distribution system which takes into account the dominant role of road freight and the potential for modal transfer to rail or inland waterways
- Evidence that the strategic role of freight distribution in the growth or regeneration of the local and regional economy has been assessed
- Evidence that efforts have been made to bring freight transport operators, businesses and the local community into the strategic thinking and planning processes
- Clear evidence of effective partnership with navigation authorities, rail infrastructure providers and freight operating companies to promote greater use of alternative modes of freight distribution
- Evidence that opportunities for the greater use of rail and water freight are being taken into account in land use planning decisions

Characteristics of a Good LTP

- Evidence of progress in establishing freight quality partnerships, identifying key organisations and companies involved
- Clear strategies to help industry develop and implement best practice
- Comprehensive assessments of existing operational and non-operational freight facilities within the area, evidence of consideration of potential for freight grants
- Clear strategies and identification of flows that could be transferred to alternative modes, including an assessment of the lorry journeys to be saved
- Strategy to balance the requirement for efficient goods distribution with the social and environmental effects, particularly in an urban environment
- Clear evidence of lorry routing strategies

Source: Crown copyright.

Table 11.5 Extract from GMPTE Land Use Planning Guide (section 3)

GMPTE is not a statutory consultee, but offers advice to District Councils on policy documents and any planning applications that appear to be significant in terms of their trip generation or impact on the existing or proposed public transport network. The type of advice given relates to the accessibility and availability of public transport; how layout and design, including the pedestrian environment can improve that accessibility; the need for developer contributions and travel plans; the mitigation of any adverse impacts on public transport services and infrastructure and the protection of routes for future public transport schemes.

The advice offered is based on government guidance and the Local Transport Plan strategy and can be summarised by the following six key principles, which are amplified in later sections of the document:

- **Accessibility of new development:** *All significant new development should be accessible by public transport.* This will ensure equality of opportunity for people who do not have access to a car, and will also provide a basis for transport policies to encourage people to use their cars less.
- **Type of development:** *Sites with the best public transport accessibility should, wherever possible, be reserved for uses (or densities) that generate a high level of trips.* This will support the LTP strategy by encouraging modal shift and will make the best use of investment in public transport infrastructure, such as stations.
- **Impact on public transport network:** *New development should not have an adverse impact on existing or future public transport operations.* Where the extra traffic generated by a development would cause delays or otherwise hinder the operation of existing services, mitigation measures will be required. Routes with potential for future public transport use should not be severed.
- **Developer contributions:** *Developers should fund any necessary enhancements to the public transport network.* PPG 13 states that developer contributions should be encouraged to secure improved accessibility to sites by public transport, walking and cycling where such measures may 'influence travel patterns to the site'.
- **Promotion of sustainable travel:** *Significant development should be accompanied by a travel plan.* In line with PPG 13 GMPTE recommend that travel plans should be submitted alongside applications that are likely to have significant transport implications, including those which involve significant expansion of on site parking.
- **Design and layout:** *The design and layout of a development should maximise the potential for public transport use and should give non-car modes priority over the car.* The aim should be to ensure that buses can, where appropriate, penetrate developments, and that there is convenient pedestrian access to stops and stations.

Source: Extract from GMPTE *Land Use Planning Guide* (section 3), reproduced with kind permission of GMPTE.

The ODPM pursued a number of broad strategies focused on securing economic growth and regeneration, whilst promoting more environmentally sustainable development forms, and rail transport was crucial to these. But an overarching aspect of Blairite regional policy was the abandonment of any attempt to restrict growth in the buoyant south east in the hope that it would be deflected to more needy regions, as the view was this will not happen and investment will be lost to other countries. The resultant growth had major impacts on job growth, particularly in London, and on demand for housing, especially affordable housing, as the overheating regional economy led to house price inflation. Strategically, to provide for this huge housing demand the Communities Plan (ODPM 2003) identified growth zones in the Milton Keynes/South Midlands corridor, the Harlow-Cambridge corridor, and the areas north and south of the Thames in the Thames Gateway. As outlined above, a sub-text of this strategy and one which has been applied generally to the supply of housing land, has been to prioritise the re-use of brownfield sites over the use of greenfield sites.

As the housing supply problem worsened, government ratcheted up the pressure on the planning system with the creation of 29 Housing Growth Zones in 2006 to increase the number of new houses built in England each year from 160,000 to 200,000 by 2016. Finally in 2007 and with a boost resulting from a personal endorsement by new Prime Minister Gordon Brown, an 'eco-towns' initiative was launched for the creation of a number of new settlements with between 5,000 and 20,000 new homes each, this initiative being squarely placed in the new towns tradition and wherein the securing of reduced car dependency is seen as one of a whole raft of environmental requirements (DCLG 2007). Nationally the housing agenda is challenging and planning around rail is just one of the transport elements to be considered in fixing the location of large areas of new housing. But, even in the broad south east, the various proposals have seemed to develop piecemeal and there has not been production of a detailed, integrated regional plan along the lines of the 1960s Strategic Plan for the South East (South East Joint Planning Team 1970) which sought to steer development into main rail corridors which subsequently received significant investment. It has not even been an explicit requirement that the 'eco-towns' should be located on a rail corridor, a major break with the new towns programme. So there has been no overall strategy for major rail network development in association with these ambitious development strategies, but some money has been set aside for infrastructure investment, which will include transport. This is through the Growth Fund, announced in 2007 with an allocation of £732m to local councils in the Growth Areas and Growth Points and the Community Infrastructure Fund wherein a further £200m was made available. The level of funding available from these sources for rail would only be sufficient for relatively minor upgrades.

Concern for the weaker economies of other regions led to publication of a 'Northern Way' strategy (ODPM 2004b) covering eight city regions wherein the three northern RDAs were invited to show how they could unlock the potential for faster economic growth. The improvement of connectivity between and to the key nodes of economic activity is an important element of the emerging response. Manchester and Leeds are perceived as the two city regions with the greatest potential to become competitive at the European level and evolving projects include the development of a Manchester rail hub and the improvement of east-west trans-Pennine rail links (Northern Way Steering Group 2004, 2005).

An exception to the absence of broad strategy for integrating railways with major developments has been planning within London itself, wherein creation of the mayor's office, the GLA and TfL has created an effective capacity for integrated rail planning. This has seen the production of further plans for development of the DLR, including an extension to London City Airport and then under the Thames to Woolwich Arsenal, and linking the new Stratford International Station and its associated Stratford City development project into the DLR network. Also plans have been developed through to the construction phase for the East London Line project which includes re-use of trackbeds closed in the 1980s when Broad Street station was demolished as part of the Broadgate project (Haywood 2008).

Overall, along with the changes in the statutory development plan process which reinforce the importance of the regional tier, these various policies comprise a complex and developing strategic policy making and delivery agenda where there is a need for close integration between railway planning and other planning activities if the railway is to be fit for purpose. The SRA's production of Route Utilisation Strategies and Regional Planning Assessments created tools to secure this which continue to be used, although the availability of finance for investment can be a severe constraint.

Conclusions

It is clear that there has been a huge amount of policy development in the post-privatisation period. It is also clear that there have been some significant differences in the approaches to rail and planning policy. Whereas there has been a degree of continuity with the pre-privatisation period in the development of planning policy, with broad support for the promotion of patterns of land-use change which facilitate use of rail for passenger and freight transport, a good deal of rail policy has been focused on addressing problems perceived as arising from privatisation. Initially this was about injecting a commitment to long term planning by creation of the SRA, which then began to develop policies with a direct focus on integration with urban and regional planning. However Hatfield, the Railtrack debacle and subsequent concerns about escalating costs, meant that expectations about expanding rail capacity to meet local authorities' aspirations about modal shift, began to be significantly talked down, although the mayor of London and the devolved governments in Wales and Scotland were able to step into the breach with regard to local services. The cost issue was eventually to lead to the demise of the SRA and this marked the end of the development of the promising thread of pro-active, planning related policy development from within the railway industry.

It wasn't until 2007 that the clouds over the national network began to clear, with some important policy commitments being made as to its future, although these still fell well short of a visionary, expansionist strategy. It is also notable that, although planning policy has continued to be broadly supportive of rail, the degree of detail and prescriptiveness has not developed along the lines that the literature suggests it could and the failure to cite rail access as a locational requirement for the eco-towns was a surprising lapse. Table 11.6 summarises the thematic analysis and with regard to the points developed at the end of Chapter 2, the railway policy agenda can be summarised as follows:

1. *rationalisation of the network*: although the drive for rationalisation and closures was relaxed, rising costs gave rise to some concerns for the future of some lightly used routes; the concern over costs held back plans for major capacity enhancements across much of the English network, although plans were brought forward for London and in Wales and Scotland, with minor enhancement projects elsewhere;

2. *development of railway services*: commitment was maintained to the WCML upgrade and the CTRL despite financial problems; acquisition of new passenger rolling stock was built into franchises and there is government commitment for more; freight operating companies have planned on the basis of expansion; there has been no national strategy for electrification, major capacity enhancement or the building of new high speed rail routes, although plans have been brought forward towards the end of the period for major upgrades at strategic bottlenecks.

3. *closing strategic gaps in the network*: no major plans for new cross city routes or re-opening of closed trunk routes have been brought forward, although plans to bring the CTRL through to St Pancras were committed; plans for route extensions and re-openings have been brought forward in London, Wales and Scotland, but only minor projects have been planned in provincial England; although plans for 25 new light rail schemes were mooted, few were actually brought forward; the upgrading of London Underground is in hand although, the process was delayed by negotiation of the PPPs and then the collapse of Metronet.

4. *development of a programme of station enhancement*: in London, Wales and Scotland plans for new routes and re-openings have been accompanied by plans for new stations, as has the CTRL; despite the scale of the project, there has been no overarching station strategy for the WCML upgrade; Railtrack, and subsequently Network Rail, developed plans for major upgrades at some major stations.

With regard to town planning policy the outcome was:

5. *patterns of urban development*: planning policy has continued to promote rail access in general terms, although this hasn't developed into more detailed and/or prescriptive policies; there has been a very strong thread in planning, regeneration and urban design policy around city and town centre regeneration in which securing high quality development at and around stations has been a priority; the CTRL and other new routes in London have been associated with polices for development around new stations; rail re-opening projects in Wales and Scotland have been associated with plans for development around new stations.

6. *management of the redevelopment process in existing urban areas*: planning policies have sought to manage the redevelopment process in ways which were predominantly concerned with road access although, in city and town centres, policies have been developed to promote high density developments accessible by rail and to develop urban design led strategies for stations and their environs; planning policy has been broadly supportive of rail freight; development of suburban areas has been less focused on rail, especially outside the south east.

7. *management of the location and character of greenfield site development*: policy with regard to greenfield areas continued to be to resist their development as far as possible and, where development has been proposed, as in the Communities Plan, it has not been associated with major rail investment projects, with funding being provided only for relatively minor upgrades; the eco-towns initiative did not prioritise location on the rail network.

Table 11.6 Summary of thematic analysis of sector policy 1994–2008

Explanatory themes	Railway sector	Interrelationships between the two sectors	Planning sector
Politics and political ideology	Initially an emphasis on private sector initiative and a reducing role for the state: replaced by increasing state involvement to secure political goals, whilst continuing to emphasise the role of the private sector in delivery. Post-1997 an emphasis on growth and integration, subsequently talked down because of cost issues. Dominance of Treasury view throughout.	Labour's vision of integrated transport embraced land use policy, but doubts over the level of commitment from government as a whole. Problems with the rail industry made development of the rail side difficult anyway, because of immediate safety and engineering priorities.	Priorities continued to be urban regeneration, housing and countryside protection. The promotion of sustainable transport and integration between land-use and public transport nodes continued throughout, but emphasis was greatest in city centres.
Professions and professional ideology	Initially in the Railtrack era there was a dilution of the introverted, engineering led culture and a focus on share price, external private sector initiatives and public sector partnerships. Post Hatfield there was a resurgence of the engineering led approach with regard to the fixed infrastructure and private sector initiative in the TOCs was constrained by the Treasury led approach to state administration of the industry.	The strongest interrelationships developed around city centre regeneration projects and where major rail investment was taking place, although they were weak around the WCML upgrade and the development of the cross-country network.	A resurgence of place making and a focus around urban regeneration. The promotion of public transport was a priority in city planning and the promotion of rail oriented development was a recognisable strand within this. But strategic policy continued to be fairly generic and could be outweighed by other considerations, especially economic ones.

Explanatory themes	Railway sector	Interrelationships between the two sectors	Planning sector
Governance and management	The initial aim of reducing government involvement was overridden, post 1997, by a concern to make the industry more responsive to government aspirations. The collapse of Railtrack presented an opportunity for greater state involvement but this was embraced reluctantly and, until 2007, was largely involved with railway housekeeping, especially cost control. The importance of private sector involvement continued to be emphasised, although its role in policy development was minimal.	The interplay between the changing and partially conflicting government stances towards the rail industry and local government made the development of integrated policy difficult.	Planning was linked to the new agenda of integration, but this was subsumed within a wider strategy to promote sustainable development and then sustainable communities. This tended to dilute the emphasis on planning to promote modal shift. The modernising and customer care agendas tended to undermine planning policy development re transport.

Chapter 12

The Post-Privatisation Period 1994–2008: Outcomes

Introduction

Notwithstanding the operational problems, rail passenger traffic grew considerably in the late 1990s, levelled off post-Hatfield and then continued to grow. This is the product of a long period of economic growth fuelling overall transport demand, growing congestion on the road network forcing people to look for alternative modes and successful marketing and customer service work by some TOCs.[1] Total passenger journeys post-privatisation have increased by approximately 25 per cent and, by 2004, were already higher than in 1950. Similarly, passenger kilometres have moved ahead of the 1950 figure[2] too. However, it has been pointed out that 70 per cent of rail trips begin or end in London and 68 per cent of all rail trips are on London and south east commuter services (SRA 2004), so there is a continuing regional bias to the pattern of rail utilisation. In addition, despite the growth, rail's market share of passenger transport (using passenger kilometres) has remained steady, at around 6 per cent, because of the increase in road traffic, so overall there has been no modal shift. This has major implications with regard to what would need to be done to enhance rail capacity if significant modal shift were to be energetically pursued. With regard to the fixed infrastructure, there have been only minimal closures since privatisation, the length of the electrified network has hardly grown, the number of stations has increased, despite some losses to light rail conversions, and there have been few outright station closures. This chapter will now go on to review the extent to which town planning outcomes were positively associated with this growth in rail traffic and will begin by focusing on the long distance passenger network focused on London, before moving on to the networks serving provincial cities, then rural routes and finally freight, with some final conclusions at the end.

---

1 The internet has, of course, made the provision of timetable information, promotions and sales of tickets much easier and TOCs have made good use of it, although there is a lack of overall coherency and consistency owing to the franchising system.

2 Changes in data recording methods by the industry make comparable measurements over time difficult, but there is general acceptance of the underlying growth trends.

Table 12.1 Passenger journeys by sector 1999–00 to 2006–07:
      Great Britain (millions)

	Long distance operators	London and SE operators	Regional operators	Total passenger journeys
1999-00	72	639	220	931
2000-01	70	664	223	957
2001-02	74	663	222	960
2002-03	77	679	219	976
2003-04	81	690	240	1012
2004-05	84	704	256	1045
2005-06	89	720	273	1082
2006-07	98	773	292	1164

Source: ORR National Rail Trends Yearbook April 06–March 07.

Table 12.2 Passenger kilometres by sector 1999–00 to 2006–07:
      Great Britain (billions)

	Long distance operators	London and SE operators	Regional operators	Total passenger kilometres
1999-00	13.2	18.4	6.9	38.5
2000-01	12.1	19.2	6.9	38.2
2001-02	12.9	19.3	7.0	39.1
2002-03	12.9	19.8	6.9	39.7
2003-04	13.3	20.1	7.5	40.9
2004-05	13.4	20.5	7.9	41.8
2005-06	14.2	20.7	8.3	43.2
2006-07	15.5	22.4	8.6	46.5

Source: ORR National Rail Trends Yearbook April 06–March 07.

Table 12.3 Railway infrastructure 1999–00 to 2006–07 (route kilometres and number of stations): Great Britain

	Route open for traffic	Of which electrified	Route open for passenger and freight traffic	Route open for freight traffic only	Passenger stations
1999-00	16,649	5,167	15,038	1,610	2,503
2000-01	16,652	5,167	15,042	1,610	2,508
2001-02	16,652	5,167	15,042	1,610	2,508
2002-03	16,670	5,167	15,042	1,610	2,508
2003-04	16,493	5,200	14,883	1,610	2,507
2004-05	16,116	5,200	14,328	1,788	2,508
2005-06	15,810	5,205	14,356	1,454	2,510
2006-07	15,795	5,250	14,353	1,442	2,520

Source: ORR National Rail Trends Yearbook April 06–March 07.

The long distance passenger network focused on London

The Channel Tunnel Rail Link (CTRL) is a branch of the French TGV system, so tried and tested technology has been applied as well as the French model of running a railway along an existing motorway corridor, in this case the M2.[3] Phase 1 opened in 2003 and Phase 2 in 2007, the whole project being on time and on budget (Table 12.4). The total length is now 109 km (68 miles) and journey times have been reduced significantly to give an air competitive 2hrs for London-Brussels and 2hrs 20 minutes London-Paris.[4] The former service from Waterloo station was unattractive to travellers from north of London and diverting the service to St Pancras offers a significant improvement, although this station is less accessible to people living south of the Thames. The line is also to have, from 2009, a high speed 'Javelin' service for Kent commuters without which it would be significantly underused (Glover 2005; Abbott 2008). The historic routes serving the depressed north Kent towns are connected to the high speed route and will get this service, which is indicative of good strategic planning, and this could stimulate their regeneration owing to the shorter commuting times, although there

---

3   This is quite different to the WCML where part of the cost escalation resulted from the abandonment of Railtrack's attempt to utilise revolutionary signalling technologies.

4   Onward travel in Belgium and France for British passengers usually necessitates a change to host country services, so even London is not hooked directly into European rail services in the way that continental cities are.

Table 12.4 Completed route re-openings and new routes 1994–2008

Date	Length of New Track km (miles)	Location
1994	8(5)	Channel Tunnel opened – new track from portal to Dollands Moor terminal
1994	12.8(8)	Blackburn-Clitheroe 'Ribble Valley' line re-opened for passenger services with new station at Clitheroe (services withdrawn 1962)
1995	0.8(0.5)	New Manchester Airport south chord opened to facilitate access from Crewe
1995	6.4(4)	Opening of Birmingham Snow Hill- Smethwick West line – 3 new stations at Jewellery Quarter, The Hawthorns and Smethwick Galton Bridge
1995	22.5(14)	Nottingham-Mansfield-Mansfield Woodhouse 'Robin Hood Line' re-opening completed with 6 new stations – 3 miles of new construction, remainder formerly freight only
1997	17.7(11)	Mansfield Woodhouse-Worksop 'Robin Hood' extension re-opened with 4 new stations – formerly freight only
1998	6.4(4)	Heathrow Express electric service between London Paddington-Heathrow Airport – no intermediate stations
2002	4 (2.5)	Kingsbury-Baddesley freight only line to access 200 acre Birch Coppice Business Park and 100 acre Baddesley Business Park developed on former colliery sites (North Warwickshire)
2003	74(46)	Channel Tunnel Rail Link phase 1: Folkestone – Fawkham junction (north Kent)
2003	4.8 (3)	Re-opening of Bristol's Portishead dock freight branch
2004	3.5(2.2)	Knockshinnoch - Greenburn (Ayrshire) – access to opencast coal site
2005	29(18)	Barry Town-Bridgend (Wales) restoration of passenger services on freight only Vale of Glamorgan line. New stations at Llantwit major and Rhoose (for Cardiff International Airport 1 mile)
2005	1.6(1)	Anniesland curve (Glasgow, Scotland) – provides additional capacity to facilitate the improved Larkhall-Dalmuir/Milngavie service. New station at Kelvindale
2005	4.8(3)	Hamilton-Larkhall to facilitate cross-city Larkhall-Dalmuir/Milngavie service with 3 new stations at Larkhall, Chatelherault and Merryton
2007	33.8(21)	Channel Tunnel Railway Line (CTRL) Phase Two – Ebbsfleet-St Pancras, new stations at Ebbsfleet and Stratford
2007	3.4/3.2 (2.1/2)	Completion of links to Heathrow T5 including new tunnels (3.4km HEx, 3.2km Piccadilly line) – 6 platform joint station. £118m project (BAA)
2008	29(18)	Ebbw Vale- funded by WAG and project managed by Blaenau Gwent Council Borough Council – re-opening to passenger services of former freight route, (passenger services withdrawn 1962) – single line but some two track sections. 6 new stations at Rogerstone, Risca, Crosskeys, Newbridge, Llanhilleth & Ebbw Vale Parkway. Cost £30m
2008	21(13)	Stirling-Alloa–Kincardine for passenger service to Alloa re-opened (closed 1968) and freight (coal to Longannet avoiding Forth Bridge, so more passenger services over latter). Cost approx £70m

Sources: Railway Development Society, 1998; Rail industry professional journals: Modern Railways, Rail, various editions.

are doubts as to the attractiveness of St Pancras for accessing jobs in the City and West End. In addition to the international station at the growth centre of Ashford in southern Kent, there are international stations at Ebbsfleet in north Kent and at the major rail hub of Stratford in East London (Perren 2005). Owing to its easy access from the M25 motorway, Ebbsfleet is a major park and ride station with 6000 parking spaces and, through a development known as Ebbsfleet Valley, is to see adjacent mixed use business development and 10,000 new homes on a site totalling some 400 ha (988 acres). There is a developing high frequency bus service, Fastrack, linking Ebbsfleet to adjoining towns experiencing growth as part of the Thames Gateway strategy, as well as the nearby out-of-town Bluewater shopping mall so, overall, there is good evidence of integration here.

At the new Stratford International there is to be a major commercial development, Stratford City, on former railway land and this, along with the existing Stratford station's excellent onward rail links, were crucial elements of London's successful bid to host the 2012 Olympics which are a key driver in the regeneration of east London. One of the links from Stratford is to Canary Wharf via the DLR which has continued to expand, with more capacity, route extensions, including a link across the Thames to Woolwich (Sully 2007), and new stations adjoining regeneration sites. Stratford is also the terminus of the Jubilee Line extension of the Underground network opened in 1999 and provides a further link to Docklands. There has been a planned association between station and property development on these networks as well as integration with other transport facilities, such as London City Airport. Overall, the Dockland regeneration has become a model of integrated land-use transport planning, despite inauspicious beginnings (Brownhill 1990), although issues remain (Hickman and Hall 2008). The area around St Pancras and the adjoining King's Cross station is very run down and the high speed rail project is closely associated with other rail developments at this important interchange which will further enhance its accessibility and this is facilitating major, private sector led regeneration in the wider locality. Overall the new railway, and particularly the new high speed commuter service, is well integrated with strategic planning developments and other public transport initiatives.

Commentators have noted the financial efficacy of the CTRL as compared with the WCML upgrade and suggested that there are important lessons here for the future. The point has also been made that the investment in the CTRL is currently of little benefit to city regions outside the south east. However, there is currently no firm proposal for a new high speed railway beyond London and the immediate prospects are poor for the upgrading of the rest of the existing main line network, outside the WCML project. With a completion date for the main works of December 2008, the latter has caused almost ten years of service disruptions during its implementation and will only be a 125 mph (200 kmph) railway, the proposal for 140 mph (225 kmph) line speed having been dropped on cost grounds. Although the 2 hour 10 minute journey time between London and Manchester is competitive with air, London-Glasgow journey times will still be around 4hrs 30 minutes, so low cost air services will continue to be competitive. It is also indicative of the traditional British approach that this high cost/high profile upgrade has not had an accompanying station upgrade strategy, let alone one for strategic and local transport and land-use planning around key stations in the corridor, in stark contrast to the situation on the new high speed line. Where stations have received attention it is as a result of operational requirements, as at Rugby and Milton Keynes and at others, such as Crewe where drastic action is necessary to help with the regeneration of this former railway town, nothing is yet committed.

Other projects which were mooted by Railtrack and/or various groupings of local authorities, such as electrification of the Great Western and Midland main lines, are currently off the agenda. The re-franchising process for the ECML completed in 2007 envisages no acceleration of services and proposed works to remove bottlenecks or to provide grade separation at conflicted junctions were dropped. However, investment by Chiltern Trains in increasing route capacity between London Marylebone and Birmingham shows what can be achieved with modest investment by a TOC with a long franchise and in-house civil engineering and financial capacity (the company was a subsidiary of Laings, although it has recently been acquired by the German state railway operator, Deutsche Bahn). This built on work in the BR era which saw the re-opening of Birmingham Snow Hill and 'total route modernisation' after closure of Marylebone had been fought off in the early 1980s: it is sobering that closure was pursued for quite some time. Chiltern has reinstated sections of double track on the Banbury-High Wycombe 'cut off' and increased capacity at Marylebone and its approaches: this project was the only significant SPV scheme to get off the ground in the Morton era at the SRA. Chiltern also opened a new station at Warwick Parkway in 2000: this was exceptionally granted planning permission despite its green belt location, as Warwickshire County Council had taken the lead in painstakingly building the case for the new station and then forming a partnership with Chiltern to deliver it. Whilst the permission was a welcome recognition of the difficulties associated in finding parkway sites which meet road and rail access requirements, it did of course preclude any housing development within a walkable radius of the station. This has taken place elsewhere in Warwick in locations not within walking distance of either of the town's two stations (Batty and Haywood 2002). A better outcome is being achieved at Aylesbury Vale Parkway which has been promoted by Chiltern and is under construction (mid 2008). This is a park and ride facility but will also serve housing developments to the north of Aylesbury. But, as further evidence of a lack of co-ordination between town planning and railway development, additional platforms at Moor Street station on the Chiltern line in Birmingham city centre, funded by developers of the adjacent Bull Ring regeneration scheme, have remained unused for several years.

Table 12.5 Completed post-privatisation minor capacity improvement works

Date	Length of Route km (miles)	Location
1998	29(18)	Re-doubling of Princess Risborough-Bicester section of Chiltern main line (Chiltern Trains)
2002	16 (10)	Re-doubling Bicester-Aynho Junction section of Chiltern main line completed – Project Evergreen 1 – came in at £53m (Chiltern Trains)
2004	12.1(7.5)	Probus-Burngullow doubling between St Austell-Truro – previously singled by BR as a cost cutter. £14.3m (SRA)
2004	n/a	Filton Junction Improvement (Bristol) (SRA)
2004	n/a	Cherwell Valley resignalling (18.5 miles Leamington-Banbury) – with extended goods loop to increase capacity to 15 trains per hour (SRA)
2004	1.2(0.75)	Reinstatement of flyover to avoid at grade crossing of WCML at Nuneaton (closed 1991) for Birmingham-Leicester services (SRA)
2004	n/a	Completion of £40m gauge enhancement work on Felixstowe/ Harwich/Tilbury/Purfleet-London-Nuneaton route for 9'6" containers, including work through to Hams Hall and Birmingham (SRA)
2005	0.45(0.28)	Allington chord – to enable Nottingham-Skegness services to access Grantham without crossing the ECML (SRA)
2006	n/a	Evergreen Phase 2 £70m – remodelling and extending of London Marylebone station (2 new platforms – 5/6) and approaches and signalling work out as far as Bicester/ Aylesbury to increase capacity, track slewed at Beaconsfield to increase track speed (Chiltern Trains)
2007	566.5 (352)	Gauge enhancement on Glasgow Mossend-Elgin (via Grangemouth, Stirling, Perth & Aberdeen) route to give clearance for 9'6" containers: cost £4m (Network Rail)
2008	12.9(8)	Annan on Glasgow and South Western route – £35m redoubling project (work includes 9'6" gauge enhancement) – singled in early 1970s, growing coal traffic from opencast and Hunterston (Network Rail)
2008	n/a	Milton Keynes – new northbound fast line and platform; new platform for Bedford services (and possible Oxford services) and better turnback facilities – £200m. (Network Rail, DfT, Milton Keynes Borough Council)

The Chiltern line runs in the same corridor as the M40 London-Oxford-Birmingham motorway which has seen significant economic growth. This has led to increased demand for rail to which Chiltern has responded by, in fact, reinstating a Birmingham-London intercity service, albeit a cheap and cheerful one. If privatisation had been successful, then this kind of private sector led strategy would have occurred in many other parts of the network but, unfortunately, Chiltern is a unique company which is operating with a long franchise in a particularly favourable corridor, so this has not happened. Other than Chiltern's work, it was left to the SRA to promote small scale capacity increases and this was done with some success, as shown in Table 12.5. But much remains to be done and corridors where single tracking took place post-Beeching and now need the kind of upgrade Chiltern has delivered include Salisbury-Exeter, Swindon-Kemble (en route for Cheltenham) and Oxford-Worcester.

The regeneration of Birmingham's Bull Ring is just one example of what has been the most notable planning and urban policy success of the past decade, the regeneration of provincial city centres. Given the importance of major CBDs to the rail mode, this has undoubtedly stimulated demand. City planning authorities and regeneration agencies have worked successfully with the property market to deliver significant increases in housing units (mainly apartments), completion of major retail schemes (see Table 12.6), growth in commercial floorspace and major improvements in the quality of the public domain so that residents and visitors alike can enjoy the delights of attractive public spaces and European-style cafe society, away from the roar of traffic. Some schemes such as Brindley Place in Birmingham, Spinningfields in Manchester and Liverpool One have been mixed use and unusually large for provincial cities. City centre residential populations have grown significantly with, for example, Manchester's being over 15,000 and even that of Sheffield (a comparatively weak CBD historically) increasing to over 5,000.

Use of rail has been further encouraged by investment by Railtrack, and subsequently Network Rail, in works to city centre stations on the intercity network, with notable examples being the Leeds station rebuilding and track remodelling (1999–2002), the renovation and partial rebuilding of Manchester Piccadilly (completed in time for the city to host the Commonwealth Games in 2002), renovation of Glasgow Central and Brighton, and capacity enhancement at Edinburgh Waverley. These activities have been reinforced by recognition of the need to improve facilities actually at and around stations. So, for example, the restrictions on the location of retail development have forced the major supermarket chains to develop a city centre or 'metro' model for a smaller unit and these have been permitted by local planning authorities at railway stations. Previously this was often resisted as it was seen as undermining retail location policy. It means that rail users can 'multi-task' during their journeys in the way that is generally so much easier by car. In addition, large trip generating developments have been steered towards stations, often in association with urban design initiatives to improve the public domain outside the station, making rail a more convenient and enjoyable mode. The £60m project to push back the inner ring road from

Table 12.6 Shopping malls over 500,000 sq ft built post-1996 and their relationship to the railway network (includes large additions to centres existing in 1996)

Location	Centre	Year Opened	Size (000 sq ft)	Size (000 sq m)	Rail Access Situation
In-Town					
Reading	Oracle	1999	850	79	5 minutes walk from station
Glasgow	Buchanan Galleries	1999	603	56	adjoins Queen Street station
Southampton	West Quay	2000	800	74	5 minutes walk from station
Basingstoke	Festival Place	2002	1,100	102	3 minutes walk from the station – this development is a rebuilding/expansion of a development started in the 1970s
Birmingham	Bull Ring	2003	1,184	110	5 minute walk from New Street and Moorgate
Croydon	Centrale	2004	1,000	100	5 minute walk from East Croydon and direct from Tramlink
Manchester	Arndale Centre	2005/6	+400	+37	5 minutes walk from Victoria, 15 minutes walk from Piccadilly
Derby	Westfield	2007	1,100	106	15 minute walk from station – 100% expansion of former Eagle Centre
High Wycombe	Eden	2008	850	79	10 minute walk from station
London	Westfield, Shepherd's Bush/White City	2008	1,615	150	New Wood Lane station and rebuilding of Shepherd's Bush on Underground and new Shepherd's Bush station on West London Line (Overground)
Liverpool	Liverpool One	2008	1,600 (807 net)	149 (75 net)	10 minute walk from Lime Street, Central, St James or Moorfields
Leicester	Highcross Centre	2008	1,184	110	10 minutes walk from Leicester Midland station

Location	Centre	Year Opened	Size (000 sq ft)	Size (000 sq m)	Rail Access Situation
Out-of Town					
Leeds	White Rose Centre	1997	650	60	not rail connected
Bristol	Cribbs Causeway	1998	725	67	not rail connected – nearest station Bristol Parkway
Manchester	Trafford Centre	1998	1,400	130	not rail connected, shuttle bus from Metrolink at Stretford
Dartford	Bluewater	1999	1,610	150	not rail connected, shuttlebus from Greenhithe station, 5 minute ride on 'Fastrack' bus service
Paisley, Glasgow	Braehead	1999	800	74	not rail connected
Pollok, Glasgow	Silverburn Centre	2007	1,500	100	not rail connected

Source: Prudential plc 2004, Wikipedia 2008 and various shopping centre websites

the entrance to Sheffield station to create a large station plaza, well linked by an attractive pedestrian route to a much improved city centre,[5] is a significant example of the effort being put in to enhance rail access in major cities. These outcomes are a step change in scale and quality above what was achieved during previous high points in the policy cycle and will stimulate use of rail for long distance and local journeys.

London commuter and airport services

In addition to the developments referred to in the previous section, there have been significant rail oriented developments across Greater London. For example, in West London the new Westfield shopping mall is associated with a new station and a station rebuilding on the Underground, and a new station on the West London line (see Table 12.6). The latter is part of the developing Overground franchise which is focused on facilitating orbital movements without the need for crossing central

5   The development of the 'station gateway' and the associated 'gold route' pedestrian link to the core of the city centre were significant elements of the Sheffield City Master Plan produced by the Sheffield One (2001) regeneration company in partnership with the City Council and others.

London and its constituent services, such as Richmond-Stratford and Clapham-Watford, have seen significant growth. To the east of London, large scale housing development in Chafford Hundred (Thurrock) was accompanied by the opening of a new station in 1993 (which also serves the adjoining Lakeside shopping centre): however as often occurs in Britain this was 'underscoped' and the station has been expanded twice subsequently, although the route which serves it continues, surprisingly so close to London, to be single track (Batty and Haywood 2002). The major suburban node of central Croydon has experienced further commercial development and the Croydon Tramlink light rail system opened in 2000.[6] This has a stop at East Croydon station as well as at six other stations, thereby enhancing rail accessibility to a wide catchment area in central and suburban Croydon and adjacent parts of Wimbledon. However, light rail projects in other secondary centres in the wider south east, such as Cambridge and Portsmouth, have been abandoned owing to lack of government support.

Further afield, Corby new town has at last been provided with a rail station, part funded by Network Rail, North Northamptonshire Development Company and English Partnerships, this being a very desirable outcome as the town is part of the Milton Keynes/South Midlands growth corridor. Train services will be provided as part of the refranchising of services on the Midland main line in 2007. Significant works are underway to expand capacity at Milton Keynes station as part of the WCML upgrade (Table 12.5), but partly funded through the Community Infrastructure Fund and by the local levy on new development by Milton Keynes Borough Council. In and out commuting continues to grow at what is Britain's most successful new town. But there is currently (Autumn 2008) no funding committed for a long standing local authority backed plan to re-open the Oxford-Bletchley/Milton Keynes-Bedford-Cambridge orbital route, despite this linking areas designated for growth in the Communities Plan and providing excellent onward travel opportunities through interchange with services on the trunk routes which it crosses. This re-opening project has been discussed for almost a decade, showing that the impacts of the excessive closure programme of the 1960s continue to reverberate down the decades and, once again, it is the local authorities which are doggedly pursuing it.

With regard to planning at and around stations more generally, the swing towards rail oriented planning is having a strong impact with station focused master plans in hand at locations right across the broad south east including Hastings, Brighton, Portsmouth, Haywards Heath, Peterborough and Bath. At Reading a new suburban station with a bus interchange is being built at Green Park as part

---

6   The contract to design, build, operate and maintain Tramlink was won by a private sector consortium in 1996. However an agreement that London Regional Transport or its successor compensates the consortium for the consequences of any changes to the fares and ticketing policy introduced since 1996 led, in 2007, to payment of £4m. With an expectation of future payments being necessary, the consortium was bought out by TfL in 2008, returning the network to the public sector.

of a mixed use business and residential development scheme and the committed main station project is to be a major scheme involving track upgrades. There is an accompanying station-focused Central Area Action Plan for the wider town centre (Reading Borough Council 2008), Reading now having become a major sub-regional centre on a par with Croydon.

Despite these positive developments, progress with major commuter rail schemes in London itself has been slow. The Central London Rail Study (DoT et al. 1989) envisaged improvements to the capacity of the central London sections of the Thameslink service so that new routes, such as to Cambridge and King's Lynn, could be hooked in, a project which became known as Thameslink 2000. It is indicative of the slow progress that this scheme only came to receive full approval and funding in 2007, despite it being a cost effective scheme which exploits existing cross-London infrastructure: completion is envisaged by 2015 (Table 12.7). There have been particular planning problems associated with this project as it involves widening railway viaducts around Southwark Cathedral (Kim Wilkie Associates 1999) and two public inquiries were necessary to resolve these, showing the continuing impacts of the Victorian railway inheritance. Another example is the East London Line Extension project to provide links between localities in north and south London and the job opportunities in the City and Docklands. This is to be part of the orbital route around central London and will provide much needed rail access to some of the most deprived parts of the East End, which hitherto had poor rail connections. It will be included in the Overground franchise and was identified by New Labour as a 'quick win' in 1997, had funding committed in 2004 and has a 2010 completion target. The project uses extant alignments in the form of an existing cross-Thames Underground route linked to an abandoned trackbed in Hackney and Tower Hamlets, showing that 'quick' for a major rail project is 'within 15 years'. This project is now being driven through by Transport for London (TfL), which illustrates the continuing importance of well resourced, local authorities to the development of local networks and the impact which an executive mayor with the capacity to directly relate railway development to economic targets and a spatial planning strategy, can make. Recent research shows there is evidence of integrated land-use planning around the proposed stations (Haywood 2008).

Another major project from the Central London Rail Study which belatedly has government support is Crossrail. The central element is an east-west tunnel under central London linking commuter services which currently terminate at Liverpool Street and Paddington. As originally envisaged, the services which would link to this tunnel would be long distance, originating 30 or more miles (50 kilometres) outside London. However, under the influence of TfL, there has developed an intra-London focus which means that services, as currently envisaged, will terminate at Maidenhead in the west and in the east at Shenfield (on the Liverpool Street-Ipswich main line) and, south of the Thames, at Abbey Wood (with a change of trains required to access the new station at Ebbsfleet on the CTRL). On completion in 2017, Crossrail will serve Canary Wharf as well as the City and West End which have all seen continuing property investment through the long boom from the mid-1990s. It is seen by the business community as essential to the continued success of London as a world city, a role based fundamentally on a concentration of global financial and business services which need to draw on a high quality, but far flung, labour force.

However Crossrail as planned is not linked to existing outer metropolitan growth corridors such as those focused on Basingstoke (on the London Waterloo-Southampton main line) and Reading (on the London Paddington-Bristol main line), or the Communities Plan growth corridors in Milton Keynes-Northampton, Harlow-Stansted-Cambridge and the Thames Gateway where people moving into new houses will need easy access to a wide job market. This led to a proposal by rail industry specialists[7] for a more broadly conceived network called "Superlink" (Thomas 2005), which would connect in main lines serving the outer growth corridors and thereby, it is claimed, generating large volumes of new traffic which would increase financial viability. Although this proposal raises additional costing and planning problems, it is more in tune with strategic planning goals for the London city region than the current proposal. Although the ODPM claimed that its Sustainable Communities strategy will not stimulate demand for access to London's job market, this would seem to presage a rerun of the 1944 Abercrombie plan and its unrealistic dependence on 'self-containment'.

With regard to airports, the opening in 1998 of the electrified Heathrow Express service between Heathrow and Paddington (amazingly all other services at this important London terminus remain diesel powered) was a product of pre-privatisation planning by BR and the British Airports Authority. However the fast link to Heathrow has served, subsequently, as the basis for the regeneration of the Paddington Canal Basin area promoted by Westminster City Council as a high density commercial and residential node. At Heathrow, Terminal Five opened in early 2008 and included substantial investment in extending the Underground and Heathrow Express into a new station under the terminal (Tables 12.4 and 12.8). Interestingly, when the Secretary of State for Transport, Local Government and the Regions gave approval for Terminal 5 to go ahead in 2001, a condition was imposed requiring these rail links to be provided before the terminal could open. Such conditions were apparently not discussed at the public inquiry, despite this lasting almost four years (Gannon 2008).

There is a need for more rail access to Heathrow as passenger numbers are expected to continue to rise and there is a need for further modal shift away from car use in any case. An Air Track Forum, led by Surrey County Council, has been developing a scheme since 2000 to help the British Airports Authority achieve its target of 50 per cent surface access by public transport. This involves a new

---

7   This includes John Prideaux, former head of BR's Inter-City sector, who first proposed the CTRL route via Stratford when the BR board was focused on the shortest, least cost option.

Table 12.7 Committed route re-openings and new routes

Target Completion Date	Length of New Route km (miles)	Location
		Scotland
2010	24 (14.9)	Airdrie-Bathgate (closed to passengers 1956/ freight 1982) reinstatement of track with 2 new stations at Armadale and Caldercruix to provide a fourth route from Edinburgh Waverley to Glasgow (this one to Queen Street Low Level). Existing Bathgate and Drumgelloch stations to be relocated and Airdrie, Livingston North and Uphall stations to be upgraded: total cost £300m
2013	49 (31)	Borders Rail Link – partial re-opening of part of former Waverley route, Edinburgh-Galashiels, with a terminus at Tweedbank: stations proposed at Shawfair, Eskbank, Newtongrange (Midlothian), Gorebridge, Stow, Galashiels and Tweedbank (Borders) – local authorities and Scottish Executive. Cost originally approx £150m, by 2008 up to £235-295m
2011	2 (1.2)	Glasgow Airport rail link – £90-£130m for a new electrified two track route between a point close to Paisley St James station and the airport
2011	18 (11.8)	Edinburgh Tram phase 1a – Edinburgh Airport- Princes Street- Newhaven (Leith), 22 stops including 3 heavy rail stations, one of which is the out-of-town Edinburgh Park business park – £592m project
		Wales
2008	n/a	£13m Upgrade of single track Cambrian line funded by WAG and NR – includes improved passing loops
		England
2010	3.6 (2.5)	East London Line – existing London Underground line to be extended along disused formation to Dalston Junction and the North London Line. New stations proposed at Shoreditch High Street, Hoxton and Haggerston, and Dalston. Southern extension from New Cross to Crystal Palace/West Croydon on existing lines – £900m
2015	n/a	Thameslink 2000 – enhancement of central London section to facilitate use of 12-car trains and addition of Peterborough/Cambridge and Guildford/Dartford routes to existing Bedford-City-Brighton axis – £3.55bn infrastructure works – committed in 2007 White Paper

Target Completion Date	Length of New Route km (miles)	Location
2017	22 (13.75) (new central tunnel)	Crossrail – approval by government for a hybrid bill in 2004 which received the Royal assent in 2008. A £16 bn funding package was agreed with public and private sector partners in 2007. The eastern links are to Shenfield and Abbey Wood and the western ones are to Maidenhead and Heathrow. Central London stations will be at Paddington, Bond St., Tottenham Court Rd, Farringdon, Liverpool Street and Whitechapel. Construction will begin in 2010.

Note: * Major resignalling projects are not included.

Sources: Rail industry professional journals: Modern Railways, Rail, various editions; transport policy professional journal, Local Transport Today, various editions.

rail line to Staines to the south west of Heathrow to connect with routes from Windsor, Woking and London Waterloo, and a new link to the Great Western main line to connect with services from the Reading direction. These would access the new tunnel already built under Terminal 5 and connect with the existing Heathrow Express route from Paddington. The estimated cost is £425m but the project is at an early stage with no statutory approval and no funding.

Gatwick airport has had a dedicated train service from London Victoria for twenty years. But, as evidence of the depth of the funding crisis facing Britain's railways, the SRA (2004a) proposed ending this so as to free off capacity for through trains to Brighton, which having trains terminate at Gatwick restricted. This curtailing of a model service because of a prior failure to invest, met with excoriating criticism in the railway press (Modern Railways 2005) and the branded service is now to be retained, although peak hour airport trains will be used by Brighton line commuters, to the detriment of both groups of passengers. On a more positive note, Luton Airport Parkway station was opened in 1999 with a good rail catchment along the Midland main line and Thameslink routes. But overall, given the government's commitment to growth in air transport and its desire to see a curb on associated growth in airport road traffic, there is a clear fault line across transport policy on the issue of surface access to London's airports. Also the lack of commitment to new high speed lines will not curb demand for flights between London and provincial cities, particularly those to Newcastle and the Scottish cities. Overall across London and the south east, despite the many positive outcomes, commentators see a lack of ambition and genuine integration between land-use planning and rail development, given the scale of new development envisaged over the next twenty years (Bolden and Harman 2008).

Table 12.8 Airport rail links 1994–2008

Date of opening	Airport	Developments in rail access
1994	Stansted	Airport rail link from the Cambridge main line opened to facilitate Liverpool Street-Stansted service
1995	Manchester International	South chord opened to facilitate access to the airport station from the Crewe direction
1998	London Heathrow	Heathrow Express service from London Paddington began 1998
1999	Luton	Luton Airport Parkway station opened on the Midland main line
2005	London City	Airport station opened along with the rest of the DLR branch to North Woolwich
2005	Cardiff	New station at Rhoose with bus link to Cardiff International Airport opened as part of the restoration of passenger services on the Vale of Glamorgan line
2006	Liverpool John Lennon	Liverpool South Parkway station opened nearby with a dedicated bus link to the airport
2008	Gatwick	Reduction in dedicated rail service as peak hour Gatwick Express trains will run through to/from Brighton mixing commuters and air passengers to maximise route capacity
2008	London Heathrow – Terminal 5	Terminal Five opened with new station underneath for the Piccadilly Line and Heathrow Express
2008	Manchester International	Opening of additional platform at the station
2009	East Midlands Nottingham Leicester Derby	East Midlands Parkway station – construction nearing completion in late 2008 – on the Midland main line from where there will be a bus link to the airport

Provincial cities

Given that the priorities for the network are the London focused long distance and commuter services, it is with regard to inter-regional and, especially, local services in provincial city regions that the shortcomings with regard to integration between the network and patterns of urban development are most obvious. One of the (partial) successes of privatisation has been the improvement of the Cross Country network operated by Virgin (until refranchising in 2007 when Arriva took over) which connects major cities, other than London. In 2002 Virgin introduced a higher frequency timetable with a £390m fleet of four and five car 'Voyager'[8] trains with a 125 mph (200 kmph) capability and there was an accompanying £200m track upgrade by Railtrack to facilitate higher speeds. This initiative was branded as 'Operation Princess' and it linked 115 regional cities and towns with Birmingham New Street as the hub of a NE-SW and NW-SE network providing half-hourly services within the inner Manchester/Sheffield/Reading/Bristol radius, and hourly within the outer Glasgow/Edinburgh/Bournemouth/Plymouth radius. But, owing to network capacity problems, the launch was marred by poor time keeping and some severe overcrowding and the scope of the new service was trimmed back to restore reliability.[9] Nevertheless, Cross Country services will have broadly doubled in frequency post-1997: Virgin claimed high growth with, for example, between 2002–4 a 63 per cent increase in trips between Birmingham-Newcastle and a 34 per cent increase between Bristol-Manchester. But despite this service improvement, once again there has been no accompanying national strategy for planning around the relevant stations. Such has been the increase in services that the capacity of Birmingham New Street has become a major constraint: it was rebuilt in the 1960s to handle 640 trains per day and in 2003 it handled 1350. However, there is now a locally led commitment to rebuild New Street and the government has committed itself to contribute significantly towards this.

Services between provincial cities not on the Cross Country network have been operated by companies other than Virgin and, typically, the quality of the routes and services are not as good. Nevertheless the city centre renaissance has triggered increased demand for rail in many cities. For example, the Association of Train Operating Companies claims 1994–2004 growth of 75 per cent between Manchester-York and there is evidence that the fairly new Trans-Pennine Express franchise is well focused on its market and is attracting more passengers. There have been proposals over the years to increase capacity on these inter-regional routes through junction improvements or even electrification (Haywood and Richardson 1996). However nothing substantial has been done and there are currently no committed major projects, despite the importance of improved rail links for the Northern Way initiative.

---

8 These are shorter and have fewer seats than the 1970s High Speed Trains which they replaced.

9 Liverpool for example currently has no Cross Country services.

Experience shows that it is the development of local services around provincial cities that is most crucially dependent on co-operation between railway management and local authority transport and land-use planning, as property markets here are very road oriented: these services account for 20 per cent of network ridership. The analysis of the BR era showed the surge in pro-rail policy and investment following the creation of the PTA/PTE structure and how this rippled out to areas dependent on county councils for support. However, it is also clear that, more recently, a good deal of effort in England has gone into developing light rail as a cheaper alternative to heavy rail in metropolitan areas such as Manchester, Sheffield, Newcastle, Birmingham and Nottingham as shown in Table 12.9 (Steer Davies Gleave 2005). These services can integrate well with heavy rail services to improve the overall rail 'offer', particularly if they are integrated with major regeneration initiatives, as is often the case, as shown in Nottingham and by extensions to the existing networks in Manchester and Tyne and Wear. But clearly the aspiration in the Ten Year Plan to open 25 light rail systems by 2010, has not been realised.

Table 12.9 Light rail systems as at March 2005

Name	Date when first opened	No. of stops	Length of route (km)	Passenger kilometres 2004/05 (millions)	Passenger boardings (millions) 2004/05
Tyne and Wear Metro*	1980	58	78	283	36.8
Docklands ** Light Railway	1987	34	27	245	50.1
Manchester Metrolink***	1992	37	39	204	19.7
Sheffield Supertram	1994	48	29	44	12.8
Midland Metro (Birmingham)	1999	23	20	52	5.0
Croydon Tramlink	2000	38	28	112	22.0
Nottingham NET	2004	23	14	37	8.5

Notes: * The Sunderland Extension was opened in 2002 comprising 14 km of running along the existing heavy rail route between Pelaw and Sunderland and a 4.5km section of new track between Sunderland and South Hylton; ** Extensions opened to Bank (1991), Lewisham (1999), London City Airport (2005); *** The 6.5km extension running through the Salford Quays regeneration area to Eccles opened in 2000.

Source: Department for Transport, Light Rail Statistics – England: Key facts, 2005.

Even in provincial city centres where investment has flowed into stations on intercity routes to London, secondary stations and their services have, typically, not received similar treatment. For example, despite partial redevelopment[10] and an increasingly favourable location vis-a-vis the retail core,[11] Manchester Victoria, which once rivalled Piccadilly, is now rather depressing aesthetically and, apart from Metrolink, has a poor quality rail service utilising DMUs and rail buses (Batty and Haywood 2002). The Merseyside PTA/PTE, however, has invested significantly in its local electric network, for which it uniquely has direct responsibility and the operator uniquely has a 25 year franchise. Investment has included new stations and station rebuilding, including the impressive Liverpool South Parkway bus-rail interchange at Garston opened in 2006, which also has a shuttle bus to the Liverpool John Lennon airport. The new Liverpool One development in the city centre is also easily accessible by rail. But the fact that parts of metropolitan city regions may actually lie outside PTE operational boundaries, means that local networks may not in fact link core cities to their natural hinterlands. Merseyside and Greater Manchester are good examples with neither city having its local electric services linked to Preston, Wigan, Widnes or Warrington which are all roughly equidistant from the two cities. The overall result is that journeys between provincial core cities and their satellite towns tend to offer a poor quality experience and take longer than those between London and its satellites, as the routes are, typically, secondary and lack investment (Lucci and Hildreth 2008). The electrification of the Leeds-Bradford/Skipton/Ilkley Aire Valley routes completed in 1995 by West Yorkshire PTA/PTE is an exception and it is notable that a local project on this scale has not been repeated post-privatisation. The RDA for Yorkshire and Humberside, Yorkshire Forward, has subsequently part-funded (£8m) extra trains on other local services into Leeds to facilitate access to its job market, an interesting development which bodes well for future RDA support for local networks in the regions (Clinnick 2008a).

Whereas the city centre renaissance has been associated with station developments of various kinds, it is very difficult to identify any high density development nodes in suburban or ex-urban areas outside the south east region which have been focused around railway stations, as opposed to major roads and use of the private car. As Table 12.6 shows, despite the policy changes of the mid-1990s and the positive outcome in the CBDs, very large out-of-town retail centres have continued to be built in locations not accessible by rail: in most, but not all, cases this is because their origins predate the policy changes, highlighting the importance of long term consistency in planning policies.

In the Dearne Valley area in South Yorkshire, there was a local rail service prior to the regeneration activity which followed the ending of coal mining in the

---

10   This includes an airspace development completed in 1995 which comprises a 21,000 seat arena.

11   This follows considerable rebuilding of parts of the central retail area, which lies closer to Victoria than Piccadilly, following the IRA bomb outrage in 1996.

early 1990s. Although supported by South Yorkshire PTE, there has been limited investment in this network and, as around many northern cities, services are largely provided by rail buses. With the collapse of coal mining there has been massive de-industrialisation and, subsequently, widespread land reclamation and regeneration activity, although this has been associated with the Enterprise Zone approach with limited evidence of strategic town planning and even less of urban design. The emphasis has been on linking employment sites to the motorway network by new roads and laying out sites in a car-friendly manner: the archetypal 'edge city' of the 1980s (Sudjic 1992), built in the late 1990s. The result is that access to new employment areas even by bus is extremely difficult, if not impossible, and the presence of railway stations has had no bearing at all on the location and design of most developments (Batty et al. 2002). More encouraging is the fact that when planning permission for the new Robin Hood Airport to the east of Doncaster was granted by the government in 2003, a condition was attached requiring construction of a station and this has subsequently been granted planning permission.

At Horwich Parkway near Bolton, in a situation where a new station has been provided as part of an edge-of-town commercial development alongside the Manchester-Bolton-Preston rail route, the associated development is car-oriented in its design with the station added as something on an afterthought, following intervention by GMPTE (Batty and Haywood 2002). However delivering new stations in a timely fashion has been difficult enough in England and, outside the PTA/PTE areas, it is the county councils which have usually taken the lead. The involvement of Warwickshire in the opening of Warwick Parkway has already been mentioned, but the county council was also instrumental in the opening in 2007 of Coleshill Parkway, located between Birmingham and Nuneaton, close to the M42. On the other hand, in Stoke-on-Trent the station at Etruria was closed in 2005 despite a good deal of local regeneration activity, but this largely ignored the presence of the station, where services had been run down in any case. Further closures have been threatened in the wider Potteries area too, demonstrating the problems arising from lack of an effective, local champion of integrated planning around rail.

Overall, despite the missed opportunities, because of continuing population dispersal and growing road traffic volumes, demand for rail services has grown significantly in many city regions and various capacity problems (often arising from earlier rationalisations) and gaps in the electrified network have become increasingly apparent. Good examples of the latter would be between Manchester-Liverpool, Liverpool-Preston, Manchester-Preston-Blackpool and Manchester-Leeds-York. English local authorities have been encouraged by national government to develop transport and land-use policies to promote greater environmental sustainability through modal shift and various junction improvements, electrification schemes, new stations and route re-openings have been mooted in local planning documents, but few have received funding and the immediate prospects are poor (see Table 12.10 for a selection of larger schemes which have been mooted).

However, Tables 12.4 and 12.7 show that a significant difference has opened up between rail investment in Scotland and Wales and the English regions. Once the tail of pre-privatisation schemes was completed in England re-openings tailed off, but several schemes have subsequently been completed in Wales and Scotland and others are committed. There is evidence of these re-openings being integrated with land-use planning too, such as the proximity of stations to new housing on the Ebbw Vale route, the Vale of Glamorgan line facilitating rail access to Cardiff airport, new housing being accessible via the Hamilton-Larkhall route in Scotland and access to new housing being part of the case for the re-opening of the Borders Rail link to Tweedbank. It is also notable that it is in Scotland that Edinburgh Park station was opened, in 2003, at an out-of-town business and retail park and this will also have an electrified service as part of the Bathgate-Airdrie re-opening and be on the proposed Edinburgh Tram network (Table 12.7) However, even in Scotland where commitment to rail development has been the greatest, experience has been mixed as Table 12.6 shows that major out-of-town shopping centres have been built with no rail access in Glasgow, at Paisley and Pollock.

Rural routes

Extensive thinning out of rural rail routes took place post Beeching and areas such as north Cornwall, north west Devon, north Norfolk, east Lincolnshire, the north Pennines and the Scottish Borders were left with no rail access at all. It is notable this had a particularly severe impact on access to national parks and other areas of natural beauty to which demand for access by car has since grown markedly. However significant lengths of single track railway have been retained in some rural areas and, of course, many trunk routes pass through rural areas and retained stations on these have become important rail heads: Oxenholme and Penrith on the WCML are good examples. The Regional Railways sector of BR became adept at working with local authorities so that external funding could be drawn in to support rural services and develop station infrastructure. The local authorities were keen to do this in order to retain rail services for those without car access, to provide alternative modes for access to the countryside and because of significant population growth in many rural areas fuelled by counter-urbanisation.

Post-privatisation, community support for rural lines has developed significantly, encouraged by the Countryside Agency (2001) and aided by the creation in 1998 of the Association of Community Rail Partnerships (ACoRP) with, subsequently, over twenty mainly rural lines being formally designated as Community Rail Partnerships. Research by the government's Social Exclusion Unit recognised that exclusion is particularly acute in rural areas, owing to the lack of good public transport (Social Exclusion Unit 2002). Local promotion has led to some significant increases in ridership and publication by the SRA of the Community Rail Development Strategy boosted confidence (SRA 2004c). The Countryside

Agency[12] was particularly active in promoting Rural Transport Partnerships and funded research to demonstrate the 'cross-sector' financial benefits of subsidised public transport: this should be part of the development of the case for rural rail services (see Batty et al. 2005). As a result of these initiatives, there have been significant increases in ridership on many routes and the subsidies involved give a good return if the wider economic, social and environmental benefits are taken into account (ACoRP 2008), but the involvement of local authorities has been threatened by the instability in the structure of English local government (Salveson 2007).

However the issue in England is whether or not *existing* routes can be retained and, perhaps, improved in some cases: timetables are often heavily constrained by operational and resource issues which mean that trains don't always run when people need them.[13] Nevertheless, there is support amongst rural bodies for re-openings with Bere Alston-Tavistock, Matlock-Chinley, and Skipton-Colne as examples, although these have the odds stacked against them, even though the latter two examples would be of much more than local interest as they would re-open interregional strategic routes. The proposed Bere Alston-Tavistock re-opening has been associated with potential funding by a house builder seeking planning permission for several hundred new homes in Tavistock, which would be accessible to the re-opened station (Harris 2008). Devon County Council has played a significant role in developing this project and is to take over ownership of the disused trackbed from one of the pre-privatisation residuary bodies, BRB Property, and the hope is that West Devon Borough Council will incorporate the project in its LDF (Clinnick 2008b). Despite privatisation, this historic association between land development and railways has been relatively rare in situations outside the main city centres. In contrast to these English, unfunded schemes (Table 12.10), re-openings which impact on rural areas have already been completed in Wales in Scotland as already mentioned and the Scottish Parliament has also committed funding for the re-opening of services along the former Waverley route between Edinburgh and Galashiels in the Borders (Table 12.7).

---

12   The Countryside Agency was created in 1999 but in 2006 was merged with parts of English nature and the Rural Development Service to form Natural England. The initiative for funding rural transport to promote social inclusion then passed to the RDAs which gave rise to concerns in rural areas, given the traditional priorities of the RDAs.

13   Also retained services may be very infrequent with poor connections with main line services – see Williams 2008 for example, with regard to the Middlesbrough-Whitby Esk Valley line.

Table 12.10 Uncommitted route re-openings and new routes

Scotland
Edinburgh south suburban line re-opening to passenger services with nine new stations
EARL: Edinburgh airport rail link – project dropped by Scottish Parliament in 2007 owing to – high costs but since replaced by the Edinburgh Tram project
Glasgow Crossrail utilising the High Street curve to link S/SW services with north-side

England
AirTrack: South western approach to Heathrow Terminal 5 from Staines
Ashington, Blyth and Tyne: use of retained freight routes for passenger services to Newcastle
East-West (Oxford-Cambridge): studies began 1996 – related to Sustainable Communities plan for expansion of Milton Keynes and other centres
Leamside line from Pelaw to Tursdale Junction: Tyne and Wear PTE and Durham County Council proposal which would provide a rail link to Washington New Town
Matlock-Chinley via Bakewell: re-opening of former Midland route through the Peak District-promoted by Derbyshire County Council to relieve road traffic congestion and promote accessibility
Portishead: 4.8 km (3 mile) extension to Portbury Dock branch to provide this growing waterside settlement with a local service to Bristol
Skipton-Colne: local authority proposal to re-open this 17.6 km (11 miles) 'missing link' between West Yorkshire (Aire Valley lines) and East Lancashire, closed in 1970. Trackbed protected in Joint Lancashire Structure Plan and district local plans
Tavistock-Bere Alston: re-opening to provide a link from Tavistock through to Plymouth
Uckfield-Lewes: floated as part of the failed re-tendering of the South Central franchise in 2001 (one of Morton's SPVs). Uckfield is the southern terminus of the route from London and re-opening would provide local people with access to Brighton as well as offering an alternative London-Brighton route when the main line is closed

Sources: Rail industry professional journals: Modern Railways, Rail, various editions; Transport policy professional journal Local Transport Today, various editions.

Freight

Research in the late 1990s (Greensmith and Haywood 1999; Haywood 2001) concluded that strategic planning policy (as set out in planning policy guidance, regional planning guidance and minerals planning guidance) had become increasingly supportive of modal shift to rail by encouraging the development of rail accessible mineral extraction sites, urban aggregates terminals, waste disposal sites (domestic, industrial and scrap metal) and distribution facilities, although policy was reactive and enabling as opposed to being proactive. However, case study research showed that experience at site level was very mixed and there was a tendency for local concerns about the negative impacts of a freight facility (often associated with the movement of lorries to and from the site, rather than the rail operation) to be given more weight than the strategic benefits to be enjoyed elsewhere as a result of modal shift. Privatisation has led to direct competition between rail freight companies and this has helped make rail attractive to the highly cost sensitive logistics sector. As a result traffic has increased and modal share, measured using goods moved, has increased from around 6 per cent to around 8 per cent. However much of the increase has been the long distance haulage of imported coal for the electricity industry which still forms the biggest sector as shown in Tables 12.11 and 12.12 Given the high level of concern about carbon emissions and the controversy around the building of a new generation of coal fired power stations, this is a doubtful long term basis for the rail freight industry. The industry has had only limited success, so far, in attracting new business such as food, drink and fast moving consumer goods, apart from the extent to which that is embraced by the maritime container traffic.

Interestingly the increase in coal haulage has triggered a need for major investment in upgrading track quality and capacity on the Settle-Carlisle line (targeted for closure in the 1980s) and the Glasgow and South Western route between Dumfries and Kilmarnock (long stretches reduced to single track in the 1970s), owing to coal for the Aire and Trent Valley power stations being imported through Hunterston on the Firth of Clyde. This again shows the need for long term vision in rail planning, something which has been lacking in the British approach over recent decades.

Table 12.11 Freight moved by sector 1999–00 to 2006–07: Great Britain (billion net tonne kilometres)

	Coal	Metals	Construction	Oil & petroleum	International	Domestic intermodal	Other	Total
1999-00	4.85	2.19	2.04	1.50	1.01	3.92	2.73	18.23
2000-01	4.77	2.09	2.43	1.36	0.99	3.84	2.60	18.09
2001-02	6.17	2.43	2.81	1.22	0.60	3.54	2.62	19.39
2002-03	5.66	2.64	2.51	1.15	0.46	3.38	2.72	18.52
2003-04	5.82	2.41	2.68	1.19	0.48	3.53	2.77	18.87
2004-05	6.66	2.59	2.86	1.22	0.54	3.96	2.53	20.35
2005-06	8.26	2.22	2.91	1.22	0.46	4.33	2.29	21.70
2006-07	8.77	2.13	2.71	1.50	0.45	4.56	1.97	22.11

Source: ORR National Rail Trends Yearbook April 06–March 07.

Table 12.12 Freight lifted 1999–00 to 2006–07: Great Britain (million tonnes)

	Coal	Other	Total
1999-00	35.9	60.6	96.5
2000-01	35.3	60.3	95.6
2001-02	39.5	54.5	93.9
2002-03	34.0	53.0	87.0
2003-04	35.2	53.7	88.9
2004-05	44.0	57.1	101.1
2005-06	48.9	58.7	107.6
2006-07	48.8	59.6	108.4

Source: ORR National Rail Trends Yearbook April 06–March 07: there is a break in the series between 2003–4 and 2004–5, and between 2004–5 and 2005–6.

Although the reasons behind the slow growth in new traffic are complex, they are partially concerned with shortcomings in the network, such as the lack of robustness because of a shortage of diversionary routes and the restricted loading gauge inherited from the Victorian era, which precludes larger loads on many routes and piggy-back haulage of trucks and trailers throughout. However there are also problems resulting from a poor interface with the planning system, such as the lack of inter-modal distribution facilities, especially around London. The failure of the LIFE project was noted in Chapter 11. With globalisation, inbound container traffic through British ports is increasing but there has been no government strategy to accommodate this, although there has been a series of ad hoc planning inquiries into privately promoted expansion projects. Expansion at Southampton (Dibden Bay) has been denied although public inquiries have yielded favourable results at Harwich Bathside Bay, Felixstowe and London Gateway (Thames Haven), all of which will put pressure on the already congested East Anglia-London route (which runs through the heart of the Olympics focused regeneration area around Stratford), showing the urgency of securing the alternative route to the north via Ely and Peterborough. Network Rail has completed a project to facilitate haulage of 9'6" containers[14] from Felixstowe to Birmingham/Manchester/Glasgow via London with the route from Glasgow to Aberdeen also improved. The projected alternative route via Peterborough, Leicester and Nuneaton or on the existing route from Southampton docks to Birmingham and the north cannot take the larger containers, but funding for this work was committed in 2007. More recently permission to expand container handling facilities has been granted at Liverpool, where re-opening of a short length of closed line will enhance capacity and Teesport (Middlesbrough) where there is a major initiative, but the implications of this for rail freight are unclear, although none of the east-west trans-Pennine routes are cleared for 9'6" containers. Overall there is a developing strategy to link railway route development with port expansion, but there has not been a related strategy with regard to inland terminal development (Woodburn 2008) which is also the product of schemes receiving planning permission on an ad hoc basis.

One of the successes of the SRA was the formation of a freight group which developed the freight strategy and was able to bridge the gap between private sector freight customers, rail FOCs and the various public planning bodies which seek modal shift to rail and the demise of the SRA has left a vacuum at this interface. The refusal of planning permission for the LIFE project in 2002, after a costly public inquiry, was a strong disincentive for the private sector to risk a similar large project around London where the need is greatest. Proposals at Colney and Radlett founded owing to local opposition and, at what near Maidstone is an ideal location in operational terms, the proposed Kent International Gateway is also meeting local opposition (Berkeley 2008). But, more optimistically, in 2007 the government gave approval for ProLogis to proceed with development of a 40 ha (2.1m sq ft) inter-modal distribution centre on a green belt site at Howbury Park (Bexley) in south London, close to the M25 and with rail access via the North Kent main line.

Outside London the more supportive planning regime has helped deliver expansion of the existing rail serviced distribution centre at Daventry and, as well as receiving more maritime containers trains, a domestic Anglo-Scottish service has been developed too. Further new rail served freight facilities have been developed at a wide spread of locations including Birch Coppice (Warwickshire), Burton on

---

14   The maritime industry is moving to 9'6" high containers and it is necessary to raise the headroom under over-bridges and tunnels to facilitate their passage: this is known in the industry as W10 gauge. This work is necessary just to retain existing market share.

Trent, Selby, Knowsley and Grangemouth, with others under construction, such as at Telford. The SRA even funded the re-opening of the branch line to Portbury docks near Bristol in 2001, a rare English re-opening scheme.

However the situation in Lincoln demonstrates the continuing problems arising from lack of a long term commitment to rail. Doncaster-Lincoln-Spalding-March was a historic freight route moving Yorkshire coal to London whilst avoiding the busy ECML, but owing to the decline of that business the Spalding-March link and the freight avoiding line around Lincoln were closed in 1982. The subsequent increase in passenger and freight traffic through Lincoln station and its associated level crossing, on one of the city centre's busiest roads, is now causing major traffic congestion. This is a significant issue needing to be addressed if the line is to carry more freight to relive the ECML, as has been suggested by Railtrack and, subsequently, Network Rail. If the avoiding line had been protected, as it could have been through the planning system, the problem would now be more manageable.

The biggest failure in rail freight policy has been the opening of the Channel Tunnel which Chapter 8 showed had led to optimism about shifting road traffic to rail and had triggered the development of inter modal distribution facilities. But cross-Channel rail freight has struggled to achieve the volumes previously carried on the train ferries. There are several reasons for this including: a serious problem between 1999–2002 caused by asylum seekers and migrant workers trying to get into the UK by illegally boarding Tunnel freight trains which virtually closed the service; the cost to train companies of using the Tunnel; the lack of priority given to freight by state owned railways on the Continent; and the impact of strikes, particularly on French railways. Recently Britain's biggest rail freight company, EWS, has been purchased by Deutsche Bahn which is developing an international capacity for rail freight and this, along with other operators' aspirations, does raise hopes that the Tunnel's earlier promise might be realised.[15]

After the removal of funding for rail freight grants in the aftermath of the Hatfield crisis, the government has made funds available again and in autumn 2008 announced increased allocations as far out as 2011–14, to demonstrate long term commitment. If rail freight volumes do increase, this will exert additional pressure on the capacity of the existing main line network. The freight companies need a more robust network with more alternative routes when the direct routes are closed: this lack of 'redundancy' in the network is a serious inheritance from the Beeching closures. Network Rail has begun to sketch out what the 'Strategic Freight Network' might look like and the need for investment in diversionary routes has been recognised (Network Rail 2008). In the medium to long term, lack of freight capacity on existing main lines may be a significant factor in triggering

---

15   In January 2008 a trial train carrying containers ran successfully from Beijing to Hamburg and the creation of a 'Eurasian landbridge' service on the North American model is a serious possibility as it would halve the time taken by ocean shipping. Such a service could be accessed by the Tunnel.

government commitment to high speed passenger rail links, which would free off capacity on the historic routes. Continued growth in rail freight will certainly lead to demand for more intermodal distribution centres and experience shows that this needs to be done on a more strategic basis.

Conclusions

Despite being completed more than ten years ago, railway privatisation continues to be highly controversial. This is not the place to explore the various views, but it has been shown that its negative impacts still affect the industry. Even the former Conservative Party Shadow Transport spokesman, Chris Grayling, said:

> We think, with hindsight, that the complete separation of track and train into separate businesses at the time of privatisation was not right for our railways (BBC 2006).

The privatisation process itself and its aftermath had strong similarities with the post-grouping and post-nationalisation periods in that the gaze of the industry was forced inwards as the impact of deep organisational change was planned, implemented and digested: as Fiennes noted, 'when you re-organise you bleed' (1967, 113). It has been shown that this created a hiatus in the development of the positive relationships between the railway and planning sectors that had developed towards the end of the BR era. The fact that, in the mid-1990s, the railway industry famously went 1064 days without ordering a single new piece of passenger rolling stock is just one example of the sort of impact the process had. It took several years for the industry to begin to consider its external relationships and, just when that was beginning to happen, came the Hatfield crash, the collapse of Railtrack and the industry experiencing what Sir Alastair Morton called a 'collective nervous breakdown'.

The underlying issue is not privatisation per se, but the form it took. The main problems are the separation of track ownership from train operation and the overall level of churn and complexity arising from the large number of companies involved in what is really only a medium sized, British based industry. It has been pointed out that several of the UK's leading supermarket chains are substantially larger businesses than the whole of the railway industry and to carve any one of them up on the railway privatisation model would be unworkable and unthinkable. The important point for this book is that railway privatisation has led to the institutional relationships between the railway and planning sectors becoming too complicated. The separation of infrastructure from train operation has created a problem in the rail industry as to where the locus of interest lies with regard to land development and its impacts on railway utilisation. Is this a matter for the track authority as monopoly owner of the fixed infrastructure, or for the train operating companies who actually manage most of the stations, run the trains, face the customers and have the prime interest in promoting growth? For freight generating developments the problem can be even more complex with, for example, the developer of a regional distribution centre having to take the lead and possibly having to drag a reluctant track authority and planning authority along. The problem is that integration with land development can involve works to fixed infrastructure as well as the enhancement of railway services on that infrastructure so, given the current structure, no single organisation can speak for the railway as a whole. The SRA was able to do this and was taking a strong lead with regard to integration with planning, as a sort of 'super PTE', and its demise has left a vacuum. There are doubts too as to whether the industry is actually incentivised to go for growth on a scale which would achieve measurable modal shift: critics have seen the government's wish to drive up fares as a continuation of the Treasury's role in BR days of choking off peak demand to minimise expenditure. The short term of most passenger franchises is a disincentive for TOCs to get involved anyway and the overall complexity makes getting things done time consuming and costly.

Matters have been further complicated as the post-privatisation period has seen a good deal of institutional change with regard to land-use planning too, which has also impacted on local transport planning. In England more unitary authorities have been created, counties have had their administrative areas reduced in size and county level Structure Plans are being abandoned. Whereas Regional Spatial Strategies and Regional Transport Strategies are now statutory documents, the attempt to create statutory regional bodies in England to produce them failed, creating problems over implementation. By comparison, the outcomes of the creation of the mayor's office in London and Welsh and Scottish devolution seem to have been more successful in facilitating integration between railway development and broader development strategies.

Notwithstanding the problems with institutional structures, the underlying ideologies in transport planning and town planning have been strongly focused on integration between land-use and railway planning. This has been reinforced by the reinvigoration of urban design as a tool to craft the detailed integration of land development with station access and development. There has also been the realisation that even rail freight facilities, such as regional distribution centres, can be environmentally friendly and visually attractive and, through careful preparation and public consultation, they can be delivered by the planning system, although often this doesn't come about owing to other policy priorities. So, overall, the policy process has moved beyond the priorities of the 1970s and 1980s, the emphasis on trackbed protection and re-opening closed routes and stations, towards the active promotion of development forms which support use of the rail mode. This can now be seen as the norm to expect in any statutory planning document, although there are exceptions, as has been shown. The problem in many cases has been in co-ordinating land side developments with timely and commensurate improvement in railway capacity, casting doubts on the degree of government commitment to integration. There are wider concerns about the direction of the government's transport policies too (Docherty and Shaw 2008).

Although there has been a plethora of government rail policy documents, the majority have been primarily concerned with matters internal to the railway industry which can be traced back to the poorly conceived privatisation. There are now a number of major rail projects going forward serving London but, as compared with say, Paris, these can be seen as a catching up operation. Other much needed enhancements on parts of the south east's network are not funded, there is as yet no commitment to extension of the high speed network beyond London, and few of the myriad improvements cited in local planning documents elsewhere in provincial England will be funded in the short term. If there is to be modal shift, much more will be required, of government and of the railway industry itself.

A summary of the thematic analysis of the 1994–2008 is shown in Table 12.13 and, with regard to the list of points developed at the end of Chapter 2, the following summarises the outcomes for the post-privatisation period with regard to the rail network:

1. *rationalisation of the network*: closures have been limited and mainly associated with de-industrialisation, only affecting freight lines and there has been a genuine attempt to promote lightly used passenger routes; re-openings continued but in England these were the culmination of BR era initiatives with major new projects only being delivered in Wales and Scotland;

2. *development of railway services*: major achievements have been the completion of High Speed 1 and Heathrow Express which are BR era initiatives although privatisation has delivered improvements to cross country services and, belatedly, the WCML upgrade will deliver significant improvements; investment in fixed infrastructure by TOCs has been associated with long franchises; there has been no strategic electrification although, generally, more passenger services are being operated across the network, but many journeys off the main lines continue to be not very competitive with car journey times; rail freight has grown but has continued to be dependent on the traditional markets of coal and deep sea containers and the Channel Tunnel has not been a success for freight;

3. *closing strategic gaps in the network*: outside of Wales and Scotland there has been little investment in new routes although there has been investment in associated networks which will promote use of the main line network: in London these include the Jubilee Line extension, extensions to the DLR and Croydon Tramlink, and elsewhere Midland Metro, Nottingham Express Transit and extensions to Manchester Metrolink and the Tyne and Wear Metro; committed projects in London are associated with creation of the mayor's office.

4. *development of a programme of station enhancement*: there have been major station enhancement projects across the network, especially in city centres, although the rate of new openings in England has turned down.

The following summarises the outcomes with regard to the operation of the planning system:

5. *patterns of urban development*: although there are exceptions, there has been a step change in planning policy towards city centres, supported by developments in urban design, which now generally seek to promote patterns of development which facilitate use of the railway network for passenger traffic; in suburban areas experience is more mixed with few rail oriented suburban nodes being developed; the promotion of freight generating activities in rail accessible locations is common but not comprehensive;

6. *management of the redevelopment process in existing urban areas*: regeneration and redevelopment, especially in city and town centres, has been managed so as to maximise access to railway stations and the quality of many schemes has been very high, but in suburban and ex-urban areas the experience has been more mixed, especially in economically depressed areas; whereas policy has been more supportive of freight, there have been difficulties in securing major rail freight generating projects, particularly in London and the south east;

7. *management of the location and character of greenfield site development*: the emphasis on regeneration and brownfield development has led to reduced utilisation of greenfield sites, but there is evidence of a continuance of the road oriented nature of much greenfield development, except in exceptional circumstances.

Table 12.13 Summary of thematic analysis of outcomes: 1994–2008

Explanatory themes	Railway sector	Interrelationships between the two sectors	Planning sector
Politics and political ideology	Once privatisation was complete the supportive context produced plans for significant improvements to main line and local services, although there were issues over delivery But the Railtrack debacle led to a focus on safety and costs which delayed delivery of capacity improvements. English regions lost out to London, Scotland and Wales.	The internal problems in the rail industry made integration between the sectors difficult, but strong local institutional structures could override the problems as in London, Wales, Scotland, some of the PTA/PTE areas and areas with committed local authorities. Continuing emphasis in rural areas on holding on to existing services, with some supportive developments and re-openings in Wales and Scotland.	The supportive context delivered many relevant developments, especially in city centres and around key transport interchanges. But outside the major cities and the south east, the emphasis on economic growth could overshadow public transport considerations. The political reluctance for high level leadership on rail investment, outside of certain key projects, held back the delivery of integrated strategies.
Professions and professional ideology	Within Railtrack there was a dilution of the engineering focus but this was strongly re-established on the creation of Network Rail. Private sector initiative was restrained because of the limitations of franchising and government concerns over costs. These internal priorities restricted the gaze towards local authorities and their aspirations.	The engineering and cost concerns constrained the railway sector's engagement with planning policies, but the two meshed well where investment was a priority for the rail industry and/or where an external body, usually a public sector one, pushed hard. This did yield very high quality, integrated projects, but in other circumstances the sectors worked in isolation from each other.	The promotion of urban regeneration and an emphasis on place making became priorities within a reinvigorated planning system and had positive implications for rail. The most notable achievements were in city and town centres where rail oriented planning was the norm, but in other situations planning outcomes were patchy.

Explanatory themes	Railway sector	Interrelationships between the two sectors	Planning sector
Governance and management	Following the demise of Railtrack, there was a confusing interplay between strong state control and the promotion of private sector initiative. The structural and ideological complexity made engagement with the industry by third parties difficult. The role of the SRA at the interface was brief but effective, given the financial constraints at that time.	The huge amount of complexity and change in each sector made the building of effective relationships difficult. The historic positive roles of county councils and PTA/PTEs was augmented by the creation of the London mayor and devolution in Wales and Scotland.	The desire to make planning more relevant to regeneration and more able to deliver improved physical outcomes tended to be eroded by wider public service policy agendas which emphasised targets, further diffused the power of local authorities and created churn in structures. Partnerships worked well when project focused.

Chapter 13

Postscript

Despite the recent plethora of railway white papers, there continues to be concerns as to what the government's long term vision for the railways really is and to what extent modal shift is seen as desirable. Notwithstanding this, the medium term prospects for the integration between planning and railway policy are relatively good with some changes in institutional structures for planning already in the pipeline, although matters in the rail industry are still problematic.

Network Rail is perceived as being a better guardian of the infrastructure than Railtrack, but there are problems as exemplified by: a crash involving a fatality at Grayrigg, Cumbria in February 2007 caused by poor track maintenance, and; during the Christmas and New Year period in 2007–8, three high profile overruns on engineering works which caused major service disruptions. The criticism is that Network Rail is remote from the industry's customers, not really accountable to anyone, over-centralised and not sufficiently well disciplined to deliver value for money. The high cost of railway projects continues to be a potential barrier to capacity enhancement. The closer co-operation with TOCs through what has been called virtual integration, i.e. jointly staffed control centres, is seen as part of the solution, but others call for better internal governance of Network Rail to secure more accountability and/or devolution of decision making down to regional boards of some kind, perhaps jointly staffed with the TOCs. Whilst this may lead to operational improvements, it will not necessarily overcome the problems of interfacing with external bodies, such as local planning and transport authorities. Also the short length of most passenger franchises mitigates against the involvement of TOCs in work with local planning authorities and the breaking up of the network into so many franchises impacts negatively on public perceptions of the scope of services on offer. Some commentators see the creation of a relatively small number of vertically integrated companies on the Big Four model (see Wragg 2004, pp. 188-189 for example), as the eventual outcome, with managers able to act on behalf of the railway as a whole on the traditional model. Although the rail freight companies may well oppose this as they require open access to the whole network and the track authority model delivers this, vertical re-integration would simplify institutional structures and, if associated with long franchises, make them more robust in the long term and thereby facilitate external liaison. Overall the saga of railway privatisation looks set to continue for a while yet and, whatever the form eventually adopted for the industry, simplification of structures and clarity and continuity of roles are necessary ingredients with regard to improved integration with planning authorities.

With regard to planning, the Planning Act 2008 acts on the recommendations of the Eddington report by creating an independent Infrastructure Planning Commission to make decisions about major projects, to be guided by National Policy Statements to be produced by ministers. This is a hugely controversial proposal as it will hand over significant decision making power to unelected individuals and is also seen as threatening the ability of local communities to ameliorate the impact of major developments upon them. However, it could expedite the delivery of railway projects, such as high speed lines or the large regional distribution centres which are necessary for modal shift for freight. The Act also contains a proposed Community Infrastructure Levy which would be a mechanism for transferring to the community part of the increases in land value enjoyed by those receiving planning permission for large developments, to be invested in the infrastructure required to support the development. Given the long term impact of rail investment in generating such increases which are not captured in railway fareboxes, then this mechanism could produce funding for local rail projects in association with large development schemes.

At the regional level in England, the currently confused pattern of plan making by various statutory and non-statutory bodies has been the subject of a plan for simplification, the Review of Sub-National Economic Development and Regeneration (HM Treasury 2007). This envisaged combining all the various regional strategies into a new 'single regional strategy' to be produced by the RDAs. Whilst this is a controversial plan too, because RDAs are appointed and not elected, integrating the regional spatial and transport plans with economic strategies does present an opportunity for simplification and closer integration and, the fact that RDAs have budgets and have invested in rail, raises the likelihood of regionally promoted rail schemes being implemented. There is also debate about how to improve governance in major urban areas through the creation of city regional authorities, perhaps with some kind of elected leader on the London model. This has implications for the relationships between local authorities and the RDAs but could, potentially, lead to more local control over funding which could also help in the development of local rail networks. The creation of bodies which can plan and finance railway development as part of a broader economic and spatial strategy in the English regions and city regions is highly desirable, given the recent investment hiatus as compared with the situation in London, Wales and Scotland.

With regard to local transport planning, the Local Transport Act 2008 gives additional powers to PTA/PTEs to intervene in the bus market to secure better services, which could lead to improved integration with rail services which can extend station catchment areas. The existing PTA/PTEs are to be renamed Integrated Transport Areas (ITAs) and are to be able to review their existing arrangements, including their boundaries, which is a potentially positive move, given the problems which overly tight boundaries have caused with regard to local rail services. Also outside the current PTA/PTE areas where two or more authorities wish to work more closely, they may be able to create an ITA so, potentially, this could improve the scope for planning around local rail networks in those areas and such extension of PTA/PTE structures is long overdue.

So, overall, institutional arrangements are moving in a favourable direction and policy remains supportive of integration. But it remains to be seen as to whether there will be the political will to make the kind of investments necessary to provide the capacity to substantially increase rail's market share and this, in turn, will impact on the degree to which local authorities are motivated to pursue more prescriptive policies to bend patterns of urban development further towards the rail network. The experience post-privatisation is that most rail investment continues to come from the public sector. Therefore the huge calls on the public purse arising from the collapse of the UK banking sector and the onset of recession, cast serious doubt over the government's ability, and possibly its desire, to invest more in rail in the short term. The collapse of the property market casts short term doubts over funding from that direction too, through planning gain mechanisms. Existing commitments may be at risk, although a return to Keynesian economic strategy could favour state investment to boost the economy, as happened on the railways in the 1930s.

Over the long term, increased investment in rail is essential to secure greater sustainability in the transport sector by securing modal shift. This book has shown that such long term commitment would be worthwhile as, despite huge changes in technology over the decades, the rail guidance system has shown great longevity and its ability to carry large volumes of traffic in relatively narrow corridors in a way which is very safe and less environmentally intrusive, on a number of counts, than road and air modes, will be a continuing asset far into the future. Also, despite huge changes in urban and rural geography and some half hearted planning along the way, the railway network remains fairly well integrated with broad patterns of urban development. Rail can get people and goods to many of the places they need to go, despite the follies of the past, because large volumes of people and goods still move along traditional axes linking long established nodes, and some new ones. This book has reviewed the sorts of institutional structures and policies which integrate rail services with patterns of urban development, noting the continuing importance of town and city centres and the fact that it is perfectly possible to link them by rail with urban extensions, new settlements and other trip generating nodes, as well as ensuring large new freight generating nodes are rail connected too.

The relationship between the railways and urban development is therefore, essentially, a long term one which requires effective, co-ordinated planning in both sectors over long time horizons measured in decades, not years: the fact that great effort is still being put in to re-opening routes closed in the 1960s shows how damaging short termism can be. The book has shown that over the post war period when, theoretically, governments have had the power to put in place the best structures and policies to secure integration, it has been pretty unusual for the optimum balance to have been in place for any length of time, owing to the ebb and flow of political and professional priorities and ideologies. The ability to implement the policies is influenced by the cyclical nature of the economy which affects railway and property investment, so this makes the long term perspective and a commitment to decisive intervention when the opportunities arise all the more important. Sadly it is notable that the rate of churn has accelerated post-privatisation, just when the need for continuity has increased, given growing road traffic congestion and our developing environmental problems. It follows that if structures and policies can be better tailored to the task and applied more consistently and continuously, the degree of integration between land development and the rail network can be increased. This, if accompanied by a convincing political narrative to secure public support, can secure modal shift and reduce the reliance on car, truck and aeroplane as a significant component of a broader transport strategy to secure a more sustainable way of living.

Appendices

Appendix 1: Development of the London Underground network 1863–2000

Railway company/Route	Year opened	Railway company/ Route	Year opened
Metropolitan*		**Metropolitan District***	
Farringdon to Paddington	1863	Kensington High Street to Westminster	1868
Paddington to Hammersmith	1864	Gloucester Road to West Brompton	1869
Farringdon to Moorgate	1865	Westminster to Blackfriars	1870
Baker Street to Swiss Cottage	1868	Earls Court to Hammersmith	1874
Paddington to Kensington	1868	Hammersmith to Richmond	1877
Swiss Cottage to Harrow-on-the-Hill	1880	Turnham Green to Ealing Broadway	1879
Harrow-on-the-Hill to Rickmansworth	1887	Acton Town to Hounslow West	1884
Rickmansworth to Verney Junction	1894	Inner Circle Completed	1884
Farringdon/Baker Street to Uxbridge electrification	1905	Putney Bridge to Wimbledon	1889
Baker Street to Hammersmith electrification	1906	Whitechapel to Upminster	1902
Rickmansworth to Watford	1925	Ealing Common to South Harrow	1903
Wembley Park to Stanmore	1932	Electrification to Hounslow, Ealing, Wimbledon, Richmond and East Ham	1905
Rickmansworth to Amersham/Chesham electrification	1960	Electrification to Barking	1908
		South Harrow to Uxbridge	1910
Waterloo and City		Barking to Upminster	1932
Waterloo to Bank	1898		
East London Railway*		*Great Northern and City Railway*	
Whitechapel to New Cross	1884	Finsbury Park to Moorgate	1904
Shoreditch to New Cross electrification	1913		
Northern Line (City and South London Railway)		*Northern Line (Hampstead Line)*	
Stockwell to King William Street	1890	Charing Cross to Golders Green with branch fron Camden Town to Archway	1907
Moorgate to Clapham Common	1900	Charing Cross to Embankment	1914
Moorgate to Angel	1901	Golders Green to Hendon	1923
Angel to Euston	1907	Hendon to Edgware	1924
Euston to Camden Town	1924	Embankment to Kennington	1926
Clapham Common to Morden	1926	Archway to High Barnet	1940
		Finchley Central to Mill Hill East	1941
Bakerloo Line		*Central Line*	
Baker Street to Elelphant and Castle	1906	Shepherd's Bush to Bank	1900
Baker Street to Marylebone and Edgware Road	1907	Shepherd's Bush to Wood Lane	1908
Edgware Road to Paddington	1913	Bank to Liverpool Street	1912
Paddington to Willesden Junction	1915	Wood Lane to Ealing Broadway	1920
Willesden Junction to Watford Junction	1917	Liverpool Street to Stratford	1946
Baker Street to Stanmore	1939	Stratford to Leytonstone	1947
Piccadilly Line		North Acton to West Ruislip	1947
Hammersmith to Finsbury Park	1906	Leytonstone to Woodford (direct)	1947
Holborn to Aldwych	1907	Leytonstone to Newbury park	1947
Hammersmith to South Harrow	1932	*Victoria Line*	

Railway company/Route	Year opened	Railway company/ Route	Year opened
Finsbury Park to Arnos Grove	1932	Walthamstow to Victoria	1968
Acton Town to Hounslow West	1933	Victoria to Brixton	1971
Arnos Grove to Cockfosters	1933	*Jubilee Line*	
South Harrow to Uxbridge	1933	Baker Street to Charing Cross	1979
Hounslow West to Heathrow	1977	Green Park to Stratford	1999

Note: * originally built as steam operated railways.

Sources: D.F. Croome, A. Jackson, *Rails Through the Clay: A History of London's Tube Railways*, Harrow Weald, Capital Transport, 1993. J. Glover, *London's Underground*, London, Ian Allan, 1991. A. Jackson, *Semi-Detached London*, Didcot, Wild Swan, 1991.

Appendix 2: Southern Railway Company*/BR Southern Region electrification: 1900–1994

Route	Year opened for electric services
London Bridge - Victoria **	1909
Victoria - Crystal Palace **	1911
Waterloo - Wimbledon	1915
Waterloo - Kingston - Waterloo Loop	1916
Waterloo - Shepperton	1916
Waterloo - Hounslow Loop	1916
Waterloo - Hampton Court	1916
Victoria/Holborn Viaduct-Orpington via Herne Hill/Shortlands	1925
Victoria/Holborn Viaduct-Catford Loop/Crystal Palace	1925
Waterloo-Guildford/Dorking South	1925
London Bridge/Victoria-Extensions to Coulsdon North/Sutton via Selhurst	1925
Charing Cross layout major works	1925
Cannon Street major works (temp. closure)	1926
All AC converted to DC	1929
Hounslow/Feltham-Windsor	1930
Wimbledon-West Croydon	1930
Dartford-Gravesend Central	1930
London-Brighton/Worthing	1933
London-Eastbourne/Hastings via Lewes	1935
Bickley/Orpington-Sevenoaks	1935
Waterloo-Portsmouth via Guildford	1937
Woking-Alton	1937
Staines-Weybridge	1937
London Bridge/Victoria-Portsmouth via Horsham	1937
Three Bridges-Horsham	1938
West Worthing-Ford (Sussex)	1938
Littlehampton-Bognor Regis Branches	1938

Route	Year opened for electric services
Motspur Park-Leatherhead via Chessington	1938
Sevenoaks-Hastings/Bexhill	1939
Strood-Maidstone	1939
Gravesend/Swanley-Gillingham	1939
Aldershot-Guildford	1939
Ascot-Aldershot	1939
Staines-Reading	1939
Gillingham-Ramsgate/Dover (Kent Coast electrification)	1959
Maidstone-Ashford (Kent Coast electrification)	1961
Sevenoaks-Ashford-Folkestone-Dover-Deal-Ramsgate (Kent Coast electrification)	1962
Woking-Bournemouth	1967
Ryde-Shanklin	1967
Tonbridge-Hastings	1986
Sanderstead-East Grinstead	1987
Branksome-Weymouth	1988
Portsmouth-Southampton-Eastleigh	1990

Notes:* and corporate predecessors; ** Originally electrified with the AC overhead catenary system, later converted to the Southern Railway third rail system.

Sources: Moody 1979; Thrower 1998.

Appendix 3: British railways electrification: summary

A: Suburban electrification outside the Southern Railway/BR Southern Region: 1900–2000

Route*	Date of opening of electric services
Seaforth-Dingle (Liverpool Overhead Railway)	1893
Liverpool-Birkenhead (Mersey Railway)	1903
Liverpool-Southport	1904
Newcastle-Tynemouth	1904
Manchester-Bury	1916
Richmond-Broad Street (North London Railway)	1916
Bury-Holcombe Brook (closed 1951)	1918
Euston/Broad Street-Watford	1922
Lancaster-Morecambe/Heysham (experimental system)	
Manchester-Altrincham	1931
Birkenhead-West Kirby/New Brighton	1938
Liverpool Street-Shenfield	1949
Manchester London Rd.-Glossop/Hadfield	1954
Shenfield-Southend	1956
Seaforth-Dingle (Liverpool Overhead Railway) demolished	1956
Liverpool Street-Hertford East/Chingford/Enfield Town/Cheshunt	1960
Glasgow Queen Street-Helensburgh/Balloch/Milngavie	1960
Glasgow Queen Street-Bridgeton/Airdrie	1960
Fenchurch Street-Southend	1961
Glasgow Central-Cathcart/Paisley	1962
South Tyneside de-electrifed	1963
Paisley-Gourock/Wemyss Bay	1967
North Tyneside de-electrified	1967
Lea Valley-Cheshunt	1969
Kings Cross/Moorgate-Welwyn/Hertford North	1976
Hertford/Welwyn-Hitchin/Royston	1977
Liverpool-Kirkby	1977
Liverpool-Garston	1977
Rutherglen-Central-Partick (Glasgow Argyle Line)	1979
Liverpool Street-Gidea Park	1980
Stockport-Hazel Grove	1981
St Pancras-Bedford	1982
Garston-Hunts Cross (Liverpool)	1983
Wickford-Southminster	1986
Ayrshire to Ardrossan/Largs	1987
Thameslink	1990
Hooton-Chester/Ellesmere Port	1993
Leeds-Bradford/Skipton/Ilkley	1995
Paddington-Heathrow	1998

Note: * all routes electrified before 1950, except the Lancaster-Morecambe/Heysham scheme used DC current: most were subsequently converted to AC.
Sources: Creer 1986; Glover 1985, 1987; Heaps 1988; Thrower 1998.

B: Main line electrification outside the Southern Railway/BR Southern Region: 1900–2008

Route*	Date of opening of electric services
Wath/Sheffield-Manchester (DC system)	1952
Shenfield-Colchester-Clacton/Walton	1959
Crewe-Manchester (WCML)	1960
Crewe-Liverpool (WCML)	1962
Euston-Crewe WCML-Trent Valley)	1966
Rugby-Birmingham (WCML)	1967
Crewe-Glasgow (WCML)	1973
Wath/Sheffield-Manchester-closed	1981
Great Eastern to Cambridge	1987
Ipswich-Norwich	1987
King's Cross-Leeds (ECML)	1988
King's Cross-York-Newcastle-Edinburgh/Glasgow *(ECML)	1991
Cambridge-King's Lynn	1991
Crewe-Kidsgrove (infill to provide diversionary route)	2003

Note:* via Carstairs to Glasgow Central.
Sources: Creer 1986; Glover 1985, 1987; Heaps 1988; Thrower 1998.

Appendix 4: The Control of Land Use: Cmd. 6537, Presented to Parliament by the Minister of Town and Country Planning and the Secretary of State for Scotland, 1944

Introduction.

1. Provision for the right use of land, in accordance with a considered policy, is an essential requirement of the Government's programme of post-war reconstruction. New houses, whether of permanent or emergency construction; the new lay-out of areas devastated by enemy action or blighted by reason of age or bad living conditions; the new schools which will be required under the Education Bill now before Parliament and under the Scottish Education Bill which it is hoped to introduce later this Session; the balanced distribution of industry which the Government's recently published proposals for maintaining active employment envisage; the requirements of sound nutrition and of a healthy and well-balanced agriculture; the preservation of land for national parks and forests, and the assurance to people of enjoyment of the sea and countryside in times of leisure; a new and safer highway system better adapted to modern industrial and other needs; the proper provision of air-fields – all these related parts of a single reconstruction programme involve the use of land, and it is essential that their various claims on land should be so harmonised as to ensure for the people of this country the greatest possible measure of individual well-being and national prosperity.

Source: Crown copyright.

Appendix 5: The Railway Network Summary Statistics: 1838–2007

	Length of British Rail Route			British Railways			British Railways		London Underground	
	length of route (kilometres)	open to passenger traffic (kilometres)	length (% of total) electrified	passenger journeys (million)	passenger kilometres (billion)	no. of stations	goods lifted (million tonnes)	goods moved (billion tonne kilometres)	passenger journeys (million)	passenger kilometres (billion)
1838										
1848	3582									
1858										
1868	13,565			322			169			
1878	15,563			596			236			
1888	17,281			796			304			
1898	29,783			1114			427			
1908	30,000			1265			522			
1918	32,420			2,064						
1928	32,565			1,250						
1938	32,081			1,237	30.6		270	16	492	
1948	31,593	23,621	1455 (4.6)	1,024	37.0		277		720	5.4
1958	30,333	15,242	1622 (5.3)	1,090	35.6	4300*	247	30	692	5.3
1968	20,080	14,396	3182 (15.8)	831	28.7		211	23	655	4.7
1978	17,901	14,309	3716 (20.8)	724	30.0	2356	171	20	568	4.5
1988	16,599	14,359	4376 (26.4)	822	34.3	2418	150	18	815	6.3
1994	16,542	14,359	4970 (30.0)	735	31.7	2493	97	13	764	5.8
1998	16,659	15,038	5166 (31.0)	892	36.3	2,499	102	17	866	6.7
2007	15,795	14,353	5250 (33.0)	1,164	46.5	2,520	(2006) 108	(2006) 22	1040	7.7

Sources: DfT, Transport Statistics Great Britain 2007.

There are some breaks in the series: see DfT sources for details.

Data for 1838–1898 rounded from various secondary sources based on Railway Returns.

Appendix 6: Select Committee on Nationalised Industries, Report on British Railways, 1960, p xciii

'What size and shape should British Railways be? The first consideration must be financial; the size and shape must be such as can enable the Commission to carry out their statutory task of balancing their accounts, taking one year with another. But if the Commission are to know which of their services are justifiable on grounds of direct financial return, they must first have some form of accounts by which the profitability of Regions and services can be judged.

However, the consideration of direct profitability is not the only one which applies in this case. Because of the cost of the roads, and of the congestion on them, the national interest may require railway services which do not in fact directly pay for themselves, but which may cost the nation less than the alternatives.

In some cases, there may be a third and different consideration – one of social need. A service may be justified on other than economic grounds, because for example the less populous parts of Britain might otherwise be left without a railway service. Account may, in other words, need to be taken of social considerations.

The consideration of profitability, mentioned above, should be left to the Commission. But if decisions are to be taken on grounds of the national economy or of social needs, then they must be taken by the Minister, and submitted by him for the approval of Parliament.

Furthermore, if Parliament is to specify that certain services should be undertaken, despite the fact that the Commission cannot profitably undertake them, then the additional cost of them should be provided, in advance, out of public funds.

If subsidies of this kind are to be paid to the Commission, then they should be paid for specific purposes, and they should be paid openly. They should not be disguised as, for instance, a payment of the track costs (which are an integral part of railway operations), nor as the writing-off of the burden of interest; and they should not be hidden away in the Commission's accounts.

The need for clarity in the accounts is important. Your Committee have suggested, at various points in this Report, that payments should be made to the Commission of appropriate sums from public funds. Provided that these payments relate to specific services dictated by the Minister, or are compensation for specific losses incurred by his actions, the Commission would be able to publish accounts for British Railways which would reflect only the matters within their control.

If this were done, there would be one important consequential advantage that both the Commission and the Minister would become much more clearly accountable to Parliament for their separate railway responsibilities.'

Source: Crown copyright.

Appendix 7: New towns and the railway network: 1945–94

Conurbation/new towns	date of designation	target population 1000s	revised target population 1000s	distance from conurbation centre miles	station prior to designation?	station present in 1994?
Greater London						
Stevenage	1946	60	80	30	yes	yes, relocated to town centre 1973
Crawley	1947	50	85	30	yes	yes
Hemel Hempstead	1947	80	85	25	yes	yes
Harlow	1947	60	80	25	yes	yes (two) new station opened 1960
Hatfield	1948	29	29	20	yes	yes
Welwyn Garden City	1948	36	50	22	yes	yes
Basildon	1949	50	130	25	no	yes, opened 1974
Bracknell	1949	25	60	28	yes	yes
Milton Keynes	1967	250	200	45	yes, Bletchley, Wolverton	yes (three) + MK Central opened 1982
Peterborough	1967	190	150	72	yes	yes
Northampton	1968	300	180	66	yes	yes
Birmingham						
Telford	1963	90	150	30	yes, Wellington	yes (two) + Telford Central 1986
Redditch	1964	90	84	14	yes	yes, relocation 1972
Merseyside						
Skelmersdale	1961	80	61	13	already closed (three)	no
Runcorn	1964	100	95	14	yes	yes (two) + Runcorn East 1983

Conurbation/new towns	date of designation	target population 1000s	revised target population 1000s	distance from conurbation centre miles	station prior to designation?	station present in 1994?
Greater Manchester						
Warrington	1968	200	170	18	yes (two)	yes (three) + Birchwood 1980
Central Lancashire	1970	430	285	30	yes	yes
Tyneside						
Washington	1964	80	80	6	yes	no (1963)
Glasgow						
East Kilbride	1947	100	90	9	yes	yes
Cumbernauld	1955	50	70	15	yes	yes (two)+ Greenfaulds 1989
Livingston	1962	100	90	29	yes	yes
Development Areas						
Newton Aycliffe	1947	10	45	n/a	yes, but closed by 1956	yes, re-opened 1978
Peterlee	1948	30	30	n/a	no	no
Glenrothes	1948	95	70	n/a	no	yes – Thornton 1992
Cwmbran	1949	55	55	n/a	yes	yes, new station 1986
Irvine	1966	90	85	25	yes	yes
Newtown	1967	11	13	n/a	yes	yes
Other						
Corby	1950	40	70	80	yes, closed 1966	no – second closure 1990

Sources: Schaffer (1970), Dupree (1987), Hurst (1992), British Transport Commission (1956b), RDS (1998).

Appendix 8: Town expansion and the railway network: 1951–94

	Population 1961	Distance from conurbation centre miles	Station at designation?	Station in 1994? (date of closure/opening)
Greater London				
Andover B	16,985	66	yes	yes
Ashford UD	27,996	54	yes	yes
Aylesbury B	27,923	40	yes	yes
Banbury B	21,004	72	yes – two	yes – one
Basingstoke B	25,980	47	yes	yes
Bletchley UD	17,095	47	yes	yes
Bodmin B	6,214	234	yes, General, North & Bodmin Road	yes, one Bodmin Road (Parkway –1967)
Braintree and Bocking UD	20,600	43	yes	no
Burnley CB	80,559	205	yes – three	yes, two – Manchester Road reopened (1986)
Bury St Edmunds B	21,179	75	yes	yes
Canvey Island UD	15,605	38	yes (Benfleet)	yes
Frimley and Camberley UD	28,552	30	yes	yes
Gainsborough UD	17,278	148	yes	yes
Grantham B	25,048	110	yes	yes
Haverhill UD	5,445	56	yes	no (1962)
Huntingdon and Godmanchester B	8,821	62	yes, one at each	yes (not Godmanchester)
Kings Lynn B	27,536	98	yes	yes
Letchworth UD	25,511	37	yes	yes
Luton CB	131,583	32	yes	yes

Luton RD	36,462	32		
Melford RD	13,317	60		
Mildenhall RD	20,458	71	yes	no (1962)
Peterborough B	62,340	81	yes	yes
Plymouth CB	204,409	211	yes	yes
St Neots UD	5,554	57	yes	yes
Sandy UD	3,963	49	yes	yes
Sudbury B	6,642	58	yes	yes
Swindon B	91,739	79	yes	yes
Thetford B	35,399	82	yes	yes
Wellingborough UD	30,583	68	yes	yes
Witham UD	9,459	40	yes	yes

Appendix 8 (continued)

	Population 1961	Distance from conurbation centre miles	Station at designation?	Station in 1994? (date of closure/opening)
English provincial cities				
Birmingham				
Aldridge-Brownhills	77,440	13	Yes – two	No (1962)
Banbury B	21,004	41	Yes one (one closure 1951)	Yes
Cannock UD	42,191	17	Yes	Yes – re-opened (1989)
Daventry B	5,860	37	Yes	No (1958)
Droitwich B	7,976	20	Yes	Yes
Leek UD	19,182	50	Yes	No (1956)
Lichfield B	14,087	16	Yes – two	Yes – two
Lichfield RD	39,935	16		
Rugeley UD	13,017	25	Yes – two	Yes – two
Stafford B	47,806	27	Yes	Yes
Stafford RD	17,930	27		
Tamworth B	13,646	15	Yes – two	Yes – two
Tutbury RD	17,597	33	Yes	Yes
Uttoxeter UD	8,185	34	Yes	Yes
Weston-super-Mare B	43,938	108	Yes	Yes

Walsall				
Aldridge UD	77,440	4	Yes	No (1962)
Brownhills UD		6	Yes	No (1962)

Wolverhampton				
Cannock RD	42,191	8	Yes (1965)	Re-opened 1989
Selsdon RD	36,981	5	?	?

Tettenhall UD	14,867	3	No	No
Wednesfield UD	33,048	3	No	No
Liverpool				
Burnley CB	80,559	51	Yes – three	Yes – see below
Ellesmere Port B	44,681	10	Yes	Yes
Widnes B	52,186	13	Yes	Yes
Winsford UD	12,760	33	Yes	Yes
Manchester				
Burnley CB	80,559	24	Yes – three	Yes – two – Manchester Road re-opened 1986
Crewe B	53,195	34	Yes	Yes
Macclesfield B	37,644	18	Yes	Yes
Winsford UD	12,760	28	Yes	Yes
Salford				
Worsley UD	40,393	3	Yes	No
Bristol				
Keynsham	15,152	5	Yes	Yes
Sodbury RD	44,884	12	Yes	No
Thornbury RD	30,679	13	Yes	No
Warmley RD	19,406	6	Yes	No
Newcastle				
Seaton Valley UD (Cramlington)	26,095	9	Yes	Yes
Longbenton UD (Killingworth)	46,530	5	Yes (1978)	Metro (1980)

Appendix 8 (continued)

	Date of agreement	Station at designation?	Station in 1994? (date of closure/opening)
Scotland			
Glasgow			
Alloa	1959	Yes	No (1968)
Alva	1963	No (1954)	No
Arbroath	1959	Yes	Yes
Barrhead	1963	Yes	Yes
Bathgate	1963	No (1956)	Yes (1986)
Bonnyrigg & Lasswade	1961	Yes	No (1962)
Denny & Dunipace	1960	No	No
Dumbarton	1963	Yes (two)	Yes (two)
Dumfries	1962	Yes	Yes
Dunbar	1961	Yes	Yes
Dumbarton County	1964	n/a	n/a
Forfar	1959	Yes	No (1967)
Fort William	1962	Yes	Yes
Galashiels	1960	Yes	No (1969-bus)
Galston	1961	Yes	No (1964)
Girvan	1959	Yes	Yes
Grangemouth	1958	Yes	No (1968)
Haddington	1958	No (1949)	No
Hamilton	1958	Yes (three)	Yes (three)
Hawick	1963	Yes	No (1969-bus)

Invergordon	1961	Yes	Yes
Inverkeithling	1962	Yes	Yes
Inverness County	1963	Yes	Yes
Irvine	1959	Yes	Yes
Jedburgh	1962	No (1948)	No
Johnstone	1965	Yes	Yes
Kelso	1963	Yes	No (1964)
Kilsyth	1967	No (1951)	No
Kirkintilloch	1961	Yes	No
Maybole	1967	Yes	Yes
Midlothian	1961	n/a	n/a
Newmilns & Greenholm	1963	Yes	No (1964)
Peebles	1961	No (1950)	No (bus)
Peebles County	1965	n/a	n/a
Renfrew County	1967	n/a	n/a
Selkirk	1962	No (1951)	No (bus)
Stevenston	1961	Yes	Yes
Stewarton	1960	Yes	Yes
Sutherland County	1960	n/a	n/a
West Lothian	1960	n/a	n/a
Whitburn (Durham)	1960	No (1953)	No
Wick	1961	Yes	Yes

Sources: BTC, 1956; Hall, 1973; Daniels and Dench, 1980; Hurst, 1992; British Rail National Timetable 1994; Jowett, 2000.

Appendix 9: The role of rail in a national project: the third London airport

Rail planning played an important role in the debate around the choice of a site for London's third airport: this had begun almost as soon as the decision had been made in 1954 to locate the second airport at Gatwick, and eventually a Royal Commission was appointed in 1968 to explore four options and recommend a preferred site. It was taken for granted that rail access would be provided to the airport and Table 7.2 shows that, although the distance from London of the options ranged from 35 to 58 miles, the difference in travelling time between the longest and shortest journeys was only 14 minutes: King's Cross was to be the London terminal in all cases. The Roskill Commission came down in favour of Cublington but Buchanan, in his Note of Dissent, favoured Foulness. This was because he could not countenance intrusive airport development in what he called, using Abercrombie's term, 'London's open background' (Roskill, 1971, 150). Although Foulness was 8 miles further away from London than Cublington, the estimated travelling time was only 5 minutes longer because it was expected that a new railway would be built to it (Roskill, 1971, fig. 10.9): this was the most expansive rail project to be countenanced since the war and was indicative of the new mood.

Table xx Rail access to the Third London Airport

	Cublington			Foulness			Nuthampstead			Thurleigh		
	High* time value	Low time value		High time value	Low time value		High time value	Low time value		High time value	Low time value	
Distance from London (miles)			48			56			35			58
Travel time form London (mins)			39			44			32			46
% surface access by rail	53	51		55	50		56	54		58	56	

Note: * Different assumptions were made as to the value of the time spent travelling by various groups of passengers.
Source: Roskill, 1971, appendix 19.

Appendix 10: Rail freight services and power stations: 1970–2005

Power Station	Approximate capacity in Megawatts	Location	Mgr* discharge by late 1970s	Mgr in operation 2005	Fitted with FGD** equipment
Aberthaw 'B'	1500	Vale of Glamorgan, coastal	Yes	Yes	
Blyth	1000	Northumberland coast	Yes	No	
Castle Donington	n/a	Trent Valley	Yes	closed	
Cockenzie	1200	Firth of Forth	Yes	Yes	
Cottam	2000	Trent Valley	Yes	Yes	
Didcot	2000	Thames Valley	Yes	Yes	
Drakelow 'C'	1000	Trent Valley	Yes	closed	
Drax	4000	Aire Valley	Yes	Yes	Yes
Eggborough	2000	Aire Valley	Yes	Yes	Yes
Ferrybridge 'C'	2000	Aire Valley	Yes	Yes	Yes
Fiddlers Ferry	2000	Mersey Valley	Yes	Yes	Yes
High Marnham	1000	Trent Valley	Yes	closed	
Ironbridge 'B'	1000	Severn Valley	Yes	Yes	
Longannet	2400		Yes	Yes	Yes
Ratcliffe	2000	Trent Valley	Yes	Yes	Yes
Rugeley 'B'	1000	Trent Valley	Yes	Yes	Yes
Staythorpe	n/a	Trent Valley	Yes	closed	
Thorpe Marsh	1000	Don Valley, Doncaster	Yes	closed	
Uskmouth	1500		No	Yes	Yes
West Burton	2000	Trent Valley	Yes	Yes	Yes
Willington	n/a	Trent Valley	Yes	closed	

Notes: * Mgr: Merry go round; **Flue Gas Desulphurisation.

Source: Shannon, 2006.

References

Abbott, J. (1992), 'Regional Railways North East', *Modern Railways*, Vol. 49, No. 529, 544-550.

Abbott, J. (2008), 'Javelins Will Be a Shot in the Arm for Kent', *Modern Railways*, Vol. 65, No. 714, 32-38.

Abercrombie, P. (1923), 'Regional Planning', *Town Planning Review*, Vol. 10, No. 2, 109-118.

Abercrombie, P. (1944a), *Town and Country Planning* (London, Oxford University Press) (first printed 1933).

Abercrombie, P. (1944b), *Greater London Plan* (London, HMSO).

Abercrombie, P. and Johnson, T.H. (1923), *The Doncaster Regional Planning Scheme* (Liverpool, University Press / London, Hodder and Stoughton).

Abercrombie, P. and Mathew, R.H. (1946), *Clyde Valley Regional Plan* (Edinburgh, HMSO).

Acworth, W.M. (1912), *The State in Relation to Railways in England* (London, Royal Economic Society).

Adley, R. (1988), *Covering My Tracks* (London, Guild Publishing).

Aldcroft, D.H. (1968), *British Railways in Transition: the Economic Problems of Britain's Railways Since 1914* (London, Macmillan).

Aldcroft, D.H. (1975), *British Transport Since 1914: An Economic History* (London, David and Charles).

Aldous, T. (1975), *Goodbye Britain* (London, Sidgwick and Jackson Ltd).

Alderman, G. (1973), *The Railway Interest* (Leicester, Leicester University Press).

Allen, C.J. (1941), 'The Development of High Speed Passenger Services on the Railways of the United States', *Journal of the Institute of Transport*, Vol. 21, No. 7, 215-220.

Allen, G.F. (1966), *British Railways After Beeching* (London, Ian Allan).

Ambrose, P. (1986), *Whatever Happened to Planning* (London, Methuen).

Anderson, P. (1996), *An Illustrated History of Liverpool's Railways* (Caernafon, Irwell Press).

Architect's Journal (1986), *Covering BR's Tracks*, Architect's Journal, Vol. 183, No. 11, 20-23.

Armitage, A. (1980), *Report of the Inquiry into Lorries, People and the Environment* (London, HMSO).

Ashworth, W. (1954), *The Genesis of Modern British Town Planning* (London, Routledge and Kegan Paul).

Association of Community Rail Partnerships (2008), *The Value of Community Rail Partnerships* (Slaithwaite, Huddersfield, AcoRP).

Audit Commission (1989), *Urban Regeneration and Economic Development: The Local Government Dimension* (London, HMSO).

BBC 2006, http://news.bbc.co.uk/1/hi/uk_politics/5186196.stm, last visited 28/11/08.

Bain, S. (1986), *Railroaded: Battle for Woodhead Pass* (London, Faber and Faber).

Bagwell, P.S. (1968), *The Railway Clearing House in the British Economy 1842 – 1922* (London, George Allan & Unwin Ltd).

Bagwell, P.S. (1984), *End of the Line? The Fate of Public Transport Under Thatcher* (London, Verso).

Banister, D. (2002), *Transport Planning – 2nd edition* (London, Spon/Routledge).

Barker, T.C. and Robbins, M. (1963), *A History of London Transport Vol One* (London, George Allan & Unwin).

Barker, T.C. and Robbins, M. (1976), *A History of London Transport Volume Two - The Twentieth Century to 1970* (London, George Allan & Unwin).

Barman, C. (1947), *Next Station*, London (Allan & Unwin).

Barman, C. (1979), *The Man Who Built London Transport: A Biography of Frank Pick* (Newton Abbott, David and Charles).

Batchelor, A. and Patterson, A. (2007), 'Political modernisation and the weakening of sustainable development in Britain', Chapter 7, 192-213 in Krueger, R. and Gibbs, D. (eds), *The Sustainable Development Paradox: Urban Political Economy in the United States and Europe* (New York, Guilford Press).

Batty, E. and Haywood, R. (2002), *Planning for Passenger Growth: Station Policy Research for the Strategic Rail Authority* (Sheffield, Centre for Regional Economic and Social Research, Sheffield Hallam University).

Batty, E., Haywood, R. and Kevill, P. (2002), *Transport Barriers to Employment in Barnsley: A Case Study of Athersley and New Lodge* (Sheffield, Centre for Regional Economic and Social Research, Sheffield Hallam University).

Batty, E., Beecham, P., Fawcett, P., Haywood, R., Kevill, P. and Solomon, J. (2005), *Transport Solutions: The Benefits of Providing Transport to Address Social Exclusion in Rural Areas* (London, Countryside Agency).

Beatty, C. and Haywood, R. (1997), 'Changes in Travel Behaviour in the English Passenger Transport Executive's areas 1981-91', *Journal of Transport Geography*, Vol. 5, No. 1, 61-72.

Beaver, S.H. (1937), 'The Railways of Great Cities', *Geography*, Vol. 22, 116-120.

Beesley, M.E. and Foster, C.D. (1965), 'Victoria Line, Social Benefits and Finances', *Journal of the Royal Statistical Society*, Series A, 67-88.

Bendixson, T. (1988), *The Peterborough Effect: Reshaping a City*, Peterborough (Peterborough Development Corporation).

Bendixson, T. and Platt, J. (1992), *Milton Keynes: Image and Reality* (Cambridge, Granta Editions).

Berkeley, T. (2008), 'Easing the Load', *Planning*, Issue 1764, 16-17.

Bertolini, L. (1999), 'Spatial Development Patterns and Public Transport: The Application of an Analytical Model in the Netherlands', *Planning Practice & Research*, Vol. 14, No. 2, 199-210.

Bertolini, L. and Spit, T. (1998), *Cities on Rails* (London, Spon).

Biddle, G. (1986), *Great Railway Stations of Britain* (Newton Abbot, David and Charles).

Biddle, G. (1990), *The Railway Surveyors* (London, Ian Allan Ltd).

Birmingham City Council (1963), *City Council Proceedings 1963-64* (Birmingham, Birmingham City Council).

Birmingham City Council (1992), *City Centre Strategy* (Birmingham, Birmingham City Council).

Birmingham City Council (1994), *Convention Centre Quarter: Planning and Urban Design Framework* (Birmingham, Birmingham City Council).

Black, E.C. (1969), *British Politics in the Nineteenth Century* (London, Harper and Row).

Blowers, A. (ed) (1993), *Planning for a Sustainable Environment* (London, Earthscan).

Bolden, T. and Harman, R. (2008), 'Railway and Spatial Strategies in the South East: Can Co-ordination and Delivery be Achieved?' *Planning Practice and Research*, Vol. 23, No. 3, 303-322.

Bolger, P. (1992), *The Dockers' Umbrella: A History of the Liverpool Overhead Railway* (Liverpool, The Bluecoat Press).

Bonavia, M.R. (1971), *The Organisation of British Railways* (London, Ian Allan).

Bonavia, M.R. (1980), *The Four Great Railways* (Newton Abbott, David & Charles).

Bonavia, M.R. (1981), *British Rail - the first 25 years* (Newton Abbott, David & Charles).

Bonavia, M.R. (1985), *Twilight of British Rail* (Newton Abbott, David & Charles).

Bonavia, M.R. (1987), *The History of the Southern Railway* (London, Unwin Hyman).

Bonavia, M.R. (1995), *The Cambridge Line* (London, Ian Allan).

Booth, A.J. (1990), *A Railway History of Denaby and Cadeby Collieries* (Bridlington, Industrial Railway Society).

Booth, C. (1901), *Improved Means of Locomotion as a First Step towards the Cure of the Housing Difficulties of London* (London, Macmillan and Co).

Boynton, J. (1989), 'New life in the West Midlands', *Modern Railways*, Vol. 46, No. 495, 630-639.

Boynton, J. (1993), *Rails Across the City: The Story of the Birmingham Cross City Line* (Kidderminster, Mid-England Books).

Breheny, M. and Congdon P. (1989), *Growth and Change in a Core Region* (London, Pion).

Breheny, M.J. (ed) (1992), *Sustainable Development and Urban Form* (London, Pion).

Breheny, M., Gent, T. and Lock, D. (1993), *Alternative Development Patterns: New Settlements: DOE Planning Research Programme* (London, HMSO).

Breheny, M. and Rookwood, R. (1993), 'Planning the Sustainable City Region', in Blowers, A., *Planning for a Sustainable Environment* (London, Earthscan).

Bressey, Sir Charles, and Lutyens, Sir Edward (1937), *Highway Development Survey 1937 (Greater London)* (London, Ministry of Transport/HMSO).

Briggs, A. (1968), *Victorian Cities* (Harmondsworth, Penguin).

British Railways Board (various years 1963-94), *Annual Reports and Accounts* (London, BRB).

British Railways Board (1963), *The Reshaping of British Railways; Part 1: Report* (London, HMSO).

British Railways Board (1965), *The Development of the Major Trunk Routes* (London, British Railways Board).

British Railways Board (1981), *The Commuters Charter* (London, British Railways Board).

British Rail Community Unit, Network South East and Hampshire County Council (1993), *Railway Environments: A Partnership in Action* (London, British Rail Community Unit).

British Roads Federation (1987), *The Way Ahead* (London, British Roads Federation).

British Rail Property Board (1986), *Heritage and the Environment* (special edition of Property Board News) (London, BR Property Board).

British Transport Commission (various years 1948-62), *Annual Reports and Accounts* (London, BTC).

British Transport Commission (1951), *Passenger Transport in Glasgow and District: Report of the Glasgow and District Transport Committee* (Edinburgh, BTC).

British Transport Commission (1955), *Modernisation and Re-Equipment of British Railways* (London, British Transport Commission).

British Transport Commission (1956), *Official Handbook of Stations* (London, BTC (Railway Clearing House)).

Brownhill, S. (1990), *Developing London's Docklands: Another Great Planning Disaster?* (London, Paul Chapman).

Browning Hall Conferences on Housing and Locomotion (1902), *Report of the Sub-Committee on Locomotion* (London, Macmillan and Co).

Bruce, R. (1945), *First Report to the Highways and Planning Committee of the Corporation of the City of Glasgow: March 1945* (Glasgow, Corporation of the City of Glasgow).

Bruce, J.G. and Croome, D.F. (1996), *The Twopenny Tube: the Story of the Central Line* (London, Capital Transport).

Buchanan, C. (1958), *Mixed Blessing: The Motor in Britain* (London, Leonard Hill).

Buchanan, C. et al (1963), *Traffic in Towns* (London, HMSO).

Burgess, E. W. (1925), *The Growth of the City,* 47-62 in Park, R. E., Burgess, E. W. and McKenzie, R. (eds), *The City: Suggestions for Investigation of Human Behavior in the Urban Environment* (Chicago, University of Chicago Press).

Butler, B. (1980), *The Dream Fulfilled: Basingstoke Town Development 1961-78* (Basingstoke, Basingstoke Borough Council).

Byers, S. (Secretary of State for Transport, Local Government and the Regions) (2001), *Planning: Delivering a Fundamental Change,* (the Planning Green Paper) (London, Department for Transport, Local Government and the Regions).

Calthorpe, P. (1993), *The Next Amercian Metropolis: Ecology, Community and the American Dream* (Princeton, Princeton Architectural Press).

Calvert, R. (1965), *The Future of Britain's Railways* (London, George Allan & Unwin).

Cambridge Traffic Planning and Liaison Select Panel (1990), *A Transport Strategy for Cambridge* (Cambridge, Cambridge County Council).

Cambridgeshire County Council (1989), *Cambridgeshire County Structure Plan* (Cambridge, Cambridgeshire County Council).

Cameron, M.A. (1953), 'Transport Users' Consultative Committees', Journal of the Institute of Transport, Vol. 26, No. 2, 54-58.

Carmona, M. (2002), *Haussman: His Life and Times, and the Making of Modern Paris* (Chicago, IR Dee).

Carson, R. (1962), *Silent Spring* (Harmondsworth, Penguin).

Central Statistical Office (1994), *Economic Trends* (London, HMSO).

Cervero, R. (1984a), 'Managing the Traffic Impacts of Suburban Office Growth', *Transportation Quarterly*, Vol. 38, No. 4, 533-550.

Cervero, R. (1984b), 'Light Rail Transit and Urban Development'*, Journal of the American Association of Planners*, Vol. 50, No. 2, 133-147.

Cervero, R. (1986), *Suburban Gridlock* (Center for Urban Policy Research, Rutgers, the State University of New Jersey, USA).

Cervero, R. (1995), 'Sustainable New Towns: Stockholm's Rail Served Satellites', *Cities*, Vol. 12, No. 1, 41-51.

Cherry, G.E. (1974), *The Evolution of British Town Planning* (London, Leonard Hill Books).

Cherry, G.E. (ed) (1981), *Pioneers in British Planning* (London, Architectural Press).

Cherry, G.E. (1988), *Cities and Plans: The Shaping of Urban Britain in the Nineteenth and Twentieth Centuries* (London, Edward Arnold).

Cherry, G.E. (1994), *Birmingham: A Study in Geography, History and Planning* (Chichester, John Wiley and Sons).

Chisholm, M. and Kivell, P. (1987), *Inner City Waste Land: Hobart Paper 108* (London, Institute of Economic Affairs).

Chorley, P. and Haggett, P. (1965), *Locational Analysis in Human Geography* (London, Arnold).

Chorley, P. and Haggett, P. (1967), *Models in Geography* (London, Methuen).

Church, A. (1990), 'Transport and Regeneration in London Docklands: A Victim of Success or a Failure to Plan?' *Cities*, November, 289-303.

City of Birmingham (1960), *City of Birmingham Development Plan: Statement and Maps* (Birmingham, City of Birmingham).

City of Birmingham Council, West Midlands County Council and West Midlands Passenger Transport Executive (1984), *Birmingham Central Area Local Plan: Written Statement* (Birmingham, City of Birmingham Council).

City of Glasgow (1951), *Glasgow Development Plan: Draft* (Glasgow, Corporation of the City of Glasgow).

City of Glasgow (1960), *Glasgow Development Plan: Quinquennial Review Survey Report* (Glasgow, Corporation of the City of Glasgow).

City of Glasgow District Council (1986), *GEAR Local Plan: Summary Written Statement* (Glasgow, City of Glasgow District Council).

City of Glasgow District Council Planning Department (1992), *The Renewal of the Merchant City* (Glasgow, City of Glasgow District Council Planning Department).

City of Liverpool et al (1969), *Merseyside Area Land Use/Transportation Study* (Liverpool, City of Liverpool et al).

City of Manchester (1961), *Manchester Development Plan: Written Statement* (Manchester, Manchester City Council).

City of Newcastle upon Tyne Planning Department (1986), *City Planning '86: Background Papers* (Newcastle, City of Newcastle upon Tyne).

Clark, C. (1958), 'Transport – Maker and Breaker of Cities', *Town Planning Review*, Vol. 28, No. 4, 237-250.

Clarke, J. (1993), *Pre-requisites for a Successful Rail Freight Industry*, paper presented at conference, 'Privatising British Railfreight', Marriott Hotel, London, 20th January 1993, The Waterfront Partnership.

Clinnick, R. (2008a), 'Yorkshire forward!' *Rail*, No. 589, April 9-22, 35-39.

Clinnick, R. (2008b), 'Devon County Council to buy Tavistock trackbed', *Rail*, No. 603, October 22- November 4, 22.

Coates, K. and Silburn, R. (1970), *Poverty: The Forgotten Englishmen* (Harmondsworth, Penguin).

Coburn, T.M., Beesley, M.E. and Reynolds, D.J. (1960), *The London-Birmingham Motorway: Traffic and Economics*, Road Research Laboratory Technical Paper No. 46.

Coleman, T. (1981), *The Railway Navvies* (London, Penguin).

Colin Buchanan and Partners (1974), *West Central Scotland: A Programme of Action: Consultative Draft Report* (Glasgow, Colin Buchanan and Partners).

Collins, M.J. (1991), *Freightliner* (Sparkford near Yeovil, Haynes Publishing Group).

Cook, E.T. and Wedderburn, A. (eds) (1996), *The Works of John Ruskin* (Cambridge, Cambridge University Press).

Cordner, K. (1990), 'St. Paul's Thameslink', *Modern Railways*, Vol. 47, No. 497, 73-76.

Cornell, J. (1993), 'The Structure of Regional Railways', 207-218 in Institution of Civil Engineers, *Modern Railway Transportation: Conference Papers* (London, ICE, May 25-27).

Corporation of the City of Glasgow (1960), *The City of Glasgow Development Plan, Quinquennial Review: Written Statement* (Glasgow, Corporation of the City of Glasgow).

Corporation of London (1986), *City of London Local Plan: Deposit Version* (London, Corporation of London).

Council for the Protection of Rural England (1992), *Where Motor Car is Master* (London, CPRE).

Countryside Agency (2001), *Great Ways to go: Good practice in rural transport* (Cheltenham, The Countryside Agency).

Creer, S. (1986), *BR Diary 1948-1957* (London, Ian Allan Ltd).

Creese, W.L. (1967), *The Legacy of Raymond Unwin: A Human Pattern for Planning* (Massachusetts, MIT Press).

Croome, D.F. and Jackson, A.A. (1993), *Rails Through the Clay: A History of London's Tube Railways*, Second Edition (London, Capital Transport).

Cullingworth, J.B. and Nadin, V. (2006), *Town and Country Planning in the UK*, 14th edition (London, Routledge).

Cumbernauld Development Corporation (1958), *Cumbernauld New Town: Preliminary Planning Proposals* (Cumbernauld, Cumbernauld Development Corporation).

Damesick, P. (1979), 'Office Location and Planning in the Manchester Conurbation', *Town Planning Review*, Vol. 50, 346-366.

Daniels, G. and Dench, L. (1980), *Passengers No More*, 3rd edition (London, Ian Allan Ltd).

Daniels, P.W. (1977), 'Office Locations in the British Conurbations: Trends and Strategies', *Urban Studies*, Vol. 14, 261-274.

Daventry District Council (1993), *Daventry District Local Plan: Topic Paper 5: Proposed International Rail Freight Terminal Near to Junction 18 of the M1 Motorway at Crick* (Daventry, Daventry District Council).

Davies, J. and Clark, R., 1996, *Valley Lines: the People's Railway* (Sheffield, Platform 5).

Department for Communities and Local Government (2007), *Eco-towns Prospectus* (London, DCLG).

Department for Transport (2004a), *The Future of Transport: A Network for 2030*, Cm 6234 (London, TSO).

Department for Transport (2004b), *The Future of Rail*, Cm 6233 (London, TSO).

Department for Transport (2004c), *Full Guidance on Local Transport Plans: Second Edition* (London, TSO).

Department for Transport (2007a), *Delivering a Sustainable Railway*, Cm 7176 (London, TSO).

Department for Transport (2007b), *Towards a Sustainable Transport System: Supporting Economic Growth in a Low carbon World*, Cm 7226 (London, TSO).

Department for Transport (2007c), *Guidance on Transport Assessment* (London, TSO).

Department for Transport (2008), *Rolling Stock Plan* (London, TSO).

Department of the Environment (1972), *Town and Country Planning (Use Classes) Order 1972* (London, HMSO).

Department of the Environment (1973), *Circular 82: Bus Operation in Residential and Industrial Areas* (London, HMSO).

Department of the Environment (1977), *Design Bulletin 32: Residential Roads and Footpaths, Layout Considerations* (London, HMSO).

Department of the Environment (1985), *Lifting the Burden (Cm.9571)* (London, HMSO).

Department of the Environment (1986), *Building Businesses Not Barriers* (London, HMSO).

Department of the Environment (1987), *Town and Country Planning (Use Classes) Order 1987* (London, HMSO).

Department of the Environment (1989), *Strategic Guidance for Greater Manchester, (Regional Policy Guidance Note 4)* (London, HMSO).

Department of the Environment (1990), *Survey of Derelict Land in England (1988)* (London, HMSO).

Department of the Environment (1991), *Minerals Policy Guidance 10: Provision of Raw Materials for the Cement Industry* (London, HMSO).

Department of the Environment (1991), *Rates of Urbanisation in England* (London, HMSO).

Department of the Environment (1992), *DB32 Second Edition Residential and Footpaths, Layout Considerations* (London, HMSO).

Department of the Environment (1993a), *Reducing Transport Emissions Through Planning* (London, HMSO).

Department of the Environment (1994a), *Sustainable Development: The UK Strategy (Cm. 2426)* (London, HMSO).

Department of the Environment (1994a), *Vital and Viable Town Centres: Meeting the Challenge* (London, HMSO).

Department of the Environment (1994b), *Quality in Town and Country* (London, HMSO).

Department of the Environment (1995), *Thames Gateway Planning Framework (RPG 9A)* (London, HMSO).

Department of the Environment (1996a), *Urban Trends in England* (London, HMSO).

Department of the Environment (1996b), *Planning Policy Guidance 6: Town Centres and Retail Developments (revised)* (London, HMSO).

Department of the Environment, Department of Transport (1977), *Design Bulletin 32: Residential roads and footpaths layout considerations* (London, HMSO).

Department of the Environment, Department of Transport (1994), *Transport (Planning Policy Guidance Note 13)* (London, HMSO).

Department of the Environment, Department of Transport (1995), *PPG13: A Guide to Better Practice* (London, HMSO).

Department of the Environment Transport and the Regions (1997), *Developing an Integrated Transport Policy: An Invitation to Contribute* (London, DETR).

Department of the Environment Transport and the Regions (1998), *A New Deal for Transport: Better for Everyone – The Government's White Paper on the Future for Transport* (London, DETR).

Department of the Environment Transport and Regions (1999), *Sustainable Distribution: A Strategy* (London, DETR).

Department for the Environment Transport and Regions (2000a), *Transport 2010: The 10 Year Plan* (London, DETR).

Department of the Environment Transport and the Regions (2000b), *Planning Policy Guidance Note No. 3: Housing* (London, DETR).

Department of the Environment Transport and the Regions (2000c), *Guidance on Full Local Transport Plans* (London, DETR).

Department of the Environment Transport and the Regions (2001), *Planning Policy Guidance Note No. 13* (London, DETR).

Department of Transport (1983), *Railway Finances: Report of a Committee Chaired by Sir David Serpell KCB CMG OBE* (London, HMSO).

Department of Transport (1989a), *National Road Traffic Forecasts (Great Britain) 1989* (London, HMSO).

Department of Transport (1989b), *Roads to Prosperity* (London, HMSO).

Department of Transport (1989c), *Circular 3/89: Section 56 Grant for Public Transport* (London, HMSO).

Department of Transport (1990), *Trunk Roads, England into the 1990's* (London, HMSO).

Department of Transport (1992), *New Opportunities for the Railways: The Privatisation of British Rail,* Cm 2012 (London, HMSO).

Department of Transport (1993), *Local Authority Circular 2/93: Transport Policies and programme Submissions for 1994-95* (London, HMSO).

Department of Transport, Scottish Development Department and Welsh Office (1977), *Transport Policy:Cmnd.6836* (London, HMSO).

Department of Transport, British Railways Board (1981), *Review of Main Line Electrification* (London, HMSO).

Department of Transport, British Rail Network South East, London Regional Transport and London Underground Limited (1989), *Central London Rail Study* (London, Department of Transport).

Dickinson, H.D. (1964), 'Is Public Transport a Social Service?', *New Society*, Vol. 12, March, 6-7.

Dickinson, R.E. (1972), *City and Region* (fifth impression) (London, Routledge and Kegan Paul Ltd).

Dittmar, H. and Ohland, G. (2004), *The New Transit Town: Best Practices in Transit-Oriented Development* (Washington DC, Island Press).

Docherty, I. and Shaw, J. (2003), *A New Deal for Transport?* (Oxford, Blackwell Publishing).

Docherty, I. and Shaw, J. (2008), *Traffic Jam: Ten Years of 'Sustainable' Transport in the UK* (Bristol, Policy Press).

Donnison, R. (1992), 'The Meadowhall Experience', Chapter 3, 19-26, in Swallow, K., *Passenger Transport: Putting it to Work: Conference Papers* (Welwyn Construction Industry Conference Centre Ltd).

Douthwaite, R. (1992), *The Growth Illusion* (Dublin, Resurgence).

Dupree, H. (1987), *Urban Transportation: The New Town Solution* (Aldershot, Gower).

Dyckhoff, N. (1999), *Portrait of the Cheshire Lines* (London, Ian Allan Publishing).

Dyos, H.J. (1973), *Victorian Suburb: A Study of the Growth of Camberwell* (Leicester, Leicester University Press).

Dyos, H.J. and Aldcroft, D.H. (1971), *British Transport: An Economic Survey from the Seventeenth Century to the Twentieth* (Leicester, Leicester University Press).

Egi (Estates Gazette) Legal (1995), *Bolton Metropolitan District Council and others v Secretary of State for the Environment and others*, wysiyg://103/http://new.egi.co.uk/LegalCases_detail.asp?case_id=PLR/51/000482:, site visited 2/15/01.

East Kilbride Development Corporation (1950), *East Kilbride New Town: the Master Plan* (East Kilbride, East Kilbride Development Corporation).

Eddington, R. (2006), *The Eddington Transport Study: The Case for Action* (London, HM Treasury).

Edwards, B. (1997), *The Modern Station: New Approaches to Railway Architecture* (London, E & FN Spon).

Edwards, C. (1898), *Railway Nationalization* (London, Methuen).

Edwards, D. and Pigram, R. (1986), *London's Underground Suburbs* (London, Baton Transport).

Edwards, D. and Pigram R. (1988), *The Final Link* (London, Bloomsbury Books).

Ellis, H. (1960a), *British Railway History 1830-1876*, Third Impression (London, George Allan & Unwin).

Ellis, H. (1960b), *British Railway History 1877-1947*, Second Imp. (London, George Allan & Unwin).

Elson, M.J. (1986), *Green Belts: Conflict Mediation in the Urban Fringe* (London, Heinemann).

Essex County Council County Planning Department (1973), *A Design Guide for Residential Areas* (Chelmsford, Essex County Council).

European Commission (2005a), *HiTrans Best Practice Guide 1: Public Transport and Land Use Planning* (European Commission Interreg IIIB North Sea).

European Commission (2005b), *HiTrans Best Practice Guide 3: Public Transport and Urban Design* (European Commission Interreg IIIB North Sea).

Farr, K. (1999), 'Far North 125', *Railway Magazine*, Vol. 145, No. 1181, 58-63.

Farrington, J., Knowles, R. and Gibb, R. (1990), 'Channel Rail Links - the Section 40 Consultation Process, *Modern Railways*, Vol. 47, No. 498, 142-143.

Fiennes, G.F. (1967), *I Tried to Run a Railway* (London, Ian Allan).

Flick, U. (1998), *An Introduction to Qualitative Research* (London, Sage).

Ford, R. (1990), 'British Rail Pursues Quality Culture', *Modern Railways*, Vol. 47, No. 503, 401-404.

Ford, R. (1991), 'B.R. Reorganises on Business Lines', *Modern Railways*, Vol. 48, No. 509, 74-78.

Ford, R. (1994), 'Managing the West Coast Route', *Modern Railways*, Vol. 51, No. 545, 90-94.

Forshaw, J.H. and Abercrombie, P. (1943), *County of London Plan* (London, Macmillan & Co.).

Foster, C., Posner, M. and Sherman, A. (1984), *A Report on the Potential for The Conversion of Some Railway Routes in London into Roads: The Steering Committee Report* (London, British Railways Board).

Freeman, Fox, Wilbur Smith and Associates (1968), *West Midlands Transportation Study* (Birmingham, Birmingham City Council).

Freeman, M., and Aldcroft, D. (1985), *The Atlas of British Railway History* (London, Routledge).

Freeman, R. and Shaw, J. (eds) (2000), *All Change British Railway Privatisation* (London, McGraw-Hill).

Frend, H.T. and Hibbert Ware, T. (1866), *Precedents of Instruments Relating to the Transfer of Land to Railway Companies*, Second Edition (London, William Maxwell).

Galbraith, J.K. (1958), *The Affluent Society* (Harmondsworth, Penguin).

Gannon, M.J. (2008), 'The Tube Flies to T5: Development of a Public Private Partnership to Fund the Piccadilly Line Extension to Heathrow Terminal 5', *Logistics and Transport Focus*, Vol.10, No. 5, 32-36.

Garbutt, P.E. (1985), *London Transport and the Politicians* (London, Ian Allan).

Geddes, P. (1915), *Cities in Evolution* (London, Williams and Norgate, reprint published 1949).

Gibberd, F. (1947) (1952 edition), *Harlow New Town Master Plan* (Harlow, Harlow Development Corporation).

Givoni, M., Brand, C. and Watkiss, P. (forthcoming), 'Are Railways "Climate Friendly"'? *Built Environment.*

Glover, J. (1985), *BR Diary 1978-1985* (London, Ian Allan Ltd).

Glover, J. (1987), *BR Diary 1958 -1967* (London, Ian Allan Ltd).

Glover, J. (1991), *London's Underground* (London, Ian Allan).

Glover, J. (2005), 'The UK's empty railway?', *Modern Railways*, Vol. 62, No. 679, 34-37.

Gold, J.R. (1995), 'The MARS Plan for London, 1933-1942', *Town Planning Review*, Vol. 66, No. 3, 243-267.

Goodwin, P.B., Bailey, J.M., Brisbourne, R.H., Clarke, M.I., Donnison, J.R., Render, T.E. and Whiteley, G.K. (1983), *Subsidised Public Transport and the Demand for Travel – the South Yorkshire Examples* (Aldershot, Hants., Gower).

Goodwin, P. et al (1991), *Transport: the New Realism* (Oxford, Transport Studies Unit, University of Oxford).

Gore, A. (1986), *The State's Estate: Landownership by Nationalised Industries in Industrial South Wales* (Cardiff, Department of Town planning, UWIST, PhD thesis).

Gough, J. (1991), 'One Railway for London and the South East' in 'Network 2000', *Rail Supplement*, 5-7.

Gourvish, T.R. (1986), *British Railways 1948-73: A Business History* (Cambridge, Cambridge University Press).

Gourvish, T.R. (2002), *British Rail 1974-97: From Integration to Privatisation* (Oxford, Oxford University Press).

Gourvish, T.R. (2006), *The Official History of Britain and the Channel Tunnel* (London, Routledge).

Grant, J. (1977), *The Politics of Urban Transport Planning* (London, Earth Resources Limited).

Greater Glasgow Transportation Study (1968), *Volume 2: Forecast and Plan* (Glasgow, Greater Glasgow Transportation Study).

Greater Glasgow Transportation Study (1971), *Volume 4: Planning for Action* (Glasgow, Greater Glasgow Transportation Study).

Greater Glasgow Transportation Study (1974), *Public Transport Demonstration Projects and Associated Studies: Effect of Rail Electrification* (Glasgow, Greater Glasgow Transportation Study).

Greater Glasgow PTE (1974), *Development of Clyderail: Application to Secretary of State for Scotland for Infrastructure Grant* (Glasgow, GGPTE).

Greater London Council (1969), *Greater London Development Plan: Written Statement (Draft version)* (London, GLC).

Greater London Council (1971), *Greater London Development Plan: Report of Studies* (London, GLC).

Greater London Council (1976), *Greater London Development Plan: Written Statement (adopted version)* (London, GLC).

Greater Manchester Council (1982), *Greater Manchester Structure Plan: Approved Written Statement* (Manchester, Greater Manchester Council).

Greater Manchester Council (1984), *Greater Manchester Council Green Belt Local Plan: Written Statement* (Manchester, Greater Manchester Council).

Greater Manchester Council (1986), *Greater Manchester Structure Plan: Approved Written Statement* (Manchester, Greater Manchester Council).

Greater Manchester Passenger Transport Executive (1995), *Trends and Statistics 1984-94* (Manchester, GMPTE).

Greater Manchester Passenger Transport Executive (1996), *Trends and Statistics 1986-96* (Manchester, GMPTE).

Greater Manchester Passenger Transport Executive (2006), *Land Use Planning Guide* (Manchester, GMPTE).

Green, C.E.W. (1989), *Congestion: A Rail Solution*, paper presented to the Chartered Institute of Transport, May 4th (London, British Rail, Network South East).

Greensmith, C. and Haywood, R. (1999), *Rail freight Growth and the Land-use Planning System* (Sheffield, Centre for Regional Economic and Social Research, Planning and Property Paper No. 8, Sheffield Hallam University).

HM Treasury (2007), *The Review of Sub-National Economic Development and Regeneration* (London, HM Treasury).

Hakim, C. (1997), *Research Design: Strategies and Choices in the Design of Social Research* (London, Routledge).

Hall, P. (1971), *London 2000* (second edition) (London, Faber).

Hall, P. (1982), *Great Planning Disasters* (Berkeley, University of California).

Hall, P. (1988), *Cities of Tomorrow* (Oxford, Basil Blackwell).

Hall, P. (1989a), *Urban and Regional Planning* (second edition) (London, Unwin Hyman).

Hall, P. (1989b), *London 2001* (London, Unwin Hyman).

Hall, P. (1992), 'Britain's Cities in Europe, *Town and Country Planning*, January, 7-13.

Hall, P. (1994), *Abercrombie's Plan for London – 50 years on* (London, Vision for London).

Hall, P., Gracey, H., Drewett, R. and Thomas R. (1973a), *The Containment of Urban England, Vol One* (London, George Allan & Unwin Ltd.).

Hall, P., Gracey, H., Drewett, R. and Thomas, R. (1973b), *The Containment of Urban England, Vol Two* (London, George Allan & Unwin Ltd.).

Hall, S. (1990), 'Clapham – cause and consequence', *Modern Railways*, Vol. 47, No. 496, 6-7.

Hall, S. (1995), *Rail Centres: Manchester* (London, Ian Allan Publishing).

Hall, P. and Hass Klau, C. (1985), *Can Rail Save the City* (London, Gower).

Hall, P. and Ward, C. (1998), *Sociable Cities: The Legacy of Ebenezer Howard* (Chichester, Wiley).

Hamer, M. (1987), *Wheels Within Wheels: A Study of the Road Lobby* (London, Routledge and Kegan Paul).

Hamilton, K. and Potter S. (1985), *Losing Track* (London, Routledge and Kegan Paul).

Hampshire County Council, Network South East and British Rail Community Unit (1993), *Railway Environments: A Partnership in Action* (Hampshire County Council).

Hardy, R.N.H. (1989), *Beeching, Champion of the Railway?* (London, Ian Allan Ltd.).

Harman, R. (1989), 'Southeast Railways and the Channel Tunnel', *Modern Railways*, Vol. 46, No. 495, 645-647.

Harris, M. (1985), 'The British Rail Property Board Today', *Modern Railways*, Vol. 42, No 443, 398-404.

Harris, N. (1996), 'Britain's Biggest New Station this Century', *Rail*, No. 285, 30-36.

Harris, N. (2008), 'Taking Trains Back to Tavistock', *Rail*, No. 590, April 28-May 6, 40-45.

Harris, N.G. and Godward, E.W. (1992), *Planning Passenger Railways* (Glossop, Transport Publishing Company).

Harris, N. and Godward, E. (1997), *The Privatisation of British Rail* (London, The Railway Consultancy).

Haughton, G. and Hunter, C. (1994), Sustainable Cities (London, Jessica Kingsley Publishers/Regional Studies Association).

Haywood, R. (1992), *Railway Re-openings and the Planning System: a Case Study in the East Midlands* (Sheffield, Centre for Regional Economic and Social Research, Working Paper No. 21, Sheffield Hallam University).

Haywood, R. (1996), 'More Flexible Office Location Controls and Public Transport Considerations', *Town Planning Review*, Vol. 67, No. 1, 65-86.

Haywood, R. (1997a), Railways, Urban Form and Town Planning in London: 1900-1947, *Planning Perspectives*, Vol. 12, No. 1, 37-69.

Haywood, R. (1997b), 'Hungerford Bridge: the Ugly Duckling Becomes a Swan', *Journal of Urban Design*, Vol. 2, No. 2, 117-142.

Haywood, R. (1998a), *South Yorkshire Supertram: Final Report on Planning Applications and Land Use Change Research* (Sheffield, Centre for Regional Economic and Social Research, Supertram Impact Series Paper No. SIS 37, Sheffield Hallam University).

Haywood, R. (1998), 'Mind the Gap: Town Planning and Manchester's Local Railway Network: 1947-1996', *European Planning Studies*, Vol. 6, No. 2, 187-210.

Haywood, R. (1999a), 'South Yorkshire Supertram: Its Property Impacts and their Implications for Integrated Land Use-Transportation Planning, *Planning Practice and Research*, Vol. 14, No. 3, 277-299.

Haywood, R. (1999b), 'Land Development Implications of the British Rail Freight Renaissance', *Journal of Transport Geography*, Vol. 7, 263-275.

Haywood, R, (2001), 'Rail Freight Growth and the Land Use Planning System', *Town Planning Review*, Vol. 72, No. 4, 445-467.

Haywood, R. (2005), 'Co-ordinating Urban Development, Stations and Railway Services as a Component of Urban Sustainability', *Planning Theory and Practice*, Vol. 6, No. 1, 71-97.

Haywood, R. (2007), 'Britain's National Railway Network: Fit for Purpose in the Twenty First Century?' *Journal of Transport Geography*, Vol. 15, 198-216.

Haywood, R. (2008), 'Underneath the Arches in the East End: An Evaluation of the Planning and Design Policy Context of the East London Line Extension Project', *Journal of Urban Design*, Vol. 13, No. 3, 361-385.

Haywood, R. and Richardson, T. (1996), 'Deconstructing Transport Planning. Lessons from Policy Breakdown in the English Pennines', *Transport Policy*, Vol. 3, No. 1/2, 43-53.

Headicar, P. and Bixby, B. (1992), *Concrete and Tyres: Local Development Effects of Major Roads: M40 Case Study* (London, CPRE).

Healey, D. (1990), *The Time of My Life* (London, Penguin).

Healey, P., McNamara, P., Elson, M. and Doak, A. (1988), *Land Use Planning and the Mediation of Urban Change* (Cambridge, Cambridge University Press).

Healey, P. (1997), *Collaborative Planning: Shaping Places in Fragmented Societies* (Basingstoke, Macmillan).

Healy, J.M.C. (1987), *Great Central Memories* (London, Baton Transport).

Heaps, C. (1988), *BR Diary 1968-1971* (London, Ian Allan Ltd.).

Heenan, G.W. (1968), 'The Economic Effect of Rapid Transit on Real Estate Development in Toronto', *The Appraisal Journal*, (April), 213-224.

Hellewell, D.S. (1964), 'Hamburg: Model of Co-ordinated Urban Transport', *Modern Railways*, Vol. 20, No. 192, 172-177.

Hellewell, D.S. (1996), *South Yorkshire's Transport* (Glossop, Venture).

Henneberry, J. (1988), 'Conflict in the Industrial Property Market', *Town Planning Review*, Vol. 59, 241-62.

Henshaw, D. (1991), *The Great Railway Conspiracy* (Hawes, Leading Edge).

Her Majesty's Stationery Office (1995), *Manchester 50 Years of Change: Post-war Planning in Manchester* (London, HMSO).

Hibbs et al (2006), *The Railways, the Market and the Government* (London, Institute of Economic Affairs).

Hickman, R. and Hall, P. (2008), 'Moving the City East: Explorations into Contextual Public Transport-orientated Development', *Planning Practice and Research*, Vol. 23, No. 3, 323-339.

Hillman, M. and Whalley, A. (1980), *The Social Consequences of Rail Closures* (London, Policy Studies Institute).

Hitches, M. (1992), *Bournville: Steam and Chocolate* (Middlesex, Irwell Press).

Hobsbawm, E.J. (1969), *The Pelican Economic History of Britain Volume 3: Industry and Empire* (Harmondsworth, Penguin Books).

Hodgkins, D. (2002), *The Second Railway King: The Life and Times of Sir Edward Watkin 1819-1901* (Cardiff, Merton Priory Press).

Home, R. (1992), 'The Evolution of the Use Classes Order', *Town Planning Review*, Vol. 63, 187-201.

Hoskins, W.G. (1955) (reprinted 1985), *The Making of the English Landscape* (London, Hodder and Stoughton).

Howard, E. (1898) (reprinted 1985), *Garden Cities of Tomorrow* (London, Attic Books).

Howard, E. (1913), 'The Transit Problem and the Working Man', *Town Planning Review*, Vol. 4, No. 2, 127-132.

Hoyle B. and Smith, J., 1998, 'Transport and Development: Conceptual Frameworks', chapter 2, 13-40, in Hoyle, B. and Knowles, R., *Modern Transport Geography: Edition 2* (Chichester, John Wiley and Sons).

Hoyt, H. (1939), *The Structure and Growth of Residential Neighbourhoods in American Cities* (Washington, Federal Housing Administration).

Hurcomb, C. (1935), 'Progress in the Co-ordination of Transport in Great Britain', *Journal of the Institute of Transport*, November, 8-27.

Hurcomb, C. (1945), 'Co-ordination of Transport: Great Britain 1935-44', *Journal of the Institute of transport*, Vol. 22, No. 3, 90-105.

Hurst, G. (1992), *Register of Closed Railways 1948-1991* (Worksop, Milestone Publications).

Ikin, C.W. (1990), *Hampstead Garden Suburb* (London, The New Hampstead Garden Suburb Trust Ltd.).

Irvine Development Corporation (1971), *Irvine New Town Plan* (Irvine, Irvine Development Corporation).

Irvine, K. (1988), *Track to the Future* (London, Adam Smith Institute).

Jackson, A.A. (1969), *London's Termini* (Newton Abbott, David and Charles).

Jackson, A.A. (1986), *London's Metropolitan Railway* (Newton Abbott, David and Charles).

Jackson, A.A. (1991), *Semi-Detached London, 2nd. Edition* (Didcot, Wild Swan).

Jackson, A.A. (1999a), *The Railway in Surrey* (Penryn, Atlantic Publishers).

Jackson, A.A. (1999b), *London's Local Railways: 2nd Edition* (Penryn, Atlantic Publishers).

Jackson, A.A. (2006), *London's Metroland* (London, Capital History).

Jacobs, J. (1962), *The Death and Life of Great American Cities* (London, Jonathan Cape).

Jacobs, M. (1991), *The Green Economy: Environment, Sustainable Development and the Politics of the Future* (London, Pluto Press).

Jones, P. and Evans, J. (2008), *Urban Regeneration in the UK* (London, Sage).

Joseph, S. (1991), *A New Future for Britain's Railways* (London, Transport 2000).

Jowett, A. (2000), *Jowett's Nationalised Railway Atlas of Great Britain and Ireland* (Penryn, Atlantic Publishers).

Joy, S. (1973), *The Train that Ran Away* (London, Ian Allan).

Katz, P. (1994), *The New Urbanism: Towards an Architecture of Community* (New York, McGraw-Hill).

Kay, P. (1996), *The London, Tilbury and Southend Railway: A History of the Company and Line, Vol 1: 1836-93* (Teignmouth, Peter Kay).

Kellett, J.R. (1979), *Railways and Victorian Cities* (London, Routledge and Kegan Paul).

Kerrigan, M. and Bull, D. (1992), *Measuring Accessibility: A Public Transport Accessibility Index* (London, London Borough of Hammersmith and Fulham, conference paper at PTRC Summer Conference).

Kim Wilkie Associates (1999), *The Borough at London Bridge* (London, English Heritage).

Klapper, C.F. (1973), *Sir Herbert Walker's Southern Railway* (London, Ian Allan).

Kitchen, T. (1993), 'The Manchester Olympic Bid', *Report of Proceedings, Town and Country Planning Summer School 1993,* 34-38 (London, Royal Town Planning Institute).

Kitchen, T. (1995), *Sustainable Transport – the Greater Manchester Experience*, notes of a presentation to the Regional Studies Association, Yorkshire and Humberside Branch (Sheffield, Sheffield Hallam University).

Kitchen, T. (1995), *People, Politics, Policies and Plans: The City Planning Process in Contemporary Britain* (London, Paul Chapman).

Knight, R.I. and Trygg, L.L. (1977), 'Evidence of Land Use Impacts of Rapid Transit Systems', *Transportation*, Vol. 6, 231-247.

Knowles, R.D. (1996), 'Transport Impacts of Greater Manchester's Metrolink Light Rail System', *Journal of Transport Geography*, Vol. 4, No. 1, 1-14.

Korn, A. and Samuely, F.J. (1942), 'A Master Plan for London', *Architectural Review*, Vol. 91, January, 143-150.

Lamb, D.R. (1948), 'Transport in Transition', *Journal of the Institute of Transport*, Vol. 23, No. 1, 6-12.

Langdon, P. (1994), *A Better Place to Live: Reshaping the American Suburbs* (Boston, University of Massachusetts Press).

Law, C.M. and Dundon-Smith, D. (1994), *Metrolink and the Greater Manchester Office Market: An Appraisal, Metrolink Impact Study (Working Paper no 13)* (Salford, Department of Geography, University of Salford).

Lawless, P. and Brown, F. (1986), *Urban Growth and Change in Britain* (London, Harper and Row).

Lawless, P. and Dabinett, G. (1995), 'Urban Regeneration and Transport Investment: A Research Agenda', *Environment and Planning A*, Vol. 27, 1029-1048.

Lawless, P. (1999), 'Transport Investment and Urban Regeneration in a Provincial City: Sheffield, 1992-96', *Environment and Planning C; Government and Policy*, Vol. 17, 211-226.

Lawson, W.R. (1913), *British Railways: A Financial and Commercial Survey* (London, Constable and Company).

Le Corbusier (1929) (reprinted 1971), *The City of Tomorrow and its Planning, 3rd edition* (London, Architectural Press).

Leibbrand, K. (1970) (1st Edition, 1964), *Transportation and Town Planning* (London, Leonard Hill).

Leicestershire County Council (1991), *Draft Structure Plan Update* (Leicester, Leicestershire County Council).

Ling, A. (1966), *Runcorn New Town, Master Plan* (Nottingham, University of Nottingham).

Ling, A. (1967), 'Urban Form or Chaos?' *Journal of the Royal Town Planning Institute*, 87-94.

Lloyd, P.E. (1980), 'Manchester: a Study in Industrial Decline and Economic Restructuring', chapter 4 in White, H.P. (1980), *The Continuing Conurbation: Change and Development in Greater Manchester: Produced for the 142nd AGM of the British Association* (Farnborough, Gower).

Local Government Board (1918), *Report of the Committee Appointed to Consider Questions of Building Construction in Connection with the Provision of Dwellings for the Working Class* (Cmnd 9191) (London, HMSO).

London Borough of Croydon (1982), *District Plan: Adopted Version* (Croydon, London Borough of Croydon).

London Borough of Hammersmith and Fulham (1988), *Borough Local Plan: Alterations and Modifications: Deposit Version* (London, London Borough of Hammersmith and Fulham).

London County Council (1951), *Administrative County of London Development Plan 1951: Statement* (London, London County Council).

London County Council (1961), *The Planning of a New Town* (London, London County Council).

London Docklands Development Corporation (1983), *Corporate Plan* (London, LDDC).

London Planning Advisory Committee (1994), *Advice on Strategic Planning for London* (London, LPAC).

Lord, R.G. (1991), *Railways From Grassroots to Management* (London, Adelphi Press).

Lucci, P. and Hildreth, P. (2008), *City Links: Integration and Isolation* (London, Report for the Northern Way by Centre for Cities).

Luttrell, B. (1992), *Regional Revival and Strategic Planning* (London, Town and Country Planning Association).

McKenna, F. (1980), *The Railway Workers 1840-1970* (London, Faber and Faber).

McLachlan, S. (1983), *The National Freight Buy-Out* (London, Macmillan Press).

McLoughlin, J.B. (1980), 'Land Use and Functional Change in the Central Business District', chapter 5 in White, H.P., *The Continuing Conurbation: Change and Development in Greater Manchester: produced for the 142nd AGM of the British Association* (Farnborough, Gower).

Manchester City Council (1984), *City Centre Local Plan* (Manchester, Manchester City Council).

Manchester City Council (1986), *Review of the 1985 Promotional Campaign* (Manchester, Manchester City Council).

Manchester City Planning Department (1981), *Housing and Urban Renewal in Manchester: A Short History* (Manchester, Manchester City Council).

Manchester City Planning Department (1983), *Manchester/Salford Inner Area: Some Basic Information* (Manchester, Manchester City Council).

Manzoni, H.J. (1940), 'Traffic Problems of a Large City – With Possible Solutions', *Journal of the Institute of Transport*, Vol. 21, No. 4, 112-117.

Marriott, O. (1969), *The Property Boom* (London, Pan).

Marshall, J. (1986), 'The Nottingham Suburban Railway', *British Railway Journal*, No. 14, Christmas 1986.

Martin and Voorhees Associates, Colin Buchanan and Partners and local authority staff (1976), *Sheffield and Rotherham: A Transportation Plan for the 1980s* (London, Martin and Voorhees Associates).

McKenna, F. (1980), *The Railway Workers 1840-1970* (London, Faber & Faber).

Meller, M. (1981), *Patrick Geddes 1854-1932*, chapter 3 in Cherry, G.E. (ed), *Pioneers in British Planning* (London, Architectural Press).

Merseyside County Council (1979), *Merseyside County Structure Plan: Report of Surveys* (Liverpool, Merseyside County Council).

Merseyside County Council (1980), *Merseyside County Structure Plan: Written Statement* (Liverpool, Merseyside County Council).

Merseyside Passenger Transport Executive (1972), *A Transport Plan for Merseyside* (Liverpool, Merseyside Passenger Transport Executive).

Millar, A. (1985), *British PTEs:1: Strathclyde* (London, Ian Allan Ltd).

Milton Keynes Development Corporation (1970), *The Plan for Milton Keynes* (Milton Keynes, MKDC).

Milton Keynes Development Corporation (1992), *The Milton Keynes Planning Manual* (Milton Keynes, MKDC).

Ministry of Housing and Local Government (1953), *Glasgow Development Plan: Inquiry: Vols I to IV* (Edinburgh, MHLG).

Ministry of Housing and Local Government (1955), *Green Belts (Circular No. 42/55)* (London, HMSO).

Ministry of Housing and Local Government (1964), *The South East Study* (London, HMSO).

Ministry of Housing and Local Government (1966), *Circular 57: Surplus Land* (London, MHLG).

Ministry of Housing and Local Government (1967), *Town and Country Planning White Paper: Cmnd 3333* (London, HMSO).

Ministry of Housing and Local Government (1969), *People and Planning: Report of the Committee on Public Participation in Planning* (London, HMSO).

Ministry of Housing and Local Government, Welsh Office (1970), *Development Plans: A Manual on Form and Content* (London, HMSO).

Ministry of Town and Country Planning (1944), *The Control of Land Use: Cmd. 6537* (London, HMSO).

Ministry of Town and Country Planning (1947), *The Redevelopment of Central Areas* (London, HMSO).

Ministry of Town and Country Planning and Department of Health for Scotland (1946), *Final Report of the New Towns Committee: Cmd. 6876* (London, HMSO).

Ministry of Town and Country Planning and Department of Health for Scotland (1950), *Report of the Committee on Qualifications of Planners: Cmd.8059* (London, HMSO).

Ministry of Transport (1949), *London Plan Working Party: Report to the Minister of Transport* (London, HMSO).

Ministry of Transport (1963), *Traffic in Towns* (London, HMSO).

Ministry of Transport (1966a), *Transport Policy: Cmnd. 3057* (London, HMSO).

Ministry of Transport (1966b), *Roads in Urban Areas* (London, HMSO).

Ministry of Transport (1967a), *Railway Policy: Cmnd.3439* (London, HMSO).

Ministry of Transport (1967b), *Public Transport and Traffic: Cmnd.3481* (London, HMSO).

Ministry of Transport (1967c), *The Transport of Freight: Cmnd. 3470* (London, HMSO).

Ministry of Transport (1969), *The Cambrian Coast Line: A Cost/Benefit Analysis of the Retention of Railway Services on the Cambrian Coast Line (Mchynleth-Pwllheli)* (London, HMSO).

Ministry of Transport (1970), *Transport Planning: The Men for the Job: A Report to the Minister of Transport by Lady Sharp* (London, HMSO).

Ministry of Transport and Civil Aviation (1954), *Railways Reorganisation Scheme: Cmnd 9191* (London, HMSO).

Ministry of Transport and British Railways Board (1967), *The Network for Development* (London, HMSO).

Ministry of War Transport (1946), *Railway (London Plan) Committee 1944* (London, HMSO).

Ministry of Works and Planning (1942), *Expert Committee on Compensation and Betterment: Final Report* (London, HMSO).

Ministry of Works and Planning (1943), *Report of the Committee on Land Utilisation in Rural Areas* (Cmnd 6876) (London, HMSO).

Mishan, E.J. (1967), *The Costs of Economic Growth* (London, Pelican).

Modern Railways (1964a), 'London Midland Region Electrification Progress: Reconstruction of Birmingham New Street', *Modern Railways*, Vol. 19, No. 189, 404-409.

Modern Railways (1964b), 'Power Station Coal by Rail Agreement – the BR-CEGB Agreement', *Modern Railways*, Vol. 19, No 186, 178-179.

Modern Railways (1975), 'Redevelopment at Liverpool Street', *Modern Railways*, Vol. 32, No. 323, 334-336.

Modern Railways (1982), 'West Coast Main-line Competition on Target', *Modern Railways*, Vol. 39, No. 402, 99.

Modern Railways (1990), 'Metro Options for Strathclyde', *Modern Railways*, Vol. 47, No. 498, 130-131.

Modern Railways (2005), *Save the Gatwick Express*, Vol. 62, No. 676, 4.

Morgan, J.C. (1994), 'On Track: Charing Cross 1954', *British Railways Illustrated*, Vol. 3, No. 8, 410-417.

Moody, G.T. (1979), *Southern Electric 1909-1979: (5th Edition)* (London, Ian Allan).

Morris, G. ed. (1948), *The Railwaymen's Year Book 1948-49* (London, Railwaymen's Publications Ltd.).

Morrison, H. (1933), *Socialisation and Transport: The Organisation of Socialised Industries with Particular Reference to the London Passenger Transport Bill* (London, Constable).

Mugliston, H.A. (1964), *Merseyside's Suburban Problem*, Modern Railways, Vol. 20, No. 192, 166-171.

Nairn, I. (1955), 'Outrage', *Architectural Review*, Vol. 117, No. 702 (Special Issue), 363-460.

National Audit Office (2004), *London Underground PPP: Were they good deals?* (London, TSO).

Network Rail (2008), *Strategic Business Plan Update: Supporting Document: Strategic Freight Network* (London, Network Rail).

New Towns Committee (1946), *Final Report*, July 1946 (London, HMSO).

Nicholas, R. (1945), *City of Manchester Plan* (Manchester, Manchester City Council).

Nock, O.S. (1966), *Britain's New Railway* (London, Ian Allan).

North West Regional Association (Transport Strategy Sub-Group), 1993, *Regional Transport Strategy for North West England* (Wigan, North West Regional Association).

North West Regional Association (1994), *Greener Growth: Regional Planning Guidance for the North West* (Wigan, North West Regional Association).

Northern Way Steering Group (2004), *Moving Forward: The Northern Way: First Growth Strategy Report* (Northern Way Steering Group).

Northern Way Steering Group (2005), *Moving Forward: The Northern Way: Action Plan – Progress Report* (Northern Way Steering Group).

Nottinghamshire County Council, Derbyshire County Council, County Borough of Derby and City Council of Nottingham (1969), *The Nottinghamshire-Derbyshire Sub-Regional Study* (Nottingham, Nottinghamshire County Council et al).

Office of the Deputy Prime Minister (2003), *The Communities Plan (Sustainable Communities: Building for the Future)* (London, ODPM).

Office of the Deputy Prime Minister (2004a), *Planning Policy Statement no 11: Regional Planning: Supplementary Guidance on Regional Spatial Strategies* (London, ODPM).

Office of the Deputy Prime Minister (2004b), *Making it Happen: The Northern Way* (London, ODPM).

Office of Rail Regulation (2007a), *ORR's Sustainable Development & Environmental Duties: Conclusion* (London, ORR).

Office of Rail Regulation (2007b), *National Rail Trends Yearbook April 06–March 07* (London, ORR).

Osborn, F.J. (1938), *Minutes of Evidence Taken before the Royal Commission on the Geographical Distribution of the Industrial Population, Twentieth Day, 5th May* (London, HMSO).

Osborn, F.J. and Whittick, A. (1969), *The New Towns: The Answer to Megalopolis* (London, Leonard Hill).

Osborn, F.J. and Whittick, A. (1977), *New Towns: Their origins, Achievements and Progress* (London, Leonard Hill).

O'Toole, M.O. (1996), *Regulation Theory and the British State: The Case of the Urban Development Corporation* (Aldershot, Avebury).

Ove Arup Partnership (1990), *Proposal for a Channel Tunnel Rail Link Leading to an Integrated, International Rail System for Passengers and Freight Serving the Whole of Britain* (London, Ove Arup Partnership).

Owens, S. and Owens, P.L. (1991), *Environment, Resources and Conservation* (Cambridge, Cambridge University Press).

Pahl, R. (1970), *Whose City* (London, Longman).

Parker, H.R. (1985), 'From Uthwatt to DLT – the End of the Road', *The Planner*, April, 21-28.

Parkinson-Bailey, J.J. (2000), *Manchester: An Architectural History* (Manchester, Manchester University Press).

Parris, H. (1965), *Government and the Railways in Nineteenth-Century Britain* (London, Routledge and Kegan Paul).

Pas, E.I. (1995), 'The Urban Transportation Planning Process', chapter 3, 53-77, in Hanson, S. *The Geography of Urban Transportation: Second Edition* (New York, Guilford Press).

Patmore, J.A. (1964), 'The Railway Network of the Manchester Conurbation', *Institute of British Geographers Transactions*, Vol. 34, 159-73.

Paul, A.H. (1980), 'Vanishing Railways and the Urban Scene: the Case of Liverpool, *Geography*, Vol. 65, No. 2, April, 119-124.

Payne, J.H.C. (1947), 'Planning and its Relation to Transport', *Journal of the Institute of Transport*, Vol. 22, No. 5, 558-564.

Pearson, A.J. (1953), 'Developments and Prospects in British Transport with Special Reference to Railways', *Journal of the Institute of Transport*, Vol. 25, No. 4, 118-126.

Pearson, A.J. (1967), *Man of the Rail* (London, George Allan & Unwin).

Pepler, G. (1949), 'Forty Years of Statutory Town Planning', *Town Planning Review*, Vol. 20, No. 2, 103-108.

Perks, R.W. (1906), *Minutes of Evidence Taken Before the Royal Commission on London Traffic*, Forty-Seventh Day, 17th March, 1904, Parliamentary Papers Vol. XL, Q 19888-9.

Perren, B. (2005), 'Stratford: 21st Century Hub', *Modern Railways*, Vol. 62, No. 679, 46-49.

Pick, F. (1927), 'Growth and Form in Modern Cities', *Journal of the Chartered Institute of Transport*, February, 156-173.

Pick, F. (1938), *Minutes of Evidence Taken before the Royal Commission on the Geographical Distribution of the Industrial Population, Twelfth Day, 5th February*, London, HMSO.

Planning Advisory Group (1965), *The Future of Development Plans* (London, HMSO).

Planning Week (1994), 'Manchester Wins First Stage in Dumplington', *Planning Week* 12, 6.

Ploeger, L. (1992), 'On the Fast Track to Rail', *Railway Gazette*, Feb. 1992, 89-92.

Plowden, S. (1972), *Towns Against Traffic* (London, Andre Deutsch).

Plowman, S. (1995), *Sustainablity? The Case of South Manchester* (Sheffield, Sheffield Hallam University, unpublished undergraduate dissertation).

Potter, S. (1997), *Vital Travel Statistics* (London, Landor Publishing).

Power, A. and Mumford, K. (1999), *The Slow Death of Great Cities: Urban Abandonment or Urban Renaissance* (York, Joseph Rowntree Foundation).

Railtrack (1998), *East Coast Main Line: The Next Generation* (London, Railtrack).

Railway Department of the Board of Trade (1845), *Report of the Railway Department of the Board of Trade on the Kentish and South Eastern Railway Schemes*, HC, 1845, Vol. XXXIX.203, 1-4.

Railway Development Society (1988), *'Bustitution': Can Bus Replace Train – The Case Exploded* (Teddington, Middlesex, Railway Development Society).

Railway Development Society (1992), *A-Z of Rail Reopenings* (Great Bookham, RDS).

Railway Development Society (1998), *A-Z of Rail Reopenings* (Great Bookham, RDS).

Railway Gazette (1944), *Coming of Age of Railway Grouping* (London, Railway Gazette).

Ravetz, A. (1980), *Remaking Cities* (London, Croom Helm).

Reade, C.C. (1913), 'The Northern Junction Railway', *Town Planning Review*, Vol. 4, No. 1, 118-126.

Reade, E. (1987), *British Town and Country Planning* (Milton Keynes, Open University Press).

Reading Borough Council (2008), *Reading Central Area Action Plan* (Reading, Reading Borough Council).

Regional Railways, Barnstaple Town Council, Devon County Council, Mid Devon District Council, North Devon District Council, the Countryside Commission and Forest Enterprise (1993), *The Tarka Line: Explore Deepest Devon* (Exeter, Devon County Council).

Rhodes, M. (1988), *The Illustrated History of British Marshalling Yards* (Yeovil, Haynes Publishing Group).

Roberts, J., Cleary, J., Hamilton, K. and Hanna, J. (eds) (1992), *Travel Sickness: The Need for a Sustainable Transport Policy for Britain* (London, Lawrence and Wishart).

Robson, B.T. (1980), 'The County Housing Market', chapter 7, 91-114, in White, H.P. (1980), *The Continuing Conurbation: Change and Development in Greater Manchester: produced for the 142nd AGM of the British Association* (Farnborough, Gower).

Rolt, L.T.C. (1998), *Red for Danger: The Classic History of British Railway Disasters* (Stroud, Sutton Publishing).

Rosehaugh Stanhope Developments (1991), *Broadgate and Liverpool Street Station* (London, Rosehaugh Stanhope Developments).

Roskill, The Hon. Mr Justice (1971), *Commission on the Third London Airport* (London, HMSO).

Ross, J. (2000), *Railway Stations: Planning, Design and Management* (Oxford, Architectural Press).

Royal Commission (1846), *Royal Commission to Investigate Projects for Establishing Railway Termini within Metropolis*, Parliamentary Papers, 17 (1846) 21.

Royal Commission (1884), *Royal Commission on the Housing of the Working Classes, 1884-85, First Report*, PRO, PP Vol. XXX.

Royal Commission (1905), *Royal Commission on London Traffic, Vol I, Cd. 2597*, PRO, PP XXX.

Royal Commission (1906), *Royal Commission on London Traffic, Vol II, Cd. 2751*, PRO, PP XL.

Royal Commission (1940), *Royal Commission on the Distribution of the Industrial Population: Report: Cmnd 6153* (London, HMSO).

Royal Commission (1994), *Royal Commission on Environmental Pollution, Eighteenth Report: Transport and the Environment* (London, HMSO).

Royal Town Planning Institute (2000), *Green Belt Policy: A Discussion Paper* (London, RTPI).

Salveson, P. (1992), 'Manchester: the Olympic Vision', *Modern Railways*, Vol. 49, No. 530, 612-614.

Salveson, P. (2007), 'Council Turmoil Unsettling for Community's Rail Future', *Rail*, No. 578, November 7-20th, 60-61.

Schaffer, F. (1970), *The New Town Story* (London, MacGibbon and Kee Ltd.).

Secretary of State for the Environment, Secretary of State for Scotland and Secretary of State for Wales (1977), *Policy for the Inner Cities: Cmnd. 6845* (London, HMSO).

Secretaries of State for Environment, Trade and Industry, Health, Education and Science, Scotland, Transport, Energy and Northern Ireland, the Minister of Agriculture, Fisheries and Food and the Secretaries of State for Employment and Wales (1990), *This Common Inheritance: Britain's Environmental Strategy (Cm. 1200)* (London, HMSO).

Secretary of State for Transport (1992), *New Opportunities for the Railways: The Privatisation of British Rail: Cm 2012* (London, HMSO).

Selbie, R.H. (1921), 'Railways and Land Development: Need for New Statutory Powers', *Modern Transport*, June 11, 3-4.

Select Committee (1844), *Select Committee on Railways, Third Report 24 May*, PRO, PP Vol. XI.

Select Committee (1863), *Select Committee of the House of Lords on Metropolitan Railway Communications, First Report*, PRO, PP VIII.

Select Committee (1960), *Report from the Select Committee on Nationalised Industries: British Railways* (London, HMSO).

Semmens, P. (1990), *Speed on the East Coast Main Line: A Century and a Half of Accelerated Services* (Wellingborough, Patrick Stephens Ltd.).

Serplan (1989), *The Channel Tunnel: Implications for the South East Region: RPC 1470* (London, Serplan).

Serplan (1992), *Serplan: Thirty Years of Regional Planning 1962-92* (London, Serplan).

Shannon, P. and Rhodes, M. (1991) 'The Life and Times of Speedlink', *Railway Magazine*, Vol. 137, No. 1086, 713-720.

Sharp, T. (1940), *Town Planning* (Harmondsworth, Pelican).

Sheffield Transport Department (1960), *The Tramway Era in Sheffield* (Sheffield, Sheffield Transport Department).

Sheffield Development Corporation (1990), *A Vision of the Lower Don Valley: Design Principles for Development* (Sheffield, SDC).

Sheffield One (2001), *City Centre Master Plan 2000* (Sheffield, Sheffield One).

Shoard, M. (1987), *This Land is Our Land* (London, Paladin).

Shore, P. (1976), *Speech at Manchester Town Hall*, 17 September 1976, Secretary of State for the Environment, Department of the Environment, 2 Marsham Street, London SW1P 3EB.

Simmie, J. (ed) (1994), *Planning London* (London, UCL Press).

Simmons, J. (1968), *The Railways of Britain: Second Edition* (London, Macmillan).

Simmons, J. (ed) (1975), *Rail 150: The Stockton and Darlington Railway and What Followed* (London, Eyre Methuen).

Simmons, J. (1986), *The Railway in Town and Country 1830-1914* (Newton Abbott, David and Charles).

Simmons, J. and Biddle, G. (eds) (1997), *The Oxford Companion to Railway History* (Oxford, Oxford University Press).

Sinclair, G. (1992), *The Lost Land: Land Use Change in England 1945-1990* (London, CPRE).

Sked, A. and Cook, C. (1993), *Post-War Britain: a Political History* (Harmondsworth, Penguin).

Skelmersdale Development Corporation (1964), *Skelmersdale New Town Planning Proposals: Report and Basic Plan* (Skelmersdale, Skelmersdale Development Corporation) (produced by Wilson and Womersley).

Smeed, R.J. (1961), *The Traffic Problem in Towns* (Manchester, Manchester Statistical Society).

Smith, M. (1996), 'Cardiff Valleys Transition – Part One', *British Railways Illustrated*, Vol. 6, No. 3, 130-143.

Smith, M. (1997), 'Cardiff Valleys Transition – Part Two', *British Railways Illustrated*, Vol. 6, No. 4, 158-169.

Smith, W.A.C. and Anderson, P. (1993), *An Illustrated History of Glasgow's Railways* (Oldham, Irwell Press).

Smith, R. and Wannop, U. (1985), *Strategic Planning in Action; The Impact of the Clyde Valley Regional Plan 1946-82* (Aldershot, Gower).

Social Exclusion Unit (2002), *Making the Connections: Transport and Social Exclusion* (London, Social Exclusion Unit).

South East Economic Planning Council (1967), *A Strategy for the South East* (London, South East Economic Planning Council).

South East Joint Planning Team (1970a), *Strategic Plan for the South East* (London, MHLG).

South East Joint Planning Team (1970b), *Strategic Plan for the South East: Volume 3 Transportation* (London, MHLG).

Standing Conference on London and the South East Regional Planning (1966), *The Conference Area in the Long-term* (London, the Standing Conference on London and the South East Regional Planning).

Stern, Sir Nicholas (2006), *Stern Review: The Economics of Climate Change* (London, HM Treasury).

Steer Davies and Gleave (2005), *What Light Rail Can Do for Cities: A Review of the Evidence* (Leeds, Passenger Transport Executive Group).

Strategic Rail Authority (2001a), *Freight Strategy* (London, SRA).

Strategic Rail Authority (2001b), *Land Use Planning Statement* (London, SRA).

Strategic Rail Authority (2001c), *Land Use Planning and the SRA: Guide for Local Planning Authorities and Regional Planning Bodies* (London, SRA).

Strategic Rail Authority (2002), *National Rail Trends* (London, SRA).

Strategic Rail Authority (2003a), *Capacity Utilisation Policy: Network Utilisation Strategy* (London, SRA).

Strategic Rail Authority (2003b), *Appraisal Criteria: A Guide to the Appraisal of Support for Passenger and Freight Rail Services* (London, SRA).

Strategic Rail Authority (2003c), *Specification of Network Outputs* (London, SRA).

Strategic Rail Authority (2003d), *West Coast Main Line Strategy* (London, SRA).

Strategic Rail Authority (2003e), *Midland Main Line Route Utilisation Strategy* (London, SRA).

Strategic Rail Authority (2003f), *Everyone's Railway: The Wider Case for Rail* (London, SRA).

Strategic Rail Authority (2003g), *Press Release: Why Rail is Important* (London, SRA).

Strategic Rail Authority (2003h), *The Railway Planning Framework: Regional Planning Assessments* (London, SRA).

Strategic Rail Authority (2004a), *Brighton Main Line: Route Utilisation Strategy* (London, SRA).

Strategic Rail Authority (2004b), West Coast Main Line: Progress Report (London, SRA).

Strategic Rail Authority (2004c), *Community Rail Development Strategy* (London, SRA).

Strategic Rail Authority (2004d), *New Stations: A Guide for Promoters* (London, SRA).

Strategic Rail Authority (2004e), *Strategic Rail Freight Interchange Policy* (London, SRA).

Strategic Rail Authority (2005), Great Western Route Utilisation Strategy (London, SRA).

Strathclyde Regional Council (1979), *Strathclyde Structure Plan: Written Statement and Decision Letter* (Glasgow, Strathclyde Regional Council).

Strathclyde Regional Council (1991), *Transport Policies and Programmes 1992-97* (Glasgow, Strathclyde Regional Council) .

Strathclyde Transport and BR Scottish Region (1983)*, Review of Strathclyde Rail Network: the Way Ahead* (Glasgow, Strathclyde Regional Council).

Struthers, W.A.K. and Brindell, M.J. (1983), 'The West Midlands: From Reconstruction to Regeneration', Chapter 3 in Cross D.T. and Bristow M.R., *English Structure Planning: a commentary on procedure and practice in the seventies* (London, Pion).

Sturt, A. (1992), 'Going Dutch', *Town and Country Planning*, Vol. 61, Feb., 48-51.

Sudjic, D. (1992), *The 100 Mile City* (London, Andre Deutsch Ltd.).

Sully, J. (1989), 'Shires Catch the Train', *Modern Railways*, Vol. 46, No. 492, 458-459.

Sully, J. (1995), 'Robin Hood Riding through the Glen', *Modern Railways*, Vol. 52, No. 565, 607-611.

Sully, J. (2007), 'Pace Picks up on DLR Expansion', *Modern Railways*, Vol. 64, No. 711, 18-21.

Summerson, J. (1962), *Georgian London* (London, Pelican).

Sutcliffe, A. (1981), *British Town Planning: the Formative Years* (Leicester, Leicester University Press).

Swenarton, M. (1981), *Homes Fit for Heroes* (Northumberland Press).

Tatton Brown, A. and Tatton Brown, W.E. (1941 and 1942), 'Three Dimensional Planning: Parts 1 and 2', *Architectural Review*, Vol. 90, 82-88, Vol. 91, 17-20.

Taylor, H.M. (1993), *The Light End of the Market*, Conference Paper, 216-280 in 'Modern Railway Transportation', Institute of Civil Engineers, London, May 25-27.

Tetlow, J. and Goss, A. (1965), *Homes, Towns and Traffic* (London, Faber and Faber).

Thames Gateway Task Force (1994), *The Thames Gateway Planning Framework: Consultation Draft* (London, DOE).

The Railway Conversion League (1970), *The Conversion of Railways into Roads in the United Kingdom: Second Report.*

The Times (1932), 'The Problem of the Railways', May 12.

Thomas, J. (1991), *The Skye Railway: The History of the Railways of the Scottish Highlands Vol. 5* (Nairn, David St Thomas Publisher).

Thomas, J.P. (1922), 'The Operation and Development of Urban Electric Railway Services', *Journal of the Institute of Transport*, January, 97-116.

Thomas, R. (2005), 'Is it Too Late to even Think about Alternative Ideas to Crossrail', *Local Transport Today*, No. 409, 12-13.

Thompson, F.M.L. (1963), *English Landed Society in the Nineteenth Century* (London, Routledge and Kegan Paul).

Thompson, W. (1913), 'The Ruislip-Northwood and Ruislip-Manor Joint Town Planning Scheme', *Town Planning Review*, Vol. 4, No. 2, 133-144.

Thornley, A. (1991), *Urban Planning Under Thatcherism: The Challenge of the Market* (London, Routledge).

Thrower, T. (1998), 'Electrification: Dead in its Tracks?' *Rail*, 334, 22-27.

Tolley, R. (1990), *Calming Traffic in Residential Areas* (Dyfed, Brefi Press).

Tomkins, R. (1991), 'Paying the Price of Traffic Jams', *Financial Times*, April 22.

Towler, J. (1990), *The Battle for the Settle and Carlisle* (Sheffield, Platform 5).

Transport and Road Research Laboratory, University of Newcastle upon Tyne, Tyne and Wear Council and Tyne and Wear PTE (1986), *The Metro Report: the Impact of Metro and Public Transport Integration in Tyne and Wear* (Newcastle, Tyne and Wear PTE.).

Tripp Alker, H. (1942), *Town Planning and Road Traffic* (London, Edward Arnold).

Tyme, J. (1978), *Motorways versus Democracy* (London, Macmillan).

Tyne and Wear County Council (1982), *Structure Plan: Written Statement* (Newcastle, Tyne and Wear County Council).

Tyneside Passenger Transport Executive (1973), *Public Transport in Tyneside: A Plan for the People* (Newcastle, Tyneside Passenger Transport Executive).

Tyrrall, D.E. (2006), 'The UK Railway: Privatisation, Efficiency and Integration', chapter 4 in Hibbs et al, *The Railways, the Market and the Government* (London, Institute of Economic Affairs).

Unwin, R. (1909), *Town Planning in Practice* (London, T. Fisher Unwin).

Urban Task Force (1999), *Towards an Urban Renaissance* (London, DETR).

Vanns, M.A. (2004), *Rail Centres: Nottingham* (Nottingham, Booklaw Publications, first published by Ian Allan Ltd 1993).

Vaughan, A. (1991), *Isambard Kingdom Brunel: Engineering Knight-Errant* (London, John Murray).

Vaughan, A. (1997), *Railwaymen, Politics and Money: The Great Age of Railways in Britain* (London, John Murray).

Velez, D. (1982), 'Late Nineteenth-century Spanish Progressivism: Arturo Soria's Linear City', *Journal of Urban History*, Vol. 9, 131-164.

Voorhess, A.M. Associates and Buchanan, C. and Partners (1972), *Tyne Wear Plan: Transport Plan for the 1980s* (Newcastle, Tyneside PTE).

Ward, B. (1986), 'Stepping out for the City', *Architects' Journal*, Vol. 183, No. 15, 40-45.

Warrington New Town Development Corporation (1973), *Birchwood District Area Plan* (Warrington, Warrington New Town Development Corporation).

Watson, J.P. and Abercrombie, P. (1943), *A Plan for Plymouth* (Plymouth, Plymouth City Council).

Webber, M. (1964), *The Urban Place and the Non-Place Urban Realm*, 79-153 in M.M. Webber et al (eds) 'Explorations into Urban Structure' (Philadelphia PA, University of Pennsylvania Press).

West Midlands County Council (1982), *West Midlands County Structure Plan: Adopted Version* (Birmingham, West Midlands County Council).

West Midlands Passenger Transport Executive (1972), *A Passenger Transport Development Plan for the West Midland* (Birmingham, WMPTE).

West Midlands Passenger Transport Executive (1992), *Keeping the West Midlands Moving: A 20 Year Strategy for Public Transport Executive* (Birmingham, WMPTE).

Wheeler, M. (ed) (1995), *Ruskin and Environment: the Storm Cloud of the Nineteenth Century* (Manchester, Manchester University Press).

White, H.P. (1979), 'Transport Moves with Technology', *Geography Magazine*, Vol. 51, 793-9.

White, H.P. (1980), *The Continuing Conurbation: Change and Development in Greater Manchester: Produced for the 142nd AGM of the British Association* (Farnborough, Gower).

White, H.P. and Senior M.L. (1983), *Transport Geography* (London, Longman).

White, P. (2002), *Public Transport: Its Planning, Management and Operation* (London, Spon Press).

Whitehouse, A. (1990), 'Provincial's Master Plan', *Modern Railways*, Vol. 47, No. 499, 176-177.

Williams, A. (2008), 'The Prospects for Whitby', *Modern Railways*, Vol. 65, No. 715, 44-47.

Williams, A.F. (1985), *Rapid Transit Systems in the U.K: Problems and Prospects* (Transport Study Group, Institute of British Geographers).

Williams, M. (1992), 'British Rail's Role in Light Rapid Transit', *Light Rail and Modern Tramway*, September, 228-231.

Willis, J. (1997), *Extending the Jubilee Line: The Planning Story* (London, London Transport).

Wilson, H. and Womersley, L. (1966), *Redditch New Town: Report on Planning Proposals* (Redditch, Redditch Development Corporation).

Winsor, T. (2004), *The Future of the Railway: Sir Robert Reid Memorial Lecture* (London, Office of the Rail Regulator).

Wolmar, C. (2001), *Broken Rails: How Privatisation Wrecked Britain's Railways* (London, Aurum Press).

Wolmar, C. (2002), *Down the Tube: The Battle for London's Underground* (London, Aurum Press).

Woodburn, A. (2008), 'Intermodal Rail Freight in Britain: A Terminal Problem?' *Planning Practice and Research*, Vol. 23, No. 3, 441-460.

Wragg, D. (2004), *Signal Failure: Politics and Britain's Railways* (Stroud, Sutton Publishing).

Yin, R.K. (1989), *Case Study Research: Design and Methods* (London, Sage).

Young, M. and Willmott, P. (1957), *Family and Kinship in East London* (London, Routledge and Kegan Paul).

Index